INDIAN SEX LIFE

Indian Sex Life

SEXUALITY AND THE COLONIAL
ORIGINS OF MODERN SOCIAL THOUGHT

DURBA MITRA

PRINCETON UNIVERSITY PRESS
PRINCETON & OXFORD

Copyright © 2020 by Princeton University Press

Published by Princeton University Press
41 William Street, Princeton, New Jersey 08540
6 Oxford Street, Woodstock, Oxfordshire OX20 1TR

press.princeton.edu

All Rights Reserved

ISBN 9780691196343
ISBN (pbk.) 9780691196350

British Library Cataloging-in-Publication Data is available

Editorial: Eric Crahan and Thalia Leaf
Production Editorial: Sara Lerner
Cover Design: Pamela Schnitter
Production: Merli Guerra
Publicity: Alyssa Sanford and Julia Hall
Copyeditor: Anne Sanow

This book has been composed in Arno

Printed on acid-free paper. ∞

Printed in the United States of America

10 9 8 7 6 5 4 3 2 1

For Dr. Rupa Chattopadhyay Mitra

CONTENTS

Introduction
Excess, a History   1

1 Origins
Philology and the Study of Indian Sex Life   23

2 Repetition
Law and the Sociology of Deviant Female Sexuality   62

3 Circularity
Forensics, Abortion, and the Evidence of Deviant Female Sexuality   99

4 Evolution
Ethnology and the Primitivity of Deviant Female Sexuality   133

5 Veracity
Life Stories and the Revelation of Social Life   176

Afterword   203

Acknowledgments 209
Notes 215
Bibliography 255
Image Credits 277
Index 279

INDIAN SEX LIFE

Introduction

EXCESS, A HISTORY

THIS BOOK is an intellectual history of a concept shaped by shame and stigma. It tells a history of social strictures that have organized, disciplined, violated, and left a void in the place of women's desires. In order to reveal this history, I return to a seemingly timeless concept, the prostitute, to make unfamiliar an idea that we think we already know.

Indian Sex Life is an account of how ideas of deviant female sexuality, often named as the "prostitute," became foundational to modern social thought in colonial India. European and Indian social analysts made scientific claims about deviant female sexuality in the constitution of new fields of knowledge about society. In these new sciences of society, the assessment of women's sexuality became essential to theories of social progress. *Indian Sex Life* makes visible this edifice of knowledge that saw deviant female sexuality as the primary way in which one could think and write about Indian society.

Dictates of shame and stigma not only were enacted in everyday forms of social control of women's sexuality but were also key in the making of disciplinary forms of social knowledge. Authorities stigmatized women in the service of new institutional and ideational forms—the philological study of origins, legal surveys of everyday social life, forensic medical investigations, social evolutionary science, and realist literature about society. Philologists, colonial administrators, scientists, lawyers, medical doctors, social scientists, and popular writers created new categories of deviant female sexuality and made them into a system of normative concepts that could be used in the diagnosis and study of Indian society. She, the sexually deviant woman, was historicized through *longue durée* antiquarian studies that posited her as the ancient origin of modern social institutions and prescribed her as the measure of social evolution from primitivity to civilization. She was mapped as the reality of a degraded social life and memorialized in first-person testimonials that made natural the terms of her exclusion.

I take the title of the book, *Indian Sex Life*, from a popular genre of social scientific texts produced in the twentieth century that linked sexual life, particularly the control of women's sexuality, to the evolutionary progress of Indian society.[1] I ask: How and why did deviant female sexuality become a primary "grid" for comprehending social life in this period?[2] The study is situated in Bengal in eastern India, with transregional networks that reached across colonial India to London, Berlin, New York, and Chicago. It spans a period from the middle of the nineteenth century to the middle of the twentieth century, which saw the height of the British colonial state as well as the rapid growth of anti-colonial nationalist movements. Ideas about deviant female sexuality were central to these intellectual and political transformations. Bengal was a key site for the development of colonial policies as well as influential institutions, intellectual networks, and publications in the Indian social sciences. The colonial state and an emerging network of Indian men extended the regulation of sexuality to far-reaching projects that sought to define what society should look like and how modern citizens should behave.

Deviant Female Sexuality as Concept History

Prostitution is the world's oldest profession, so the saying goes. Its origins are attributed to British writer and colonial enthusiast Rudyard Kipling, from his 1889 story "On the City Wall." The story concerns a woman, Lalun, who orchestrates the escape of an Indian prisoner from the British during the violence of a communal riot in the colonial city of Lahore.[3] Kipling authored the phrase "the most ancient profession" in the same moment and in the same register that rendered colonial India—its histories, customs, traditions—as timeless, static, without agency or history.[4] This was no accident, for the prostitute was critical to an episteme that took India as an object of knowledge and investigation. Let us look at Kipling's opening paragraph of "On the City Wall," narrated by a young British colonial officer, who tells us of Lalun's place in colonial society:

> Lalun is a member of the most ancient profession in the world. Lilith was her very great grand-mamma, and that was before the days of Eve as every one knows. In the West, people say rude things about Lalun's profession, and write lectures about it, and distribute the lectures to young persons in order

that morality may be preserved. In the East where the profession is hereditary, descending from mother to daughter, nobody writes lectures or takes any notice; and that is a distinct proof of the inability of the East to manage its own affairs.[5]

Lalun's ancient profession remains unnamed throughout the story. Kipling describes its origins and contours with evocative knowing to his audience. Indeed, there was no need to explain it. The reference is clear: *as every one knows*. Lalun was the direct descendant of Lilith, the first woman created by God, born of the same earth as Adam, a female demon who is the very genesis of the dangerous sexual desire intrinsic to woman. Lalun's timeless profession extends beyond her person, to her ancestry, to India's ancient past and corrupt present. She embodies the distinction between the incorrigible East and the moral West. Kipling links the most ancient profession to the insidious nature of woman's sexuality at the origin of humanity.

Later, Lalun defies description. Kipling writes: "Lalun *is* Lalun, and when you have said that, you have only come to the Beginnings of Knowledge."[6] Lalun is Lilith, who asserted her carnal dominance at the very inception of knowing. Lalun appears in the story as an omniscient viewer of the colony, a calculating woman who held total knowledge of the deceptive world of Indians. Ultimately, Kipling's colonial narrator is seduced and deceived by Lalun. He becomes Lalun's pawn, an unknowing co-conspirator in the escape of the prisoner from the colonial fort. Through her sexuality, she becomes the master of the narrator. In the face of Lalun, British conquest over its colony is woefully inadequate. Lalun is a woman who escapes knowing, who sets forth an agenda of mastery for the colonial narrator. Lalun eludes language and exceeds any account that seeks to encompass her, despite the best efforts of men. The narrator later utters the phrase again, anew, in an attempt to convince himself that Lalun is indeed a mere mortal: "Lalun is nothing else but Lalun."[7] Described again and again as Lalun, she is a closed loop. Lalun is the Beginnings of Knowledge as well as its limit. She, a woman who rules men with her sexuality, must be named again and again, described in detail, reiterated, and sought across fields of knowledge. Lalun is the genesis of the colonial knowledge project, a testament to its inadequacy, but also the engine that drives it.

I first encountered the category of "prostitute" as I began research in an archive of colonial eastern India from the 1880s, created in the same period as Kipling's tale. When I began this project, I had set out to do a social history of the many social classes of women classified as prostitutes. I had been unsatisfied with explanations in scholarly and public discourses that saw British colonial mores, or so-called Victorian morality, as the sole reason for strict sexual norms in India and much of the postcolonial world. This kind of "derivative discourse" of sexual repression seemed an inadequate historical account of long-standing patriarchal strictures, virulent misogyny, and endemic issues of sexual violence in South Asia.[8] As I began to follow this archival category, there were many things that were not clear to me.

I found the prostitute everywhere, across different archives from colonial India, appearing, disappearing, and then reappearing in files that seemingly had little to do with the regulation of sexual commerce. She was ubiquitous in the analysis of Indian social life—foundational in Hindu and Muslim social reform movements; practices of evidence in criminal law; studies of ancient Indian marriage and erotics; medical science texts on women's diseases; theories of racial evolution; debates about consent, gender, and family; caste hierarchies; anti-Muslim rhetoric; and everyday dictates of food, health, and bodily comportment. In colonial India, the term "prostitute" was used to describe virtually all women outside of monogamous Hindu upper-caste marriage, including the *tawa'if*, the courtesan, the dancing girl, the *devadasi*, high-caste Hindu widows, Hindu and Muslim polygamous women, low-class Muslim women workers, indentured women transported across the British empire, beggars and vagrants, women followers of religious sects, mendicant performers, professional singers, the wives of sailors, women theater actors, saleswomen, nurses, urban industrial laborers, and domestic servants.[9]

How could I account for the excess of this archival presence as a historical phenomenon? It seemed clear to me that something systematic was occurring—a system of thinking for which we had not yet fully accounted. To understand this haunting presence required a different practice of reading that linked together seemingly disparate archives.

Our historical imaginations have focused primarily on a politics of recuperation of the prostitute. Indeed, the subject par excellence of comparative feminist historiography since the rise of women's history in the 1970s has been the prostitute. Here, the prostitute was made visible as a "sex worker," the woman for hire, famously described by Judith Walkowitz as the "proletariat of prostitution" in her field-defining study of Victorian society.[10] She has been recovered as a social actor through historical accounts of the legal regulation of commercial sex.[11]

We have largely lingered in this mode of recuperation, where the prostitute in our archives appears as a historical subject primarily as a sex worker and solely through the lens of the regulation of commercial sex. Yet we know little of the vast array of people, forms of labor, and social practices encompassed by the concept of the prostitute. What we do know comes from archives of those social scientific projects of colonial law, public health and medicine, policing and detection, housing, and social reform that initiated new practices of knowledge from the nineteenth century onward. Most often, when women appear in these archives, they are already marked as prostitutes.[12] These archived categories and taxonomies are too often taken at face value, a practice of reading that produces a limited archival hermeneutics for our histories.

I argue that at the core of the modern understanding of the prostitute is a definitional fluidity that requires a history.[13] That is, the prostitute, when dislocated from the urge to recuperate her as an identity, takes on a different history: as a concept foundational to the making of social life as an object of study. In colonial India, she was trafficked *as a concept* in the service of the development of colonial social science, claims to scientific expertise, and new social theories on the progress of Indian society. This book offers a critical genealogy of the concept of the prostitute to make visible these structures of intellectual life.[14] It considers the work of the concept as it was invented, homogenized, and circulated by British colonial and Bengali men. It accounts for how the concept of the prostitute became essential to new methods of social study and new practices of empiricism that condensed manifold social practices into strict taxonomies. As such, it traces the concept of the prostitute—and the many, many varied forms of social and sexual practices she came to encompass—in her ambiguities, multiplicities, and contradictions as she gained momentum as a coherent concept for social study.[15]

A range of social and political authorities utilized the concept of the prostitute to delineate social life as a bounded object of study. She was critical to debates about social exclusion, caste strictures, widowhood and inheritance, sexual condemnation, women's labor, and religious and sectarian ideologies about the dangers of Muslim sexuality. This was a world of racialized intellectual networks and institutions built through the colonial encounter in India. With the turn of the twentieth century came new claims to expertise and the rise of transcontinental disciplines of study. Increasingly stringent sexual norms defined these new multilingual networks of people, ideas, and institutions. What resulted were numerous studies, often hundreds of pages long, of sexual life and prostitution published and republished through the twentieth century, comprehensive colonial questionnaires that initiated new social scientific practices in the most intimate domains of social life, as well as a proliferative print culture that claimed to represent the reality of the underworld of sexual life.

What authorities—colonial and "native" men—sought to create in these social studies differed. While the state built new structures of legal dominance and scientific knowledge through the study of sexuality, an emerging group of Bengali men, primarily upper-caste Hindus, constituted new social theories of sexual transgression in pursuit of social and political authority. They argued for the dramatic reorganization of society around strict upper-caste Hindu monogamous ideals. Yet it is through the colonial encounter that the "European colonialist and the indigene are united in one analytic field."[16] The colonial state and Bengali elites utilized a common language of the control of female sexuality in "an exchange of mutual self-representation."[17] The concept of the prostitute served as a seemingly endless resource that could be used to explain nearly all forms of social behavior, ancient and modern.

I use the phrase *deviant female sexuality* to account for the surplus of ideas and classifications that circulated around the category of the prostitute. The concept history of the prostitute, I suggest, reveals a broad history of how ideas about the dangers and excesses of women's sexuality shaped modern social thought. There were a wide range of women who were stigmatized as sexual deviants, marked as aberrant, sexually unchaste, outside of respectable society, socially ill, criminally dangerous, or sexually unbound. I employ this phrase to encompass the multilingual sexual classification and translation of diverse social practices into this classificatory imagination, where many different women were named "prostitute" in English and a wide range of Sanskrit and Bengali terms. In multiple archives from eastern India, the prostitute and different Bengali terms for "deviant women" are almost uniformly gendered as woman and described as female.[18]

"Deviant," as I use it in this study, is not meant to characterize historical subjects *as* sexual deviants. Instead, I use the term "deviant" to suggest that the delineation of deviance was an integral part of the social scientific enterprise in this moment, a knowledge economy that stretched from the metropole to colony and back. This is the idea of deviance as civilizational difference that defined early positivist sociological thought, an idea that would become formalized as a distinct object of sociological study by the middle of the twentieth century. In theories premised on models of ethnological social evolution, from Herbert Spencer to Francis Galton to Émile Durkheim, social deviance was a necessity that provoked new limits and norms of social good.[19] This approach saw interdictions against deviance as critical to modern social development from "primitive" to modern forms. In the evolution of societies, moral boundaries were to be built and transgressions were to be defined, all in order to demonstrate how modern society differed from the promiscuity and normlessness of primitive societies. These normative boundaries, and the many people that transgressed these limits, became a critical site of knowledge production and self-reflection for social scientific writers in colonial India.

Diverse ideas, categories, and behaviors were classified as deviant in the making of new sexual norms and moral boundaries in social thought. For the colonial state, any woman engaged in a nonmonogamous relationship was deviant. This demarcation was achieved through large-scale surveys that classified essentially every woman as a potential prostitute. The unknowability of the prostitute posed her as an ever-present threat. Indeed, administrators even viewed monogamous marriage among the lower classes, especially Muslims, as an elaborate conspiracy to hide women who they argued were actually prostitutes. In Bengali social thought, a wide range of types of women came to be understood as aberrant, socially transgressive, and criminally deviant, labeled as prostitutes and a wide range of Sanskrit and Bengali terms. Terminological charts and scientific taxonomies grew in popularity with the rapid expansion of print in the late nineteenth century. This classificatory impulse reveals how transgression—of social domains, of public spaces, of caste strictures, of an idealized domesticity based in monogamy—shaped the reorganization of normative social life around upper-caste marriage.[20] Elaborate taxonomical charts of the prostitute brought together different Sanskrit, Bengali, and English categories for women.[21]

While this study takes as its subject the concept of the prostitute in colonial India, much could be said about the objectification of social life through the study of the prostitute across the modern world. She is a critical concept in canonical studies that introduce new methods of social scientific inquiry, from Alexandre Parent-Duchâtelet's taxonomical survey in Paris to William Acton's study in London to William Sanger's medico-social study in New York City to Cesare Lombroso in his creation of positivist criminology in Italy.[22] Across modern Europe and its colonies, discussions of prostitutes and sexually deviant women were not limited to the increasingly specialized subfield of the sexual sciences but appeared across modern social thought, and this was certainly the case in colonial India.[23] The prostitute, as a concept, thus shaped manifold approaches to social study across the modern world. In colonial India, ideas of the prostitute and more broadly deviant female sexuality defined new modes of inquiry—from positivist methods of antiquarianism in Indology, to early state practices of empirical taxonomy and social inquiry, to ethnological models of evolutionary social development, to early practices of evidence, detection, and criminology, to lay sociologies of urban space.

This book is the first full-length monograph on the history of sexual sciences in India and also an argument for the critical place of sexuality in the constitution of diverse fields of modern social thought beyond the subfield of the sexual sciences. I argue that deviant female sexuality was not an isolated object of specialized study. It was "at the heart of the social sciences," to use Kath Weston's formulation, constituting the very "bread and butter" of the study of social life upon which modern disciplines were built. I ask: What history might we tell when we ask not only about the objectification of sexuality, but "study the infusion of sexuality into the very pursuit of knowledge"?[24] Ideas of deviant female sexuality were infused into diverse universalist theories of comparative societies, studies often based in the empirical study of India. The control of female sexuality—especially through stringent forms of patriarchal marriage—served as the primary model for major social scientific concepts from the nineteenth century, from marriage, descent, and kinship to "normality, evolution, progress, organization, development, and change."[25] The traffic in women, as Gayle Rubin's groundbreaking 1975 essay suggests, was the central premise for modern social scientific understandings of social relations.[26] Whether it was philology, ethnology, comparative jurisprudence, political economy, or sociology—from Henry Maine to Lewis Henry Morgan to John McLennan to Friedrich Engels—female sexuality, restrained within compulsory heterosexual marriage, was foundational for universalist models of social life.

By arguing for a concept history of the prostitute, this book complicates historical projects that treat the heterosexual/homosexual definition as the singular motor that drives the making of modern sexuality from the nineteenth century.[27] I propose that the concept of the prostitute is critical to the reorganization of modern sexualities. My study of the concept of the prostitute in modern South Asia is not meant to be an additive account that globalizes already-established frameworks from Europe and America with empirical evidence from South Asia.[28] Instead, this history denaturalizes underlying assumptions about the universality of the hetero/homo divide that have long shaped practices of reading in the history of sexuality. *Indian Sex Life* reveals how ideas of deviant female sexuality, particularly through the concept of the prostitute, were foundational to modern social thought in India, while also accounting for the place of Indian sexuality as a key empirical referent in the constitution of universalist theories of civilizational and racial development. By linking ideas of female sexuality to the origins of modern social thought, this project suggests new avenues for writing histories of women's sexuality and more global histories of sexuality.[29]

I build on rich traditions of critical scholarship that interrogate historical methods and practices of reading in archives of marginalized pasts—from groundbreaking South Asian feminist historical critiques, to methods in queer history and the history of sexuality, to debates about colonial knowledge and the historiographic challenge of subaltern histories.[30] The critique of the recuperation of sexuality is powerfully reframed by Anjali Arondekar as a paradoxical question of loss and discovery in histories of sexuality. What would it mean to write histories "unmoored" from our attachment to ideas of loss and absence in the archives of marginalized pasts?[31] What we know is that multiple forms of heterosexual and same-sex practices were marginalized, racialized, criminalized, or forcefully disappeared through strictures of law, science, and social norms. Yet the archives that remain are not just fragments of the past but a testament to a prolific sociological imaginary that was systematically built through ideas of deviant female sexuality.[32]

In the wake of this intellectual history of colonial sexual strictures and social stigma, life in postcolonial South Asia reflects these histories in dictates of marriage and the ruthless condemnation of peoples, social practices, gendered labor, and public behavior through ideas about sexual propriety. The afterlife of this history of deviant female sexuality can be found in public debates in South Asia today—in the moral denunciation of the public performances of so-called bar girls, in claims that women are to blame for acts of rape and sexual violence, in violent attacks against intercaste and interreligious marriages, and in acts of gendered violence that kill women to protect their "honor." Debates about women's sexuality are shaped by the inheritance of mutable concepts like "custom" and "Indian culture," where monogamous patriarchal marriage appears as the only legitimate means through which to reproduce "tradition" and normative values.[33]

The Sciences of Society

This modern understanding of tradition emerged as the result of the comprehensive study of Indian society over the last three hundred years. Over the course of the colonial period, India—its landscapes, peoples, "social customs"— became a site of ongoing social scientific investigation. European studies of social life introduced practices of positivist description and classification through extensive, evocative descriptions and images of women's victimhood and sexuality in the Hindu "custom" of *sati* in travelogues, paintings, and treatises from the seventeenth century onward.[34] Colonial studies on the nature of Indian society were to become the empirical basis for universalist theories of comparative societies. Indeed, the colonial state in India was, at its inception, an experiment in new forms of scientific and social scientific practices that were to influence state practices and the formation of disciplinary knowledge in the colony and metropole.[35]

As the seat of the British Empire, Bengal was an important site for many early institutions of learning that came to shape the structure and development of social study across colonial India. These institutions were essential to the earliest expansion of the colonial project, most notably the Asiatic Society of Bengal. The Asiatic Society critically focused on issues of female sexuality (i.e., in the textual basis of practices like *sati*) and textual dictates around marriage and reproduction, a selective basis for early colonial law.[36] Founded in 1784 in Calcutta by William Jones, the Asiatic Society of Bengal was part of an ambitious project to massively expand the Indological project of compiling and translating Indian language texts. The society was committed to the systematic acquisition, arrangement, cataloging, and translation of the classical literatures of the colony in Persian, Arabic, and Sanskrit. Through this widescale project, Jones and his contemporaries began what was to be a centuries-long pursuit of knowledge that saw a selective set of ancient and medieval texts as fundamentally representative of the past, present, and futures of Indian civilizations.

Bengal also holds a critical place in the institutionalization of education and the creation of scientific and social scientific knowledge about India. Colonial legal, scientific, and social concepts that came to encompass the study of India originated in the study of social life in colonial Bengal from the earliest British conquest of territory in 1757. The philological inquiries of the Asiatic Society were to shift by the early nineteenth century to surveys and scientific studies of everything from pathology to botany to race science and demography. Ideas of normative womanhood and pathological female sexuality emerge again and again across these comprehensive studies. These influential texts included everything from medicine and science to geography, situated ethnographies, and the descriptive cataloging of the peoples of India, including Allan Webb's *Pathologica Indica* (1844); the forensic manuals of Norman Chevers in his *A Manual of Medical Jurisprudence for Bengal and the Northwest Provinces* (1856); Edward Dalton's *Descriptive Ethnology of Bengal* (1876); W. W. Hunter's twenty-volume study (with Herbert H. Risley) *A Statistical Account of Bengal*

(1875–1877); and perhaps the most influential ethnographic survey, Risley's *Tribes and Castes of Bengal* (1891), which defined the modern study of caste.

By the first decades of the nineteenth century, the capital city of Calcutta was home to many emerging projects of social study that focused on the nature of Indian womanhood and the control of women's sexuality and reproduction through marriage. These projects were institutionalized in the form of university education in Hindu College (1817), professional scientific education in the founding of the Calcutta Medical College (1835), and organizations dedicated to creating learned societies in the arts and sciences.[37] These included the Society for the Acquisition of General Knowledge (1838), which published papers from "Civil and Social Reform" to "Interests of the Female Sex" and "A Sketch on the Condition of Hindu Women," to the Tattwabodhini Sabha (Truth-seekers Society, 1839), to the Bengal Social Science Association (1867), among many others.[38] These organizations proliferated with membership from colonial administrators, British missionaries, and Bengali elites. They disseminated ideas that shaped the study of India in the colonial period, from Comtean positivism to liberal political thought.[39] In the last decades of the nineteenth century, institutions of education expanded rapidly at the initiative of a growing literate public, with over one hundred private institutions of education in the region by 1902.[40] By the 1900s, spurred by the uproar of the Swadeshi movement, social organizations began to rapidly publish and disseminate different forms of knowledge, from nationalist pamphlets to ancient histories to textbooks on health and medicine. Alongside the fervor in a growing nationalist movement, higher education expanded rapidly in Bengal. By 1918, the University of Calcutta had become the largest university anywhere in the world.[41] The earliest master's degrees in sociology in India were awarded at University of Calcutta in the first decade of the twentieth century.

Social scientific education and thought expanded in Indian languages across the subcontinent in the last decades of the nineteenth century. As institutions of learning in Calcutta began to train students in overlapping fields of Indology, sociology, and ethnology, Indians rapidly built new institutions of social scientific learning, everywhere from Lahore, Pune, and Bombay in western India to Madras and Hyderabad in southern India to Aligarh and Lucknow in the north.[42] Questions of female sexuality and its foundational place as the diagnostic of social evolution pervaded early studies from scholars trained in these institutions.[43]

These new practices of social study reflect the growth of "scientism" in nineteenth-century social thought. These new sciences of society could objectively encompass and limit the study of the social world in the colony. Social thought in Bengal produced an abstract notion of Indian society as a coherent and immanently knowable object of study. For anti-colonial nationalists, this was a science that could objectively explain their lack of autonomy in the colonial present and predict the future of Indian society. Distinct archives of texts constituted this multilingual domain of social analysis where Indian social life was delineated as a bounded object of study. These multilingual texts treated the social world as an object of inquiry, a veritable and verifiable science of society. Many terms were used for these hybrid genres of writing: social analysis, social theory, social reform, sociology, social thought, and occasionally those texts formally called social *science*.

I refer to these emerging fields of modern social thought in and about India as the sciences of society, overlapping fields of social scientific knowledge that took Indian society as an object of investigation.[44] The sciences of society included everything from the earliest texts formally classified as "sociology" in the indexes of the India Office collections, to the growing disciplines of Indology, history, forensic science, ethnology, and popular literature.[45] Diverse genres of texts, often classified together in contemporary scholarship under the unified category of "social reform," were deeply invested in social scientific ideas.[46] Influential texts and ideas that focused on women's sexuality, relegated to the broad domain of social reform literature, have been largely written out of the canon of social science in the twentieth century, despite the widespread influence of these ideas and concepts for modern social theory.[47] This was "partly for want of method, but mostly for want of 'theoretical concerns,' the trope by which an emerging academic discipline came to define itself."[48]

A diverse repertoire of social scientific thought based on sexual ideas circulated through networks of people and texts that moved across the colonial world, from the colony to the metropole and back. This transnational exchange of ideas emerged in a world of multidisciplinary experts who studied a breadth of subjects, including antiquity, law, sociology and anthropology, history, the forensic sciences and criminology, and literature. While the colonial state sought to precisely define Indian subjects as populations in these new practices of data collection and analysis, Indians soon looked to this social scientific repertoire to create new models of social and political autonomy. Drawing upon Andrew Abbott's formulation for the global authors of modern social thought, I describe these professionals and intellectuals as *social analysts*. Social analysts are administrators, public intellectuals, social reformers, and intellectual classes who produced social scientific thought before and alongside the formalization of academic social sciences in Europe, North America, and the colonies.[49] Indeed, as Abbott describes, the sites of the social sciences in the colonies were always multifold, "born of storm and strife," between powerful practices of social description by the colonial state and an emerging world of educated elites who used multiple genres to systematize the study of social life.[50] Modern social thought was constituted by everyone from state administrators building complex apparatuses of the census to early Indian social scientists and lay sociologists writing on the past and future of Indian society.[51]

The social analysts explored in the chapters that follow were British colonial officials, British, German, and American scholars, and Bengali elites—mostly upper-caste Hindu intellectuals. They were men who were administrators, medical doctors, natural scientists, educators, dentists, university professors, and lawyers. At some points, women also engaged in these social scientific discourses in limited ways.[52] Many of these Bengali men would be understood as nationalists, yet most of their publications do not describe the content or import of their social scientific ideas within the framework of "nation." Rather, men used the language of the past and potential futures of Indian society. I therefore use the term "social analysts" in order to preserve the historical specificity of their ideas and to account for the analytical work of claims to scientific objectivity in these social theories.[53]

These writers utilized and exchanged a set of concepts of female sexuality, ideas that they used to cohere new practices of social analysis and description. Colonial administrators, empowered in midlevel positions in the British colonial state, were simultaneously social scientists, doctors, and military personnel. Many elite Bengali men were not formally trained in the disciplines of the social sciences. These men, often self-trained, produced exhaustive studies of Indian social life. Their studies are not often the subject of intellectual history, despite their prodigious written production and the widespread citation of their texts.[54]

Written alongside the establishment of boundaries between academic disciplines of sociology, anthropology, or history, social thought in colonial spaces was multifold, written by polyglot writers and social commentators. These publications often had a "vertiginous quality" in their claims to expertise.[55] As social analysts built social theories through a multilingual hermeneutic, they claimed a range of disciplinary forms, circulated and cited canonical texts in their claim to authority, and performed repetitions within their own texts, where reiteration was to be understood as a demonstration of expertise.[56] These formal fields were only to be differentiated and institutionalized as formal disciplines in India decades into the twentieth century.

The archives left in the wake of these men and their intellectual worlds are piecemeal. Often, biographical information about the authors is difficult or impossible to obtain, with disembodied texts that moved thousands of miles from the sites of their production, haphazardly kept in archives and libraries across present-day India, Bangladesh, England, and the United States. The scattered archives of these sciences of society reflect the travel of texts as a result of unequal projects of knowledge acquisition in the colonial and postcolonial world.

The Context of Colonial India

At the heart of these sciences of society was a concern about structuring, tracing, and mapping the social world of colonial India through the assessment of women's sexuality. These histories reveal the way key debates about gender, caste, communal difference, and social hierarchy in India became objects of social scientific analysis through the description and evaluation of female sexuality. By the nineteenth century, ideologies about women's potential transgression of sexual and social strictures became essential to projects that sought to define the contours of ideologies of caste, communalism, and social difference. Female sexuality could be used to describe, enforce, and explain exclusionary institutions and ideologies of social difference.

Normative ideas of female sexuality shaped the contours of the nascent nationalism fostered by upper-caste elite Bengali Hindus who, at the turn of the twentieth century, faced challenges to their social authority in contentious claims to be counted by the colonial census, shifts in regional political authority, and access to education. These men—largely upper-caste Brahman and Kayastha castes—utilized discourses of women's chastity to create idealized visions of Hindu womanhood as wife and mother. As Tanika Sarkar demonstrates, with the idealization of the upper-caste Hindu woman and Hindu marriage came the reorganization of gendered norms around an increasingly restricted vision of Hindu conjugality and domesticity, one exclusive of the many social forms that existed alongside upper-caste social norms.[57] They simultaneously condemned lower-caste people and Muslims as sexual deviants, prostitutes, and criminals.[58]

These men trafficked in ideas of deviant female sexuality in order to position themselves as the natural inheritors of the ruling apparatus of India. Yet scholarship on colonial power, anti-colonial nationalist ideologies, or the material conditions of colonialism in South Asia has often treated sexuality as epiphenomenal to "true" objects of historical inquiry. I reject such a formulation. I deliberately do not use the language of figuration to describe ideas of the prostitute and deviant female sexuality. In my telling, women and ideas of female sexuality are not solely significations, representations, or symbols of broader social and political challenges of social reform, ideas of colonial power, or anti-colonial Indian nationalism. Instead, *Indian Sex Life* demonstrates that the control of female sexuality is a central driving force in the very conceptualization of social life itself as an object of study, intervention, and reform.

This project builds on rich debates in critical feminist histories of South Asia.[59] Feminist histories have focused on the critical place of gender for claims to autonomy in anti-colonial nationalism, in laws that organize colonial and postcolonial marriage and women's rights, and in the enforcement of upper-caste ideologies of family and domesticity along rigidified strictures of caste and communitarian differences.[60] I foreground sexuality as a central analytic for intellectual histories of South Asia in order to bring normative concepts of modern social thought fully into view.[61]

In these new sciences of society, increasingly narrow, strict understandings of sexual norms were transplanted into the language of objectivity and science. Those social sciences concerned with the study of the social world, past and present, were seemingly contradictory sites. While they produced the study of caste and community as a social scientific object, they also created theories that simultaneously and systematically normalized caste difference and discrimination and anti-Muslim communal thought through the language of an objective science of society.[62] This claim to objectivity by Hindu elites reflected the cruel irony of colonial histories of knowledge, where colonial ideologies utilized exclusionary claims of scientific expertise to insist that the colonized were to be "robbed of their autonomy in order to qualify to receive it back from the robbers."[63] For Bengali social analysts, the philological study of ancient text, the condensed colonial survey data, and universalist ethnological models of social development were to be used to explain the necessity of strict social and sexual norms in the pursuit for social and political autonomy.

This objective of naturalizing upper-caste Hindu supremacy was achieved through a double move. First, in social scientific arguments for caste difference, social analysts presented caste hierarchy as a natural development of modern Indian society. Hindu intellectuals produced, through scientific ideas of sexuality, a vision of an ideal society in the model of an idealized upper-caste monogamous conjugality. Second, social analysts claimed historical and positivist sociological objectivity in the condemnation of Muslim rule and conquest in South Asia. In the Muslim, cast as sexually deviant and dangerous, many Hindu social analysts found simultaneous explanations for the lack and lag of Hindu societies (sexual degradation at the hands of Muslim rulers) and a mechanism through which to regain social power and progress (Muslim exclusion and social control). Muslims were produced as the devolution of true Hindu civilization.

The claim to social scientific expertise by Bengali social analysts was exclusive and exclusionary, where caste supremacy and anti-Muslim communal biases were recast as pure, objective science.[64] These ideas appeared in claims to the bodily difference of lower-castes and Muslims that mapped ideas of purity and pollution onto the language of public health and the body, through ideas of the natural evolution of Indian society as one progressively developed through caste stratification, and arguments about the historical necessity of caste as occupation. In these sciences of society, caste difference was the result of occupational, racial, and sexual differentiation and reproduction for the purpose of social advancement across time. In the same theories, the natural evolution of Hindu society was retarded by Muslim conquest. Indeed, perhaps no space in the public sphere naturalized caste and religious difference while reinforcing upper-caste power and anti-Muslim ideologies more strategically than the new sciences of society.

Toward a History of Deviant Female Sexuality

This social scientific imaginary had extraordinary reach. Let me turn to another literary scene, which, like Kipling and Lalun, was to become a paradigmatic locus for the knowledge project. Perhaps the most widely read Bengali novel in the twentieth century was Saratchandra Chattapadhyay's *Devdas* (1917), a tale of a man torn between two women, the woman denoted as a prostitute who cares for him, Chandramukhi, and his unrequited love, the housewife Parbati, who is forced to marry an elderly man. *Devdas* was immediately popular at the time of its publication and continued to dominate a popular imagination fascinated with women's sexuality in postcolonial South Asia as the most remade movie in Indian cinema. The most recent interpretation of *Devdas* in film was released in 2018.[65] Known for his many fictional depictions of the problem of female sexuality, Chattapadhyay's projects in literature were legitimated by his claims to social realism. In a nonfiction essay purportedly drafted in the same moment as *Devdas*, Chattapadhyay produces an argument about social progress after he claimed to have collected the firsthand accounts of hundreds of "fallen" women of Calcutta and why they fell into disrepute.[66] What resulted was the study "Narir Mulya" (The value of a woman, 1923?), an extended exegesis on the fallen woman's condition and the evolution of Indian society to true monogamy.[67] For Saratchandra Chattapadhyay and writers like him, literature was not simply a figurative engagement with the sexually transgressive woman, but a way of bearing witness to the degradation of modern social life.

Through the comparative ethnology of primitive societies, Christian ethics, and positivist sociology, Chattapadhyay produces an intricate schematic on the evolution of sexual strictures on women. The essay betrays Chattapadhyay's phantasmatic empiricism, his desire to fix an indeterminate idea of the prostitute as a knowable object through exhaustive descriptions and claims to expertise. His argument brings together many themes, including the control of female sexuality from promiscuity to marriage in modern society, the sexual traffic of women, and widow immolation. The essay culminates in the need for both sexes to commit to monogamy. He compares the degraded condition of Indian womanhood to the traffic in women as gifts among tribes of Africa, the sexual promiscuity of Eskimos and native tribes of the Americas, and primitive modes of marriage. Chattapadhyay builds a theory of the plight of women through theories of primitive promiscuity, citing everything from the epic tales of the *Mahabharata* and *Ramayana* to St. Augustine and John Stuart Mill. His essay creates a complex citational apparatus, from Gaston Maspero's study of Egypt in *The Dawn of Civilization* (1894), John Lubbock's *The Origin of Civilisation and the Primitive Condition of Man* (1870), Henry Sumner Maine's comparative jurisprudence in *Ancient Law* (1861), and Alfred C. Haddon's *Head-Hunters: Black, White, Brown* (1901), to John McLennan's *Primitive Marriage* (1865). Most especially, Chattapadhyay looks to Herbert Spencer's *Descriptive Sociology* (1873) for a diagnosis of the ills of Indian society.

Chattapadhyay saw social evolutionary schema as an essential way to explain the everyday oppression of women and those pitiable women who became prostitutes. In Chattapadhyay's scheme, the prostitute was akin to an array of primitive counterparts across the world. A woman of "the oldest profession," the prostitute was the ultimate sign of sexual primitivity and its lingering effects in society.[68] A woman's continued traffic, her worth (or lack thereof) revealed the present-day incivility of society. Chattapadhyay claimed a progressive ethics through the pitiable condition of women. But pity is not politics, and ultimately, the women of "Narir Mulya" appear only as archetypes of primitivity, social degradation, and suffering.

Saratchandra Chattapadhyay's desire to discover the true reality of the prostitute and emplot her in time—where the prostitute linked Sanskrit epics to scientific theories of evolution and positivist sociology—was by no means novel. Over the course of *Indian Sex Life*, I analyze how this logic became a foundational apparatus for different sciences of society—essential for the search for the origins of social life in Sanskrit texts, scientific treatises that populated sociological classifications with bodies of evidence, evolutionary models that saw the prostitute as primitive sex, early sociological surveys of fallen women, and proliferative eyewitness accounts that claimed to tell the reality of the prostitute. Whether it was a historico-sociological study, a survey of women workers in the factories, or a Calcutta newspaper exposé on the causes of a woman's fall, the concept of the prostitute was used to govern, explain, describe, and contest the domain of social life and knowledge. Indeed, everyone was invested in an explanatory reasoning that could narrate the failures of female sexuality as a symptom of uneven social development. These complex theories linked women's vulnerability and victimhood to their inherent sexual proclivities and the excess of their desires.

In colonial India the prostitute was a powerful exemplar, used to argue for new techniques of social analysis. Authorities used the concept to bring the limits of social life into focus and normative models of social organization into fruition.[69] Social analysts invoked the prostitute to organize debates about the nature of Indian society and its progress toward modern forms, to proliferate and secure new modes of knowledge that could be used to argue for social and political autonomy.[70] The prostitute, as a concept, was used by different authorities to produce fixity and to enslave different customs, social practices, and people into its ranks, even when the idea of the prostitute itself was consistently questioned and interrogated for its indeterminacy.[71]

The chapter themes and divisions literalize the itinerary of the concept of the prostitute across diverse archives. In the chapters that follow, the reader will encounter how the concept of the prostitute, and more broadly, multilingual categories of deviant female sexuality, shaped different fields of knowledge—philology, criminal law, forensic medicine, ethnology, and popular literature. Each chapter traces an individual field of knowledge from the middle of the nineteenth century until the first decades of the twentieth century. Focusing on the foundational role of ideas of deviant female sexuality, I bring diverse fields of knowledge together into a single framework.

In eluding definition, the concept of the prostitute was critical to the development of key methods in modern social thought. The concept was integral to a comprehensive project of origins, where ideas of deviant female sexuality were foundational for methods of antiquarian study that posited ancient Sanskrit knowledge of female sexuality as the textual basis for modern social practice. In chapter 1, "Origins," I analyze how such premodern texts were taken as the source of social fact—a diagnostic and predictive tool that could define the limits of female sexuality in present-day society. For social analysts from Germany, England, America, and India, the Indological study of female sexuality in the ancient and medieval past was critical to the present and future of society. In chapter 2, "Repetition," I trace the role of deviant female sexuality in comprehensive practices of positivist description in the colonial legal survey. Authorities developed a mutable idea of the prostitute as a coherent and immanently knowable object, a concept they linked to everything from solicitation to trafficking to abortion and infanticide. Ideas of deviant sexuality shaped colonial methods of counting, creating a category and populating it with bodies, and new modes of taxonomizing through questionnaires and seemingly endless lists that brought together disparate social practices through diagrams and charts. The prostitute was produced as a fact that could be reiterated across fields of social thought—a classification used, in Durkheim's phrase, "to consider social facts as things."[72]

Classifications of deviant female sexuality were also critical to a project of pathologizing, explored in chapter 3, "Circularity," where I analyze the development of forensic evidence of female sexual deviance in cases of abortion. I argue that medico-legal experts mapped ideas of female sexual deviance onto bodies and peoples, and then folded the detailed anatomies of bodies back into social scientific descriptions that linked the alleged sexual depravity of Indian women to the idea of timeless Indian "social custom." This circular form of thinking shaped new claims of expertise in forensic medicine. In chapter 4, "Evolution," I analyze how European and Bengali social scientists utilized female sexuality to create universalist models of the evolution of civilizations. The assessment of women's sexual evolution was the primary site of comparison between civilizations. Bengali social analysts made female sexuality the primary site of commensurability between stages of societies and utilized the concept of the prostitute to assimilate Indian society into universalist theories of social development. Finally, ideas of deviant female sexuality were critical to claims of objective truth, explored in chapter 5, "Veracity," which traces the reach of the sciences of society into the domain of popular literature. I analyze social analysts who published popular print publications, including lay sociologies and the "autobiographies" of so-called prostitutes, which claimed to reveal the hidden truths of society.

Mindful scholars have asked: What of women's voices, of women's lives, of subaltern perspectives that resist these patriarchal notions of women's dangerous will, desire, and sexuality? What is at stake for us in returning to this canon that stretches across different fields of knowledge, written primarily by men? It is my hope that in mapping the construction of these enduring forms of modern social scientific thought, we may account for the way that sexual norms shape the descriptive practices, methods, and categories we use in writing marginalized subjects into history. The history of sexual taxonomy and social description is infused into the very categories through which we approach the study of our social worlds, the modes and language through which we describe our subjects, and perhaps most critically, the fragmented archives upon which we rely to write our social histories and name marginalized historical subjects.

Even as I trace the universalizing impulses that appear across these exclusionary visions of modern society, I do not concede the domain of totalizing knowledge to these social analysts. Instead, I am interested in how infinitely changeable concepts of women's sexuality created by social analysts were used to hide their anxieties, ambiguities, and failures—those excesses of social life, those polymorphic sexual and social forms that were not to be comprehended in positivist sociological writing. There is immense power in these *claims* to totality in the social sciences, particularly those assertions of neutral objectivity and detached expertise in the name of science. To recognize the biases, the powerful effects, and the enduring legacy of this history of social thought is not to adhere to their total view of Indian society.

To think this history, we must turn askew the seemingly neutral methods and practices—from positivist description to sexual taxonomies to aggregation to comparison—that were essential to the objectification of the social world. This was the systematic naming of women as prostitutes and sexual deviants in the form of lists, numbers, and genealogical charts. These texts aspired to be science—indeed, *social science*—and too often we have felt it necessary to accept the terms of their objectification, even as we try to undermine their conclusions with important social histories of subaltern peoples that rely on evidence, and categories, from these archives. The myriad ways in which women inhabited and defied precarity, social stricture, and exclusion were not to be captured by a term, taxonomy, or chart. Too often, the sociological typologies of women are taken at face value.

In asking about the categories we inherit, I do not offer a deconstructive critique born solely of suspicion, a skeptic's view of whether or not a woman was *really* a prostitute. Rather, I shift the object of historical investigation from the state and legal regulation of sexual commerce to construct an intellectual history of sexuality in the making of new modes of social analysis. The project reconfigures the historical investigation to reveal the systematic role of deviant female sexuality in new practices of knowledge and expertise that claimed Indian society as an immanently knowable object. Put simply, this book asks why the concept of the prostitute is ubiquitous across modern social thought in and about colonial India. I return to these archives to excavate the role of these ideas in the objectification of society and the methods and categories used in the making of the social sciences. In mapping the pervasive appearance of deviant female sexuality in the formation of modern social thought—including key concepts like kinship, family, marriage, descent, social evolution—it is my hope that we may be able to differently approach how we write womanhood, with a critical distance from the overwhelming and powerful epistemologies that create our archives.

Social scientific thought, in its aspiration for objectivity, sought to produce in its language a strict limit to the affective experience of its audience. How might we face the artifacts of these archives and confront the mood and feeling of these texts? Over the course of this book I dwell on materials and descriptions contained within archives of law, science, medicine, ethnological thought, and literature. I include detailed descriptions from source material—be they of elaborate social taxonomies or invasive autopsies. These archives are often banal, at many points predictable and repetitive, and at other times profoundly violent. In the detailed texture, sensibility, and narrative effect of these different sites of social scientific thought, the reader may feel that there are obvious ideological biases of colonial administrators and elite men. There may be moments of palpable exhaustion after reading, frustration with the redundancies or nonsensical statements in the source material, or a visceral reaction to the graphic nature of scientifically objectified narratives of violence inflicted onto women's bodies.

Through extensive descriptions and taxonomies in these archives, the reader will see a social scientific imaginary that was, again and again, predicated on the ongoing assessment of women through their sexuality: their failure at sexual restraint, their proclivity for sexual transgression, their secrecy, their victimhood, their deaths. The chapters that follow highlight the textual detail of social scientific texts, medical studies, and administrative reports, texts that often appear to have no affective register at all, those forms and structures of social thought that unwrote experience as they claimed to capture and encompass it in its totality.

At the heart of the project is a commitment to multilingual source reading as an essential approach to the history of sexuality in the colonial and postcolonial world. By shifting focus away from solely the colonizer's understanding of sexuality in colonial archives, we may write histories of transnational, multilingual epistemologies in the sciences and social sciences that reorganized sexual norms long after the formal end of colonialism.[73] The fateful imaginations of elite Indian men, spurred by the emerging sciences of society, built enduring institutional and ideational structures on the control and erasure of women's sexuality often couched in the language of progressive politics. These social studies of female sexuality were to become critical to nationalist anticolonial movements and political and social structures in postcolonial South Asia deeply invested in patriarchal visions of the past and future. I detail new modes of analysis of female sexuality in social science—powerful claims to expertise, assertions of scientific authority through comparison, vigorous practices of citation—that helped these men consolidate authority. I do so to analyze the effects and excesses of the social world that are captured, and so often fail to be captured (or, perhaps more accurately, escape capture), in the new sciences of society born of the colonial encounter.

Ultimately, the project is centrally concerned with those epistemic structures that claimed to apprehend the lived contours of social life in India, even as I analyze texts that so often have little to do with the actual matter of living. The intellectual history of these concepts of female sexuality requires us to think anew the life and ideational structures of social stigma and how they continue to shape us today. We must trace the creation and inhabitation of strictures, be they conspiracies of silence, the violence of concealment, the power of secrecy, the weight of shame, and the intimate, often vicious surveillance of the many social regimes that did that shaming. This book is an intellectual history of the simultaneous *objectification and erasure*, through the language and methods of social science, of women who persisted through immense hardship, who transgressed and defied boundaries, who abided by social strictures that were constructed at every turn of their lives, who worked in homes and industries under the persistent threat of sexual violence, who were forcibly moved across space in systems of indentured labor—women who at many points died as a result of strict epistemic, legal, and social regimes. These women, their choices and contradictions, were not to be grasped in the cold hands of social science.

1

Origins

PHILOLOGY AND THE STUDY OF INDIAN SEX LIFE

A PROFOUND contempt for women's sexuality was built into the foundations of modern social thought in and about colonial India. Men driven by this contempt sought to explain it by searching for justifications in a corpus of Sanskrit texts. They claimed that the philological study of Sanskrit, as the science of originary languages and texts, was essential to excavating the truth of women's sexuality, past and present. One philologist, Abinash Chandra Ghose, argued that premodern Sanskrit classifications made the sexually deviant woman knowable in the service of theories of modern Indian social progress. In 1894 Ghose published *Rati-Sastram: or, The Hindu System of Sexual Science*, a gloss of a medieval Sanskrit work, *Ratirahasya*, also known as the *Koka Shastra*. This popular study was purportedly a scientific manual based in classical Sanskrit knowledge about sexuality and reproduction, what Ghose termed "Hindu sexual science." He argued that Sanskrit texts provided a comprehensive typology of women and systematically assessed them for their potential impurity and social pollution as a result of anything from menstruation to sexual deviance. Based in his Hindu sexual science, Ghose produces an evocative description of the sexually dangerous woman through a hierarchical classificatory scheme. Consider, for instance, his description of the *Hastini*, the "elephant kind of woman," who exhibits the primary features of female sexual deviance:

> Always given to foul practices, her body smells of wine, fallen from womanly ways, fat, scanty haired, of smiling lips, with eyes of reddish tint her breasts uncommonly high and fat, she is grave, boisterous, tolerably beautiful, deep-voiced, void of modesty in satisfying her carnal appetites, always

mad after lustful desires, inclined to coming together sexually with men, and engaged in enjoying with men other than her husband. This class of woman always unmanageable and untruthful to their husbands. Most of them leave their husband's protection and pass their lives in a shameful manner.[1]

A smile ever-present on her lips, the *Hastini* woman was the negation of good femininity, a woman who embodied indelicacy and perversity. She was empowered by her lustful sexual desire, willing to leave the safety of marriage in pursuit of sexual pleasure. Ghose argued that reproductive marital sex, as dictated in the hierarchical typologies of Sanskrit text, was the only way to control the unbound sexual desires of the *Hastini* woman and her "carnal appetites." She was a woman "mad after lustful desires," a type of woman that required textual elucidation and comprehensive analysis.

For Ghose, the study of ancient and medieval Sanskrit texts on sexual strictures was critical for modern social science. Sanskrit texts were universally applicable treatises that Ghosh argued could make "any subject . . . intelligible to all."[2] Ghose insisted that a return to Sanskrit textual origins would provide strict moral guidelines for modern social life, dictates that ensured healthy reproduction for future generations in modernizing India: "As the progress of the world depends upon coming generations . . . the *Rati-Sastram* deals upon those features of sexual enjoyment as are productive of good progeny."[3]

Ghose's *Rati-Sastram* reflects the rapid popularization of the *Kokasastra* and other Hindu sexual science texts that occurred at the turn of the twentieth century among reading publics in India and beyond. Ghose's *Rati-Sastram* and other editions of *Ratirahasya* were widely popular. *Rati-Sastram* had six editions by 1921, and remained in publication until at least 1977.[4] *Ratirahasya* was translated and transmutated into English, German, Japanese, and into different Indian languages in the first decades of the twentieth century.[5] By 1964, Dr. Alex Comfort, the soon to be famous author of *The Joy of Sex* (1972), published an English rendition of the *Ratirahasya* with a preface by ethnologist W. G. Archer that circulated widely in Europe and America.[6]

The modern study of society in India was built on the philological study of sex. The emergence of a popular literature in India on sexual sciences in the late nineteenth century was part of a global moment when philology reigned supreme and sexuality became its primary object.[7] These studies asserted the central place of Sanskrit texts on deviant female sexuality and prostitution in the study and assessment of the progress of modern society. The study of ancient Indian sex life focused on the "discovery" of ancient texts and the creation of a fixed set of Sanskrit texts that systematized the study of ancient Indian erotics.

A network of men—British colonial officers and scientists, American and German Indologists, and Bengali social analysts and public intellectuals—collectively engaged in researching and writing about the textual basis of Indian erotics, particularly strictures on female sexuality. They investigated the origins of female sexual control through the translation, interpretation, and canonization of a set of premodern Sanskrit works, such as the *Kamasutra*, *Anangaranga*, and the *Kokasastra*, alongside epics and foundational treatises like the *Mahabharata*, the *Ramayana*, and the *Manusmriti*. Interest in the Sanskrit sexual sciences extended from scholarly discourse to a wide popular readership, with diverse reading publics including philologists in academic institutions across the world, specialized scholars of medical science, biology, and sociology, and a wide variety of people who consumed pulp "foot path" (street) literature on ancient Hindu erotics.

By the mid-nineteenth century, the field of philology encompassed the study of classical and "Oriental" literatures as well as the comparative analysis of languages and language families. Philology was a historical science, its methods genealogical. It was concerned first and foremost with the question of the origins of languages and civilizations but came to include the full range of antiquarian studies of ancient and medieval texts.[8] Throughout Western Europe philology was considered the "king of the sciences," encompassing the formal linguistic study of texts as well the interpretation of premodern texts. Philological method shaped the development of various modern academic disciplines, from literature and anthropology to history and comparative religious studies.[9] Indology—the study of Sanskrit, Pali, Prakrit, and other languages and textual practices of India—was arguably the most influential subfield in this broad discipline, largely due to the influence of Sanskrit scholars like Max Müller and William Dwight Whitney. Through the comparative study of language families and "Aryan" consanguine "races," it powerfully shaped the development of a widespread understanding that Indians and Europeans shared not only a common linguistic heritage but also a common racial past.[10] As Ronald Inden has argued, Indology and its methods of linguistic derivation and comparative analysis became hegemonic in many fields of knowledge that took as their object Indian culture and civilization.[11] Philology, as imagined by Max Müller and others, was a parallel project to the natural sciences, a *scientific* understanding of the essences of language and enduring nature of Indian "social custom" that these ancient languages and premodern texts represented.[12]

Within this form of reasoning, ancient Sanskrit texts were the only sources required to comprehend all parts of historical and contemporary Indian life. Indological study produced a widely influential interpretative practice that utilized the narrow textual interpretations of Indian society in the creation of exclusionary models for Indian social futures. Philological studies defined a singular vision of a timeless and unchanging Hindu society by enforcing fixed practices of interpretation and constituting a selective canon of Sanskrit texts. It was from this notion of the static essence of Hindus that particular concepts—kingship, caste, *sati*, and, as Uma Chakravarti brilliantly shows, Aryan womanhood—became exemplary of the past and present of Hindu society. The philological study of Sanskrit texts on ancient sex life from marriage to prostitution occupied a primary role in the study of Indian society.

In this chapter, I offer a conceptual history of the modern study of ancient Indian sex. I trace the intellectual history of how the philology of Sanskrit erotics, particularly through concepts of deviant female sexuality, shaped the modern study of social life. To be clear, I am not producing either an exhaustive account of all Sanskrit texts on erotics or an interpretation of the true meaning of these texts. Rather I offer a different history—of how modern philological inquiry produced deviant female sexuality, as found in premodern Sanskrit text, as an originary object for the study of modern Indian society. What was lost in these new fixed structures of knowledge was the multiplicity of interpretations of different texts on premodern social life.

This chapter examines the transregional rise of the field of Indological erotics in the period between the 1880s and the 1950s and beyond. Beginning my narrative with the publication of *The Kama Sutra of Vatsayana* by Sir Richard F. Burton in 1883, I trace how *kama*—that amorphous concept variously understood as desire, love, sex, erotics, sexuality—became an object of knowledge. Burton's *The Kama Sutra* defined the new modern study of erotics in Sanskrit texts, with an explicit focus on the sexuality of Indian women. I then turn to how the study of sexual life in India became primarily an Indological project at the turn of the twentieth century by Indologists in Germany and the United States, most famously in the extensive scholarship on Indian women by Richard Schmidt and Johann Jakob Meyer.

Alongside the highly sensationalist publications of Burton and the detailed philological studies of Schmidt and Meyer, a network of Bengali philologists and scientists produced their own studies. They argued that the philology of Indian sex life was essential to the sociological study of modern Indian society. The second part of the chapter explores how these Bengali social analysts constituted Sanskrit texts as originary guides for masculinity and patriarchal power. Through claims to philological mastery and authority, elite Hindu men constituted new theories of caste and racial hierarchy. In their analysis, social transgression was the result of women's sexual deviance. These men included well-known academic philologists like H. C. Chakladar, medical doctors like Santosh Kumar Mukherji, and public intellectuals, including S. N. Sinha, Nripendra Kumar Basu, and Chandra Chakraberty. The Indology of Sanskrit erotics, particularly the sexuality of women, defined new forms of modern social scientific inquiry.

Kama as a Modern Object of Knowledge

The *Kamasutra* is one of the most widely circulated ancient Indian texts in the modern world. It has been described as everything from the first scientific study of sex, to a vital book of Hindu erotics, to an ancient treatise on love, to a sexological manual, to the definitive account of ancient Indian society. It became an object of fascination in the 1880s with the translation and wide circulation of the text by East India Company political agent Richard F. Burton (1821–1890) in his *The Kama Sutra of Vatsayana*. Burton is well known for his role in shaping colonial knowledge across the empire and for his many publications on regions as diverse as Africa and Central and South Asia.[13] A self-proclaimed explorer, translator, commentator, and ethnographer, he imagined the East as a timeless archive of unchanging social practices from the ancient to the colonial world. He wrote prolifically about his travels and produced interpretive translations of Sanskrit, Arabic, and Persian texts that became definitive representations of the region. He was perhaps most famous for his transcreation of *The Book of The Thousand Nights and a Night*, which shaped nineteenth- and twentieth-century Orientalist notions of despotism, sexual transgression, and wonder of the Muslim world.[14] Likewise, his travel writings through Sindh and Africa and his erotic publications were critical for popular understandings of "native" sexuality. Through exaggerated representations of sexual practices and religious superstition, Burton claimed to capture the true social lives of colonized subjects.

Burton's early translation and interpretation of *Kamasutra* has become emblematic of the fantastical Orientalism that shaped the late nineteenth-century imagination about India. In truth, Burton himself did little of the translation; instead, it was the product of his collaborators Forster Fitzgerald Arbuthnot (1833–1901) and two Indian men, Bhagavanlal Indrajit and

Shivaram Parashuram Bhide. The text gained widespread popularity as Burton's *The Kama Sutra*, circulating all over the world (it remains in print today).[15] As Anjali Arondekar has demonstrated, even the rumor of Burton's travels produced a furor. People sought Burton's fantastical depictions of a "perverse" Indian sexuality. The fascination with Burton led to an almost obsessive interest in searching for his lost accounts.[16]

The *kama* texts that fascinated Burton were in fact not simply treatises on sex but broader inquiries that addressed subjects ranging from domestic practices to cosmetics to gardens.[17] What was presented to the colonial world as *The Kama Sutra* and taken to be a literal translation of Vatsayana's *Kamasutra* was in fact the selective (and poor) translation of one part of a multipart disquisition on erotics and manners. Burton's *The Kama Sutra* was a phantasmatic claim to empiricism based in imagination—the selective translation, interpretation, and reinvention of texts, rather than a comprehensive translation of a Sanskrit treatise.[18] Burton's *The Kama Sutra* was initially based on the partial translations of a fifteenth-century text, *Anangaranga*. He claimed that he collected parts of manuscripts from across India with the help of Hindu pundits. These manuscripts, Burton asserted, were compared for their facticity through the tools of comparative philology. In later editions, Burton merged his original text with selections from Vatsayana's *Kamasutra*, as well as with a thirteenth-century Sanskrit commentary.[19]

What I would like to highlight here is the generative energy of Burton's publications for a new field of inquiry. Burton's *The Kama Sutra* fueled the widespread interest in Sanskrit texts on *kama*.[20] Its publication was followed by decades of extended translations and critical editions of the Sanskrit texts across Europe and led to a new interest in the study of *kama* into other ancient and medieval Sanskrit treatises among German and Indian Indologists and sociologists. Widely circulated by the fictitious Hindoo Kama Shastra Society, it immediately gained an audience across Europe, fueling the public fascination in the metropole for texts that animated ancient Indian sex life.[21] For his part, Burton claimed the text was meant to be read beyond its titillating details, as a science; *The Kama Sutra* was a scientific understanding of what he termed the "Hindu art of love."[22] Burton sought to assimilate Sanskrit erotics in a comprehensive canon of Oriental texts, which were in his view interchangeable and representative of the highly sexualized and unchanging nature of colonized societies. In his prefatory remarks to the first edition, he drew links between the classificatory regimes of Sanskrit texts that he paralleled to classification of animals in the natural sciences: "Men and women are divided into classes and divisions in the same way that Buffon and other writers on natural history have classified and divided the animal world."²³ Burton's sensational accounts led scholars of the late nineteenth century to address *kama* as an object of knowledge in learned, detailed philological studies.

Indeed, Burton asserted that his *The Kama Sutra* should be placed alongside British scientific texts, most notably the pseudonymous medical doctor Thomas Bell's *Kalogynomia: or the Laws of Female Beauty* (1821)—itself a pseudo-scientific sex manual on the dangerous sexualities of women, from polygamy to prostitution to infidelity.²⁴ For Burton, the theme of "Hindoo" conceptions of love found in the Sanskrit *Kamasutra* and *Anangaranga* were to be read by the learned scholar as parallel and in conversation with this English scientific study of female beauty and sexuality. Burton made a conceptual equivalence between the European sciences of female sexuality and ancient *kama* texts. His interpretation of *Kamasutra* merged his understanding of premodern Indian sexual practices with scientific studies circulating in the nineteenth century on the status of women, their beauty, and their role in marriage and prostitution.²⁵

In *The Kama Sutra*, Burton produced a comprehensive canon of Oriental erotics, and even extended the analysis to other times and places. All texts on ancient "ars erotica" across the colonial world were to be taken as equivalent and interchangeable. This project was transhistorical in application, trans-geographical in scope. In India, he argued, there was an ancient urtext on *kama*, composed by Vatsayana, which appeared as *Anangaranga* later and then morphed into the sixth-century Arabic text *Lizzat al-Nisa*, from which emerged Persian and Turkish versions.

Indeed, as the preface to Burton's *Ananga-Ranga* proclaims, the knowledge of Hindu erotics was so commonplace as to be the very natural world of all societies of the near and far East: "In these days the Ananga-Ranga enjoys deserved celebrity. Lithographed copies have been printed by hundreds of thousands, and the book is in the hands of both sexes and all ages throughout the nearer East, and possibly it may extend to China and Japan. It has become a part of natural life."²⁶ Put another way, the book was to be treated as an anthropological study of the very nature of Hindu society, naturalized across all of the East. He writes in the preface that "the book becomes an ethnological treasure, which tells us as much of Hindu human nature as the 'Thousand Nights and a Night' of Arab manners and customs in the *cinquecento*."²⁷ Burton argues that Hindu erotics were valuable precisely because they were a social science that could be used to comprehend the whole history and present of the people of India: "*The*

Kama Sutra of Vatsyayana, concerning which more presently, and *Ananga-Ranga* must be regarded as two valuable and interesting works on Social Science: they bear repeated readings."[28]

The publication of Burton's *The Kama Sutra* was a signal event. Alongside his exaggerated Orientalist depictions of Indian sexuality, we may consider the enormous impact of Burton's claims about the systematic study of Indian social life. Burton's project of reading Sanskrit treatises produced new *methods* based in the search for origins that constituted a new episteme built on a set of texts. After Burton, sociological inquiry about modern Indian society was to be based in a canon of Sanskrit sources about the sexual practices of ancient and medieval India.

Analytically key in Burton's *The Kama Sutra* is his insistence that female sexuality was critical in the past and present of Indian social life. Deviant female sexuality was thus the metric through which to measure timeless characteristics of Indian society. In discussing the nature of women in *The Kama Sutra*, he describes how typical social gatherings in India always consisted of men who "sit together in company with public women" and engage in discourse.[29] Through the idea of public women, he draws an analogy between the women who appeared in Sanskrit texts at social gatherings with a comparative history of the Greek courtesan. He cites the early nineteenth-century Orientalist H. H. Wilson's *Select Specimens of Theatre of the Hindoos* (1826) to describe courtesans—equated with the Sanskrit *vesya*—as women who were "unfriendly" to married women in society.[30] Burton argues that the courtesans, or *vesya*, were equivalent to the Hetaerae of the Greeks. This comparison between ancient Greece and ancient India was to become an integral part of the study of modern India, for it proved that India had an ancient golden age, parallel to the status of Greek philosophy and ancient civilization, which was critical to claims of philosophical origins in modern Europe. Burton argues that the courtesan of India, like the Hetaerae of ancient Greece, was essential to the very workings of "Hindoo society."[31] But unlike Europe, which had successfully progressed and overcome the sexual proclivities of the ancient Greeks, Indian society was timeless and unchanging.

Burton's citation of H. H. Wilson is itself part of this philological genealogy. Wilson was a prominent British Orientalist and author of the first Sanskrit-English dictionary. His *Select Specimens of Theatre of the Hindoos* studied the most influential representation of Indian womanhood in the late eighteenth and early nineteenth centuries: the story of Sakuntala, first told in the epic *Mahabharata*, then dramatized in a play by the poet Kalidasa and later translated in 1789 by William Jones, the philologist and East India Company jurist. Jones is now most famous for his translation and early codification of a Hindu legal structure based on *Manava-Dharmasastra* (*The Laws of Manu*) and his critical role in founding the Asiatic Society. Jones had translated Sakuntala into English in his 1789 *Sacontalá or The Fatal Ring: An Indian Drama* to wide acclaim.[32] Jones's translation of Sakuntala circulated widely in Europe, influencing European Romantic writers, most famously Johann W. von Goethe. Jones had long fostered an interest in thinking about primitive promiscuity as a fundamental characteristic of Indian women. In 1784 he had composed, among other poems like hymns to Indira, Lakshmi, Durga, and Bhavani, an ode to "The Hindu Wife."[33] In his verses, Jones transposes the biblical story of the original forbidden fruit onto the story of Draupadi and her five husbands from the *Mahabharata* to illustrate how the Hindu wife was forever tempted by her sexual excess. As early as the 1780s, Jones had treated women's sexual deviance as essential to the Indological enterprise.

Almost a century later Burton replicated Jones's framework, repeatedly returning to the critical place of Indian women's sexuality in Sanskrit texts for the study of Indian society. Burton described women's sexuality primarily through the concept of the courtesan. Importantly, he constructed an inextricable nexus between the courtesan and prostitute that was to become an essential part of the modern study of Sanskrit erotic texts. He argued the courtesan was representative of the essence of *all* Indian women: "But while some women are born courtesans, and follow the instincts of their nature in every class of society, it has been truly said by some authors that every woman has got an inkling of the profession in her nature."[34] Burton insisted that all women across social rank and community, married or unmarried, across the history of India, were sexually deviant. He conceived of Sanskrit texts as tools that could be used to combat and control female sexuality.

In his preface, Burton narrates an origin story for the ancient production of *Kamasutra*. The story was of a woman with a voracious sexual appetite who needed to be disciplined through a systematic study that would give written guidelines for controlling women. According to Burton, there was once a notorious sexually voracious woman who "was burning with love and could find none to satisfy her inordinate desires threw off her clothes and swore she would wander the world naked until she met her match."[35] Her lust was unmatched, her desires never satisfied. Left without any satiation from inadequate male lovers, she finally experienced satisfaction from the learned skills of "Koka Pandit." He was a priest who had requested permission from the King to "tame the shrew." Koka Pandit, with his breadth of techniques and his ability to control her sexuality, finally satisfied her carnal appetite, in essence, domesticating her desires through sex. Impressed with his domination, the King beseeched Koka Pandit to write a universal guide for controlling the dangerous sexual appetites of all unrestrained women.[36] For Burton, this tale of Koka Pandit was the origin of all *kama* texts, created to control the insatiable nature of Indian women's sexuality.

Burton proclaimed that the purpose of *kama* texts in the modern world was to control female sexuality, just as it had been in ancient India. His project made two pivotal shifts that shaped the study of Indian erotics. First, it posited the necessity of a global comparative approach to the study of sexual life and second, it argued for the foundational place of female sexuality in apprehending the past and present condition of Indian society. With Burton's study of *kama*, Hindu erotics became a primary site for the philological investigation of Indian social life and structure. Burton's project transformed into a whole field of knowledge on the science of Indian sexuality.

The *Wissenschaft* of Ancient Indian Sexual Life

Richard Schmidt (1866–1939), a professor of Sanskrit at Halle University, was a comparative Indologist. He was the next important figure to engage in the field of Indian erotics. Schmidt published a key translation of Vatsayana's *Kamasutra* that appeared in 1897 (the 1904 cover appears in Figure 1) and followed it with several studies that produced a scholarly treatment of the *Kamasutra* as well as a wide array of treatises from the Sanskrit canon on erotics.[37]

In his most significant work, *Beiträge zur indischen Erotik* (Contribution to the study of Indian erotics, 1902), Schmidt places *Kamasutra* as the earliest text in a comprehensive canon of ancient and medieval Hindu erotic treatises. In his 660-page study that combined bibliographical compilation with textual analysis, Schmidt examines the *Kamasutra* and the *Anangaranga*, as well as other *kama* texts, with an extended scholarly commentary about language and context of Sanskrit erotic materials. It is an encyclopedic study that created a canon of Sanskrit *kama* texts and provided a detailed exegesis of key concepts.

Schmidt poses *kama* as part of a triumvirate of concepts, alongside *dharma* and *artha*, that explained ancient Indian lives. *Kama* dealt with love and sexuality, *dharma* with "morality and piety," and *artha* with the principles of privilege, money, and property.[38] This same tripartite philological structure of Hindu culture and civilization also shaped colonial law, from the codification of the *dharmasastras* of Manu (*The Laws of Manu*) to the later "discovery," in the early twentieth century, of an edition of the *Arthashastra*, the primary ancient

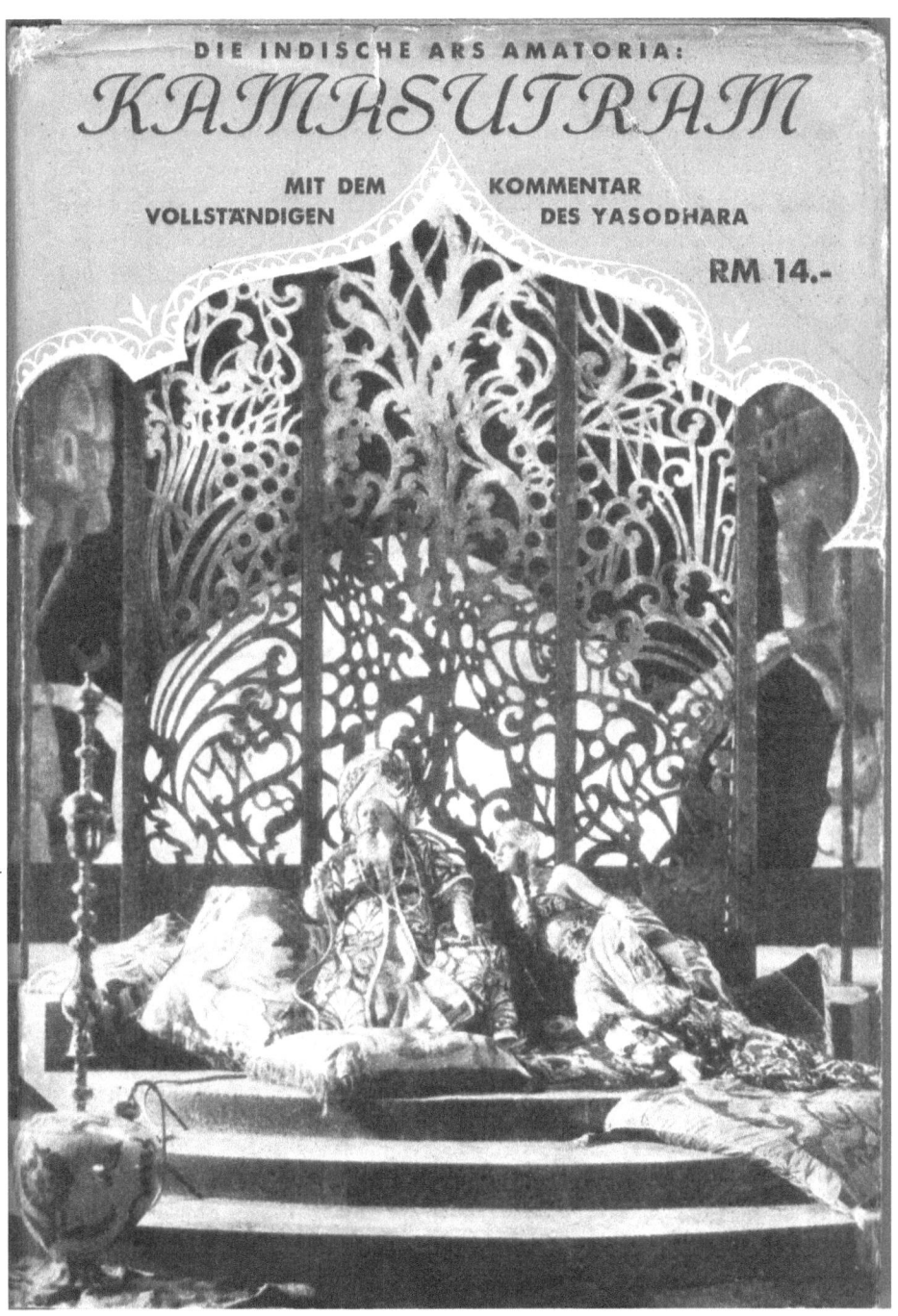

FIGURE 1. Richard Schmidt, *Kamasutram* (1904), cover.

Sanskrit treatise of political theory.[39] Following his extended study of *kama*, Schmidt published a detailed annotated translation of the *Arthashastra* in 1923.[40] Schmidt described his work as a "collection of documents" with philological annotations, emphasizing that it was of scholarly value as both a comprehensive description of the texts and a broad interpretation of Hindu erotics.[41] With the publication of *Beiträge,* Schmidt became the definitive expert on Sanskrit love and erotics at a moment when the study of ancient Sanskrit texts was permeating not only German philology but also new studies of religion, sociology, and history.[42]

In his preface to the first edition, Schmidt situates his study of *kama* texts alongside a growing field of sexual sciences emerging at the end of the nineteenth century in Germany. Indeed, he described it as *Wissenschaft,* or a systematic science, of Hindu erotics. Like Burton, Schmidt claimed it was not a study meant to produce titillation for the reader, but one with pure *scientific* value. Where Burton had placed *The Kama Sutra* in conversation with an emerging British scientific literature on women's excessive sexuality, Schmidt equated his study with the foundational text of a new German sexual science, *Psychopathia Sexualis* (1884), authored by the so-called father of modern sexology, Richard Krafft-Ebing, as well as with the works of prominent sexologist Albert Moll. Like Krafft-Ebing, Schmidt argued, he translated all "titillating" or "sensitive" sexual material into Latin to shield the reader. He emphasizes his chaste, purely scientific outlook:

> It is easily conceivable that my book will find readers, who do not study with the pure eyes of the researcher, but devour it with the lustful greed of libertine will. To them alone I say that my book is a very serious, strictly scientific study, and to note the fact that I everywhere use selected Latin terms, written similar to what Moll or Krafft-Ebing have done in their scientific books about libido or Psychopathia Sexualis.[43]

Schmidt believed he was performing important comparative work by reading the *Kamasutra* and *Anangaranga* in dialogue with other Sanskrit texts.[44] He further argued that his study should be read in conjunction with other philological studies. Notably, Schmidt also saw his project in conversation with the modern sociology of Max Weber, whose study of modern religion was based in a comparative analysis of Western and Hindu texts.[45]

Schmidt addressed the sexuality of women across a wide variety of Sanskrit texts. In constituting a canon of erotics, Schmidt took a taxonomical approach. His chapters outline typologies of women's sexual temperaments, provide extended analysis of the four classes of women and their associated sexual characteristics, and describe at length the physical attributes of women's bodies (particularly the vulva as well as the physical changes of pregnancy). Drawing on a wide range of Sanskrit sources, Schmidt analyzes the effects of pregnancy, abortion, and the power of the female orgasm. He also describes in detail the role of women in marriage, in particular as a bride and then as a married woman, specifically intercourse of married women with other men who were not their husbands. Most strikingly, Schmidt devotes over a hundred pages to an extended analysis of Indian courtesans and the art of the courtesan beauty. Paying attention to details—particularly, penis size and enlargement and different sexual positions—he sketches out multiple sex acts and the effects of arousal on the body, stories that had elicited fascination and marvel from audiences of Burton's *The Kama Sutra*.

Schmidt considered love to be a universal human condition, and argued that its significance was most amplified in India—whose climate itself made love all-encompassing in a land of extremes.

> If love is so important universally, we must not be surprised to learn that under special conditions, particularly climatic, its already great importance is amplified to proportions by which the relatively humble standards of us northerners seem fabulous, even grotesque. Such is the case in India, that land of opposites, where the human temperament oscillates between the sublime and the vile, the gracious and the monstrous, the beautiful and the hideous, and desire extends from the most atrocious asceticism to the craziest of debauchery. The blast-furnace heat of the Indian sun, the fairy splendor of the vegetation, the enchanting poetry of the moonlight nights permeated with the fragrance of the lotus flower, finally—and by no means least—the peculiar role the Indian people have played from time immemorial, the role of world-forsaking dreamers, philosophers, impractical enthusiasts, all unite to make the Indian a true virtuoso in love. Thus love in India, in theory and practice, is an engrossing preoccupation of whose paramount importance we can hardly comprehend.[46]

Like Burton and other colonial administrators, Schmidt argues the climate of India fostered a kind of racialized sensuality that was timeless. This idea of an erotic love, one that was the sensory experience, language, and very sensibility of a transhistorical Indian people, was the most cited passage from Schmidt's work. It became the reigning sentiment about Indian social life in the field of Indology.

Schmidt's study of Sanskrit erotics had a profound impact on another key field of knowledge emerging at that time: sexology. A survey of significant German sexological literature of the period demonstrates the extraordinary reach of Indology in shaping universalist and essentialist theories of the civilizational origins and development of sexual difference and modern sexuality.[47] The sexuality of ancient civilizations was foundational to European scholarship on texts and ideas that had structured modern civilizations. Schmidt's comprehensive analysis of Hindu erotics is widely cited, notably by famous German sexologist Havelock Ellis in his 1921 *Studies in the Psychology of Sex* and by Iwan Bloch the physician and sexologist who, with Magnus Hirschfeld and Albert Eulenburg, coined the concept of *Sexualwissenschaft* or sexology.[48] Bloch relied on Schmidt to demonstrate the critical importance of "Hindu love" in creating a set of universal principles that governed social and sexual life.[49] Magnus Hirschfeld, who founded the the Institute of Sexual Science in Berlin, delivered a lecture on "Hindu Sexology" in his tour of India in 1931, where he lamented that the modern world had yet to understand the complexity of the Hindu sexual sciences, which he argued were the world's first sexology.[50]

As Schmidt was producing scholarship on *kama*, American scholars had initiated new studies in the field of Indology. In the United States, Indo-European philology had solidified as a growing field by the 1880s, creating a generation of American-born philologists invested in the study of Sanskrit as necessary to any comparative project in the social sciences. US universities had fashioned themselves after the German model, and in Germany, no field of study had more influence than comparative philology. American Indologists, most famously William Dwight Whitney at Yale University, participated in the emergence of a field of comparative philology that proliferated alongside the growing field of comparative ethnology. In 1892, Carl Darling Buck, an American who studied Sanskrit in Germany, was appointed the first chair of Indology at the newly founded University of Chicago. Buck trained a new generation of Indologists, including a student who would go on to write the definitive study of ancient sexual life in India, Johann Jakob Meyer.[51]

Meyer (1870–1939) was appointed professor of Sanskrit and German at the University of Chicago in 1899.[52] Meyer was famous in the American and European academy as a scholar who interpreted and translated texts relating to all three Hindu principles—*dharma, artha,* and *kama*—for a wider audience. He produced a widely cited German translation of the *Arthashastra* (1927) and numerous studies on ancient Indian society and erotics.[53] But he was best known for his ambitious investigation of ancient Indian sex life in Sanskrit epics in his *Sexual Life in Ancient India: A Study in the Comparative History of Indian Culture* (1929). *Sexual Life* was the English adaptation and translation of his 1915 German publication, *Das Weib im altindischen Epos: Ein Beitrag zur indischen und zur vergleichenden Kulturgeschichte* (The woman in the ancient Indian epic: A contribution to Indian and comparative cultural history), a book that Meyer dedicated to the German scholar Schmidt: "Richard Schmidt, in Verehrung und Freundshaft."[54] With over seventy editions across the world, *Sexual Life in Ancient India* is still in print today.

Sexual Life in Ancient India has received little scholarly treatment despite being one of the most widely circulated philological studies of India in the twentieth century. Meyer offers romantic stories in the style of early colonial Indologists alongside positivist interpretations of Sanskrit erotics along universal schemes of primitivity and civilization. While his title proclaims the book to be a study of sexual life, Meyer primarily addresses the question of women's sexuality and their role in marriage. We have already seen how the philological approach to Indian sex life—from Burton to Schmidt—focused on the status and sexuality of Indian women in ancient and medieval texts. It is no accident that Meyer presents women as representative of all of "sexual life" for India. Indeed, Meyer equates the study of women with the Indological investigation of ancient sex—an equivalence between the whole of ancient sexuality and womanhood, past and present, that is taken up again and again by Indian writers in the 1920s and 1930s. Together with Schmidt's classificatory systems, Meyer's comparative hermeneutic linked the philological study of Indian sexual life to the study of female sex.

Meyer suggested that his reading of Indian sexual life was based on the translation and interpretation of narrative tales that detailed women as sexual and social subjects, from the *Mahabharata* and *Ramayana*. His chapters include "The Maiden," which relates the status of women in the *Mahabharata* and *Ramayana* to contemporary Hindu womanhood and society. The extended detailing of the maiden is followed by an exegesis of the characteristics of the fallen maiden, the woman who falls outside of monogamous marriage. Following the section on "The Maiden," Meyer then analyzes the nature of kinship and women in a chapter on marriage. His study of sexual life travels from chapters on motherhood, women's sexuality, and most extensively on the "public woman" who enjoyed "venal love."[55] The Hindu epic could be used to understand the nature of woman in different stages of her development as well as in her sexuality, in and out of marriage.[56]

Meyer emphasizes how the *Mahabharata* and *Ramayana* conveyed the very essence of what it meant to be Indian, now and then. He describes how an exhaustive chronicling of texts from "old India" is essential to understand a new India.[57] In this description, the timeless nature of the Indian could be found in their forms and structures of knowledge, which were in essence a contradiction: "Thus, in very many points, we can look for no inner consistency in either of the two great national Epics of India. In every human being, indeed, we can find a host of contradictions side by side; how much the more will they be found where many minds have helped in the building up of one work."[58] To Meyer, the dualism of Indian society was best understood through the metaphysical and philological study of the nature of the Indian woman. Like Schmidt, Meyer describes how the foundation of Indian life was defined through this dualism:

> Woman and all belonging to her, or to speak more exactly, on the subject of the reflection of this object in the brain and heart of Man, the two great Epics ... contain very contradictory utterances ... This lies first of all in the nature of the Indian ... In the soul of the Indian there dwells that twin pair, burning sensuality and stark renunciation of the world and the flesh. What a delight and torment then must woman be to him![59]

There were two personalities that in essence defined India: "the voluptuary and the renouncer."[60] Meyer opens his text by emphasizing the dichotomous nature of Hindu society across time. He suggests that these oppositional characteristics of desire and renunciation permeated all of ancient and contemporary social life in India. These epics "still exerted an influence to-day on the mind and the life of the Hindu people."[61] Meyer annotates this declaration by extensively citing studies that revealed how the epic shaped the contemporary Indian mind. His references include Nisikantha Chattopadhyay and his study of Hindu society in his *Indian Essays,* Ramkrishna and his wide influence as a Bengali spiritual leader, and the famed poet and Nobel laureate Rabindranath Tagore.[62]

Meyer's citations are so wide ranging that his commentarial para text takes up most of the pages of his study. He repeatedly references Schmidt's 1902 *Beiträge zur indischen Erotik,* James Tod's *Annals and Antiquities of Rajasthan* (1829), and the German ethnology journal *Anthropos,* edited by Wilhelm Schmidt. Meyer correlates his interpretation of Sanskrit text with widely influential ethnological ideas of social evolution from primitive societies to modern society based in monogamy. He consistently mentions ideas about female promiscuity and primitivity in order to correlate Sanskrit epic depictions of women to the science of social evolution. In particular, he cites the unbounded sexuality of women in jurist John Ferguson McLennan's *Primitive Marriage* (1865) and Edwin Sidney Hartland's *Primitive Paternity* (1909) multiple times in the book.

Meyer's extensive references demonstrate his comparative method of study and the essential role of ethnological concepts of female sexuality in so-called primitive society and the evolution of marriage for the philological study of sex. As I show in chapter 4, "Evolution," ethnological models of comparative human development hinged on the control of female sexuality, an idea that was to be widely influential in social scientific thought throughout the twentieth century. The assessment of social stage, from primitive promiscuity to civility, was based in one's proximity to patriarchal monogamy.

Meyer further cites texts by Indian writers of the time on what he describes as the degraded social condition of the country's women, most notably Pandita Ramabai's *The High Caste Hindu Woman* (1887), as well as comprehensive books on Hindu society by Bengali writers, including S. C. Bose, *The Hindoos as They Are* (1881) and Bulloram Mullick, *Home Life in Bengal* (1885).[63] Meyer thus constructs a comparative hermeneutical method to comprehend Indian sexual life, providing extensive analogs to Hindu epics in comparative contexts from Finnish erotics, to medieval Europe, to the medieval 'Abbasid, to the ancient sexual practices of the Greeks and Romans. This project of comparative ancient sexualities was linked to ethnological models of social evolution based in monogamy, as well as in colonial social critiques that sought the reform of social custom in Indian society.

The Indological studies of Schmidt and Meyer, like other philological work of the period, were invested in the dating of ancient Sanskrit texts, the bibliographical compilation and canonization of manuscripts, and readings of the meaning of *kama* in Sanskrit texts through a comparative citational apparatus. For scholars like Richard Schmidt and Johann Jakob Meyer, the study of Sanskrit erotics was a scientific endeavor that could elucidate the origins of those essential characteristics that defined the timeless nature of Indian society, which they argued was made up of unchanging people mired in contradictions. With the widespread publication and citation of these texts across disciplines, languages, and geographies, here was an intellectual moment where the study of ancient Indian sex life, focused in particular on the subordination and erasure of female sexual desire, became the first step to the modern study of sex.[64]

In this archive of Sanskrit erotics, one encounters the myriad ways Indian history and social life were collapsed and flattened in time. A logic of equivalence produced as comparable objects different societies, a project of aggregation and juxtaposition that linked vast geographies, texts, and peoples through the status of women. Like Max Müller, European and American social analysts sought to produce a field akin to the natural history of female sexuality. Female sex appears as the very essence of a timeless Indian culture, its very nature, used to comprehend its past, present, and future of Indian society.

The Indology of sex told a story of origins: not only of those structures of sexual control and patriarchal marriage that shaped Indian society, but of a universal science of sexuality, as famed German sexologist Magnus Hirschfeld himself proclaimed. This mode of inquiry, whereby ancient sex came to define modern social scientific inquiry, extended far beyond European intellectual circles. Concurrent with the rise of European studies of ancient Indian sex life, there was a resurgence of interest in intellectual histories of sex and sexuality that arose in Calcutta and, eventually, in other parts of India. In the section that follows, I explore how, in Calcutta and elsewhere, a new genre of scientific history writing on ancient Indian sex life emerged from the late nineteenth century to the 1930s. A network of Bengali intellectuals treated the philological origins of ancient sexuality as a foundational site for social scientific study. This project culminated in systematic, totalizing studies of prostitution in the 1920s and 1930s as well as broad studies of Indian social life and polity.

The Indology of Sex as the Study of Modern Social Life

A global history of studies of ancient Indian sexuality connected Europe, America, and India. In this transregional movement of texts and ideas on the origins of Indian sex life, comparison emerged as a key method. Like their European and American counterparts, a network of Bengali intellectuals utilized the philological study of ancient sexuality in Sanskrit texts to describe the temporal progress of Indian civilization.[65] Richard Schmidt had praised the philological work of Rajendralal Mitra, who produced a critical bibliography of key ancient texts in the late nineteenth century in Calcutta, which was to become essential in the creation of a canon of erotic treatises. There were a number of other prominent philologists and scientists studying Sanskrit texts in Calcutta. These men, in addition to being philologists and social analysts, were medical doctors, bureaucrats, legislators; they shaped state policies based in these texts, made new scientific and educational institutions, and led social movements. Although Indological studies often did not explicitly refer to anti-colonial nationalism, upper-caste Bengali elites looked to ancient Sanskrit texts to constitute normative models of modern society in pursuit of social and political autonomy.

With the rise of print in Calcutta came new studies of contemporary society that also demanded an account of the ancient past. This conceptual link between the ancient past and the present permeated Bengali social scientific inquiry about an array of sociological subjects. This temporal reasoning, whereby progress could be measured through the assessment and rejection of practices treated as remnants of a nonmodern past, produced the vacillation between modern and traditional that was to become a central paradox for ideas of social progress in the colonial world. As Prathama Banerjee argues, linear progress was the primary indicator of political capability or social exclusion—the central problematic of modern politics in India.[66] An "unprecedented temporal judgment" became essential to assess the legitimacy of collective political action and the value of social norms, as well as the possibility of one's belonging to a social or political community.[67]

Let us return to Abinash Chandra Ghose's *Rati-Sastram* (1894), a text published in the same year as Schmidt's definitive translation of *Kamasutra*. Ghose claimed Sanskrit textual origins as the basis of his taxonomical scheme of sex and marriage in modern India. Ghose offers an essentialist argument about the Sanskrit origins of Indian sexual practices. Sanskrit text appears here as prescriptive, essential to the study and control of women's sexuality. Like many subsequent Bengali publications, Ghose classifies men and women into four types based in what he terms, in the title of his study, the "Hindu sexual sciences." While it addresses male sexuality, the manual focuses on the textual mandates for women's sexuality, from dictates about their body and comportment, to chastity, to their segregation and pollution. The typological scheme of sexuality was mapped onto a taxonomy of caste hierarchies—for example, the feminine comportment of high-caste women versus the attributed masculinity of low-caste women. Ghose provides extensive details about women's behavior, their menstruation cycles, and the relationship between women's behavior and the health of future progeny.

In his hierarchy of social types, Ghose labels *Padmini* as women of the highest order—feminine and chaste—as opposed to the *Hastini*—who were the most unchaste of women, with masculine characteristics and brash sexuality. For him, Sanskrit categories served to differentiate women in terms of their proximity to appropriate norms of femininity, monogamous marriage, and caste stricture. Ghose presents the typology as a timeless model for womanhood, a usable guide that could be used to classify women in the present. This impulse toward typology, where women with physically masculine traits are hypersexual, aggressive, and socially dangerous, was not Ghose's alone, pervading many critical interpretations of Sanskrit categories of women.

In his *Rati-Sastram*, Ghose appropriates premodern text and asserts the authoritative place of Sanskrit knowledge for a theory of the dangers of women's sexual impurity. Women were fundamentally a paradox, always in proximity to sexual transgression and suffused with the potential for excessive expressions of sexual desire. This contradiction was a potential threat for both the housewife and the public woman. Ghose asserts that it was this ongoing danger of women's proximity to impurity that necessitated the social regulation of their movement in public spaces as well their most intimate social relationships, a regulation to be enforced by men.[68] Menstruation was a time of particular danger, a sign of the reproductive potential and bodily pollution that existed within every woman's body. According to Ghose, during the time of a woman's menstruation, even a woman of the highest social caste was nothing more than an outcaste woman, an untouchable, prone to social transgression and sexual deviance. Menstruation was absolute untouchability: "On the first day of her menstruation the impurity of a female is that of a Chandal woman. On the second day her impurity amounts to that of a woman who has slain a Brahman. On the third day her impurity amounts to that of a washer woman. On the fourth day she becomes pure."[69] In the footnote, he describes the degradation of women on their first day of menstruation:

> The Chandals form the lowest type of Hindu-society, they are looked upon with contempt as the most impure of men by the pious Hindus for their cruel profession of hunting harmless animals with dogs, and for their bodily uncleanliness, the act of killing an animal for food or for any other purpose being regarded as sinful.[70]

Menstruation was the height of a woman's impurity, a time when all women lost social status. Ghose considers her so debased as to be equivalent to those in society that committed acts of animal cruelty as well as other social sins. Deploying the rhetoric of ritual purity and citing practices of isolating Hindu women during menstruation, he systematically claims the dictates of an ancient Hindu sexual science to produce strict patriarchal, upper-caste strictures for women's behavior and social and spatial exclusion. Ghose is clear: the contemporary use of ancient texts was a necessity for the future of Indian society, as ancient dictates cautioned against the dangers of low-caste and outcaste women. Sanskrit origins served to mandate caste hierarchy and women's social exclusion, and to bring women under the authority of the patriarchal household. The relationship between the Indology of *kama* and the study of modern social life took on many forms as it developed in Ghose's wake. It was, in the aftermath of Ghose, a field of knowledge inextricably linked to caste difference.

Yet the study of Sanskrit *kama* texts yielded not only a typology of women but also a comprehensive framework that served to explain regional identity, geography, and kinship structures. The *Kamasutra*, according to the scholar Haran Chandra Chakladar in his 1929 *Social Life in Ancient India*, offered sociological insight into the "avowedly secular matter of social life" in ancient India. For Chakladar, *kama* texts provided a rationalist method for which to examine long enduring social customs in India. Chakladar (active ca. 1910–1937) was a professor at Calcutta University from 1917 to 1937, where he first taught in the Department of Ancient Indian History and Culture and later moved to the Department of Anthropology, of which he was made chair in the 1930s. Described by his peers as a devout Hindu, Chakladar left his faculty position at the university in 1937 to become a devotee at a small temple in the city of Puri.[71] His major work, *The Aryan Occupation of Eastern India* (1925), makes an originary claim for the modern region of Bengal, which he argues was the first place in the subcontinent to be occupied by Vedic Aryans. According to Chakladar, these Aryans likely composed the *Rg Veda* in eastern India, based on his assessment of the fauna prevalent in Bengal. Thus, according to Chakladar, the first Sanskrit text was Bengali. He sought to establish the origins of Bengali identity in the Aryan roots of the earliest Vedic texts.[72] His *Social Life in Ancient India* was translated in 1929 into French and was republished through the twentieth century, with the most recent version issued in 1990.

In *Social Life*, Chakladar notes that while the history of Indian politics and religion had received scholarly treatment, Indian social life had been neglected in modern studies of India, a thoroughly modern subject that required a *longue durée* perspective that only an Indologist could give. As he observes in his foreword to *Social Life in Ancient India*:

> Before a synthetic history embracing a long period, through which Indian society has grown and developed, is attempted, an intensive study has to be made of the different ages through which it has come. It was with this object that I took up the study of Vatsayana's *Kamasutra* which gives a beautifully vivid picture of Indian society in the early centuries of the Christian era.

Dealing with an avowedly secular matter as it does, it depicts society from an independent point of view, and gives details, especially of the darker features of social life, with a fullness that we naturally miss in the sacred texts.[73]

Chakladar took the *Kamasutra* to be a comprehensive manual on social life, necessary for understanding everyday secular practices. He emphasizes that *Kamasutra* was an ideal source for positivist interpretations of enduring customs, the origins of the essential character of Indian people. According to his argument, while the ancient Sanskrit texts of the *Dharmasastra* were used to determine Hindu marriage and religious dictates for caste difference and ritual practice, the *Kamasutra* and other *kama* texts were sociological texts about secular life: "The science of erotics had in the third century A.D. obtained equal footing with the sister sciences of Dharma and Artha as branches of learning."[74] *Kama* texts were critical to modern sociology in two ways. First, they were avowedly secular and scientific and thus could be disentangled from colonial critiques of the mythic nature of Sanskrit epics. Second, the *Kamasutra* and other texts on the science of erotics were the only ancient texts that addressed the civic norms that organized ancient and now modern society, from marriage to reproduction.

Like other philological studies, Chakladar emphasized the scientific authority of his inquiry. He claimed that in addition to its insights on everyday life, anyone could use the content of the *Kamasutra* to map the precise physical geography of India. Indeed, he begins *Social Life* with a detailed map of ancient India based on the *Vedas*, *Ramayana*, and the *Mahabharata*. To produce this cartography, he draws on *Kamasutra*'s descriptions of different regions as well as details about places in the *Arthashastra*. He also suggests that the geographies described in ancient texts could be used to accurately date these ancient texts. Chakladar attempts to show that *Kamasutra* was a direct descendant of the *Rg Veda* and the *Mahabharata*. He cites different philological studies to demonstrate how, by the third century, *Kamasutra* had completed the three principles of Hindu thought, as the first textual treatment of *kama* following manuscripts that addressed *dharma* and *artha*. This dating placed *Kamasutra* as an ancient, originary text, an essential treatise written among the earliest and most important Sanskrit works.[75]

While Chakladar describes the *Kamasutra* as a book of erotics, he does not address the sexually explicit aspects of the treatise. Rather he treats *Kamasutra* as a *scientific* manual on social life, an originary document that described structural aspects of Indian society, particularly marriage and women's roles. Chakladar draws on *Kamasutra* for information about caste, occupation, marriage and courtship, urban growth and expansion, domestic arrangements, and social events. Indeed, most of the book on ancient social life focused on issues of marriage, urbanization, and ideal domesticity that could be easily translated to modern India. Chakladar looks to *Kamasutra* to understand pressing social issues of the 1920s. He details doctrines of Hindu marriage and the joint family, female domestic seclusion, women's education, and Hindu widow remarriage. In this comprehensive study of the social life depicted in *Kamasutra*, Chakladar insists that the *ganika*—depicted as a courtesan in Burton's translation and as a prostitute in other adaptations—is only a master of the arts and a bearer of "aesthetic refinement parallel to the devoted wives," entirely devoid of sexuality.[76] His study of *Kamasutra* was framed through reform discourses about social issues, from normative models of marriage to the place of the woman in the joint family, that surrounded him in early twentieth-century Calcutta.

Chakladar also produced a critical edition of *Kamasutra* (1919?), today the most respected scholarly edition of the text produced in India. It served as the basis of the many studies of "Hindu positivism" and philological studies of Aryanism that followed.[77] Prominent sociologist Benoy Kumar Sarkar, who founded the department of sociology at Calcutta University, cites Chakladar's study as an essential guide to scientific philological study. In his 1937 *The Positive Background of Hindu Sociology: Introduction to Hindu Positivism*, Sarkar reads Chakladar's *Kamasutra* as an exemplary model of Hindu positivism in its dating of a secular text. Sarkar emphasizes the importance of Chakladar's study for demonstrating the parallel development of a Hindu positivist science of *kama* and *artha*.[78]

For Ghose and Chakladar, ancient Sanskrit texts were not only a site of scholarly study but also a resource for political possibilities for the present. These Bengali authors, writing in the same moment as European philologists, looked to ancient texts for a different purpose: to determine normative practices of marriage and reproduction for contemporary Indian society. Likewise, in the early twentieth century, the intelligentsia—including public intellectuals, doctors, and social scientists—turned to the *Kamasutra, Kokasastra*, and other ancient erotic texts for scientific guidelines for Indian social life. If *Manu* dictated Hindu religious law and practice through the dictates of *dharma*, and Kautilya's *Arthasastra* and other texts dictated the laws of governance and capital, *artha*, what was to govern the scientific study of the social? The answer, for this network of Bengali intellectuals, was the philological treatment of Sanskrit treatises on *kama* and sex outside of a paradigm of sexual positions, love, or desire.

Through the modern study of erotic texts, these men initiated a project that saw social life as a distinct and bounded object of study. Social life, as a conceptual category, encompassed everything from marriage practices to reproduction to social comportment to normative sexuality. For these intellectuals, philological inquiry into ancient Indian sex provided the essential toolkit for understanding modern social life, through a classificatory regime based in the systematic typology of women's sexuality.

The Origins of Indian Prostitution

Nothing spurred the proliferation of philological studies of marriage and sex life more than the subject of prostitution. Indeed, by the 1920s, prostitution had emerged as a site for totalizing study—where philological, historical, scientific, and sociological modes of knowledge systematically and institutionally converged. It was widely considered the oldest and most universal of all forms of social degradation—characterized by nineteenth-century jurists, scholars, and writers as a timeless, unchanging institution. For social scientists, the existence of prostitution and efforts for its control required a combination of the study of social origins, the science of social development, and positivist sociology.

Following Burton's usage, several scholars adopted the typology of courtesans, whom different social analysts equated with prostitutes. This courtesan–prostitute nexus dominated studies of women's sexuality in India, from interpretations of Sanskrit text to understandings of women in Muslim courtly traditions. Scholars had sought to produce a more precise and all-encompassing comparative taxonomy that could describe the totality of women's many different sexual behaviors.

Sex Life in India was anonymously published in 1909 "by a Member of The Royal Asiatic Society of London" and was one of many texts that focused primarily on the history of the Indian courtesan-prostitute to comprehend Indian social life.[79] The author variously describes the Indian courtesan with numerous Sanskrit and English terms, including *ganika* (purportedly, a woman who has many partners); *vesya* (often translated as "prostitute," purportedly, a promiscuous woman); *devadasi* (literally, a temple devotee); *kalavatis* (described by the author as a "women possessed of the arts of Kala"); *apsaras* (literally, a temple deity); and *nautch* girl (literally, a dancing girl). A series of these popular scientific texts on sex, love, and erotics in Hindu society were published as medical treatises by Calcutta's Medical Book Company, which also put out several editions of the *Kamasutra, Anangaranga,* and *Ratirahasya* for a general reading public.[80] They may have been termed "medical" to avoid colonial obscenity laws.

A key sociological text explicitly on the past and present of prostitution was written by the polyglot Nripendra Kumar Basu (active ca. 1930–1965), a self-made man who migrated to Calcutta from rural Bengal, eventually becoming a public intellectual in the 1920s. His book *The History of Prostitution,* written with S. N. Sinha, is a philological study of prostitution from the Vedic age to the time of Vatsayana.[81] Basu published sociohistorical studies of Indian society in Bengali and English.

With the passage of the first anti-trafficking law in Calcutta, the Calcutta Suppression of Immoral Traffic Act of 1923, accounts of so-called prostitutes circulated widely in Bengal. This act, and the many others against "immoral traffic" that followed, emerged in the wake of colonial laws that regulated prostitution in the colonies from the Contagious Diseases Acts onward, as discussed in the following chapter, "Repetition." The anti-trafficking laws of the 1920s were a result of reform efforts to end "white slavery" across the British Empire.[82] Basu and Sinha's *History of Prostitution* was published under the auspices of the Bengal Social Hygiene Association, an organization purportedly created as part of the new activism against the trafficking of women. Introduced by well-known Indologist B. M. Barua, Basu and Sinha's *History of Prostitution* was meant to be a scholarly book that could also claim a wider audience, from policy makers to professionalized middle-class reading publics in Calcutta.

Basu and Sinha felt that the study of prostitution from its origins in Sanskrit text was an urgent necessity required to understand social practices and create new modes of regulation for women in modern society. Sanskrit texts were essential to comprehending social practices from the ancient past that endured in contemporary society. This era of the social regulation of prostitution, with laws that claimed to regulate vice in the 1920s, would benefit from insights into the ancient regulation of women and prostitution.[83] They declare at the beginning of their study that "only the following of modern Western methods was not deemed sufficient to cope with the situation here, and the Association keenly felt the necessity of a workable knowledge of the previous records of the Indian prostitute, her favourable environment, peculiar traits, customs and traditions, and the old provision of law either for her protection or her efficient control."[84] They argue their book was of particular importance to social reformers and note the keen interest and support given to them by members of the Legislative Council of Bengal, J. N. Basu and K. C. Chowdhury, and two local members of the League of Nations, A. Chatterjee and S. Ghosh.

Basu and Sinha's study of ancient prostitution is organized chronologically, extending from the *Rg Veda* to the *Mahabharata* to *Manusmriti* to the *Puranas* to Vatsayana's *Kamasutra*. They use ethnology, sexology, Aryan race theory, and comparative philology in making the case for a totalizing study of Indian prostitution. In the style of Meyer, the book features detailed tales of notable men, women, and gods, as well as epic tales of love and marriage. Laws and social practices are read through social issues that shaped the contemporary world of Calcutta in the 1920s and 1930s. Thus, one chapter details immoral traffic laws in the *Smritis*, while another describes prostitutes in the *Puranas*.[85]

The authors argue that prostitution was a necessary social institution that captured the excesses of male sexuality in earlier stages of civilization. Prostitution naturally existed alongside marriage, which existed alongside an ideal chaste Aryan womanhood: "If *Ramayana* and the *Mahabharata* contain beautiful descriptions of the best type and embodiment of perfect womanhood" of Sita, then these books too depicted "'Rambha, Urbasi, Menaka,' a vast array of 'celestial nymphs, who could frustrate the penitential vows of even the most austere sage.'"[86]

To build this comprehensive ancient history, Basu and Sinha integrated the study of a canon of Sanskrit texts with nineteenth-century ethnological theories of social development, as well as early German sexology. They cite and extensively borrow ideas from a range of sexological, ethnological, and medicolegal treatises, including Leon Henri Thoinot and A. W. Weysse's study of medical jurisprudence, *Medicolegal Aspects of Moral Offenses* (1858), Edwin Hartland's *Primitive Paternity* (1909), Magnus Hirschfeld's *Sexualpathologie* (1921), and Chakladar's *Social Life in Ancient India*. Like the Indologists of Europe and America, they emphasize that the development of marriage in the *Vedas* could be mapped onto ethnological evolutionary theories of McLennan, Hartland, and others, marking the transition from primitive promiscuity to early forms of marriage. Basu and Sinha further correlate ethnological theory and Sanskrit philology with German sexologist Iwan Bloch's study of human sexuality. They argue that sexology as a discipline verified the importance of the transition from primitive sexual practices of promiscuity to polygamous marriage. Evidence of the transitions in stages of civilization could be found in early Sanskrit texts. They also build on philological studies of Aryan language that equated Aryan languages with racial origins. In their argument about India's Aryan past, philological evidence in *kama* texts factually verified the intermingling of Aryans in India, who were related to Europeans, unlike the Dravidians of South India.

Throughout their study, Basu and Sinha provide detailed etymologies for Sanskrit terms that they translate as "prostitute" and outline comparative philological taxonomies that accounted for the range of social types across the world that were to be understood as prostitutes. These social types—classified in different parts of the study as *apsaras, baijees, ganika, beshya*, and *devadasees*—are placed alongside taxonomies from comparative antiquities, including ancient Egypt, Greece, and Rome.[87] The etymological project is paired with a comparative taxonomy across space and time. For Basu and Sinha, the origins of the prostitute necessitated comparative philology, while the etymology of the most common Sanskrit term, *vesya*, could be tied to the names of low-caste people. They argue that the historical origins of prostitution could be found via the Sanskrit terms that systematically demonstrated the place of low-caste women in the social hierarchy—terms that evolved over time to encompass those women who were "approachable by all."

> The prostitutes were then called *Vishya*. Probably this class had been created originally to minister to the "Vish" or Vaishya caste (i.e., traders and merchants who mostly led a town-life cut off from their hearth and home); afterwards it was thrown open to all, and a fresh meaning as "any gentile" was added to the word "Vish." Vishya of the Brahmana period gradually changed into "Beshya," which lost its original derivative root and was framed from the root "Besh" (to enter, to decorate) and which meant "one who is approachable to and by all" or "one who nicely bedecks herself."[88]

The taxonomy culminates with a detailed list and a genealogical kinship chart of the subdivisions of the *rupajivas*, women who lived by their beauty. The classes under the term covered a wide range of women, essentially encompassing every form of womanhood, including married high-caste women and public women that were social outcasts.

Basu and Sinha provide evocative descriptions of the many women who should be equated with the prostitute:

> (a) *Paricharika*, a maid of honour or a lady-in-waiting in a respectable house who gradually ... was dragged into forming a secret alliance with either the master of the house or a member of his family.
>
> (b) The *Kulata* was a married woman who secretly and occasionally slipped out of her house to enjoy the embraces of one or more lovers. She was afraid of her husband and his relatives, and went astray not so much for the sake of money as for the romanticity of love or the satisfaction of her lust.

(c) The *Svairini* goes another step forward. She is not afraid of her husband, who, almost in all cases, is mealymouthed and devoid of the least sense of personality. She snubs him on his face and entertains her lovers either in her own house or that of another.

(d) The *Nati* who professedly lives by dancing, music and acting on the stage, has often a fixed "man," with or without whose approval, she entertains people of her choice for earning "extra."

(e) The *Silpakirika* is the wife (or sometimes the daughter) of a man engaged in independent labour or petty handicrafts, such as the washerman, the weaver, the carpenter, the potter, etc. The husband or the father often connives at the misconduct, provided he receives a big fraction of the fruits of her labour.[89]

According to the authors, this extensive list of women constituted "clandestine prostitutes" whose secrecy necessitated social scientific inquiries into the vast subdivisions of sexual deviance hidden from view. Basu and Sinha emphasize how all sexual and social practices of the *rupajivas*, from married women to those provocative women who publicly performed, must be seen as prostitution. Note that in their list, the taxonomy of ancient terminology uses the present tense, with detailed descriptions of the characteristics of prostitute women that map onto past and present. The *kulata* is in the past tense as an explanation of her present condition. She is presumed to have once been a married woman but in the present tense had assumed the position of a prostitute.

Sinha and Basu created visual verifications of their extended taxonomies through graphs and genealogical charts of the "*veshya*" akin to the genealogical charts of kin relations (as shown in Figure 2). The authors argue that the Sanskrit texts, distilled into charts and lists, could be made into usable guides

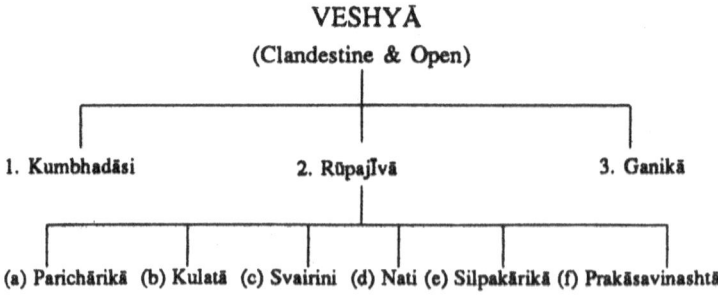

FIGURE 2. Taxonomy of classifications from Basu and Sinha's *The History of Prostitution* (1929).

for present-day society. *The History of Prostitution* explicitly rejects colonial critiques of Indian society that treated the *Mahabharata* and *Ramayana* as simply mythical stories. For Sinha and Basu, these texts could be used for a vast positivist project of ancient origins. As they note in a statement on the role of ancient history in the making of the nation, the study of Indian antiquity had developed significantly through the nineteenth century and provided an accurate picture of social life. Indological study in India revealed the scientific facts held within Sanskrit texts, and had "weakened the foundation of Elphinstone and Cowell's proposition" that no dates could be found in Sanskrit text prior to the invasion of Alexander.[90] European Indologists had "done a great injustice to Vedic and Epic chronology." The authors criticize Müller and his contemporaries for their "short-sightedness" and for their "incorrect dating" that further hindered a comprehensive understanding of Indic antiquity.[91] In their critique of European Indologists, Basu and Sinha cite archaeological excavations in Mahenjodaro (Sind), Harappa (Punjab), and Lauriya Nandangarh as proof of the false nature of the "conservative theories of the old Mullerian school and the calculations of Whitney."[92] They thus recount a history of prostitution from a Vedic period that existed long before the dates given by prominent Indologists.

The authors further provide dictates of appropriate and desirable behavior for women. Analyzing excerpts of *Kamasutra* in their study, they emphasize the submissive position of all women, both the wife and courtesan, according to Sanskrit texts. Here we see the literal, selective reading of *Kamasutra* as an origin manual that provided normative dictates for modern social life. In their view, *Kamasutra* mandated that married women were required to submit to the sexual will of their husbands: "She should carefully keep from his view her anal region, axilla, etc. (lest they should excite disgust) ... when he wants to touch her private parts, should yield herself readily to him; should kiss and embrace him while he is falling asleep."[93] In effect, these social analysts utilized the Indological study of sexuality—the claim to authoritative origins—to produce a textual justification for marriage as complete and unrestricted sexual access to a woman's body. Indeed, according to Basu and Sinha, marriage as dictated in Sanskrit text was a *necessity* in the face of the otherwise unrestrained sexuality of women. Women were always at risk of eliciting disgust, and dictates were required to regulate that perpetual danger of women's impurity.

This study appealed to audiences well beyond the moment of its initial publication in the 1930s. In 1992, Jawarharlal Nehru University professor R. D. Sil reissued the book to great success, with a second edition of his republished version appearing just two years later in 1994. Sil asserted that the study of prostitution in Sanskrit texts was essential to understand contemporary trends of prostitution and marriage in 1990s India.[94]

At the same time as Basu and Sinha, Santosh Kumar Mukherji was writing foundational studies on prostitution and Indian sex life. Mukherji (active ca. 1922–1970) was a prominent medical doctor and public intellectual who won the Padma Shri award—India's fourth highest civilian honor—for medicine in 1962. He authored numerous medical textbooks, sociological studies, and social commentaries. He was the editor of the *Indian Medical Record* and a lecturer at the Calcutta Medical School.[95] His studies of prostitution and ancient Indian sex life appeared between the 1920s to the 1960s. The philology of sex became the premise of a range of Mukherji's treatises on the reform and modernization of society. According to him, Sanskrit dictates on sex life were also essential to the study of population control and the problem of poverty. In both *Prostitution in India* (1934) and his study of marriage and prostitution, *Sex Life and Prostitution in India* (n.d.), he used prostitution to sociologically analyze structures of marriage, family, kinship, and reproduction in Indian society. His publications have been widely cited as scientific accounts by scholars working on prostitution in colonial and postcolonial India. *Prostitution in India*, first published in 1934, was republished by the well-known sociologist Biswanath Joardar in 1986. In his introduction, Joardar insists on the scientific nature of the text and the importance of Mukherji's study as the one true source on the history of prostitution in the early twentieth century. He describes Mukherji as a physician of great repute who worked extensively with "real prostitutes" in the city of Calcutta in the 1930s—work that gave Mukherji an "insider view of the life and world of the prostitutes."[96] Joardar claimed the status of a sociologist who had firsthand knowledge of the social conditions of prostitutes in 1970s and 1980s Calcutta, an expertise he likens to Mukherji's in medicine. As Joardar describes, Mukherji had continued significance in contemporary India, serving "the need of the many specialist engaged in this endeavour, Sociologist, Psychologist, Medical personnel, Social workers."[97]

Mukherji opens *Prostitution in India* (1934), his comprehensive multidisciplinary study, with an epic scene of conflict and contradiction between man's sexual desire and his pursuit of civility. The scene is from the *Mahabharata*. In Mukherji's telling, the sage Swetaketu as a child sat with his mother when, all of a sudden, a man appeared and took her away. The boy became angry. What kind of world would remove a mother from her child? But his father explained: "This is the eternal custom; though a woman be attached to hundreds of men, she commits no sin." From that day forward, Swetaketu pronounced: "A woman who cohabits with a man other than her husband, and a man who becomes attached to a woman other than his wife, the sin of that woman and that man will be equal to that of infanticide." To Mukherji, women's sexual transgression was equivalent to the murder of an infant.[98]

For Mukherji his declaration was nothing less than a turning point in Indian history, for it ended the custom of sexual promiscuity. He in fact saw it as the dawn of civilization because it brought an end to the unrestrained promiscuity of primitive humans. Marriage thus became the very mark of civilization. For Mukherji, Swetaketu was the founding myth of all civilizations because India was the most ancient civilization in the world. From this atavistic formulation, Mukherji develops his central problematic: How does one account for women's promiscuity and prostitution in modern Indian society?

Prostitution in India is comprised of three parts: the first provides a detailed philological study of the origins of prostitution; part 2 is a sociological study titled "The Modern Prostitute"; and part 3 offers a genealogy of laws against prostitution, merging Sanskrit texts with colonial jurisprudence. Mukherji traces the role of prostitute in India via epochs from the "prehistoric period," to Buddhist and Hindu periods, the Muhammedan period, to early European society in India. He draws on canonical Sanskrit texts including the *Mahabharata, Ramayana, Arthashastra, Manusmriti,* and *Kamasutra.* Like his contemporaries, he also participated in the network of knowledge that circulated around him—citing sexologists like Bloch, Ellis, and Hirschfeld, Chakladar's *Social Life in Ancient India*, McLennan's *Primitive Marriage*, Meyer's *Sexual Life in Ancient India*, and R. C. Dutt's *History of India*, as well as a range of Bengali translations of Sanskrit texts. He extensively taxonomizes the many women and social practices understood as equivalent to the English term "prostitute," and provides evocative visual representations of his scientific project through his genealogical charts of the types of prostitutes (as shown in Figure 3), paintings and drawings of "dancing girls," and exemplary images of what he describes as primitive women.

Importantly, and much like other philologists, Mukherji understood modern prostitution to be equivalent to primitive promiscuity, which existed as a by-product of the "marriage system." For him, there was a temporal difference between the prostitute and modern marriage, one representing the promiscuity of the past, the other a modern institution. The persistence of the prostitute in modern India was the result of the anachronistic sexuality of women who reverted to a primitive sexual promiscuity when left unrestrained. He thus saw

Classification of Prostitutes

The Hindu sexologists classified the prostitutes according to their beauty and the power of charming by dance, music and other entertainments.

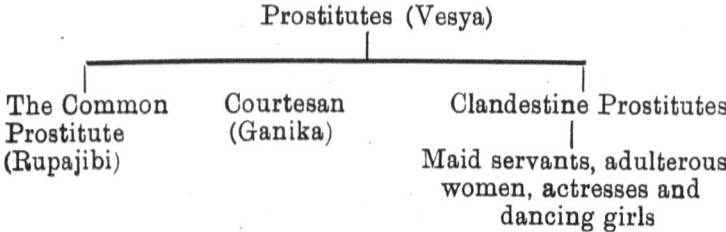

FIGURE 3. Mukherji's diagram of "prostitutes" from Hindu sexology, from *Indian Sex Life and Prostitution* (1934).

the continued existence of women's sexual acts outside the bounds of marriage as an urgent problem that necessitated the systematic study of prostitution from its origins to modern-day India.[99]

What accounted for prostitution in modern India? Mukherji offers a decidedly communalist answer, based in anti-Muslim, Hindu majoritarian ideologies that permeated colonial histories of premodern India. He argues that modern prostitution grew out of the Muslim conquest of India, which was first and foremost a sexual conquest. In his depiction, the persistence of the prostitute in modern India reflected the subjugation of Hindus, and more specifically Hindu patriarchy, by violent and sexually depraved despotic Muslims, exemplified by the Mughals. In Mukherji's telling, as in the colonial historiography that had come before him, Muslim rule was a time of sexual "debauchery": "Nabobs and nobles were so degraded that they did not feel any shame in keeping concubines and prostitutes even in their houses."[100] Mukherji denounces the Muslim nobility for having harems with women that passed from generation to generation like property and for indoctrinating their sons into the harem lifestyle.

For Mukherji, the women enslaved into harems represented the violence of Muslim conquest across India. More specifically, Shia Muslims used temporary marriage, or "*muta* marriage," to acquire "wives on hire" who were essentially prostitutes. Mukherji further argues that Muslim men had a particular affinity for sodomy. He also insists that famous women of Mughal India, including Anarkhali and Lal Kunwar, were courtesans equivalent to a kind of high-class prostitute for the Mughals.[101] Mukherji proclaims that the degradation of Hindus by Muslims persisted into his present, particularly through the act of gang rape, which he described as an act committed by gangs of men, "mostly Muhammedans" who abduct "married and unmarried women and after outraging them return the poor half-dead creatures to their own doors."[102] His inflammatory, communalist anti-Muslim language adopts the guise of a scientific Indological study that also functioned as sociology.[103]

A range of Santosh Kumar Mukherji's studies—from treatises on Hindu rationalism, to books on caste and marriage, to his study of birth control—relied on Sanskrit textual origins for Indian sex life. Indeed, he published his own translation of the *Kamasutra* in the 1940s, which was reprinted in 1945. In his introduction to his rendition of the *Kamasutra*, Mukherji stresses his expertise as a doctor, and that the *Kamasutra* was a "work on Sexual Science."[104] Mukherji also produces a detailed taxonomy of prostitutes and their social roles, like that of Sinha and Basu.

So why does one encounter so many lists and typologies in these studies of prostitution? Because, according to writers like Mukherji, the multiplicity and indeterminacy of the concept of the prostitute required as much exegesis as possible. Here was the generativity of the process of translation: how diverse categories, social practices, and social classes of women could all be translated into the prostitute, and through that translational process, become acts that were equivalent to prostitution itself.[105] Mukherji equated an impressively wide range of women outside the bounds of marriage with the prostitute:

Vatsayana mentions the following clandestine prostitutes who also lent their body for money.
1. The Adultress: A woman who commits adultery for money secretly is called a Secret Adultress (Kulata); while one doing so openly is an Open Adultress (Swairini).
2. The Deserted Wife is one who leaves her husband and lives with another man for money.
3. The Actress and female artists.

The Prostitutes may be classified as follows:
1. The Common Prostitute (Kumbha-Dasi)
2. A woman living on her beauty (Rupa-jibi)
3. The Courtesan (Ganika)
4. The Attendant (Paricharika)
5. The Secret Adultress (Kulata)

6. The open Adultress (Swairini)
7. A woman who has left her home (Prakasa binashta)
8. The Actress (Nati)
9. The female artisan (Silpa-karika)[106]

Mukherji emphasizes the pedagogical utility of these classifications from the *Kamasutra* for a science of contemporary society: "In the modern medical curriculum the sexual science does not find a place though its importance cannot be denied."[107]

Mukherji deploys the ancient past as the premise of social scientific reasoning for contraception in his *Birth Control for the Millions*, published in 1944. He, like many of his contemporaries, sets out the problem of overpopulation, citing Malthusian theories of population.[108] More striking in Mukherji's *Birth Control* is the chapter on the history of contraception, which includes an extended exegesis on the history of ancient Hindu civilization in India. As Mukherji states, the problem of population as it appeared in India was a necessary result of "civilizational progress": "With the development of civilization and struggle for existence the problem of too many children gradually appeared."[109] In ancient India, knowledge of contraception was found in "the Kama-Sutra (Sexual Science)."[110] Sanskrit knowledge of ancient sex life constituted the foundation for a medical and sociological manual on contraception.

Across these texts, one finds the history of an emerging civil society in a colonized space—an epistemic history embedded in a social history of colonized men who sought to study society through a range of emerging disciplines. These social analysts in India were academics, sociologists, and medical doctors, as well as amateur philologists. Some, like Basu and Sinha, were in conversation with bureaucrats and legislators making decisions on early laws against the trafficking of women. Others, like Chakladar, shaped academic fields, trained scholars, and built institutions. Their texts appear in print through the twentieth century until today, and can be found at libraries and footpath bookstalls in Kolkata.

Bengali social analysts constructed a universalizing discourse in their elaborate multilingual taxonomies of women's behavior, where all women outside of man's supervision were always potentially prostitutes. Sexual difference defined the terrain of sexual norms, where men had the capacity for sexual restraint, while women were to be restrained by and surveilled under social strictures because of the supposedly weak nature of their bodies and the uncontrollability of their desire. Marriage, according to these limited interpretations of text, was the mandatory sexual access to women and the control of their unrestrained sexuality. Premodern textual dictates were the primary solution to the problem of the prostitute.

Sex as Sociology

The work of Chandra Chakraberty (b. 1881, active ca. 1910–1970), a public intellectual and Indian nationalist who traveled across the world, exemplifies the popularity of these studies of ancient sexual life as sociology. Chakraberty was a polyglot who emigrated to New York after traveling to Germany in the first decades of the twentieth century. Chakraberty was tried as part of the Hindu-German conspiracy trials in the United States for the transnational organizing of Indian nationalists for an alliance with the Germans from 1915 to 1917. He was imprisoned in the United States for several months for his involvement in a pro-German movement among diasporic anti-colonial Indians during World War I. He was the first person convicted in these highly sensational trials. A photograph of Chakraberty in court, a "Hindoo" associated with conspiracy, appeared in the *San Francisco Chronicle* in 1917.[111] The first of eight men arrested, this moment made Chakraberty visible across a transnational Indian nationalist movement (Chakraberty is pictured on the right in Figure 4). Indian revolutionary M. N. Roy, who encountered Chakraberty as a leader among New York Indians in the 1910s, described Chakraberty as insincere, an "imposter" with a large ego, in his 1960s memoir about his travels.[112]

Chakraberty was one of the most prolific writers about social life in India, the author of texts on everything from ancient races and myths to Hindu sexology to dyspepsia and diabetes. His texts were widely reviewed, published in several editions, circulated transnationally, and continue to be reissued in India today. His 1944 study of the racial history of India, which argued for the Aryan descent of high-caste Hindus, the racial differences between the peoples of North and South India, and differences of sexual perversion and practice based in racial difference, was most recently republished in India in 1997, while his study of ancient Hindu medicine, with an extended discussion of ancient sex life and medicine, was republished in 2013.[113] His most popular books include *Ancient Indian Sex Life, Sexology of the Hindus,* and *The Racial History of India*. His texts had a global reach, with positive reviews across major journals in India and abroad. A founder of the history of science, George Sarton, in a review in the journal *Isis* in 1925, described Chakraberty's "interesting introduction to the

FIGURE 4. Chandra Chakraberty, photograph with Ernst Sekunna, German intelligence officer, undated, Library of Congress collection.

study of India and its peoples, by one equally steeped in Hindu and Western learning."[114]

What is most striking across Chakraberty's many publications is the consistent appearance of the philological study of sex at the heart of a wide range of sociological studies, from food and health to rationalism to the racial heritage of India. In Chakraberty's synthetic philological and scientific works the comparative method is key, where broad racial types, physical characteristics of bodies, and even linguistic traits serve to demonstrate the scientific nature of Hindu sexology and their enduring significance for contemporary society. To a reader today, his writing is an unusual synthesis of different social theories. Many ideas and concepts in one text appear again in another study. The writing is steeped in comparative etymology, word derivations, and citations. His studies provide detailed accounts of race theories, linguistic derivation, and physiology and medical terminology. What results is a claim to scientific authority through the combination of expert modes of knowledge and forms of writing: medical and physiological terminology, explanatory modeling from physics and biology, detailed comparative philology, and narratives of social evolution based in ethnology and race science. At certain points his narratives seem to devolve into a kind of free association, where biological sciences, physics, anthropological terminology, sexual sciences, and ancient Sanskrit and comparative philological categories all blend together.

Take, for example, his comprehensive treatise *Sexology of the Hindus: A Study in the Hindu Psychology of Sex with Modern Interpretations*, which was likely first published in the 1920s, with a third edition published by the late 1930s. *Sexology of the Hindus* combines racial science with the biology of sexuality as well as the philology of Sanskrit treatises, with detailed interpretations of the *Kamasutra, Anangaranga, Ratirahasya, Panchasayaka, Rg Veda, Mahabharata,* and more.

In his introduction to this study, Chakraberty makes an explicit link between the philology of ancient Sanskrit texts and modern science. He argues that philological knowledge should be interpreted through the natural sciences to create a usable guide to social life in India: "Our ancient sages (rishis) approached the subject rightly . . . but their keen observations and psychological conclusions need new interpretations in the light of modern physiology, endocrinology and ethnology."[115] He asserts that his study is a systematic overview of the typology of races and their resultant sexual behavior, according to Hindu sexologists, with four major race groups, including the "Negro," "Semite," "Aryan," and finally, the "Mongolian." He describes how racial typology maps onto the sensory experiences of sexual intercourse, and then details the physiological transformations of the human body in sexual interactions.

It is in the evocative language of the text that one gets a full sense of the tone of Chakraberty's *Sexology*. These descriptions of sex are the most graphic of any published in this period. On women's sexuality, Chakraberty observes that the "sexual impulse is so powerful and congress so intoxicating and voluptuous to her that she abandons to it nonchalantly as to personal risk of pregnancy, infection of venereal diseases, position, prestige, and family honour."[116] He provides extensive physiological descriptions of genitalia, including evocative details of sexual acts. He describes sexual intercourse as the moment when "the penis like a red-hot blunt iron rod of delicious warmth and vigor forces its entrance into the vaginal vestibule," which then adjusts "to the volume of the penis and to increase not only its turgescence but also that of the vaginal bulbs which clasp tightly the penis and the clitoris by the presence of the blood driven into them."[117] Alongside the detailed description of genitalia, in the footnotes he describes the racial typologies of Indian women and how their racial makeup related to their physical and sexual constitution and the "eugenic" results of racial heredity. Women are characterized by their "race": Dravidian, Assamese, Punjabi, Bengali. While the women of Bengal are "delicate like flowers," who enjoy copulation with men whose "penis corresponds to vaginal depth," the women of southern Punjab are "addicted to the phallus" and "very fond of cunnilingus."[118] Chakraberty cites Sanskrit texts to create a regional geography of the subcontinent, much like Chakladar. He further relates the sexual categories of Sanskrit texts to racial types and sexual and social disorders, including sexual hyperesthesia, nymphomania, impotence, the frigidity of women, masturbation, and prostitution.

The fact of women's sexual perversion and prostitution in contemporary India could be explained through a comparative method that created parallel contexts in ancient civilizations that had comparable systems of extramarital sexual relationships. For Chakraberty, like his contemporaries, the presence of prostitution in modern India was explained through "Muslim conquest."[119] Here, as in Mukherji's work, Chakraberty betrayed his deeply anti-Muslim perspective, tying women's sexual exploitation and prostitution to Muslims in India. The comparative method is used to create equivalence between ancient India and other ancient civilizations, including the Babylonians, Greeks, Corinthians, Assyrians, and Egyptians. Using this lens, India's ancient sexual science of Sanskrit texts appear as a universal science, as widely applicable as the physiological and social evolutionary sciences.

This comparative method of the philological origins of women's sexuality and racial difference appears across Chakraberty's wide-ranging publications. For him, the study of sex—through a combination of Indology and the natural and medical sciences—served a key component of all social scientific studies of life in India. Chapters on sexual physiology and the Indology of sex, particularly the sexual excess in women, can be found in everything from his *Food and Health* (1922), a medical manual on foods and practices that lead to healthier bodies; *Principles of Education* (1922), on the education of Indian men and women for the sake of social advancement; *Endocrine Glands* (1923), on endocrinology and physiology; *The Outline of Rationalism* (1938), on science and rationalism in modern Indian society; and *The Racial History of India* (1944), on eugenics and the differentiation of the races (particularly Aryans) and the development of Indian society.[120]

Chakraberty's texts may offer the most explicit form of this combined science. However, when read in tandem with this transnational network of public intellectuals, doctors, and social scientists, the logic that governs his work no longer seems so piecemeal or aspirational in its claims to science. Indeed, his studies combine many of the important features of the philology of sex: the Sanskrit text was a resource for a multidisciplinary study of society that combined history, sexology, biology, archaeology, etymology and linguistics, and sociology. The Indology of sex life fit quite seamlessly with sociological studies charged with the task of assessing Indian society with an eye toward its future.

This model of writing social life through a claim to originary text continued through much of the twentieth century, most notably in the multiple publications of Sures Chandra Banerji.[121] Banerji was a professor of Sanskrit and secretary of the Education Department for the Government of West Bengal in the 1960s and 1970s. His books include an extended study of prostitution in India since Vedic times to the present, *The Castaway of Indian Society* (1989), as well numerous studies on sex, crime, and prostitution that posed Sanskrit texts on erotics as the origin of guidelines for contemporary social life.[122]

I have demonstrated ways in which the philology of sex was the central premise of a wide range of sociological inquiries. The study of ancient female sexuality—whether for the sake of social propriety, family and kinship structures, or contraception—lay at the heart of modern sociological inquiry. The philological study of originary Sanskrit texts constituted hierarchies of caste and gender, defined the difference between Hindus and Muslims, and explained through an evolutionary model normative kinship structures and social and biological reproduction.

From Sanskrit texts came the solution to the urgent threat of female sexual deviance, in the language of Ghose, that unfeminine *Hastini* who would do anything to fulfill her "carnal appetites."[123] The philology of ancient sex, as the textual origins of social life, became foundational to social scientific study. The project of a "Hindu sexual science" for Indian society was perhaps most powerfully and effectively argued by a wide range of men through the publication of these philological approaches to Indian sex life and the Hindu sexual sciences. This field of knowledge, constituted entirely by male philologists and public intellectuals, saw the control of female sexuality as the primary index for stages of civilization. Philology established women's sexuality, structured through the Indology of marriage and prostitution, as the primary terrain for establishing social and political authority—from juridical to scientific to sociological structures that took society as an object of knowledge.

2

Repetition

LAW AND THE SOCIOLOGY OF DEVIANT FEMALE SEXUALITY

Female Sexuality as Explanation

For the colonial state in India, secrecy necessitated social scientific inquiry. The secrets of Indian social life were to be excavated, compiled, and described in detail through comprehensive surveys, questionnaires, and circulars sent to local officials across India. The responses of local magistrates were to be understood as generalizable for all of Indian society. The colonial state saw the questionnaire as a comprehensive archive of social fact.

In 1872, the British colonial state initiated its most ambitious and extensive knowledge-gathering survey about Indian women.[1] The inquiry was spurred by a new law against the buying and selling of girls for the purpose of prostitution, passed under the 1860 Indian Penal Code—perhaps the first law against trafficking anywhere in the world. In this widely distributed questionnaire, the Government of India asked a deceptively simple question: Who was a prostitute in India?

In the responses, local colonial administrators answered that *all* Indian women were potential prostitutes. Take for example the handwritten response to the questionnaire by the deputy commissioner of the Police in Calcutta, A. H. Giles, who argued that all women outside of high-caste monogamous marriage could be classified as one of five types of prostitutes:

> The prostitute community is recruited in various ways from all classes and castes. The greatest number of prostitutes are perhaps Hindoo widows who have been seduced in their native village, and being out-casted have come to Calcutta to practise as prostitutes ... A second section are hereditary

prostitutes that is their mothers were prostitutes before them and they were reared into the profession from infancy . . . Hindoo widows however who were not prostitutes previous to the birth of the child but afterwards became so contribute the greatest number of children of this class. A third section consists of women (both Hindoo and Mohamedans) who have run away from their husbands on account of ill treatment or because they object to polygamy. Among the Hindoos many of these are the wives of Kulin Brahmans whose fate it is to share a husband in Common with 40 or 50 other women. A fourth and not innumerous section is composed of married women who practise as prostitutes with the full knowledge and consent of their husbands. Numbers of Mohamedan prostitutes are the wives of sailors . . . They drive a profitable trade by prostituting themselves, but confine themselves to connubial embraces when their husbands are in port . . . Among the Hindoos, the lower castes such as Harees, Bagdees, etc commonly connive at the prostitution of their wives, for the sake of gain. A fifth section is no doubt composed of women who when young have been made over to brothel-keepers by their parents.[2]

Extending his typology, Giles stressed that a wide range of women of different communities were clandestine prostitutes. According to his response to the questionnaire, Indian women were particularly prone to dangerous and illegal behavior, hidden from state view by a society that conspired to keep secrets. In replies to the questionnaire, dozens of magistrates, policemen, and doctors mapped social networks, caste and religious authority, and strictures of kinship in handwritten letters (a response to this survey appears in Figure 5). A query purportedly about the protection of minors became the broadest single inquiry into the intimacies of social life.[3]

The deputy police commissioner's letter is preserved in a rare archived file of handwritten survey responses in the B proceedings in the archives for the Bengal Presidency. In Bengal alone, the survey generated hundreds and hundreds of pages of repetitive, descriptive prose in letters and lists. The responses detailed taxonomies of Indian social practices and typologies of women deemed prostitutes. A. Mackenzie, secretary to the Government of Bengal, emphasized that the responses of local authorities were "very voluminous, and contain a vast amount of repetition."[4] It was the very sociological detail and recurrent categories that constituted the fact of the prostitute for the colonial state.

My concern is the methods of cataloging and description that these colonial social analysts employed to illustrate the social lives of women through legal share of course the lot common to all who follow their calling. In this country many succumb to the ignorant use of the most dangerous drugs and medicines, many die of diseases induced or fostered by the character of the life they lead some are supported into old age by the girls whom they have in their turn brought up to follow their own profession and a good many turn Boistubs and live by begging — Among Musulman women many get some sort of menial service to do for a living —

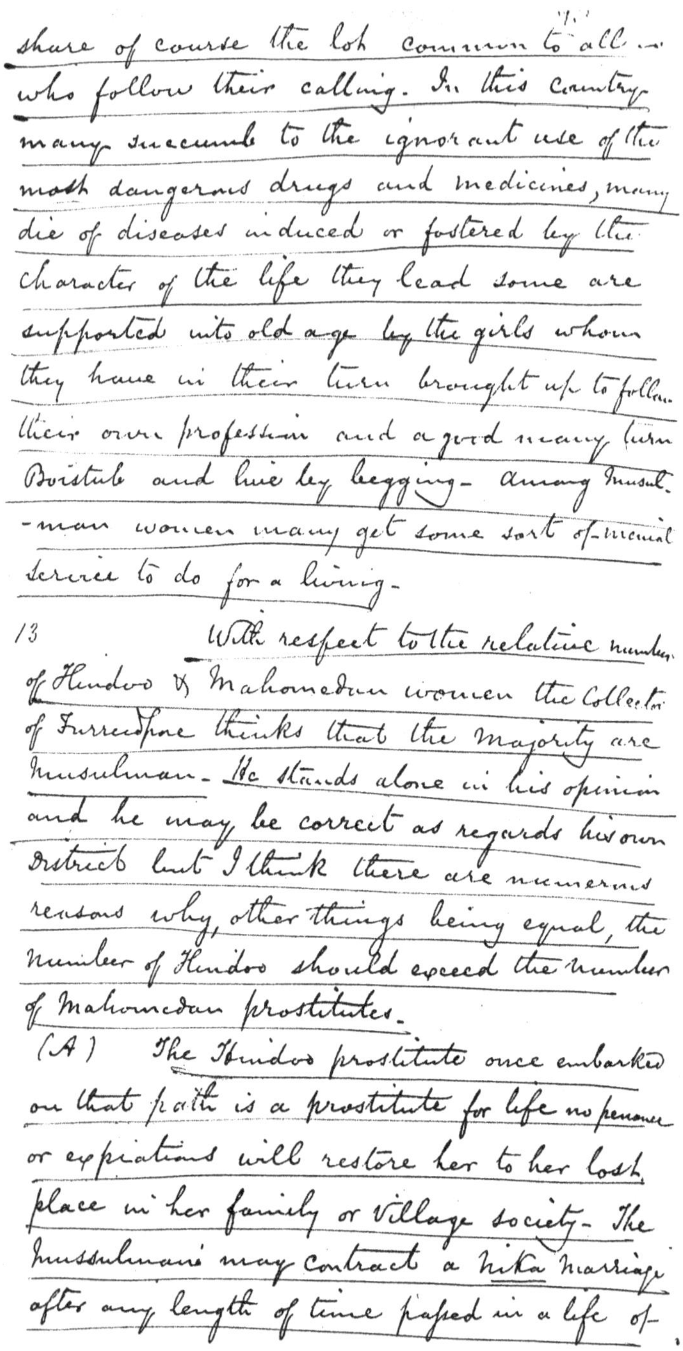

13. With respect to the relative number of Hindoo & Mahomedan women the Collector of Furreedpore thinks that the majority are Musulman. He stands alone in his opinion and he may be correct as regards his own district but I think there are numerous reasons why other things being equal, the number of Hindoo should exceed the number of Mahomedan prostitutes.

(A) The Hindoo prostitute once embarked on that path is a prostitute for life no penance or expiations will restore her to her lost place in her family or village society — The Mussulmani may contract a Nika marriage after any length of time passed in a life of

FIGURE 5. Letter from Deputy Magistrate Bankim Chandra Chatterjee to Government of Bengal, 1872, WBSA.

surveys. They found in the concept of the prostitute not only a name that could encompass a range of social behaviors and types of women but an *explanation* as well.[5] The questionnaire responses produced definitive descriptions of women's social types that could exhaustively account for the deviant nature of the social world in India. The state initiated a "process of objectification," in the words of Bernard Cohn, which held colonial commentary on Indian society as sociological *fact*.[6] As Lata Mani argues in her groundbreaking study of *sati* debates of the early nineteenth century, the "very formulation of official questions" defined the terms of what could be answered. The structure of the question and answer constituted a network of experts and authorities who were to explain Indian "social custom" in extended sociological projects in the service of the codification of colonial law.[7]

When we trace the chain of movement of this sociological survey, we see the systematic distillation of ideas about female sexuality into usable forms of knowledge. The questionnaire first commissioned by the colonial Government of India in London was distributed across state and regional administrators. The responses traveled from local questionnaires across regional districts to the Bengal Presidency offices to the central government offices in London. Administrators at the local level responded to the inquiry with detailed handwritten responses, named as the "B proceedings" when catalogued by the state in the colonial state archives. In their handwritten letters, regional magistrates produced extended accounts of the many details of social life through exhaustive oral reports and testimonies submitted by local policemen, doctors, and deputy magistrates. These letters were then submitted to the Government of Bengal. The Government of Bengal summarized the detailed letters into taxonomies in typed reports that charted the women deemed as prostitutes from each locality (an excerpt from the summary A file appears in Figure 6). These summaries enter the archive as the condensed files of the "A proceedings." The A files traveled from the Government of Bengal to the central colonial Government of India. The pages and pages of voluminous details of the facts of social life from local magistrates were condensed in the final report as typed succinct paragraphs that reported the region, the official's name and title, and summary abstract of the letter. As Mackenzie describes in his final statement from the Bengal Presidency to the Government of India, "the following abstract of their opinions are reproduced only in sufficient detail to give a correct idea of the general result."[8] The Report of A proceedings produced the general, and *generalizable*, schematic of the prostitute. The positivist sexual typology—condensed from

Index No.

JUDICIAL.

HOME DEPT. PROCEEDINGS, JULY 1873.

Progs. No.

Commissioner of Dacca (Mr. A. Abercrombie).—There is no reason to doubt that the practice of prostitutes bringing up young girls to follow their mode of life prevails largely all over India. The proposed prohibition to be effectual must be general and absolute—there must be no qualifications. Simultaneously with the proposed prohibition some arrangement for the care of the children must be made. The prostitutes are generally Hindus, owing to the prejudice against re-marriage, strictness of Hindu social law, Kulinism, &c.; the children in their possession are either their own or made over by poor parents. Remembers no instance of wholesale kidnapping of girls. The prohibition against allowing prostitutes to keep girls not their own will not in itself present any difficulty in carrying out. A proclamation on any given day by beat of drum, that all prostitutes in possession of unregistered girls not their own by birth would be prosecuted, would be effectual. The girls reclaimed will never be able to get rid of their original taint; they will never attain any respectable place in Native society; they will so feel this to be their destiny that they will themselves accept it as inevitable and turn prostitutes on the first opportunity; has no very certain knowledge of the ultimate fate of prostitutes; they share the lot common to all who follow the calling; they succumb to the ignorant use of most dangerous drugs and medicines, and die of diseases contracted from the character of the life they lead; while others in old age are supported by the girls they have in turn brought up to the profession; others turn *boistumees* and live by beggary. The Mussulman women obtain menial employment.

No. 156.

Magistrate of Dacca (Mr. D. R. Lyall)—Is not aware of any case in which young girls were kidnapped; occasionally a case of child-purchase arises, but the money is called a payment of a debt or bond, and proof to the contrary is hard to get. As a registering officer frequent cases have come before him where women wanted to register a deed giving their children to prostitutes, which of course was refused. It is difficult to give the caste of young girls who are apprenticed to prostitutes, as the vast majority are Hindu bastards, and it is questionable whether the closing of the only means of disposing of such children that now exists would not lead to an increase of child-murder—a form of murder which is very difficult to find out. Young girls are kept by prostitutes chiefly for support in old age, and the claim is very generally admitted.

Magistrate of Furreedpore (Mr. W. S. Wells)—Believes the evil of educating young girls to a prostitute's life exists to a very large extent; in fact, women of the town are mainly recruited by purchase, and sometimes by adoption; children are seldom born to prostitutes except when they first commence as public women, and by no chance are they found to possess sons, which indicates the existence of infanticide among them. Prostitution is encouraged by Native landlords, who in starting a new bazaar or *hât* consider it their first care to settle prostitutes on the land, who are sure to attract customers. There is now pending in the district a case in which a landlord sold a little orphan girl for Rs. 25 to a prostitute.

Deputy Commissioner of Cachar (Mr. O. G. R. McWilliam).—The evil is so small here that it calls for no remark. The prostitute class are recruited principally from low caste Hindus who have gone astray; a considerable number of Munnipooree women live in a state of concubinage, which is not considered a disgrace among them, and they are almost invariably received by their relations on the cessation of the temporary connections.

Commissioner of Rajshahye (Mr. W. LeF. Robinson)—Does not believe that the ranks of prostitutes are recruited to a large extent by girls under ten years of age, except, perhaps, in great towns. Instances of course occur where prostitutes and brothel-keepers get hold of children by unlawful means with a view of profiting by their prostitution. The following are some of the difficulties in the way to forbidding the possession of girls by prostitutes; the prohibition would always be easily evaded; if it would not, then Government would have to support a considerable number of girls until they were old enough to become prostitutes, which, in nine cases out of ten, would be the result of the girls being brought up by Government as out-castes. It seems to him unwise to prohibit when the prohibition cannot be enforced. It is a fallacy to suppose that the prohibition would check prostitution. The girls apprenticed to a prostitute's life are usually of the lowest caste, the children of some poor out-caste women who sells her child; their fate, after some years of prostitution, is that they either carry on the trade of prostitution through younger women, live on any savings they have made during their own career, or, if that has not been a successful one, lapse into beggary or menial labor of the lowest sort; knows of no instance where young girls had been kidnapped. If the prohibition is enforced, the limit of age should be ten years. Orphanages, at the expense of Government, would have to be established for the girls reclaimed, and this would give rise to far greater

b

FIGURE 6. Secretary Mackenzie's summary of district commissioner reports in Bengal to Government of India, 1873, NAI.

extended exegesis to a succinct empirical taxonomy—could be circulated, translated, and repeated across the empire.

In the condensation of knowledge into the A files, it is the B proceedings, the handwritten answers to the questionnaire—their internal logic, graphic detail, elaborate redundancies and contradictions, opinions from local authorities—that rarely survived except in the trace summary. Often the B file is not to be found, unavailable to the historian who enters the colonial archive today. Yet it is in the B file, when it does survive, that we find more contradiction than fact. The B file, when preserved in the archives, rather than solely being culled for *proof* of life for our social histories, may instead help us consider the contradictions of what is written, summarized, and abstracted into an object of study.

In this chapter, I analyze how new modes of sociological inquiry created categories of women's sexuality that defined colonial legal interventions into Indian social life. My contention is that Indian social practice became an object of knowledge in large part through the repetition and traffic in a recurring set of ideas about women's sexual deviance, in particular through the concept of the prostitute. The idea of the prostitute appears as an epistemological horizon: if only she could be known fully, then the colonial state could know everything about "native" society. Women's sexuality thus became a primary object of the legal survey, spurring controversies about the application and workings of new criminal laws.

This process of objectification emerged with the rise of codified criminal laws that sought to regulate intimate social behavior. The prostitute was produced as social *fact*—repeated again and again as an organizing principle used to comprehend diverse social and sexual practices.[9] Colonial social analysts—including administrators, judges, doctors, and policemen—drew on this reasoning to constitute the domain of social relations outside of companionate marriage as an object of knowledge and legal intervention.

The chapter examines the expanding field of criminal law from the 1860s until around the 1930s, focusing in particular on legal questionnaires that sought to objectify Indian social life in the second half of the nineteenth century. Such surveys detailed a wide array of social behavior that was to be subsumed under the category of prostitute. These social types were outside the domain of high-caste Hindu marriage and included women who were part of mendicant religious sects, high-caste Hindu polygamy, Brahman widowhood, forms of public performance, Muslim marriage practices, women's migration, women laborers, and caste strictures. I reveal how legal social scientific inquiry defined a new terrain of legal intervention into some of the most intimate aspects of social life. In the first part of the chapter, I read in detail the 1872 survey with which I began. I then examine the Contagious Diseases Act of 1868, the wide-reaching law that regulated prostitution in major Indian cities. While there is considerable scholarship on this act, I reframe and complicate its history to consider how debates about the ambiguities and imprecision of the category of prostitute shaped the broader legal production of sexual knowledge. I then turn to another survey, an enquiry sent to judges across Bengal in 1877 for a law against infanticide. I analyze how ideas of women's sexual deviance framed debates about the infanticide of so-called illegitimate children in Bengal. Finally, I briefly look at the reach of these survey practices in the first decades of the twentieth century.

Charting the Range of Prostitutes

The middle of the nineteenth century saw a shift from early colonial reforms of civil law to new approaches to regulating India through criminal laws.[10] Perhaps no effort for systematization of state practice was as successful as the Indian Penal Code of 1860, a watershed set of criminal laws that shaped the development of penal codes across the colonial world. This code brought subjects of the colonial state under a uniform code of criminal law.[11] The 1860 Indian Penal Code introduced an expansive set of laws that regulated the bodies of women and controlled their sexual and reproductive behavior. These laws included foeticide (sections 315 and 316); infanticide (section 315); the procurement of minor girls for illicit intercourse (section 366a); the selling and buying of girls for prostitution (sections 372 and 373); and rape (sections 375 and 376).

The 1860 code featured the category of prostitution across different sections, including laws on the buying and selling of girls and solicitation in public places, which were not originally in an earlier 1837 draft of the legislation.[12] In the 1837 debates about a uniform criminal code, the commission emphasized that while there were no laws against abortion in England, the proposed criminal code must have laws against foeticide because of its widespread prevalence in India, where illicit sex led to illegitimate pregnancies.[13] The 1860 Penal Code also introduced a set of vaguely worded laws, such as the mandates against public nuisance (section 268), which gave the police broad discretionary power and was subsequently used by the colonial state to regulate the behavior of women and sexual minorities in public. The provisions on abortion and infanticide were linked directly to the need to govern the sexual transgressions of Indian women.

Alongside the Indian Penal Code, the state instituted new specialized laws that systematized the sociological survey, including the Cantonment Acts of 1864 and the expansive Contagious Diseases Act of 1868 that regulated women's movement.[14] These laws controlled a diverse range of social behaviors through the classification and criminalization of women's sexual behavior. On the other hand, men's sexual practices remained almost entirely outside the formal purview of the state, with the notable exception of the provision against sodomy in section 377, which was primarily used in practice to regulate gender non-normative people in the colonial period.[15] The resulting inequality created a legal system where sexual regulation of Indian society by the state occurred almost solely through the control and classification of women.[16]

The colonial state defined the monogamous conjugal home as the sole space of legitimate sexual behavior. Conversely, it condemned behaviors that transgressed the bounds of monogamous marriage as dangerous and potentially criminal. Indeed, this division was clear in the earliest forms of social scientific practice. The 1881 census of Bengal deemed all unmarried women over the age of fifteen years as prostitutes. According to the census, "every member of the female population" was married by that age. If they were unmarried by fifteen, the 1881 census assumed that they would permanently remain outside of the realm of marriage.[17] Through an elaborate system of classification that tied social behavior with crime, the colonial state consistently saw women outside the conjugal home as sexually promiscuous, often naming them prostitutes.

Let me return to the 1872 survey with which I begin this chapter. These are the B proceedings—the circulars and replies, those detailed letters that answered the questionnaire—that were used in the creation of the condensed A proceedings, the summary reports and the condensed census reports that compiled extended descriptions of social life as an archive of sociological fact. Who was this dangerous prostitute who required elucidation in the survey? To find out, the state launched a wide-ranging inquisition into the types of women who were imagined to act as prostitutes in rural and urban areas of the Bengal Presidency. It asked magistrates, police officers, and civil surgeons to elaborate on the same questions: Who was to be categorized as prostitute, and what Indian social practices should the state understand as prostitution?[18] It is here that we may begin not only to cull the content of these rare archives for proof of women's lives but to construct a history of knowledge where the concept of the prostitute shaped the very study of Indian social life.

Following the passage of laws that prohibited the buying and selling of minors under the Indian Penal Code in 1860, the Government of Bengal received appeals from local magistrates and police officers across the presidency to rescue girls in the possession of women suspected of being prostitutes.[19] Through Indian Penal Code laws against the buying and selling of minors for prostitution, the state differentiated people who were considered dangerous from those categories of people that the state deemed vulnerable. Yet the extent of the danger of prostitutes to minor children remained unclear. According to officials, children were acquired by women under the guise of charity but were in fact used for the purpose of prostitution. These children, after being sold, were permanently lost to a life of "disrepute."[20] Throughout the nineteenth century, colonial administrators emphasized that once a female minor had come into contact with a prostitute, she was irredeemable in the eyes of Indian society.

In the 1872 survey, the government solicited as much sociological knowledge about the prostitute as magistrates could furnish, asking authorities to comment on the race, caste, religion, and social behavior of all possible prostitutes in their jurisdiction.[21] In response, officials claimed that women rarely possessed children for prostitution, and that the buying and selling of children was negligible. Rather, they stressed there was a secret world of illicit sexual practices that the state must see as the true source of clandestine prostitution. All social behaviors were to be observed and all social types counted by the state; no terrain of social activity was free of scrutiny.

The Vaishnav religious sect was a subject of extended scrutiny in these B files of the 1872 survey. Colonial administrators insisted that Vaishnav religious practices were really a guise for diverse women who were actually prostitutes. Derisively labeling them as *neris* (shaved head), magistrates emphasized that mendicant women endlessly engaged in prostitution while publicly proclaiming their loyal membership in the religious sect of Vaishnav Hinduism. Magistrate Baboo Kasi Kenkur Sen, Rajshahye (Rajshahi), argued that Vaishnav women were often engaged in prostitution, a result of lax social dictates among women who were naturally sexually promiscuous. For Sen, the religious sect allowed women to rear children and introduce them to prostitution. These women were beggars who hid their promiscuity in claims to religiosity:

> They are found to be the daughters of Vaishnabs, a class of religiousts who recognise no distinction of caste and receive proselytes from all, men who are habitually idle and averse to work or who are very poor become generally converts to Vaishnabism, in as much as it holds out to them as easy means of subsistence by begging which is the profession of this class of people. Domestic misfortunes and want of connubial fidelity drive some to such

consolation in Vaishnabism. Females also under similar circumstances become converts to this religion, particularly women who have been prostitutes. Polygamy exists to a certain extent among them. Children born of these people are very little taken care of by their parents and are usually sold for the most trifling consolation or given away to any one who undertakes to bring them up.[22]

Sen links idleness to women's infidelity, lax morals, and polygamy. As Magistrate Sen emphasized how Vaishnav Hindus practiced prostitution, he also claimed that the majority of these women came from Muslim communities. Sen proclaimed that Vaishnav practices paralleled Muslim practices of divorce, widow remarriage, and short-term marriages. For Sen, these practices of nonmonogamous, impermanent marriage among Vaishnav sects and widespread among Muslims were all to be judged through the rubric of immorality and prostitution. As Sen proclaimed, the only reason that the number of prostitutes seemed so much greater among Hindus than Muslims was because Muslims passed for Hindus in order to become prostitutes.[23]

Other responses to the questionnaire also cited the widespread sexual laxity and clandestine prostitution among Vaishnav sects. According to the Magistrate of Dinajpore, Hindu prostitutes "called themselves Bhostobees or devotees of Vishnoo," whether or not they actually followed Vaishnav religious practices.[24] Other colonial survey responses equated the practices of Vaishnavs with characteristics ranging from the rejection of caste, divorce, and widow remarriage to prostitution. The census of 1871 includes a quote from Magistrate W. H. Verner, where he describes in detail the "Baisnabs" of Bengal as a casteless group, where "any Hindu can join the Baisnabs, from the lowest Chandal to the highest Brahman."[25] The freedom from caste strictures led many to join Vaishnav sects. Those Baisnabs called "Bairagi" were those individuals who were "free from the control of the passions."[26] For Verner, a "very large number of prostitutes are Baisnabs."[27] Ten years later, in the census of 1881, the author suggested that there was a semantic slippage between the Vaishnav and the common prostitute, the *beshya*, a Bengali term for promiscuous woman or prostitute: "It is a common practice among public women to assume the style of Baishnabs, while the similarity between that name and the word Vaisya which denotes their profession is near enough to have led to some mistakes."[28]

A remarkable example of the power of descriptive taxonomies comes from the detailed report of Deputy Magistrate Bankim Chandra Chatterjee—a one-time deputy collector in Midnapore who eventually would become the most celebrated modern novelist of Bengal and the author of India's national song, "Vande Mataram" (1882). His report rests on a stringent belief in monogamous marriage and high Hinduism. His time as a deputy magistrate may have shaped his later ideas of domesticity and sexual difference. Chatterjee's response to the questionnaire reveals that a diverse array of women practiced clandestine prostitution. In Chatterjee's view, secrecy shrouded the social and sexual transgression that was rampant in society. Chatterjee claims his taxonomy of social types would make visible those diverse social practices found in Bengal that were to be equated with prostitution. In narrating these secrets through his "insider" knowledge as a member of society, Chatterjee positioned himself as a privileged viewer and narrator with a systematic understanding of Bengali social life. In his explanatory descriptions of the many types of deviant women, he constructs an exhaustive classificatory hierarchy of social and mental conditions that led women to become prostitutes:

> Prostitutes in general are recruited from all classes of society and do not belong to "any hereditary prostitute caste." . . . Enquiry into the personal history of most of these unfortunate classes in the towns will probably show that prostitutes generally come from the following classes:
> I. The daughters of prostitutes: These creatures have scarcely any other life to choose. They labour under a fearful social stigma by reason of their birth and are outcastes for life. Consequently, a married life to them is impossible; no one, however low caste and low in society will accept them in marriage . . .
> II. Women belonging to ordinary society who voluntarily adopt a prostitute's life. A very large proportion of the prostitute classes are recruited from this source. Grown up women, brought up in the houses of their families, often all of a sudden leave their houses, come to a town, and there take up a prostitute's life. It may be interesting to know which are the causes or histories which lead women deliberately to prefer such a degraded and miserable life to domestic virtues and comforts. It may be desirable to enumerate the principal among them:
>   1. Seduction. Unprincipled villains who seduce women from their households often leave them to their fate after the novelty wears off.

2. Domestic misery. The cruelty of a husband, or of a relative, often renders home intolerable to the wife; the woman maltreated deserts him, and when she can find no other shelter, she takes herself to the brothel.
3. Ennui and love of excitement. The life of a Hindu family woman is peculiarly lonely and secluded; and the restraints of the seclusion are sometimes upsetting to women of particular temperaments, however prized by the rest . . . These women are found to lead the prostitute's life for want of a better one.
4. Constitutions unfavourable to moral restraints. The extreme vigilance with which Hindu society watches female propriety reduces indulgence . . . Women with vicious tendencies are therefore obliged to place themselves beyond its power.
5. Poverty.[29]

Chatterjee offers a contradictory vision of female sexual deviance, with a taxonomy that encompasses the pitiable condition of women and what he argues was the natural tendency of women with poor moral constitutions to fail at sexual restraint. Prostitutes existed as a result of the insatiable sexual nature of Hindu women, who were unable to restrain themselves despite strict Hindu strictures because of their love of excitement. He offers compassion and condemnation in the same epistemic register: deviant women are helpless, vulnerable, and sometimes mistreated by Hindu society, yet women will almost inevitably defy social stricture because they are naturally prone to sexual transgression and moral failure.

Chatterjee, like other magistrates, further describes how "Baisnavis" had a "loose morality." They were, in his language, the "utter negation of feminine morality," clandestine prostitutes who had no regard for respectability.[30] According to him, the Vaishnav social world lacked necessary regulations of caste hierarchy that could be found in traditional Hindu society. The Vaishnav woman defied the respectability of the conjugal home and exercised an unprecedented level of choice because of the lax practices of marriage and divorce among Vaishnavs. Vaishnav sects allowed diverse women from all castes to live together and pursue independent modes of living outside the monogamous conjugal household. For Chatterjee, the Vaishnav sect blurred caste lines and created false egalitarian social structures of marriage and divorce that hid the reality of prostitution. Administrators like Chatterjee depended on this idea of a vulnerable yet inevitably deviant womanhood to determine the regulation of social practice.

Concurrent with the colonial survey, as we saw in the chapter "Origins," philologists were creating their own taxonomies that could account for the prostitute as the genesis of deviance in Indian society. Women's sexuality could be the premise for the scientific study of social life, as an investigation into ancient orginary tests and through legal surveys that would generate new codes for Indian social life. The sexual deviance of diverse women, brought into view through the practice of the survey, was not only an object of knowledge but also a potential site for state intervention.

W. Wavell, magistrate of Moorshedabad and the superior of Bankim Chatterjee, had commissioned Chatterjee's report for the sake of accuracy; he argued that the perspective of a Bengali man was the most accurate depiction of "native" society. Wavell distilled Chatterjee's extensive descriptions into a systematic taxonomy of all women who the state must mark as prostitutes.[31] His list includes Muslim women living under the "guise of *nika* marriage," girl children forced into Hindu marriage, high-caste widows barred from remarriage, and the "Hindoo form of polygamy known as Coolinism."[32] According to Wavell, women became prostitutes as a result of ancient Hindu law: "There are bad ones among the wealthiest or the highest in social rank and I think perhaps they have here more excuse in consequence of the unhappy law laid down by Manu."[33] This explanatory mode attributed contemporary Hindu social practices to the laws laid down in ancient texts. The widow was, in the view of Wavell, an inevitable prostitute. This form of reasoning placed ancient texts as the primary origin of the Indian prostitute.[34] According to Wavell, the secrecy of a woman's sexual transgression resulted from the static nature of timeless social customs that led to an inevitable problem of widowhood and prostitution.

With a similar inventory of women, Alexander Abercrombie, the commissioner of Dacca (Dhaka), differentiated Hindu prostitutes who fell into prostitution as a result of religious stricture from Muslim prostitutes in his response to the 1872 query. According to Abercrombie, Muslim women prostitutes hid their sexual deviance in false marriages. He understood this difference in sociological terms. According to Abercrombie, women who turned to prostitution had fallen permanently out of society. If Muslim, women could find menial jobs like housekeeping because of the relative tolerance of sexual promiscuity among Muslims. As a result, they had a more stopgap or casual relationship to the act, and often were at once prostitutes and workers. "Mussulmans," Abercrombie claimed, "may contract a nika marriage . . . and a Mahomedan thinks nothing of contracting such an alliance."[35] When the Muslim couple became "thoroughly tired of each other," they separated "without difficulty and the woman is free to go nika with another man or set up again for herself in the bazar."[36] Hindu women, on the other hand, had no means of earning a living after falling out of society. Disreputable Hindu women converted en masse to Islam to be free from social condemnation, as Islam had "nothing conservative in its tenet."[37] While Muslim women were sexually promiscuous, they were unregulated by regimes of shame and social condemnation like their Hindu counterparts.

In these taxonomies, Muslim women were characterized as more sexually brazen than their Hindu counterparts, with insatiable sexual appetites and a dangerous promiscuity unleashed by the system of temporary marriages. That said, administrators stressed that women of *all* religious communities were potential prostitutes. Across these letters, the same categories and social behaviors are linked to prostitution. Babu Taraknath Mullick, deputy magistrate of Madaripur, insisted that the marriage customs of Hindus led to widowhood and the polygamy of Muslims led to prostitution. For Mullick, Muslims were always leading lives of disrepute:

> The Mohamedan religion, I think, affords greater facilities for leading an irregular life with intercourse with prostitutes than any other religion on the face of the Globe. A Mohammedan, if he chooses, can marry a woman today and renounce her tomorrow, and a wife so given can again marry another. His religion sanctions this. But the case is quite different with a Hindoo. His religion is very jealous in this respect . . . Hence it is that a Mohamedan of loose character gratifies his inclination by contracting temporary marriages, while a Hindoo of the same character does the same by visiting prostitutes.[38]

Similarly, explaining how Muslim women were prostitutes as often as Hindus but hid under the guise of marriage, D. R. Lyall, magistrate of Dacca, argued that officials must broaden the definition of what constituted prostitution. If prostitution meant "simply one that indiscriminately carries on intercourse with men whether openly professing prostitution or not," then the number of Hindus acting as prostitutes would be significantly less than "that of Mohamedan prostitutes."[39] Lyall describes how "respectable men" of elite Muslim families had official wives who were, in fact, prostitutes, alongside their ayahs, nannies, who were "mostly prostitutes who escape notice."[40] The other important segment of Muslim prostitutes were the well-known dancing girls who continued in courtesan traditions, described variously as "Nottees" and "Nautch" by administrators.[41]

Stressing the "extreme" nature of Muslim temporary marriages and the inevitable return of these women to prostitution, Magistrate Mullick emphasized the fluidity of Muslim social institutions and the virtual absence of propriety when compared to Hindus. The only redeeming feature of Muslim polygamy, when compared to Hindu Kulinism, was that wives lived under the supervision of their husband:

> Polygamy and Coolinism also augment the number of Hindoo prostitutes. The Mohamedans, indeed, indulge in the plurality of wives, but their customs in this respect are very different from those of the Hindoos. A Mohamedan, whatever may be the number of his wives, keeps all within his harem but the wives of a Hindoo lie scattered over different places and districts. A Mohamedan woman who is united to a man having many wives has at least the consolation of living under her husband's roof, eating his bread, and seeing him frequently, but a Hindoo woman who happens to be married to a Koolin having a plurality of wives, remains all her days at the house of her parents, and considers herself very fortunate if her husband sees her even once in the interval of 4 or 5 years ... Under the Shastras she cannot on any account marry during the lifetime of her husband. Sometimes for the sake of Koolinism, parents or other guardians of young girls marry or rather sacrifice them to men old enough to be their grandpapas. It is not therefore surprising that the wives of such Koolins and polygamists should become prostitutes.⁴²

Here, Muslim polygamy is the foundation of the harem, governed at all points by the Muslim man. Mullick notes there is a "Shastric" dictate for Kulin Brahman polygamy, a textual origin for a social practice that left women outside of the domain of the conjugal home. Like the prohibition of widow remarriage among high-castes, polygamy of the Hindus created a class of unrestrained women who existed outside of monogamous marriage. In his formulation the harem, despite all of its dangers and perversions, was a means for women's sexual regulation, whereas Hindu dictates left high-caste women exposed to the dangerous result of their own sexual desire.

Many officials, including Mullick and Lyall, cited texts like *Manu* and the *shastras* as the primary reason Hindu women transgressed social bounds. For these administrators, it was not economic circumstance but the strict religious dictates of caste and ancient Hindu law that led women who were outside of a monogamous conjugal home and without the oversight of a husband to sexual transgression. Ancient law, defined through colonial engagement with a particular canon of Sanskrit text, was thus essential to the state-sponsored sociological project. Sexual transgression was hidden by the façade of caste, and required exposure through authoritative practices of description from administrative experts who would illuminate the true facts of sexual transgression. Ultimately, according to this colonial sociological survey, women who resided outside the conjugal home were almost inevitably sexual deviants—no matter the context that would have led them to desperate conditions or absolute social exclusion and condemnation.

What could be done to end prostitution? Mullick offered a sociological answer in his extensive response to the query. Since he saw prostitution as an inevitability because of social custom, Mullick argued that no law could truly bring about an enduring change against unchanging customs without internal reforms in society. It was thus the burden of Hindu society to expose the hidden practices of their society and end prostitution through systematic reform: "I may only add that it is with the Hindoos themselves to remedy the evil. The Government can abolish sati rites. It can put a stop to infanticide. It can legalize widow remarriage ... The nation itself must exhort to put a stop to this disgraceful state of things and as long as it does not do so earnestly there is no hope."[43] The sociology of the prostitute was the lens through which a range of social evils could be placed in the same sociological register: *sati*, the prohibition of widow marriage, and the killing of illegitimate children.

It is striking how often these correlated typologies of women's deviant sexuality are repeated across the hundreds of pages of responses to the questionnaire. Officials could create parallel lists of the types of prostitutes through the common reasoning that all nonmonogamous forms of sexuality for women was akin to prostitution. The inquiry framed the detailed sociological answers that followed. In their redundancy, these extensive descriptions became a foundational apparatus to comprehend the secrets that organized everyday social life. The B files feature practices of taxonomical sociology that utilized the prostitute to explain key concepts in a growing science of society in India: Muslim and Hindu difference, caste hierarchy, patriarchy, companionate marriage, polygamy, widowhood, infanticide. Here we see an extraordinary logic at work that allowed for the colonial state to initiate comprehensive sociological studies into the most intimate domains of everyday life. The concept of the prostitute was the difference, a named boundary constantly in flux between legitimate forms of social relations recognized by the state in civil law and the secret realm of sexual transgression outside of Hindu monogamous marriage. This domain, outside of monogamy, was to be the subject of systematic inquiry under numerous new criminal laws.

The Contagious Diseases
Acts and the Clandestine Prostitute

"I did not attend for examination twice a month as I have not been a prostitute."[44] In 1868, Sukhimonee Raur was sentenced to prison for evading a genital examination, mandatory for all women made to register as prostitutes, a process systematized under the newly passed Act XIV of 1868, the Contagious Diseases Act. Sukhimonee had insisted she was not now nor had ever been a prostitute. She testified that she had been forced by the police to take a registration ticket and explained that they had misrecognized her as a prostitute. Despite having a state-issued ticket in her possession, she refused to appear for the genital examination. Responding to the appeal of her conviction, the Appellate High Court of Calcutta reversed the decision on March 22, 1869. The court stated that while Sukhimonee had failed to appear for the exam, "the mere possession of a registration ticket under Act XIV does not necessarily make the holder of it a registered public prostitute under that Act . . . The registration must be voluntary."[45] It held that the police were expected to bring a summons against those women whom they identified as clandestine prostitutes. However, because of criminal procedure codes, they could not force a woman to register as a prostitute.

Sukhimonee Raur's case offers us a window into the complex world of classification and procedure under new forms of governance by the colonial state. Hers was not a unique protest by a woman against the new law but was a rare case that reached the courts. The Contagious Diseases Act inaugurated a new era of the regulation of sexuality in India, regulating criminal behavior through the classification, registration, and examination of women seen as prostitutes in major cities of India.[46] In this archive of legal inquiry about contagious diseases, we encounter only fragmented histories of the people who came under the broad category of the prostitute. The classification encompassed so-called dancing girls, widows, Vaishnav women, low-class Muslim married women, Kulin Brahman polygamous wives, women factory laborers, maidservants, and many more. This social typology of women enters the colonial archive solely through the language of the regulation of the prostitute. The social history of these diverse social practices and communities in the nineteenth century is limited and distorted by an archive that presents women solely through their proximity to prostitution.

Yet in histories of the Contagious Diseases Act, women who came under the new law are most often historicized as "sex workers" or otherwise as part of the sex trade.[47] In contrast to the histories of prostitution that equate the historical appearance of the archival category of prostitute with sex worker, the prostitute here appears as an ambiguous and indeterminate concept that often encompassed women who were not directly (or solely) engaged in sexual commerce. Indeed, a different picture emerges when we situate the sociological project of the Contagious Diseases Act of 1868 alongside other modes of criminal legal inquiry that sought to enumerate deviant sexuality from the 1860s. The introduction of the act led to an epistemic shift, a pivotal change where Indian sexual practices became a primary object of knowledge for the British colonial state. In this framework the prostitute appears as a concept, invented, circulated, and repeated in the service of new forms of social scientific inquiry. Administrators correlated a systematic typology of Indian social practices through the repeated use of the category of the prostitute. The Contagious Diseases Act produced a new language and spurred new modes of social description and explanation. The concept could be used to comprehend everything from marriage practices to venereal disease control to urban policing to abortion and infanticide. Administrators used the prostitute to count populations, diagnose the legitimacy of marriage structures, and justify broad sociological inquiries into sexual relationships. Legal surveys about women's sexual practices relied on this form of reasoning—whereby distinct and often incongruous types of women were collapsed into a bounded category of the prostitute.

The *concept* of the prostitute was thus "trafficked" by the colonial state in the service of new modes of sociological survey and social scientific explanation. These descriptive methods—of taxonomical classification, inferential identification, legal speculation—informed a wide practice of colonial governance over social life in India beyond the Contagious Diseases Act, from the buying and selling of girls to infanticide and abortion. The colonial state insisted that a sociological explanation was needed to comprehend sexual secrets. That explanation, for colonial administrators, was to be found in the repeated use of the concept, the same and yet different in its iteration. Newly empowered officials of the state—from administrators to policemen to doctors—produced as natural the categorical equivalence between the prostitute, a flexible and indeterminate idea, and the many types of sexual and social behaviors of Indian women.

Like Sukhimonee Raur, thousands of women were arrested by the police for failing to abide by rules of registration and examination mandated under the act; many of the arrested women denied their participation in prostitution and petitioned against their classification as prostitutes.[48] The colonial census created new modes of enumeration and description that homogenized diverse networks of women under the classification of prostitute. The Government of India produced the most systematic assessment of its colonial subjects through the first official census of India, taken in 1871, just three years after the passage of the Contagious Diseases Act of 1868. The census counted women, detailing and categorizing their employment in urban and rural areas, with the largest count of women appearing under the category of prostitutes. Out of a population of about 145,000 women, the first complete census of Calcutta and its surrounding areas from 1871 counted 12,228 known prostitutes.[49] By the 1891 census the number of women classified as prostitutes rose to 20,126, perhaps based on a broader understanding of what constituted the prostitute by census surveyors. The 1891 census accounted for the discrepancy and substantial increase in the number of prostitutes, claiming that "the Contagious Diseases Act . . . may have caused some concealment" that no longer existed in the aftermath of the act, which was officially repealed in 1888.[50]

Almost immediately following Sukhimonee's case and others that followed, authorities began to debate the efficacy of the Contagious Diseases Acts in apprehending the prostitute. One such heated exchange, between the police commissioner for Calcutta, Stuart Hogg, and Dr. Robert Payne, the head superintendent of Lock Hospitals in Calcutta, reveals how the concept of the prostitute generated extensive controversy. Extraordinarily, Payne pleaded with Hogg for the right to register women without their consent. Payne felt that the Contagious Disease Act failed because authorities fundamentally misunderstood the nature of prostitution in India. Indeed, Commissioner Hogg and Dr. Payne, two of the most powerful city officials in the 1860s and 1870s, consistently cited the "clandestine prostitute" who evaded registration and examination as the greatest threat to the success of the acts.[51]

What compelled these officials to so vehemently argue for such stringent regulations on Indian women? And what exactly was Payne referring to when he warned against the murky social world of Bengal? Payne argued that the police did not comprehend the complex social terrain of Indians, hidden from view from the state. He warned that women were often secretly prostitutes, and some under the guise of marriage existed outside the domain of state regulation. He described how he consistently saw women slip away from the grasp of the act because of the law's inability to regulate all women in the city.[52] Though women continued to appeal the requirement of registration under the Contagious Diseases Act, the state consistently rejected the addition of an official amendment that would legally mandate the forcible registration of women. Despite no official policy, there were ongoing extralegal uses of the act to regulate the diverse women understood to be clandestine prostitutes but who were not on the registers.[53]

As Payne described in 1870, regulating the prostitute of Bengal was an almost impossible task. She was everywhere and nowhere because every woman had a potential to come under the classification. As an invisible yet pervasive presence, the prostitute could not be identified through visual indicators. Prostitution thus required the ability to socially decipher the behavior of women through comprehensive social scientific tools. He asserted that "the movements of so large a number of women" was an immense task in itself, and the fact that they were "licentious and disorderly and by nature suspicious of legislation" only added to the extraordinary difficulty of regulating the unfamiliar terrain of Indian women's illicit behavior.[54] The prostitute functioned as social fact and explanation in every domain of governance, from the census accounts of women, to regulatory efforts of women in the name of public health, to a newly empowered police. The police were authorized to arrest any registered woman who had failed to attend her periodic examination. Between the 1870s and 1888, on average, twelve women were arrested daily for breach of the rules of the Contagious Diseases Act in Calcutta alone.[55] According to Commissioner Hogg, women became alarmed and exited en masse out of Calcutta upon finding out that they were under police supervision. Hogg claimed these women secretly returned to the city without registering or complying with the act.[56]

According to Payne, "knowledge of the indigenous evil" that was the Indian prostitute was essential to the effective enforcement of the Contagious Diseases Act.[57] He argued that a huge range of women from different communities made up the population of prostitutes who came to Calcutta. Payne argued that women consistently "introduced afresh" the diseases regulated by the act by secretly acting as prostitutes without any government oversight. He further asserted that the social scientific study of women's sexual deviance was essential for the effective working of the act. It was the "great difficulty of proof" of the woman's role in prostitution that prevented effective legislation.[58] In his view, the system of law itself was inadequate for the context of Calcutta, as the state had "little knowledge and experience of details":

> The estimates of numbers itself was conjectural and information on the several forms of prostitution was fragmentary and indefinite . . . Added to this was the necessity for proceeding cautiously in a measure which was to impose restriction on the freedom of a class of people licentious and disorderly in their habits and by nature suspicious of legislation.[59]

Payne provides extensive sociological details of the many types of social behaviors that were to be equated with prostitution. He includes many classes that we have encountered in the survey for the buying and selling of girls, from married women clandestinely acting as prostitutes to Muslim women who were protected under *nika* marriage.

We see in Payne's reports a taxonomy of the many types of prostitute that parallels contemporaneous surveys into intimate social practices.

> It is convenient to mention here, as illustrating the great difficulty of proof, some of the peculiar phases of prostitution in Calcutta. Calcutta has a large company of clandestine prostitutes, and here, as elsewhere, they are a most mischievous class. Many married women, especially among the lower Eurasians, are of this class . . . In some cases it is known to the Police that prostitution is carried on with connivance of the husbands.
>
> A second class are the so-called nika wives of khalassies and other Mohamedans employed in sea-going and coasting vessels . . . They are the first recipients of venereal disease brought from other ports where there is traffic, and there is perhaps no class of women in the place so pernicious to the public health as they are.
>
> A third class are women employed as labourers in various factories, and in rough labour under artisans . . . They are protected from the liabilities of prostitutes by the testimony of employers in their diurnal industry. Over all of these classes the Police are, they say, powerless. If an attempt is made to bring them under control the result is most discouraging.
>
> In addition to the above methods of sheltering themselves while they injure the public the women of a neighborhood occasionally contrive to place themselves under the direct protection of a man of influence. A man of property has constituted himself guardian of all prostitutes in the vicinity.
>
> It is not necessary to describe the various forms of less public concubinage which prevail in this town . . . Some of these forms are such that there can be little security for those who approach the kept women of Calcutta.[60]

Payne argued that some women would even go as far as dressing in men's clothing in order to enter military barracks and ply their trade without detection.[61] Like the many officials charting the terrain of the prostitute, Payne deduced that many types of women who resided outside monogamous Hindu marriage, from temporary wives to women laborers to mistresses, were clandestine prostitutes who threatened the efficacy of law. He concluded that the police were helpless in the face of the clandestine prostitutes who pervaded social life: "That the best efforts of the Police are hopeless in the presence of existing obstacles and limitation of powers, that the evidence of prostitution requires authoritative definition, and that neither marriage nor other protection should be suffered to shield a woman from the liabilities of a life of prostitution."[62]

The police agreed with Payne's diagnosis of the problem, expressing their frustration with the failure of the classification of prostitute for regulating "native" sexual practices. In a letter to the secretary of Bengal, Hogg emphasizes that despite the best efforts of the police, women would continue to infect men with venereal diseases because of the limited reach of the act for those women formally classified as prostitutes. He suggests that the act would be effective only if it was widened: "The Contagious Diseases Act must be worked with a rigor which will bring within its scope all scope of women" who engaged in deviant behavior to come under supervision by the state. It was the job of the police to name those women who acted as prostitutes and decipher those acts that counted as prostitution in Calcutta.[63] Hogg emphasizes that it was difficult to prove in the legal sense that the wide range of social types in Bengal were prostitutes: "To establish in court, except inferentially, that a woman is a common prostitute, is most difficult."[64] Comprehending the prostitute required inferential thinking because the sexual deviance of women was always concealed under the guise of respectability.

The Cantonment and Contagious Diseases Acts were unsuccessful in curbing venereal disease through the new system of regulation and mandatory medical examination and treatment. Officials in Bengal explained this failure of the acts by arguing that Indian women were often clandestine prostitutes who evaded classification. For officials, the result of these legal limitations was a conspiracy of secrecy among women, making them virtually ungovernable. Hidden at every turn was the possibility of prostitution. According to one police officer, women in Calcutta regularly evaded examination but often "lurked" in shadows:

> When the police proceed to the woman's place of abode they find that perhaps ten days or a week previously, she had absconded and left the jurisdiction ... It is very certain that none of her friends or relatives will afford the slightest clue to her whereabouts. It is possible she is lurking within the jurisdiction and so the warrant is kept in hand.[65]

Officials described how women evaded examination and maintained dangerous sexual relationships despite the best efforts of local authorities. The danger of the unknown was real and resulted from the secret nature of Indian women's social liaisons and the possibly virulent results of their illicit relationships. This threat existed even among those women who purported to be respectable. Horace Cockerell, secretary to the Government of Bengal, insisted that diseased women, even if they were registered on the prostitute roll, would send "healthy friends to attend examination for them" to avoid problems.[66] There were further challenges assumed by the colonial state—for there were "the higher classes of women who are not mere kept women, but who are no doubt common prostitutes" and who were protected under the guise of legitimacy.[67]

Over the period of enforcement of the Contagious Diseases Act in Calcutta, the commissioner maintained that police should be empowered not only to arrest women for public solicitation under the Indian Penal Code, but also summarily arrest any woman suspected of being a prostitute.[68] The secretary to the Government of Bengal, S. C. Bayley, warned that any lax approach to the classification of women would lead to the failure of the act.

> When among so great a prostitute population and amid so much resistance to the Act only nine women have been subjected to very light punishments for failing to register . . . His Honor apprehends that women who are induced to come on the register by admonition and police arrest, and who are determined to resist, probably do so successfully. The Lieutenant-Governor cannot say what evidence should satisfy Magistrates that a woman is a common prostitute.[69]

The question of who was to be named as a prostitute was a site of profound disagreement. Payne, in his role as superintendent of Lock Hospitals, blamed the police for the failure of the acts to curb venereal disease. He criticized Hogg for failing to apprehend the wide range of women who were prostitutes and forcibly register them under the act. Hogg vehemently refuted Payne's account of the failure of the police.[70]

Petitions against the police in the colonial archives reveal the broad discretionary power that police wielded in registering women as prostitutes. Charges of extortion and inappropriate behavior were so numerous that the police were unable to keep an accurate record of the complaints.[71] A small number of petitions from elite, upper-caste Bengali men accused the police of harassing respectable women, while most petitions from women bearing the brunt of the act alleged gross misconduct and rampant blackmail under the fear of registration and forcible detention. For example, one petition, against a head constable, alleged that the officer blackmailed women for gratification in exchange for exemption, while another was accused of forcibly entering a woman's house in order to obtain evidence against a woman accused of being a prostitute. Numerous petitions revealed that police officers took bribes from women who refused to be registered. Yet the Government of India rejected all petitions and deemed them to be without merit. The police conducted the forcible registration and examination of women with little interference from the local government.[72]

The Contagious Diseases Act also provoked a dramatic response from women who were classified as prostitutes. The indexes of the archives of the Bengal Presidency testify to the number of petitions against the act submitted to the state by women classified as prostitutes and contained within "Lock Hospitals."[73] But according to archivists, most petitions were lost in a fire that destroyed these detailed documents—the B proceedings, notes, and supplemental materials that described the everyday workings of law.[74]

In July 1869, following the passing of the Contagious Diseases Act, one particular petition by "certain prostitutes of Calcutta" circulated among officials in the Government of Bengal. In this rare document transcribed by a court clerk in English, which survived in the state archives of West Bengal, an anonymous group of women protested their classification as prostitutes. They accused colonial authorities of "violating their womanhood" by making them register and comply with the medical examination and detention mandates of the act.[75] The petition highlighted the suffering of women who were brought under Act XIV:

> We are undergone to suffer a great deal . . . compelled to leave our lodge in town . . . out of the jurisdiction of Calcutta and its suburbs police, in order to save ourselves from their oppression. Therefore we are gone to lose much, and suffer thereby beyond description. We are at a loss to understand why the Legislatures come to force us for registration and let us to undergo the process of hateful examination, which is in other words *gross exposure*. The few who are caught hold of by the police are forced to expose themselves to the Doctor and his subordinates, whether they are diseased or not . . . The sense of female honour is not wholly blotted from our hearts.[76]

By appealing to the state as vulnerable subjects, rather than "dishonored" criminals who were to be harmed through examination, these women indicted the legislature as well as the police for categorizing them as disreputable women, indeed, as prostitutes. They presented themselves as defenseless women who were to supposed to be protected by the state. They also pointed to the double bind of the act, where a woman, if not already perceived as a dishonored woman, would become dishonored through the forced genital examination. Like many other petitions, the petition was quickly dismissed by the secretary of Bengal, deemed as "entirely general," the kind of action that "might be expected from women who are straining their utmost to resist the operation of the Act, and whose obedience to it has to be enforced by means of the Police."[77]

By 1881, officials found it increasingly difficult to justify the act in the face of growing opposition in Britain as well as in India.[78] The Contagious Disease Acts of 1864 and 1868 were suspended briefly in 1883 in Calcutta. They were officially repealed in 1888 following years of contention about the issue of prostitution and the critique from British movements that saw the Contagious Diseases Acts as tantamount to state-regulated vice.[79] Officials emphasized that the colonial state's inability to stop the spread of venereal disease was a result of the wide range of clandestine sexual relationships and the façade of social propriety in India. But this failure only further fueled the taxonomical method of the sociological project, with methods of homogenization and aggregation used for decades following the acts.

In the last decades of the nineteenth century, colonial administrators utilized the survey and questionnaire directly in social scientific practices of colonial ethnography. Herbert Hope Risley (1851–1911), colonial ethnographer and census commissioner after 1901, relied on extensive questionnaires about marital status and sexual practices to write his definitive 1891 study, *The Tribes and Castes of Bengal*.[80] In collaboration with historian and statistician William Wilson Hunter (1840–1900) in their comprehensive statistical study of India, Risley introduced the marital status of women as the primary category to understand Indian society. The study that resulted, *A Statistical Account of Bengal* (1875–1879), repeatedly uses the category of prostitute over the course of its twenty volumes. Risley and Hunter distinguish legitimate marriage practices and illegitimate social practices of different caste groups across Bengal. They describe as definitive fact the wide range of women who were prostitutes in Bengal: Vaishnav women, Kulin Brahman women, dancing girls, Muslim women engaging in *nika* marriage, Muslim courtesans known as *tawa'ifs*, vagabond women, and caste groups including "gandarbaha," "nats," "kheltas," "kasbi," and "Maljadi," who "prostitute their women" or were "the children of prostitutes."[81] The prostitute, enumerated at length in the multivolume statistical survey, was now undeniably a social fact.

Infanticide and the Concealment of Transgression

In the 1872 questionnaire and the debates about the Contagious Diseases Acts, I have traced how colonial administrators utilized the concept of the prostitute to constitute everyday social practice as an object of inquiry. I now turn to a controversial issue in the late nineteenth century, infanticide, that spurred an almost obsessive interest by the colonial state in the social silence around women's sexual behavior. In response to growing state concerns, the colonial government issued a questionnaire to all administrators and judges about the occurrence of infanticide in 1877, which, like the 1872 query, was a knowledge-gathering project that sought to elucidate quotidian social practices. This time, the colonial state surveyed judges across Bengal, asking them to explain the roots of infanticide in Indian society. Legal debates in the late nineteenth century framed infanticide as a critical problem that resulted from Indian women's deviant sexuality. The category of prostitute became emblematic of the perversion of femininity, the "inherent" proclivity among Indian women to commit violent crimes to keep secrets. The responses to the survey about infanticide emphasized the absolute irrationality of Indian women as a result of their sexual desire.

In the Indian Penal Code of 1860, women who committed infanticide against newborn infants were deemed to be criminal subjects in need of the most stringent forms of state regulation. The code produced the perpetrator of infanticide as a capital criminal, subject to the toughest punishment under the law. A woman could be sentenced to "transportation for life"—indentured servitude—to a penal or work colony, or she could be sentenced to death. Following the Indian Penal Code, the colonial state passed the Female Infanticide Act of 1870 to regulate what was perceived as a "customary" problem of killing female infants in parts of North India.[82]

According to judges and magistrates, cases of infanticide in Bengal were distinct, differing from colonial inquiries about female infanticide in other regions. For colonial authorities, these practices of infanticide were different because infanticide itself was not a customary practice to reduce the population of girls. Instead, authorities insisted that the infanticide outside of the tribes of the Northwestern Provinces resulted from entire systems of unchanging social customs, including widowhood, polygamy, and caste. In the logic of the state, the rigid social strictures of Hindu society led women to be sexually unrestrained and become pregnant. This formulation was explicitly a claim to the need of the survey to create an empirical data set that could serve as an archive of social fact. Rather than colonial understandings of femicide, depicted as innate tribal or caste practices that devalued girl children, administrators and judges insisted that general infanticide was directly attributable to women's proclivity for sexual deviance and prostitution. Administrators argued that Indian women committed infanticide on illegitimate children with little regard for human life—that is, for entirely selfish reasons, to maintain social status and hide illicit sexual relationships. The state emphasized that the law was necessary to *expose* the clandestine social networks that sought to conceal abortion and infanticide. It is in the moment of the revelatory questionnaire that numerous accounts of women committing abortion and infanticide enter into the state archive as A and B files.[83]

Authorities in the Bengal Presidency debated the role of evidence in investigating abortions and infanticide from 1860 on, but judicial decisions about the sentencing of women convicted of infanticide went largely unchallenged by elite Indian men.[84] Then, in 1876, T. Madhav Rao, the Dewan of Baroda, Gujarat, published "Considerations on the Crime of Infanticide and Its Punishment in India" in the *Journal of the National Indian Association*.[85] Rao advocated the abolition of capital punishment for widows who committed infanticide, arguing that the punishment was excessive and cruel because social custom, including child marriage and caste rules, prohibited widow marriage. For Rao, women were never culpable for such crimes because they were incapable of rational thought in the face of oppressive customs like enforced widowhood. Rao responded to the colonial explanation of linking infanticide to irrationality by claiming that Indian women were to be pitied, as they were naturally inclined to infanticide because of their fears of social exclusion. Both arguments saw women's sexual deviance and the willingness among women to kill infants as inevitable, the direct result of their natural irrationality. While the state saw it as a regulatory problem, Rao saw the "infanticidal woman" as the ultimate object of pity.[86]

In response to growing indictments of the state in the Indian press, the Government of India initiated a systematic inquiry about infanticide and the sentencing of women who were accused of the crime. The secretary to the Government of Bengal, Judicial Department, sent a mandatory circular with questions to all judges across the state on September 21, 1876. Like the inquiry into the types of prostitutes across Bengal in 1872, this survey posed questions to administrators to create a full sociological schematic of Indian infanticide. The questionnaire constituted an archive of explanation, where administrators built a foundation for legal intervention and reform through descriptions of the reasons for women's behavior and taxonomies of their sexual and social deviance.

In response to the query, the Government of Bengal received detailed reports on the causes of infanticide, particular case histories, and recommendations for legal reforms. Alongside case details, the reports provided extended commentaries on the nature of infanticide in India. Officials reflected on the distinct features of the social world in the region, depicting how women's lives were haunted by the specter of shame, illegitimacy, and sexual deviance that led as if inevitably to the "heinous" crime of infanticide. The cases reported were particularly important because they exclusively addressed the birth and possible infanticide of children born as a result of illicit sexual relationships outside of monogamous marriage. In hundreds of letters sent between 1876 and 1877, judges across Bengal provided detailed charts and narratives of cases of infanticide they had encountered in their courts. They stressed that the infanticide of illegitimate children occurred more often in this region than in any other part of India.

Judges in Bengal insisted that the numerous cases that appeared before them in court represented only a small fraction of what they termed "crimes of concealment." Indeed, they stressed that the crime of abortion was undetectable, since it was consistently hidden by the family and community because of caste strictures. The idea of timeless social custom was cited again and again by judges and magistrates as a complete explanation for infanticide. Judge W. Macpherson, officiating judge in Bengal, emphasized it was widowhood among high-caste women and the illicit pregnancies of Kulin wives who did not reside with their husbands that led to the crime of infanticide.[87] He argued that it was difficult to successfully prosecute a woman on charges of infanticide in court because of this "conspiracy" of concealment.

Sessions Judge J. M. Lowis of Bhagulpore gave voice to his colleagues' collective fear when he wrote:

> I do not on this account believe, nor would I wish the Government to believe, that information is given freely regarding the commission of such offences. Looking at the low state of morality which exists among the masses on the one hand, and the very small percentage of illegitimate children on the other, it is impossible to avoid the conclusion that abortion and child-murder are practised to a very large extent.[88]

Lowis reflects the paranoia of administrators and policemen about clandestine sexuality that could not be controlled. Indeed, the nature of the question and answer of the survey itself *created* this fear of the unknown by figuring women's deviant sexuality as an immanently productive field of social inquiry. Rather, for many administrators, the purpose of laws against infanticide were necessary to control the results of Indian's women's sexual transgression. The law thus was productive of a new paranoia while also quelling it. It was a punitive measure, meant to punish those criminal women, as well as a necessary deterrent for any future secret crime that would be outside the reach of the state. As S. C. Bayley, secretary to the Government of Bengal, explained, the secret nature of the crime itself almost invariably meant that abortion and infanticide escaped detection by the state. He thus insisted that "punishment should be made deterrent in proportion to the strength of the temptation that exists to commit the crime."[89]

Colonial officials felt that women's illicit acts would become visible to the state only through close observation of local communities. The state needed to be attuned to rumors or suspicions of pregnancies spread by neighbors and community authorities. Rumors were reported to local authorities, who acted on the information and often arrested the outcast women for acts of violent concealment. Following the prohibition of abortion and infanticide in 1860, police officers and local communities submitted testimonials and petitions to the Government of Bengal that detailed suspicious activity of unmarried women suspected of pregnancy. Young widows were singled out; it was suggested that they intended to abort or had already aborted unborn fetuses that resulted from illicit sex.[90]

In this way, the state created a new environment of intimate surveillance. Colonial administrators promoted new practices of collusion with families, neighbors, and communities in everyday life, a network of snitches and men who blackmailed women that would monitor and report on the sexual transgressions of women and the potential for their secret crimes. These individuals included the *dhobi*, the washerman, and the local *chowkidar*, the neighborhood watchman. Officiating Judge W. Macpherson narrated a sociological reason for why women commit infanticide and how the crime of infanticide was made visible to the colonial state:

> A widow becomes pregnant by illicit intercourse; the dhobi comes to know of this owing to certain clothes not being sent to the wash as usual or . . . the woman's personal appearance betrays her. The dhobi, if his mouth is not closed, tells the village chowkeedar; the latter questions the woman and makes public her shame, at the same time he informs the police of her pregnancy. Should she take an opportunity of procuring abortion, as she generally does, detection is almost sure to follow. If the vigilance of the

chowkeedar prevents this, the birth is only too often concealed, and the body disposed of in such a way as would constitute an offence under section 318.[91]

Judges wove legal case decisions with evocative narratives of the event of infanticide. With lurid narratives and detailed charts, their letters feature systematic descriptions that explained how widows killed their babies—how they drowned, poisoned, or choked the child. The cause of death was narrated alongside details of how mothers discarded the body and the forensic medical appearance of the infant after death. Records reproduced detailed case diagrams that name the case, the suspect, and acts of violence used to inflict death upon the infant. Through these comprehensive charts of infanticide cases (see Figure 7), judges linked the nature of the violent act directly to the nature of the woman. Authorities demonstrated the degree of calculation of women who committed infanticide. The motive of the crime was critical—judges explained the difference between immediate, irrational acts of violence by pitiable women and carefully planned out, insidious acts of depravity.

What was ultimately at stake in these narratives of infanticide was not the crime itself but the motive for concealment. According to judges across Bengal, Hindu social custom forced sexually unrestrained women outside the safe confines of companionate, monogamous marriage. It was the backward marriage traditions of Hindus that enabled women's sexual deviance and inclination toward prostitution. In their narratives about infanticide, Indian men appear unable to control unruly women in social institutions like polygamy and enforced widowhood, which officials insisted led to women's sexual transgression by leaving them exposed outside the conjugal home. The depictions of the infanticidal woman in surveys were often contradictory, as objects of pity and yet sexually and morally depraved. Indeed, judge after judge sought to understand if the Indian woman was even capable of rational thought and reasoned judgment. While Hindu social custom was offered as an explanation for the perversion of women, judges emphasized that there was a more fundamental issue at play: the innate irrational character of Indian women. The logic of the judge went like this: with sexual promiscuity inevitably came illicit pregnancy. With the possibility of social shame through pregnancy, these women fulfilled their natural inclination to conceal their pregnancy through abortion and infanticide. These explanations could be systematized in charts that summarized the typology and highlights of each case for easy use by the state in the assessment of the law.

(2)

Cases of Infanticide from 1871 to 1875.

Names.	Sections under which tried.	Date of Sentence.	Brief narrative of cases.
1. Mussamut Lukrunia ...	302, Indian Penal Code	19th January 1871	1. The prisoner was charged with the offence of murdering her child. Before this court she states that the child was born alive, that when it died she threw it into the tank where it was found. The fact of the child being born alive and death being caused by drowning is deposed to by medical evidence. The assessor found her guilty, and the Judge, concurring with his opinion, sentenced the prisoner to transportation for life. Appeal preferred to the High Court and was dismissed.
2. Mussamut Seokulea ...	304, Indian Penal Code	5th February 1872	2. She was charged with the offence of culpable homicide not amounting to murder. The evidence discloses that a child was born to the prisoner, and that the identical child was found in the river. The child was alive when it was taken out, but died the next day. Medical evidence proves that the child's death was caused by exposure. The assessors convicted her guilty, and the Judge, concurring with their opinion, sentenced the prisoner to five years' rigorous imprisonment. No appeal preferred to the High Court.
3. Mussamut Husebea ...	304 and 317, Indian Penal Code.	6th Ditto	3. The prisoner was charged with the offence of culpable homicide not amounting to murder. It is proved that a child was born to the prisoner and was abandoned in a ruhur field. Medical evidence showed that death was caused by exposure. The Court, concurring with the assessors, convicted the prisoner and sentenced her to five years' rigorous imprisonment. No appeal preferred to the High Court.
4. Mussamut Chirounji ...	304 and 318, Indian Penal Code.	2nd March 1872	4. The Court, discrediting the evidence of witnesses as to the fact of their seeing the child born alive and taken away alive by the prisoner, agrees with the assessors in acquitting the prisoner under section 304; but, differing from their opinion, convicted her of the offence of secretly disposing of the dead body of her newly-born son with the intention of concealing the birth of the said son, and sentenced her to two years' rigorous imprisonment. No appeal preferred.
5. Mussamut Surehea ...	304 and 317, Indian Penal Code.	11th January 1873	5. Is charged with the offence of exposing and abandoning her infant child. It is proved that the child was born alive and was abandoned in a dhan field. The medical evidence attributes desertion and neglect as the probable cause of death. The Court, concurring with the assessors, convicted the prisoner; but, considering that she was abetted by another to commit the offence, inflicted a lighter punishment, and sentenced her to three years' rigorous imprisonment. No appeal preferred.
6. Mussamut Deorunea ...	302, 304, and 317, Indian Penal Code.	10th July 1874	6. Proves not guilty of the offences under sections 302 and 304. Is found guilty of the offence of exposing and abandoning her infant child in a low ditch, where it was found by a workman and taken out alive. The child subsequently died. The evidence of the Civil Surgeon shows that death was probably caused by want of food and exposure. The Judge, concurring with the opinion of the assessors, sentenced her to three years' rigorous imprisonment. On appeal being preferred to the High Court, the punishment was modified to six months' rigorous imprisonment.
7. Mussamut Subhugea ...	302, Indian Penal Code	10th July 1874	7. The prisoner was delivered of a live child, which she threw into water, from where it was taken out and sent to the medical officer, where it died. Medical testimony shows that it died from exposure and the result of immersion. The assessors were of opinion that the case should be tried under section 317, Indian Penal Code, but the Judge, differing from them, convicted her of the offence of committing murder by causing the death of her child by throwing it into water under section 302, Indian Penal Code, and sentenced her to transportation for life. On appeal being preferred to the High Court, the conviction and sentence were set aside.
8. Mussamut Suntokhea...	302 and 318, Indian Penal Code.	16th August 1875	8. Charges were brought against the accused under sections 302 and 318, Indian Penal Code. The Judge, concurring with the opinion of the assessors, acquitted her of the first charge, but convicted her of the offence of secretly concealing the dead body of her infant child with the intention of concealing the birth of such child under section 318, Indian Penal Code, and sentenced her to one year's rigorous imprisonment. Appeal rejected by the High Court.

A. V. PALMER,
Sessions Judge of Shahabad.

The 17th November 1876.

FIGURE 7. Chart of infanticide cases in Bengal, 1871–1875, Shahabad, WBSA.

For most judges, infanticide could be directly linked to women's clandestine sexual relationships and their potential link to prostitution. From Dacca, Sessions Judge C. B. Garrett questioned the principle of extenuating circumstances, for women who were so often prone to sexual deviance:

> A woman of a respectable family, but habitually unchaste (and there are many such) finds herself pregnant. She deliberately makes up her mind to conceal her condition and destroy her child if born alive. She makes her preparations accordingly; is such an act sufficiently punished by an imprisonment for seven years? Again, a prostitute finds herself pregnant and resolves to destroy her child, because its existence is inconvenient to her; what extenuation is there for such conduct?[92]

Judge Tottenham of Midnapore emphasized to the lieutenant governor of Bengal that the truthfulness of Indian women was to be doubted at all points. Women acted with selfish intent:

> The motive which prompts women to take the lives of their own illegitimate children is after all a purely selfish one. They deliberately sacrifice their children for the purpose of maintaining their position in society; and when the offence is established against them, they ought, in my opinion, to be severely dealt with, not merely as a punishment for the act, but for the purpose of affording an example to others. I cannot but think that if the penalty now prescribed by law for this class of crime were lessened, the crime would be far more common than it is.[93]

Judges further emphasized the difficulty of legally demonstrating that a woman committed the crime of infanticide. It was impossible to prove scientifically whether the child was illegitimate, and the possibility of social shame from illicit sexual liaisons led women to shocking acts of violence. In the extensive responses to the questionnaire, women's violent behavior was linked again and again to an inherently perverse motherhood. Colonial administrators and judges argued that women had a natural proclivity to commit cruel acts of violence to rid themselves of infants and secretly fulfill their own sexual desires. The women who committed infanticide in these letters also appear naturally inclined to prostitution.

In Judge Rampini's view, Indian women were often clandestine prostitutes, and they sought to reject any natural role as a mother for the purpose of pursuing sexual pleasure and passion. He believed that infanticide and abortion were common in India, whether or not a woman was ashamed of her deviance:

It would be very difficult to decide whether a woman who had murdered her illegitimate child had really been under the influence of an overpowering sense of shame or not. I should think it not unlikely that some women, though not openly prostitutes, might yet murder their illegitimate children simply with the view of getting rid of them, of saving themselves the trouble of nurturing them, and of removing an obstacle in the way of their indulging their passions, and they would not be fit objects for mercy.[94]

Should the motive of women influence the adjudication of law? Most officials answered with an emphatic no. If the law were to accommodate the motive behind the crime, Baboo Juggadanund Mookerjee, government pleader before the High Court, argued there was no place for mercy for the infanticidal woman, who was "murdering her own child" to avoid shame.[95]

Judges across Bengal argued that the standardized punishment mandated in the code was the greatest deterrent to what they considered the perverse social behavior of women.[96] These laws, predicated on punishment and the criminalization of behavior, stood in contrast to the reform-oriented regulations of the early nineteenth century, including the 1856 act that created a legal provision for widow remarriage. In the case of widow remarriage, the colonial state, upon the advice of Hindu social reformers like the prominent Ishwar Chandra Vidyasagar in the 1840s and 1850s, looked to accommodate the "helpless" widow within the paternal protection of the institution of marriage. For Vidyasagar, the threat of widows' sexual desire was dangerous to the health of society, and it outweighed the potential violation of caste status brought with the remarriage of widows.

This debate about civil versus criminal legal regulations for social custom had in fact appeared earlier in the Law Commission of 1837. According to the commission, the most effective deterrent against the criminal concealment of illicit pregnancies was not criminal law or the "negative" structures of law that criminalized acts. Rather, it was "positive" civil legal reform that could legitimize sexual liaisons for widows and bring them under the control of the conjugal household through provisions for widow remarriage. Discussions recorded in the Law Commission for India cited the cultural difference of Indian custom as justification for punitive laws. As the commission observed, while there were no such laws in England, the proposed criminal code for India must have laws against abortion because of its widespread prevalence in India.[97]

The stringent, punitive law against infanticide first introduced by the 1837 commission was meant to produce a symbolic retribution for the "heinous" crime of infanticide.[98] Yet some officials insisted that rather than being sentenced to death, women ought to be the sentenced to deportation for life, to become part of a growing system of indentured women across the British Empire.[99] Administrators consistently linked migrant labor and the indenture system to the liberation of outcast women. Indenture, for many judges, was a compassionate, even humanitarian answer to the problem of the infanticidal Indian woman. In this logic, indenture was the way in which the state could compassionately liberate women from the sexual shame and caste exclusion they would confront in their own communities. The officials noted that the labor of indenture was, in many ways, a kind of freedom. Officials argued that many widows were available to remarry male indentured laborers because in their displacement, they no longer adhered to the strict constraints of their own communities.[100] In this logic, indenture was a *privilege* granted by sentencing judges, one that gave sexually deviant women access to redemption and surveillance in the safety of a new conjugal arrangement free of caste. As the secretary to the Government of Bengal, S. C. Bayley, asserted in his summary statement to the Government of India, "Transportation, as giving her a fresh chance under fresh conditions, is not altogether an inappropriate sentence, and means, perhaps a less miserable future for her in practice than would be involved in her life as an outcast at home."[101] Ultimately, the sentencing mandates for women convicted of crimes of abortion and infanticide remained the same in the last decades of the nineteenth century, and the judicial discretion of judges residing over their cases remained intact. Judges felt that their sentencing practices had in fact saved women from social condemnation because the shortened sentences and deportation of women revealed a sympathetic state unjustly vilified by the Indian press.

From 1880 onward, the Government of Bengal ordered the police to regularly send detailed accounts that described all cases of infanticide of illegitimate children, institutionalizing a regular government survey of social practices.[102] Cases of infanticide that appeared before judges were to be disclosed to the local government with a full report of the final opinion, so that the discretionary power of the executive government could be exercised, if needed, to temper Indian opposition to harsh criminal sentences in the most visible cases.[103] Reports of infanticide cases of children born out of wedlock continued at least until the early twentieth century.[104]

In this period, one case of infanticide contributed to a growing critique of the colonial state and its approach to Indian women by Indian men.[105] Adding to the fervor of denunciations of state punishments for infanticide and its interference into Hindu marriage in child marriage debates in 1889, the Calcutta newspapers *Reis and Rayyat* and *Amrita Bazar Patrika* reported the trial of a young mother convicted of burying her child alive to cover an illicit relationship. The woman was sentenced to transportation for life. The *Amrita Bazar Patrika* declared that the woman "could not confess her guilt—in more senses than one," and that "with the evidence of her illicit love, the girl could not live in society, and she did the unnatural act for mercy to herself and the child."[106]

News editorials argued that no law could go against the popular sentiment that shunned illicit sexual relationships. The Bengali press indicted the state for cruelly punishing Indian women while British domestic courts hypocritically gave light sentences to British women out of compassion. After all, Indian women did not have the choice to remarry like their British counterparts, and the shame in England "was not so strong there" as it was in India.[107] For the editors of *Amrita Bazar Patrika*, the sentences passed on women convicted of infanticide revealed the inhumane and unjust nature of the colonial state, which treated Indians as different and refused to recognize the woman who committed infanticide as a subject of pity. The Bengali press contested the social descriptions of the state, claiming that women were pitiable. In this logic Indian women required the protection of Indian men, not state intervention into social practice.

Policing Women, Controlling Space

The legacy of this form of reasoning that linked ideas of women's sexual deviance to criminality was long lasting. The genre of the colonial questionnaire repeatedly brought together in the same epistemic register diverse taxonomies of women's behavior and social types with sociological descriptions of sexual deviance and prostitution. This mode of reasoning traveled well beyond early criminal legal surveys of the mid-nineteenth century. Despite the growing public outcry against the appearance of "social evil" in respectable areas of Calcutta at the turn of the century, the Government of Bengal failed to institute other provisions to explicitly rule women considered prostitutes.[108]

In 1907, the Government of Bengal passed the East Bengal and Assam Disorderly Houses Act to suppress the expansion of brothels in these areas, including the city of Dhaka. From 1907 until 1923, there were no initiatives to introduce new legislation that governed women's criminal behavior and prostitution until the wave of the pivotal Trafficking Prevention Acts of the 1920s and

1930s. Influenced by a growing movement against white slavery and an international movement to curb the trafficking of vulnerable subjects by criminals of the sex trade, a new wave of prevention laws began in the 1920s in Calcutta. On February 9, 1923, Professor S. C. Mukherjee introduced the Calcutta Suppression of Immoral Traffic Bill to the Bengal Legislative Council. This law was the first of a series of immoral traffic laws to pass across India and across other British colonies. Its main object was the suppression of brothels and the immoral traffic of girls and women into the world of prostitution. This bill was based on the Indian Penal Code laws against the buying and selling of girls that led to a comprehensive sociology with which this chapter began, the watershed sociological survey conducted more than fifty years before. Just as Deputy Chief of Police Giles declared in 1872 in his letter to the Government of Bengal that "the prostitute community is recruited in various ways from all classes and castes," authorities in the 1920s expressed their suspicion of the potential of *all* girls and women to be prostitutes.[109]

Despite changes to the structure of criminal law, the perceived threat of women's sexual deviance and criminality continued in twentieth-century knowledge projects of the colonial state that sought to describe and diagnose women outside the household. Like the Contagious Diseases Act of 1868, these survey practices sat at the nexus of medical knowledge, public health, policing, and state policy. An eerie continuity in the explanatory diagnostic of the prostitute appears again in the surveys conducted by state health officials who created reports about women who worked in the jute mills of early twentieth-century Calcutta. These women were deemed clandestine prostitutes, some of the most dangerous types to appear in the public spaces of Calcutta. In reports about jute mills, women are uniformly described as secret prostitutes who earned an independent income and often resided outside of a monogamous conjugal home.[110] For example, in the Curjel Report of 1923 on the conditions of the mills, Dagmar Curjel, a physician in the Women's Medical Service of India, detailed how jute mill labor disguised clandestine practices of prostitution that dominated the lives of working women.[111]

The idea of the clandestine prostitute remained relevant to state regulations around health and behavior more broadly. The 1921 census of India took note of the sexual deviance of maidservants, stating that maids should be understood as prostitutes, and that the "actual number is almost certainly understated" in the census, which, like the 1872 survey fifty years before, linked Muslim marriage, Hindu widowhood, unmarried women, and now vagrancy and beggars to the statistical project of counting the number of prostitutes. According to census officials, there were "many more loose women than will admit to following the profession of prostitutes."[112] The conflation of female workers and many other types of women with prostitutes did not begin with the survey of jute mill workers of the early twentieth century, and it certainly did not end there. Exhaustive typologies of women continued through the 1930s with the new laws against trafficking.[113]

The colonial legal questionnaire utilized women's sexuality as a mode of explanation that could encompass an otherwise inaccessible social world of Bengal. This archive of social fact, constituted through thousands of responses to the questionnaire, was the sole domain of men in the colonial administration. Through the reiterative use of the concept of the prostitute, social analysts launched a comprehensive knowledge project that linked a wide range of sexual types and behaviors and brought them under the domain of the Indian Penal Code and Contagious Diseases Acts. While introducing new forms of sociological description based in new forms of medical regulation and policing, criminal law in India caused a pivotal shift by naturalizing monogamous Hindu marriage as the only legitimate and legally exempt social space. The survey created a rubric through which one could easily replicate a systematic social typology of the prostitute. Through the new legal sociology of Indian sexual practices, women outside of monogamous marriage or who appeared in public spaces, participated in the labor force, and practiced kinship forms seen as backward and sexually promiscuous were equivalent to prostitutes. By exploring the circulation of repeated classification in the survey of intimate practices, this chapter has traced a new mode of sociological description based in a repeated taxonomy that equated diverse social practices with prostitution. This logic of correlation linked a wide set of social practices to an increasingly coherent concept of the prostitute. Over time, the concept of the prostitute sedimented as a legal idea and shaped new modes of colonial governance that intervened in the intimate, everyday lives of women, from their sexual relationships to their reproductive choices. Colonial legal sociologies transformed multiple fields of knowledge. In the chapter that follows I trace the rise of a forensics of female sexual deviance, particularly through new evidentiary imperatives in cases of abortions. The new forensic science surveilled and criminalized women's reproduction while making the woman's body open to public viewing.

3

Circularity

FORENSICS, ABORTION, AND THE EVIDENCE OF DEVIANT FEMALE SEXUALITY

KALLY BEWAH experienced many social deaths before she actually died in 1885, alone in a dilapidated house, where she lay naked, bleeding profusely from an alleged abortion.

It is in the coroner's investigation of Kally's death that we find fragmentary details of her life story.[1] We learn that Kally belonged to a high-caste Hindu family of colonial Calcutta. We learn that she was married at the age of ten or eleven and that three years into her marriage her elderly husband died. In 1863, after this death, Kally's brother-in-law forced her to leave her inherited property. Her own relatives rejected her as well, and accused Kally of having an illegitimate pregnancy. One relative even claimed to authorities that Kally visited him four days prior to her death, vomiting and stained with blood. He did not let her inside his house. In the coroner's telling of her life, Kally was thrown out by all of her kin. According to the report, she would ask her sister Prosonno shortly before dying: "How will I show my face among so many people?"[2] A few days later, Prosonno found Kally dead in a shack, yards away from the house in which she was born. Her nude body was found decomposing, strewn across the floor, with bundles of bloody clothing under her head. The coroner concludes that Kally was abandoned by her family, neglected until her death: "There was nothing in the house to show that the deceased had any attention paid to her. There was neither food, water nor any ordinary country lamp. In fact the wonder is how the corpse escaped the ravaging attempt of the jackals."[3]

Kally's death was recorded by E. W. Chambers, coroner of West Bengal, in the official Coroner's Inquiry, narrated in detail in a letter to the Jury of Inquest.[4] It was he who named the body before him as Bewah, the colloquial Persian word for "widow." He observed that the violent case before the Jury of Inquest was in fact commonplace in colonial Bengal, where women took extreme measures to conceal their sexual transgressions. The "evidence revealed," he claimed, "facts which are ordinarily connected with the life of a Hindu widow." Namely, it was *ordinary* that Kally, like other Hindu widows, had after her husband's death led an "unchaste life" that resulted in her pregnancy. She was forcefully expelled by her family and prohibited from leading a "respectable" life. Her pregnancy increasingly visible to others, Kally was "literally hunted from house to house, even from the ancestral dwelling of her father and the family property of her late husband," never to return home again.[5]

In his report, Chambers narrated Kally's social world to explain the physical evidence at hand. At stake for the coroner were the scientific facts that surrounded the dead body. The description of Kally's life anticipates the violent circumstances of her death. The presumptive purpose of the Coroner's Inquiry was to define the cause of death. In the language of the report, Kally's body betrayed both the physical violence inflicted on it as well as an underlying social violence that made her death a social inevitability. Rather than solely reading the physical evidence of the body, Chambers reads Kally's physical form as a manifestation of characteristics of social life for any and all widowed Hindu women, a death so commonplace that the particular medical facts of the inquiry represented a generalizable social phenomenon. Chambers emphasizes that the violence of Kally's physical death was only the end result of a life of shame and "ill-fame." In his view, her body demonstrated how traditions of Indian society were culpable for her transgressions and subsequent social and physical degradation.

The jury's verdict in the case of "one Kally Bewah deceased" condemned the dead body before them, and anyone who may have assisted in the abortion, as criminal under the Indian Penal Code:

> We are of opinion that Kally Bewah was really pregnant and that the inflammation of the womb from the effects of which Kally died was the result of criminal abortion or miscarriage; under such circumstance that the persons Bewah committed a rash and negligent act, and she should be committed under Section 304 of IP code and for concealing birth under Section 318 I.P.C code.

In the end, all that remained of Kally's life was her body, the sole testimony to her life and death.

Abortion and the Speculative Social Sciences

In this chapter, I offer glimpses of how women appear in forensic medical descriptions as sexually deviant bodies—often disembodied, always empirically verifiable. I analyze medico-legal accounts of abortion, descriptions that overlapped with the forensic assessment of rape, virginity testing, and infanticide. It is telling that multiple authorities lay claim to Kally's death, including the Jury of Inquest, the law, and the colonial archive, where her death was recorded and then quickly dismissed.[6] Yet colonial science endowed the coroner with the power to narrate Kally's death into an event, not only to speculate about the facts of the physical evidence on the body, but to use her material remains to articulate the terms of her life and character. Chambers treats the corpse under his purview as an archive of common fact, where the dead offered proof of the degradation of the living. The body was named *bewah*, widow, and even after death was taken only as proof of a criminal act. The Official Inquest detailed Kally's physical body and social world. Importantly, his narrative produced evidentiary truths premised on his claim to a specialized knowledge of the body.

Why do such details of a woman's life and the violent circumstances of her death come to be narrated in the archive? There are brief, constrained appearances of the precarious lives of women in official medico-legal narratives. Yet medical and legal archives offer exhaustive, exacting, and repetitive descriptions of these women's bodies: narratives saturated with details of bodily trauma and death. Experts claimed these women's lives, and deaths, for their own purposes. Different authorities, including coroners, medical doctors, policemen, state administrators, and social commentators, utilized a circular form of reasoning where anatomical description was united with a speculative sociology of Indian women's sexuality, and then read back onto the body to discern the meaning of the anatomical violence on the body. Like the coroner's report, these case studies of the body utilized typological categories that link women's social status to their sexual behavior. Over the course of individual case studies, social typologies were *read back* onto parts of women's bodies to comprehend the meaning of physical evidence.

This circularity appears in legal medicine as a natural form of reasoning: a logic that seamlessly united anatomical descriptions of sexualized bodies with the ethno-scientific assessment of social identity. Medico-legal narratives traveled from the particularities of the physical body to broad and fluid sociological categories. Women's social types were subsequently invoked by investigators to interpret the legal meaning of the anatomical features of the body. In this circular reasoning, an array of social types of sexual deviants became permanently anchored to the act of abortion. By the middle of the twentieth century, the widespread use of legal medicine in debates about women's sexual propriety had become commonsense.

The social analysts involved in the production of forensic medical knowledge were medical, legal, and military authorities. Doctors and colonial administrators published manuals, reports, and guidelines on the application of medical knowledge and anatomical description in law.[7] Their publications reveal how forensic interventions into Indian social practice created a continuum of knowledge that linked military practice, medical expertise, and police enforcement. As Elizabeth Kolsky has argued, medical jurisprudence textbooks deployed discourses about the status of Indian women as a marker of civilizational difference; in the language of Partha Chatterjee, "the rule of colonial difference."[8] In cases of abortion in India, racial difference resulted from unchanging "social customs" that compelled women to commit violent acts.

Forensic description became a unique site where new claims of scientific objectivity, legal veracity, and social scientific authority silently converged.[9] This knowledge economy trafficked in descriptions of female sexuality as body and social type. The case study of the Indian woman's body circulated from missionary accounts, travelogues, military reports, civil administrative surveys, philological studies, firsthand examination accounts by colonial and "native" doctors, *back* to legal medical textbooks. Forensic medicine was constitutive of and constituted by diverse modes of social scientific knowledge—philology, law, and history, as well as sociology. These fields of social knowledge cohered through the repetition and circulation of medico-legal concepts about female sexuality.

What could account for this seemingly natural mode of circular reasoning that read physical evidence through the rubric of the idea of timeless Indian social custom? Debates about abortion in India differed significantly from nineteenth-century Christian discourses on the sanctity of life that emerged in Western Europe and America.[10] In the context of colonial India, discourses about abortion were driven by a system of criminal law that saw the practice as a paradigmatic example of the Indian perversion that resulted from social custom. It was the colonial state's desire—what they framed as a *right*—to know and comprehend Indian social and sexual behavior, especially those sexual practices that transgressed the bounds of monogamous marriage. As I argue in the previous chapter, authorities initiated a knowledge project that explained Indian social deviance through a diverse taxonomy of social behavior linked to the concept of the prostitute. The act of abortion, rather than being the sole object of forensic study, was narrated as an inevitable criminal aftereffect of women's deviant sexuality.

Social analysts and state authorities saw abortion, as well as infanticide, as inevitable crimes of concealment, crimes that hid secrets of women's sexual transgression.[11] Concealment required new methods of scientific inquiry and revelation that could prove the truth of the crime. Colonial authorities defined abortion as a unique site of investigation, the ultimate test of the objectivity of new practices of forensic science introduced in the colonies. As medical and administrative authorities proclaimed, a comprehensive forensic science of abortion unique to India could reveal the prevalence of sexual transgression. Authorities emphasized the revelatory efficacy of forensics, which provided scientific truth in the face of opaque Indian social customs. In this logic, the secret sexual indiscretions of Indian women were so hidden that they could be found only within the body. The medical investigation of an abortion could expose the unknown social and sexual behavior of the Indian woman as well as the lengths she and others took to conceal the act.

This chapter analyzes the expansion of the field of forensic medicine, focusing on the forensics of deviant female sexuality, in the period between the 1840s and the first decades of the twentieth century. I first analyze how colonial social analysts produced a range of social types in a bounded epistemic field through detailed descriptions of violence enacted on bodies—named in sources as widows, child brides, Muslim women, Kulin Brahmans, prostitutes. I then show how forensic investigations extended beyond claims to legal truth to create new authoritative forms of knowledge that constituted female sexuality as the foundation for sociological and scientific inquiry. Recursive practices of medico-legal description became foundational to invasive state surveillance into everyday life. In response to this surveillance, people across the region of Bengal began to utilize forensic medicine to blackmail unmarried and widowed women. Medico-legal knowledge also shaped new forms of Bengali sociological thought in the late nineteenth century. This emerging field of forensic medical knowledge continued to structure practices evident through the postcolonial period across South Asia.

I wish to account for the constitution of women's bodies as social fact—named as Kally Bewah and countless others in the archive, courts, and in many historical accounts that follow.[12] What if we view forensic testimonies, autopsies, forensic case studies, manuals, and reports as the original site of new modes of social scientific description? What methods of description appear in these accounts?[13]

The Anatomy Museum and the Forensics of Abortion

By the early nineteenth century, colonial doctors and administrators in India insisted on a new field of medico-legal knowledge that would address the unique social and "climatic" circumstances that shaped crime in India. With changing legal codes and standards for evidence, a new literature emerged on forensic medicine specific to India. The intersection of law and medicine was codified in the Indian Penal Code of 1860 and the Criminal Procedure Code of 1861, which became the basis for an emerging literature on legal medicine.[14] Evidence became crucial to legal proceedings through the Indian Evidence Act of 1872, which determined the types of evidence that colonial officials ascertained as objective fact. The act defined the role of evidence in demonstrating motive, and established the status of medical experts in legal proceedings.[15] As we saw in the previous chapter, "Repetition," the Penal Code introduced an expansive set of laws that pertained to women and their sexual and reproductive behavior, including laws against foeticide, infanticide, sodomy, and rape. The criminal code thus set forth legal standards that outlawed crimes carried out in private, intimate spaces, a new legal sanction for state intervention into everyday social life.[16]

Forensic typologies of Indian practices of abortion appeared in medical education and textbooks as early as the 1840s. First published in 1844, Allan Webb's influential *Pathologica Indica, or the Anatomy of Indian Diseases, Medical and Surgical: Based Upon Morbid Specimens from All Parts of India in the Museum of the Calcutta Medical College; Illustrated by Detailed Cases, with the Prescriptions and Treatment Employed, and Comments, Physiological, Historical and Practical* became foundational to legal medicine in India (the title page appears in Figure 8). Webb, professor of medicine at the Calcutta Medical College, built a pathological museum of physical specimens for medical pedagogy at the Calcutta Medical College. Webb's textbook, *Pathologica Indica*, recorded the event of the pathological museum in a usable medical textbook and catalog of the museum. In *Pathologica Indica*, Webb describes in detail the social conditions of India as well as the physical specimens that were put on display at Calcutta Medical College. Webb insisted in his record of the museum that the textbook captured the unique pathology of India.[17]

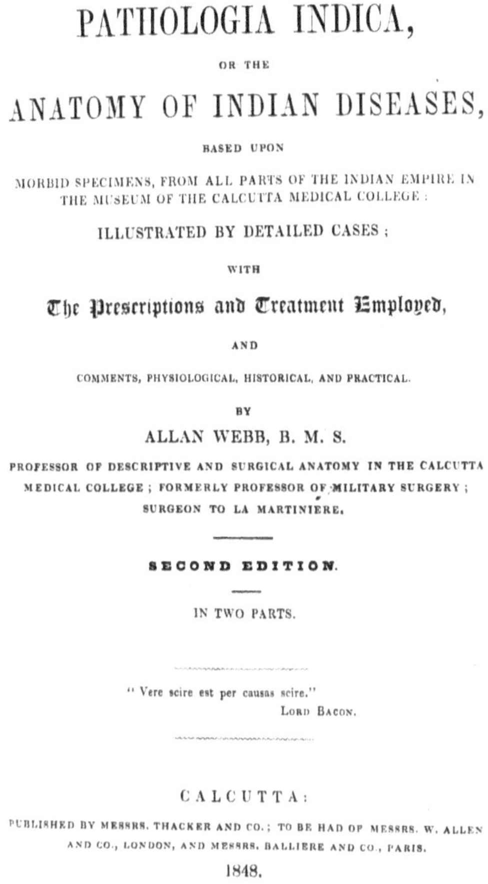

FIGURE 8. Allan Webb, *Pathologica Indica* (1848), title page.

Webb's discussions of abortion are an early example of circular reasoning. He describes physical specimens that he argues exemplified abortion, available for view in his pathological museum of the 1840s:

> ABORTION PRODUCED BY VIOLENCE INDUCING ACUTE PERITONITIS AND DEATH. Shama, a Hindoo woman, about the age of 30, was brought into Hospital by the Police . . . She distinctly denied having received any injury whatever sufficient to cause abortion . . . She sank, however, and died in the course of the following morning.

Autopsy. The post-mortem examination was conducted in the lecture-room. On opening the abdomen, a large quantity of thin milky fluid mixed with flakes of free lymph was discharged, and the whole of the viscera were found agglutinated together by extensive peritoneal adhesions... On the discovery of this the examination was made to find the passage by which the foreign body had found its way into such a situation, it being known that a very general practice prevails among the natives of this country to produce abortion by introducing some foreign and irritating body through the vagina into the uterus...

Remarks by Dr. D. Stewart, (Professor of Midwifery) Medical College. This is a melancholy example of the fatal consequences of the ignorant and wicked attempts, which I fear are extremely common though unsuspected to produce miscarriages, among the natives of India, the practice alluded to by Mr. Thomas of effecting this by penetrating into the womb itself is of daily occurrence.[18]

How might we understand the "melancholy example" of women's bodies dissected for evidence? In his description of these anatomical samples in the museum, Webb integrates extensive descriptions of bodily injuries and organ removal for the purpose of pedagogical display. Shama's body was placed on display in the lecture room as the autopsy was performed. In Webb's narrative, the public performance of the autopsy was of forensic as well as social scientific value. We learn she was Hindu and that she committed an abortion through the practice of inserting a stick to open the cervix and puncture the uterus. The use of a stick to cause injury and procure an abortion is characterized as "common," and knowledge of the evidence of this injury was necessary for any colonial forensic expert. Webb merges commentary on the frequency and immoral nature of social practices with expert language of anatomical determinations. Importantly, the forensic medical account negates what he recounts as Shama's own words shortly before her death, her denial that she had no "injury... sufficient to cause abortion." Like Kally, Shama's body proves her culpability for the crime.

In another case, a uterus, removed from the body of a dead woman, is isolated and sent as an exemplary sample to Webb for his anatomical museum. Attached to the disembodied uterus as it travels to be displayed is a short, seemingly benign description of its context.

No. 1025. DEATH FROM CRIMINAL ABORTION. By Dr. Greene. I send you an uterus with the placenta taken from a *poor native woman* who died last night from uterine haemorrhage, with which the foetus must have been expelled... The placenta (as I suppose) was found lying in the vagina, together with large coagula of dark blood. I could discover no organized or shaped mass amongst the coagnia... *The woman was a widow. Miscarriage in all probability produced by foul means.* The os uteri was patulous. Howrah, January 15th 1848.[19]

The women who appear in these accounts of their body parts are described in terms of their sociological status: a Hindu, a poor native woman, a widow, followed by a category that explained the bodily condition and nature of the crime, from poor to foul. Acts of abortion are "very general," of "daily occurrence," and "ignorant and wicked."

Pathologica Indica is an early example of the pedagogical forensic textbook that merged sociological generalization with the case study. In the preface to the first edition *of Pathologica Indica*, Webb claims as his inspiration the widely influential military pathological museum in Chatham, England, which had been created by Sir James McGrigor and other Army Surgeons of the Royal Service for the purpose of military medical education.[20] Webb's textbook contains over 650 pages of detailed descriptions of tissue and organ samples that displayed the pathological maladies unique to India. Webb's Calcutta pathological museum had nearly two thousand specimens of preserved body parts on display, like those of Shama and others. He included samples of genitalia and reproductive organs as representative of issues of abortion, infanticide, and the science of "generation," of reproduction. These exemplary specimens, Webb proclaimed, were representative of common crimes and afflictions of women in Bengal.[21]

Webb's anatomical museum, and its memorialization in his pedagogical text, was an important epistemic event. As perhaps the earliest example of such a museum in the colonies, it signified the increasing importance of pathological and forensic sciences across the empire, particularly the role of the physical specimen as social scientific exemplar. The pathological museum was a military institution that was to be a "central depot for pathological contributions, from every part of the Indian Empire."[22] Webb believed that the museum was an essential tool in the training of new classes of medical authorities. As he argues in his introductory framework, "the value of a good museum, well arranged and accurately described to the *students of medicine* is incalculable."[23] The exhibits displayed pedagogical specimens of bodies, preserved parts saved from decomposition. The museum reflected a critical turn in early nineteenth-century forms of knowledge of evidence, namely, the exultation of visual observation as the primary claim to objectivity and expertise.

The critical place of practices of scientific description was institutionalized in Webb's title at Calcutta Medical College after the publication of his *Pathologica Indica*. He was the first Professor of Descriptive and Surgical Anatomy (formerly, Webb had been Professor of Military Surgery). In this new science of dissection, anatomy, and social pathology, the eye became the most capable tool of the expert. The book abstracted the museumization of bodies into a textual narrative that could be circulated widely for teaching and learning.

What was Webb's understanding of Indian women's pathology? The answer appears in an extended section of *Pathologica Indica* titled "Generation," which addresses women's sexuality, reproduction, and abortion. As the title of Webb's text proclaims, the science of the morbid specimen was at once "Physiological, Historical and Practical." The chapter on "Generation," as a pathology of Indian social custom, most powerfully deploys this unified claim—the ancient, the historical, sociological, and physiological. In this chapter, Webb weaves together a comparative philological study of ancient marriage practice, a racially differentiated science of Indian women's menstruation, and detailed descriptions of customary social practice. In his schematic of Indian pathology of generation, Webb unites detailed anatomical description of women's bodies with an extended discussion of comparative ancient societies that Webb saw as equivalent to present-day Indian social life. Pathology was not simply a science of body tissue or disembodied parts preserved and displayed; it was science that required correlation with theories of comparative studies of ancient social origins, as well as Indian sociological types.

Like other studies that compared ancient sexual practices, Webb's exegesis of generation depends on a complex citational apparatus. He compares the status of women and sex in Myhtta of the Babylonians, Isis of the Egyptians, Cybele or Tellus of the Phrygians and Greeks, Magna Mater of the Romans, and *lingam* worship of India. According to Webb, comparative knowledge of practices in honor of the *lingam* were essential to a "full understanding of the female organs of generation in this country; since many of their most serious lesions, result from vicious institutions or practices connected with this very idolatry, so fatal to that only safeguard of chastity, purity of mind."[24] Comparative philological studies of ancient society—that search for the origins of sexual life in premodern text explored in the first chapter—were a powerful tool to the colonial pathological science of sexuality and reproduction.

Webb's scheme of comparative ancient societies set up those ancient customs that he uses to explain how women in the present violate their chastity. He elaborates on an extensive discussion of the social circumstances of abortion in Bengal:

> Nay, if a Hindoo girl be but one only of the hundred wives of a Koolin Bramin, whose only trade is marriage, she can never be released at his death even, but must always remain a widow . . . Thousands of women are thus living in hopeless celibacy, surrounded by institutions and practices if not wholly subversive of chastity, at least very unfavorable to it . . .
>
> The result of this state of things is a fearful amount of crime. Perhaps no country on earth has immolated so many new-born infants as India, nor has any race of mankind more generally practised the abominable art of murdering children when yet in the womb of the mother. The art of producing abortion and all its long train of evils . . . is but too openly practised even now. Whilst the strong arm of a humane Government has done much to cleanse the land from the foul stain of child murder, it has not been able to reach this more common and secret practice of abortion, as many of the preparations in the museum sufficiently attest.[25]

Note Webb's deft movement between different archetypal critiques of Hindu society. First, he offers a critique of Kulinism, the practice of polygamy among high-caste Hindus of Bengal. Second, Webb's use of "immolation" in relation to child murder reflects broader discourses about Indian society. Webb connects immolation and child murder to colonial debates about high-caste widow immolation, or *sati*, in the 1820s. Kulin polygamy and *sati* appears in the same epistemic register as abortion, alongside a social landscape that bore the "stain" of child murder. We see a paradigmatic use of this knowledge economy: the forensic medical specimen is read through a flexible sociology that at once links *lingam* worship to *sati*, Hindu polygamy, the abortion of fetuses, and child murder.

Webb uses caste stricture as an umbrella explanation for women's sexual deviance and criminality. He links Hindu polygamy to abortion and describes in detail the relationship between abortion and caste status for women. He insists that women transgressed caste strictures in pursuit of their sexual desires. They had an almost inevitable "unchastity," reinforced through crimes of concealment. According to Webb, abortion was so common that it was resorted to over and over by women: "In two instances reported to me, women acknowledged to have effected abortion in order to preserve their caste, as many as eight times in one instance, and ten times in another."[26]

In the decade that followed the publication of Webb's textbook, numerous forensic treatises and reports were published for use by colonial administrators and doctors. These pedagogical treatises and reports produced similar representational strategies that linked general theories of women's crimes with illustrative case studies. In their textbooks medical authorities united ancient origins of social custom, sociological typologies, and descriptions of bodily evidence of abortion. In 1854, C. R. Baynes, civil and sessions judge of Madura, published *Hints on Medical Jurisprudence, Adapted and Intended for the Use of Those Engaged in Judicial and Magisterial Duties in British India*, in which abortion is described as one of the most common crimes of India.[27] In 1856, Norman Chevers, civil assistant surgeon in Calcutta, published *A Manual of Medical Jurisprudence for Bengal and the North-Western Provinces* (1856), a 608-page manual with extensive appendices of case studies, and several chapters that address the forensics of women's bodies. Chevers later expanded his Bengal manual into an edition for all of India, which became *A Manual of Medical Jurisprudence for India* (1870), an 861-page exegesis on forensic medicine for India (the title page and frontispiece appear in Figure 9).[28] Numerous publications on forensic medicine followed, in journals, textbooks, and administrative reports. These textbooks and articles continued to gain prominence from the middle of the nineteenth century through the twentieth century.[29]

Like Webb, Chevers's account is an extended sociological and anatomical exegesis that links women's sociological status to their bodies. In Chevers's manuals, we see a knowledge economy that utilizes multiple forms of expertise that circulated in mid-nineteenth-century India. Chevers draws upon the following widely circulating books and reports: Allan Webb and his *Pathologica Indica*; texts by William Ward, a Baptist missionary and founder of the first printing presses in Calcutta; reports of Dr. Arthur J. Payne, the colonial doctor we encountered in the previous chapter in charge of Lock Hospitals and the Contagious Diseases Act; texts by Johann Ludwig Burckhardt, a Swiss traveler who wrote extensively on his travels to Mecca; and writing by a subassistant surgeon at Calcutta Medical College, Baboo Kanny Lall Dey. Again, as in Webb's Indian pathology, we see forensic medicine established through and sustained by a complex network of practice and publication. Different intersecting fields of social knowledge were required to make the body a true scientific object.

The 1856 edition of Chevers's *Manual of Medical Jurisprudence* outlined categories, including virginity, rape, foeticide, infanticide, and "unnatural

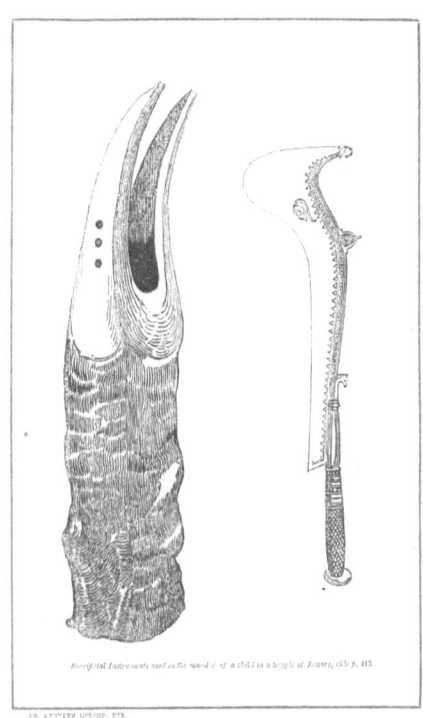

FIGURE 9. Opening pages of Norman Chevers, *A Manual of Medical Jurisprudence for India* (1870), illustration with the caption "Sacrifical Instruments used in the murder of a child in a temple at Jessore."

offences" that continued to be used in textbooks on forensic medicine through the twentieth century.[30] In his chapters on women, Chevers regularly invokes colonial classifications of Indian social custom to describe the significance of physical evidence of the female body. For these crimes, he emphasizes the scientific need for the *forced* genital examination of women: "The question of compulsory examination is beset with some difficulty. In cases with native women of questionable character, examination becomes a matter of legal necessity."[31]

In an extended discussion of abortion in the 1870 edition of the manual, Chevers describes the frequency and violent nature of Indian abortion through his detailed citations of a diversity of authoritative texts, from medical texts to missionary ethnographies to colonial travelogues. His forensics of abortion utilizes a wide-ranging citational apparatus in its claim to expertise. Chevers explicitly builds on Webb's understanding of generation in his opening proclamation about the nature of abortion. This opening assertion was to become standard in texts that were widely cited by colonial administrators who insisted on the forced genital examination of Indian women. For Chevers, the crime in India should be understood as common because Indian women were naturally prone to transgress social strictures and propriety. He emphasizes that in India, "immorality" was the sole reason for the act:

> In a country like India, where true morality is almost unknown, but where the laws of society exercise the most rigorous and vigilant control imaginable over the conduct of females, and where six-sevenths of the widows, whatever their age or position in life may be, are absolutely debarred from re-marriage, and are compelled to rely upon the uncertain support of their relatives, it is scarcely surprising that great crimes should be frequently practised to conceal the results of immorality, and that the procuring of Criminal Abortion should, especially, be an act of almost daily commission, and should have become a trade among certain of the lower midwives, or dhaees.[32]

Evidence of abortion could prove the inevitable unchastity of unmarried, widowed, and polygamous women in India. Chevers argues that Indian women had a natural tendency toward frequent sexual transgression and subsequently, acts of concealment like abortion. The picture of social life sketched by Webb and Chevers is rife with sexual transgression, oppressive social strictures, and secret conspiracies between women who committed crimes of abortion almost every day.

By the 1870s, practices of forensic medicine had become widely used in the colonial administration of law. Robert Harvey, surgeon-general for Bengal, published exemplary case studies in the *Indian Medical Gazette* for use by colonial administrators and medical authorities. In his "Report on Medico-Legal Returns for Bengal for 1870–1872," Harvey models his inquiry on the studies of Webb and Chevers, arguing that Indian women were immoral in nature and committed acts of abortion to conceal their pregnancies. He insists that alongside the physical characteristics of the body, nonmedical observations were essential for determining women's criminality: "Criminal Abortion is believed to be an exceedingly common practice in India, where the prohibition of widow marriage leads to much immorality . . . In these cases it is important to know the *whole history of the person,* and those in the returns treated purely in their medical aspect throw little new light on the subject."[33] For Harvey, the whole history of the woman's person, including her social type and sexual behavior, was necessary to understand the anatomical facts of her body and the crimes these descriptions evidenced. The purely medical had little value for an episteme that sought to narrate bodies into events. The Indian woman's physicality revealed her identity as a criminal subject, while her identity defined the contours of her anatomy.

The Medico-legal Case as Sociological Study

Let me now turn to the detailed language of case studies of abortion as they appeared in these textbooks. In Robert Harvey's 1870s reports from Bengal, he narrated medico-legal cases with a primary focus on the forensic evidence of women's bodies. According to Harvey, these cases detailed how Indian women employed violent practices to induce abortion:

> In a case at Dinajpur a stick was thrust up the vagina of a *prostitute* aged 16, and caused her to abort. Mr. Webber found, "the mucous membrane of the vagina entirely torn away and pushed upwards probably into the uterus" and gave it as his opinion that the woman would die. No post-mortem is recorded.[34]

In a subsequent report in the *Indian Medical Gazette* from December 1, 1875, we again see how Harvey invokes sociological categories in the narrative of the anatomy of the body:

> INJURIES TO THE FEMALE GENITALS—25 cases are returned, where a stick or some hard substance has been thrust into the vagina, potentially to procure abortion. The motives of the crimes are seldom mentioned, but jealousy or desire to cover unchastity are the most common ones.
>
> Subject, *a Mussalmani widow,* aged 45 . . . Entrance to the vagina contused and ruptured, upper part of the vagina and cavity of the cervix filled with blood, partly fluid, partly coagulated. Uterus was twice its normal size . . . The woman, *a loose disreputable character,* charged three men with an assault . . . Opinion—Death resulted from shock and hemorrhage consequent by the introduction of a blunt instrument. Only one of the accused was convicted. *The statements of the woman were considered wholly untrustworthy by the magistrate.*

In the next case, Harvey again invokes chastity in his scientific assessment:

> A girl, age 10, was found dead with a lacerated wound ¼ of an inch long in the anterior wall of the vagina, with an inflamed uterus scraped of its contents. *Absence of the hymen showed that she had long been accustomed to intercourse.*[35]

In these case studies, the clinical writing seamlessly unites the anatomy of women with an assessment of their sexual behavior. Each account narrated sociological descriptions of sexual behavior and violent concealment with details of anatomical wounds into an anatomical description of internal and external genitalia that is sayable, knowable, and medicalized in each case of a girl or widow. We see the entry of different colonized subjects into the official archive through a distillation of occurrences into the category of an event by the authority of a colonial official.[36] Social practices were entered into an archive of criminal evidence, which in turn testified to the event of the crime. In this event the chastity (or lack thereof) of the prostitute girl, the widow, and the dead child are critical to Harvey's assessment of the crime as well to his understanding of the body itself.

In the accounts of each case, there is a preoccupation with graphic descriptions of violence, devices, and anatomies that authorities argued portrayed the true reality of the crime through the body. These scientific investigations read the character of the woman solely through an assessment of her genitalia. Indeed, the narrative of the case study seems to do little except to objectify the violence inflicted on the body. The description heightens the claim of scientific objectivity that could explain the violence inflicted on women's genitalia through generalizations about "native" sexuality. Yet it is *through* these circular modes of citation, anatomical description, and social commentary that the medico-legal investigation produced an epistemic correlation between observations of bodies, female sexual deviance, and the everyday event of a woman's death.

Doctors and administrators extensively detailed bodily trauma in case study after case study, which, according to the medico-legal expert, represented all of Indian society. They provided evocative details of the body, where the appearance, texture, and comparison of women's genitalia—from the state of the hymen to bodily injuries—appear as exemplary of a generalizable truth about Indian social practice. State authorities produced new modes of expertise and novel claims of objectivity through an equation that saw the individual medico-legal case as an all-encompassing, generalizable explanation of social phenomena.[37] The extraordinary violence on a woman's body was narrated through detailed descriptions of the body, casual commentary about the unethical nature of Indian society, and observations that elaborated on a woman's character and social type.

The juridico-medical abstraction defines a document that sets its own epistemological limits. Even as the event of violent acts was reconstructed through evidence of medical knowledge, the violence within the case study seems to resist the writers' claims to an objective study of evidence. Indeed, the extensive description of every aspect of women's internal sexual organs reveals their interest in the sexual anatomy of the female body. It is as if Harvey recognized the visceral effects that his narrative produced, even while he was detailing the anatomical descriptions of these women. He warns his readers that "the cases [of rape and 'unnatural crimes'] for the most part are of very little interest," cautioning against seeing these accounts beyond their objective value as a pedagogical tool for forensic science. He continues, noting, "there is a general tendency to treat them with a reticence, which takes away all their medico-legal value—a reticence which savors of squeamishness in an enquiry which aims at the extirpation of the crime by making its detection easy."[38] Harvey insists on the scientific necessity of explicit description of histories, injured organs, and violent acts. He trains his reader to anticipate the affective effects of forensic case studies—reticence and squeamishness—and to consciously focus on the scientific value of such evidence. Even as he insists that colonial authorities must document these events for their scientific value, he recognizes that medical description produces undesirable effects. For Harvey, forensic analysis did not entail feelings of hesitation or reticence; rather, it required the expert viewer and reader to maintain the gaze on the body and produce objective descriptions of body parts and bodily trauma.

Harvey's account traveled widely and shaped broad understandings of the forensics of abortion. The British medical journal *The Lancet* cited the "admirable" work of Robert Harvey in his reports on medico-legal issues. According to the reviewer, from "a section on criminal abortion we gather that the practice is exceedingly common in India, where the prohibition of widow marriage leads to much immorality."[39] As Harvey's reports circulated, authorities insisted that the crime of abortion was commonplace in India because of the social landscape, much like Webb and Chevers stated in the decades before these reports. The bodies of Indian women testified to the extreme violence of everyday acts. Early editions of Isidore B. Lyon's textbook *Medical Jurisprudence for India* (1889), citing Harvey, describe how Indians commonly employed tools for "local violence," including the introduction of plant irritants and sticks.⁴⁰ Later editions of Lyon asserted that Harvey's case studies show how Indians were "prone" to use extreme forms of violence to hide their "immorality" and commit crimes of abortion: "In India, cases of injury by thrusting a stick into the vagina are not uncommon. Harvey states that twenty-five such cases, ten of them fatal, were included in the Bengal, etc., returns for 1870–72."⁴¹

The stick, used to inflict injury and induce abortion in a woman's body, became a singular object of fascination for forensic authorities. For these men, it represented the violent nature of acts of abortion in India. The act of abortion by stick signified the racial difference of these acts and the willingness of Indian women to go to extreme measures to cover up their sexual transgressions. Chevers (1870) presents two case studies of "Mussalmanee" (Muslim) women that unite sociological categories and extensive descriptions of violence:

> In August 1854, I examined the body of a Mussalmaunee, dead three days, who was alleged to have died in consequence of the employment of means to produce Abortion. I found that this had been effected by the introduction of a portion of Lal Chitra root, about four inches and-a-half long, and rather more than half as thick as a common cedar pencil . . .
>
> It appeared, in a trial at Mymensing, that a widow, *having entered upon a disreputable course of life,* and becoming pregnant, she and one of her paramours had recourse to a woman of the bearer caste, who was " acquainted with medicine," to procure Abortion. This hag furnished "a twig of a creeping plant," which she procured on the bank of the river. This was introduced into the womb: it immediately began to cause pain, but she was entreated by her paramour to bear it for the sake of preserving their reputation. On the following day, she began to complain of severe pain in her stomach, saying that it was owing to some medicine which had been given her for the purpose of procuring Abortion. Her death occurred three days after this. The Civil Surgeon deposed that death was caused by miscarriage; that the womb was enlarged; that there was no foetus in the womb; it must have been thrown away, and death ensued from haemorrhage; that there was a large sore [?] on the surface of the womb, to which the fetus had been attached, with effusion of blood in and around it; that the miscarriage must have been caused by the introduction of a stick of a highly irritating nature into the womb, such as the piece of stick shown to him in Court, which was found in the womb. That it was called akhidmendee (Lawsonia inermis?), and is universally used by the natives for procuring Abortion by introducing it into the womb.⁴²

Using conjecture from the medical evidence before him, Chevers draws broad sociological conclusions about the event of the abortion. In his account, the absence of a fetus in the body indicates not only that it had been expelled from the body but that the woman had "thrown away" the fetus. He highlights the length and thickness of the stick in his examination of the body and remarks that the same material evidence could be used in the courtroom. In this case, it was quite literally held up as proof the violence of abortion in India. Chevers describes how the stick was a "universal" fact of abortion cases in India. In his extensive descriptions of case after case of abortion, he produces a comprehensive corpus of exemplary case studies of bodies that repeat anatomical detail, material evidence, and sociological conclusions on the social status of women.

The stick is identified by Chevers as *lal chitra*. Chevers describes in detail the discovery of *lal chitra*, or as he translates into Latin, *Plumbago rosea*. Beyond Chevers's manual, *lal chitra* is described again and again in medico-legal textbooks for India (Figure 10 shows an illustration from Lyon's 1921 textbook). As Baynes footnotes in the section "Rape-Abortion" in his early 1854 treatise *Hints on Medical Jurisprudence*, "it may be feared that this crime prevails in this country to a far greater extent ... and I am inclined to believe that mechanical means are very usually resorted to."[43] Webb, Chevers, and Harvey describe *lal chitra* as a site of absolute difference, and use it to describe crimes named both abortion and rape. He describes the color and use of the plant: "It will be seen, in the remarks on Criminal Abortion, that this root is frequently used with far more violence than is here described."[44] In the second edition of his manual, he cites E. J. Waring's *Pharmacopoeia for India* (1868) and M. Dulong's 1824 discovery of the *Plumbagin* to build a comprehensive expertise that utilized pharmacology and botany in the work of forensic medicine.[45]

Doctors and administrators insisted that abortions in India were unique because of the violent techniques used to commit the crime. For these medico-legal men, the natural landscape provided a wide array of common everyday materials that functioned as abortifacients, from flowers to spices to opium. Forensic medicine was thus an essential tool for the botanical sciences and the botanical sciences were essential for forensics, united fields of knowledge that helped experts catalog the array of local substances that functioned as poisons or mechanical tools used to procure an abortion.

The suspected case of abortion required multiple forms of expertise, including diverse natural sciences and social sciences—everything from gross anatomy, pathology, botany, and pharmacology, to sociology and philology. Women's sexuality was critical not only to the constitution of a sociological knowledge

582   VEGETABLE IRRITANTS.

with a paste made from the powdered roots; and I once met with a case in which a lump of such paste was simply thrust into the upper part of the vagina, and was found there after death. It is also used as an irritant to skin by malingerers or to support false charges, see *Case* below.

DETECTION.—The roots are ¼ to ½ an inch in diameter, dark brown externally, and reddish within; from them and matters

FIG. 48.—Plumbago zeylanica.

containing it, plumbagin may be extracted by digesting the substance under examination with alcohol, straining this off, and evaporating the tincture to dryness. The dry residue from the tincture should then be digested with a small quantity of water rendered slightly alkaline with caustic potash, the solution obtained filtered, acidulated with hydrochloric acid, and shaken

FIGURE 10. I. B. Lyon, *Medical Jurisprudence for India, with Illustrative Cases* (1921), illustration of *lal chitra*.

of sexual transgression but also in investigations of the flora and fauna unique to India. The typologies of natural history were akin to the taxonomies of female sexual deviance used in the medico-legal narrative. Manuals and reports featured extensive detail of other natural artifacts that were essential to understanding the unique crime of abortion in India. Medico-legal experts produced extensive taxonomical studies of the "poisons" and abortifacients in India that they claimed were a common cause of death. In medico-legal texts, forensic authorities argued that women's deaths by poisoning hid the true crime of abortion. Like the tree branches of India used in the commission of an abortion, the poisonous substance represented Indian racial difference.[46] Isidore Lyon's manual offers case studies of deaths by poisoning, which he links to abortifacients and their deleterious effects. He details cases of supposed suicides, opining that the deceased more likely died from botched abortions. Lyon emphasizes that these cases of "suicide" required extensive sociological details to understand the true nature of each death:

> A. A widow seven months gone with child died rather suddenly; an inquest was held by the police, and a verdict returned of death from dysentery. Suspicion, however, being excited, a post-mortem examination was ordered, the result of which was the discovery of the pregnant condition of the woman (which had been concealed in the inquest report furnished by the police), and of the fact that the cause of death was arsenical poisoning. The district magistrate remarks . . . that there is every reason to believe that all engaged in the inquest tried to conceal the true cause of death. Bo. Chem. An. Rep. for 1884, reported by the District Magistrate of Bassim, Hyderabad Assigned Districts.
> B. In this case, which occurred in the Surat district, as in above case, the cause of death was arsenical poisoning, and the deceased was a widow far gone in pregnancy. The brother and sister of the deceased confessed to having given her eight annas' worth of opium in order to procure abortion or to cause death, so as to avoid the disgrace arising out of her condition. No opium, however, could be discovered in the viscera of the deceased. Ibid . . .
> D. Case of poisoning by arsenic reported by medical officer, Tatta, Sind. Deceased was promised in marriage to a man of her caste (Mussulman), but before marriage she cohabited with him and became pregnant, and was advanced to above the fourth or fifth month, when her parents, to avoid disgrace, it is said, tried very much to procure abortion, but failed (much against her intended husband's will); so having failed to procure abortion, her

parents, to save their reputation, it is suspected, gave her poison in her food. Bo. Chem. An. Bep., 1876–77.[47]

Though these medical men swore absolute fidelity to *science*, the narrative effect of their manuals extended far beyond the limits of scientific reason. Indeed, the redundancies and exhaustive detail reveal the compulsive preoccupations of men who claimed the mantle of science, from the evocative narratives of women's genitalia to the obsessive fascination with the psychology of pitiable characters that fell victim to Indian traditions. A range of sociological types appear, from promiscuous Hindu widows barred from the legitimate realm of marriage, young girls forced into child marriage, and women who engaged in sexual relationships outside of the confines of marriage. For these medico-legal experts, the narrative of the case study of abortion also necessitated extensive descriptions of sociological type: the inevitability of a widow's sexual unchastity, the regularity with which women transgressed caste stricture, the naturalness of Muslim women's sexual impropriety, the failure of Hindu polygamous wives to remain chaste. Abortion appears as an exalted site of evidentiary truth—one that revealed the complex social milieu of everyday crime in India.

Indeed, as Harvey had warned in his reports, medico-legal writing recounted the body and described the events of violence with such detail that they risked titillating the reader. The genital examination was a process wherein the investigator gradually closed in on the facts of the crime, beginning with observations about the general appearance of the woman to a close and detailed reading of her internal organs and the state of her genitalia, a description that moved from outside to inside. The Indian woman's body was perceived as finite, sanctioning a mode of "inferential thinking that moved from visible indicators on the surface to invisible traits held inside the body."[48]

Perhaps no words featured in these forensic cases of abortion more than "common," "daily," "general," and "universal." In this widely circulating knowledge economy, doctors and administrators produced and reproduced a claim to objectivity in their abstraction from the particular to the universality of difference. In the process they created a comprehensive and recognizable genre of forensic medicine that reached far beyond the textbook. Built on the structure of knowledge in Webb's study, an entire landscape of sexual types and acts converged in the forensic study of abortion.

Over the course of a number of cases, the reader encounters a cumulative body of knowledge of the women who commit abortion. Case study after case study we encounter Indian women described through a repeated set of characteristics and social types. We see the same list of crimes and the tools deployed for the act of abortion, and we learn of the limited emotive range that was permissible to the investigator of the case. It is this circularity, between anatomy, deviant typologies, and criminal acts, that unites this episteme. Here, I render these categories as a list in the same formal language of the social science under investigation. The reader of the forensic case study of abortion bears witness to the cumulative force of the case study as generalized episteme.

Diverse social types united in an epistemic field:

- Kulin Brahman polygamous wives of Bengal
- women of "questionable character"
- "immoral" women
- Hindu widows
- prostitutes
- girls (as young as age ten) "accustomed to intercourse"
- child brides
- Muslim widows
- unmarried Muslim women
- loose, disreputable characters
- disgraced women
- hags

A range of violent acts tied to these social types:

- murdered children of the womb
- abortion by a stick "thrust" into the womb
- child murder
- child immolation
- rape
- poisoning

Affective registers used to describe these acts:

- hopeless
- evil
- fearful
- foul
- melancholy
- wicked

This was the fact of women's sexual deviance.

Abortion, Rape, and the Problem of the Prostitute

In these case narratives, the prostitute appears as a central concept that linked women's criminality to the problem of tradition in Indian society. In invoking concepts of chastity and sexual propriety in their medical assessment of the body, forensic authorities like Chevers and Harvey regularly narrated the motive of crimes of concealment. In these accounts, women's sexual deviance appears as the sole reason behind these crimes.

Colonial administrators and doctors regularly cited strictures against widow remarriage and the inherent danger of unbridled widow sexuality as the most important factors that led to the prevalence of the crime. In the first edition of his textbook (1856), Chevers proclaims the banality of the crimes of abortion and infanticide; that is, those acts that were "of almost daily commission."[49] It was so prevalent that according to him, "in the family of a single Koolin Brahmin, it was common for each daughter to destroy a child in the womb annually. The pundit who gave me this information supposed that 10,000 children were thus murdered in the province of Bengal, every month!"[50] In the 1870 revision of his textbook, Chevers connects the crime of abortion to prostitution and highlights the link between Indian women's promiscuity and the Contagious Diseases Act of 1868. He cites statistical data from Dr. Payne on the workings of the act. Chevers argues that perverse traditions fostered the existence of prostitutes in Bengal, "a most striking illustration of the folly of the present system of preventing re-marriage of widows. Calcutta, with a population of 416,000, supports 12,419 women of ill-fame."[51] According to Chevers, widowhood led to the culturally specific daily practice of abortion and to large numbers of prostitutes in the city.

Chevers even claimed that prostitutes were responsible for crimes conducted on the bodies of men as well. His *Manual* for Bengal features a section titled "Rape by Females on Males" that detailed the supposed marks of rape on men who manifested venereal disease. Chevers declared that prostitutes committed crimes that marked the bodies of young Indian boys in order to free themselves of the diseases acquired through prostitution. Explaining the appearance of syphilis and gonorrhea in young boys, Chevers declared "debauched women have an idea that they can rid themselves of venereal disease by having connexion with a child."[52]

Lyon's *Medical Jurisprudence for India* links "criminal miscarriage" to other sexual crimes. Abortion was "especially common in India" because of the proclivity of Indian women to sexual indiscretion and criminal concealment of the resultant pregnancies. As he describes, abortion was "resorted to by both single and married women in order to get rid of the product of illicit intercourse. In India the custom of preventing the remarriage of widows tends directly to increase the prevalence of the offence."[53] The criminal nature of social custom was to be found in a wide spectrum of sexual crimes:

> Abortion and child-murder are most common amongst the unfortunate class of young Hindu widows, for whom re-marriage and social rights are denied by their religion. Amongst Mohammedans sexual crimes are much more frequent than amongst Hindus. Prostitution is much more extensively practised amongst the former, and sexual jealousy resulting in the murder of paramours and favoured rivals is probably the most frequent case of homicide amongst Mohammedans. In Bengal, for example, the greatest number of rape cases are reported from the Mohammedan districts of Mymensingh and Dacca. That fanatical form of homicidal insanity "running amok" is more common amongst Mohammedan fanatics than Hindus.[54]

Lyon's narrative technique unites a disparate set of sociological types in the same epistemological field. He makes abortion, prostitution, sexual transgression, and communalist anti-Muslim depictions of rape equivalent and interchangeable. This series of associations, whereby Hindu widowhood is correlated with child murder, placed alongside prostitution, and linked with the frequency of rape among "Mohammedans," was emblematic of a wider pedagogy of sexual deviance that appeared across these reports and textbooks.

Women's bodies were repeatedly identified by colonial forensic authorities as concealing the truth of crime. Medico-legal authorities, from Chevers to Harvey to Lyon, insisted that the medical investigator must be at all points skeptical of the testimony and claims of the Indian woman. In medico-legal textbooks, they produced equivalence between what they called "false charges" of rape and the concealment of abortion and infanticide. Chapters that appear consecutively in the textbook were conceptually linked, from cases of virginity to rape to abortion and infanticide. Indeed, the forensic study of women's bodies was predicated on skepticism and doubt, beginning with a presumption of sexual deviancy and guilt for crimes of concealment.

The forensic assessment of rape cases, like case descriptions of abortion, used categories like "prostitute" to explain the true meaning of the physical evidence at hand. Categories of sexual deviance were invoked to disprove the testimony of women. In sections on rape, the question of false charges made by women define the intent of the investigation, while those on abortion and infanticide center on the practices of concealment used by women to hide illicit pregnancies. False charges of rape, the concealment of sexual deviance, and women's willingness to hide their behavior to avoid social stigma are linked throughout. Lyon emphasizes this point in his insistence that doctors investigate the presence of the hymen: "Virginity. Is a certain female '*virgo intacta*' or not? The question arises in cases where women are falsely accusing rape, or an unmarried female is alleged to be a prostitute, a matter that is dealt with under the Contagious Diseases Act."[55] Later textbooks on legal medicine for India feature more and more elaborate chapters on virginity and rape. These textbooks feature extensive scientific discussions about the physical appearance and quality of the hymen of girls, especially those girls who make the accusation of rape. These girls, according to the textbooks, showed evidence of being "habituated" or "accustomed to intercourse." Forensic medical men produced in the medico-legal assessment of rape the same circular reasoning as abortion and infanticide.[56]

The Institutionalization of the Forensics of Abortion

Legal medicine was an essential tool in state interventions into everyday social practices in nineteenth-century India as well as a new epistemological basis for Indian social scientific thought. In this section, I analyze the way these forms of circular knowledge about abortion were foundational to new practices of intimate state surveillance as well as Bengali-language treatises on abortion and social progress.

With the enactment of a uniform set of criminal laws in the Indian Penal Code, new institutional apparatuses emerged to monitor and regulate women, and new types of experts were appointed by the state to decipher acts of crime. The police emerged as a key actor in the detection of women's crimes as they were charged with the duty of discovering and investigating them. The Indian Police Act of 1861 established the Imperial Police and provided guidelines that led to a new system of policing in India.[57] Forensic textbooks, reports, and surveys were used by the police to justify an expanding apparatus of colonial state surveillance and legal detection. The colonized body became a site of state intervention. Nineteenth-century records from the colonial Government of Bengal reflect this growing concern for the scientific power of medical evidence. From the 1860s through the 1890s, the Government of India debated whether police in Bengal could legally conduct genital examinations on women who were accused of becoming pregnant and conducting either abortion or infanticide.[58] Local authorities argued that testimony on crimes of immorality was not to be trusted. Only scientific facts of the body, collected by doctors and the police, could demonstrate the truth of the criminal act. Police authorities continued to use the forced genital exam into the twentieth century, citing it as an essential tool in the collection of objective evidence in criminal cases of abortion and infanticide.

Magistrates cited forensic medical texts to empower local police forces and justify the necessity of social and sexual surveillance. In insisting that police must be empowered to conduct genital exams, colonial administrators argued that forensic evidence would reveal the criminal acts that otherwise went undetected. Magistrates, utilizing the language of forensic medical experts, suggested that women in India were prone to lie to cover up sexual relationships outside of marriage.

With the prohibition of abortion and infanticide in 1860, people across Bengal submitted petitions to the police that detailed suspicious activity of unmarried women suspected of pregnancy. These petitions were speculative in nature and reveal social networks that utilized new regulations from the colonial state in order to blackmail unmarried and widowed women.[59] Widows were singled out, with the insinuation that they intended to abort or had already aborted unborn fetuses, or had been secretly pregnant and had killed their infant and disposed of the body.[60] Petitions to the state became a new site for social policing of women's sexuality. The entrance of the state into sexual policing distorted and reorganized social hierarchies and practices of the everyday surveillance of women's bodies. In appealing to the state for official social regulation, these petitions from people in local communities utilized new structures of colonial criminal law to scrutinize the daily practices of women.

Local authorities, everyone from the village or neighborhood elders to the lowest caste washerman, were to surveil potentially criminal women and to report any attempts at abortion to the subinspector of the police. Guardians of the suspect woman would then submit a sworn statement or deposition assuring that the suspect would be carefully surveilled to ensure that no abortion took place and that they would report any suspicious activity to the police. In cases in which the accused woman denied the pregnancy, the subassistant surgeon would examine the suspected woman regardless of her consent.[61]

According to police procedure, suspect women were not to be forcibly genitally examined at the *thana* (police station) by the police; rather, they were to be examined by the local medical authority, a state-designated surgeon. However, policemen regularly violated this mandated procedure. When women were suspected of crimes requiring a genital exam, police officers would often publicly accuse women of abortion and force them to go to the police station. There, they would conduct the exam themselves without any medical authority present. According to one official reviewing the state policy, "in some places where it is known or suspected that a widow is pregnant, she is summoned to the Thannah [police station] ... and that in cases in which the pregnancy is denied an examination takes place in order to ascertain the fact."[62] In some instances the local *chowkidar* (watchman) sent weekly reports to the police of the pregnancy of widows in their village. As a district magistrate suggests in an 1861 report on the medical examination of widows suspected of abortion, village members and the police would use a suspected pregnancy to extort women for money or property rights. Upon learning that a widow had become pregnant, neighbors or the local police immediately accused her of planning an abortion. They would ask for hefty bribes to prevent a public accusation and forced genital examination at the local *thana*.[63]

Complex networks of local and colonial authorities produced knowledge about women's sexual practices and their potential criminal behavior. The police consistently cited the *dhobi* (washerman) as the primary informant on the sexual liaisons of women, like judges in cases of infanticide in the previous chapter. Gribble and Heher's 1892 *Outlines of Medical Jurisprudence for India* provides a sociological explanation, positing the knowledge of the *dhobi* as essential to the workings of criminal law:

> In this country, it is generally impossible to obtain evidence regarding the exact time of a woman's pregnancy, and it is only from an examination of the body that it can be decided whether it is that of a foetus or a viable child. If the former, the woman might be convicted of having caused an abortion, but it is only when the latter is proved that she could be convicted of infanticide or of concealment of birth. The statements made by the woman as to her condition are, for medico-legal purposes, untrustworthy ... The evidence generally produced to prove a woman's pregnancy is that of neighbours who have observed her figure, or that of a washerman who says that for many months she has not menstruated, judging from the clothes sent to him to be washed.[64]

Later, the textbook describes a case where the *dhobi* played a pivotal role in implicating a woman in a crime: "A woman was arraigned on a charge of infanticide and also of having caused abortion. The evidence against her was that of the washerman to prove her pregnancy, a cloth stained with blood."[65] Because of his social power and his knowledge of the intimate life of women, the neighbor and *dhobi* were designated as key watch guards to monitor female sexual propriety and deviance. Colonial forensic medicine fostered new structures of social scrutiny.

As the state employed social networks in the formal surveillance of women's criminality, local communities utilized state power to regulate social hierarchies and prevail in monetary and property disputes related to widow inheritance. Until 1873, families who brought civil property disputes to colonial courts could compel widows to give up their property rights on the basis of their "unchastity," a requirement of forfeiture parallel to remarriage under conservative interpretations of Hindu law. In the adjudication of inheritance cases for Hindus, any relation with another man voided a widow's property rights.[66]

In the Great Unchastity Case of 1873, the Calcutta High Court decided, against the public opinion of outspoken Hindu elites, that a widow who had not remarried but was considered unchaste or to have committed adultery would retain her share of her husband's property regardless of her sexual indiscretions. Disputing families utilized colonial laws on abortion and infanticide. They not only used evidence of women's unchastity to shame women but identified the widow as a criminal with the hope of recovering family property from her. Petitions to the state demanding the investigation of women accused of abortion and infanticide continued through the end of the nineteenth century.[67]

One magistrate strongly felt that without the compulsory genital examinations of women, "false cases of rape and procuring abortion will largely increase, and we shall have scarcely any means of distinguishing between true and false cases."[68] Another magistrate argued that requiring consent from women for genital examinations had the potential to "cripple" the "administration of justice." Citing Chevers's 1856 *Manual*, he described in detail the untrustworthiness of Indians and the special significance of medical evidence in crimes hidden from the view of the state.[69] I reproduce again the introduction to Chevers's section on abortion, cited word for word by a district magistrate in his insistence on forced genital exams:

> In a country like India . . . it is scarcely surprising that great crimes should be frequently practiced to conceal the result of immorality, and that the procuring of criminal abortion should especially be an act of almost daily commission . . . It is necessary that every facility should be given to obtain evidence.[70]

The magistrate emphasized the frequency of concealed crimes committed by Indian women, and the role of truth in the face of the false claims of women who went to great lengths to conceal their sexual behavior and subsequent crime. He warned against policies that would require women's permission in their own genital exam, which he believed would render the colonial state powerless. In his view, scientific evidence was more useful than any woman's testimony.

State authorities insisted that local police had the right to assess a woman's genitalia, regardless of consent. In response to calls to end compulsory genital exams of women against their will, magistrates unanimously concluded that the examination was essential to obtain true facts to substantiate crimes perpetrated by Indian women: "When a charge of the commission of any of these offences (rape, abortion, or infanticide) is instituted, the Court must proceed with the examination *irrespective of the wishes of the women*."[71] The genital examination, an evidentiary imperative mandated by medico-legal textbooks and enforced by new structures of surveillance and policing, shaped knowledge about and governance over social behavior, family structures, and contentions over inheritance.

Another site of the institutionalization of the circular mode of reasoning in the forensics of abortion was the Bengali-language forensic manual, where medical evidence was deemed critical to the control of women's sexuality. During the second half of the nineteenth century the growing circulation of legal medical knowledge extended beyond officers of the colonial state, appearing in popular Indian-language publications that assessed the nature and progress of Indian society. Bengali social scientific studies sought to produce a comprehensive catalog of Indian problems that arose from customary practices in Hindu society. Elite, upper-caste Bengali social analysts argued that women's sexual acts outside of monogamous Hindu marriage caused degeneracy. They produced systematic studies of practices and claimed objectivity through colonial scientific knowledge. Bengali publications expanded rapidly in the nineteenth century, with Bengali men producing new manuals and chapbooks that united medical science and sociological study, particularly through novel commentaries about science, caste-based social relations, and customary practice. These lay social scientists created a popular literature on medicine and society for an increasingly literate consumer moving through urban spaces like Calcutta.

The forensics of female sexuality appeared in this burgeoning literature as an important method for a new science of social diagnosis. An 1875 manual on women's medicine, *Gurbini Bandhab* (A guide to pregnancy), details the natural causes of abortion and the detection of abortion, as well as the symptoms of pregnancy and possible complications.[72] The author Harinarayan Bandhyopadhyay was subassistant surgeon in Kandi, Murshidabad, chief surgeon at the charitable dispensary, and the writer of several medical textbooks.[73] In a section on *papasrido gorbhosrab*, the criminal disposal of the womb, Bandhyopadhyay explains the reasons for unnatural abortion in colonial Bengal and the instruments and poisons used to induce abortion.

In his introduction to the subject of criminal abortion, Bandhyopadhyay argues that although he despised "this hateful subject," he was compelled to discuss criminal abortion to understand why India had become renowned for its frequency. According to Bandyopadhyay, abortion had ruined the very essence of Indian culture, and the contemporary study of the reasons behind the violent act required both a scientific and sociological lens. He emphasizes the past glory of Indian civilization—its historic intellect and previous respect for women. But now Bengal had become the scene of thousands of fetal murders. Why? According to Bandyopadhyay, with the rise of Hindu polygamy in Bengal—a system where one man married more than a hundred wives—Bengalis had degenerated into a farce, feigning respectability while committing endless disreputable acts. People committed secret crimes to conceal their true nature; they drank alcohol and committed acts of debauchery that were, in Bandyopadhyay's depiction, "too terrible to describe." All men in colonial Bengal now visited *barbilashini* (public women). Women too succumbed to their own desires, adding to the population of *barangana* (those women outside of the home, or public women).[74]

Bandhyopadhyay believed that all women outside of monogamous Hindu marriage committed abortions regularly. He traces the failure of traditional social institutions and the decline of Indian women. The polygamous wives, unrestrained by their husbands and sexually unsatisfied, formed a critical part of the population of women who were sexually available. Bandhyopadhyay refers to Dr. Payne, surgeon-general in charge of Lock Hospitals for prostitutes under the Contagious Diseases Act, and he lists the numbers of "Hindu, Mussalman, and Christian" prostitutes. He claims that they were responsible for the "over 10,000 unborn children who are murdered in Bengal every month."[75] The "darkness covering India" was the presence of these women, who murdered their own children to hide their daily indiscretions and feign respectability.

In *Gurbini Bandhab*, Bandhyopadhyay utilizes different classifications to describe sexually deviant women and define their exclusion from legitimate social realms. Both *barbilashini* and *barangana* describe women who were in public: women who resided outside the space of monogamous marriage. The public woman was the sign of social degradation. Importantly, his text uses multiple designations to describe the act of abortion. Bandhyopadhyay sought precision in the use of technical terms that designated the act of abortion. In the title of the section, Bandhyopadhyay uses a word that explicitly references a criminal act: *papasrido gorbhosrab*, the criminal disposal of the womb. Other phrases in his text describe the loss of the fetus, including *petphela* (the expelled womb) and *gorbhonashto* (the ruined womb). But Bandhyopadhyay intertwines his description of the degeneration of society with more dramatic words that condemned abortion as illegal and immoral, especially in his continued use of *bhrunahatya* (the murder of the fetus) in his introduction to the medical detection of criminal abortion.[76]

In his assessment of criminal abortion, he extensively catalogs the methods and plant derivatives used to commit abortion in Bengal. Bandhyopadhyay emphasizes the danger of abortion, as most of these methods killed the mother as well as the fetus.[77] He lists the external applications of sticks to induce the abortion through invasive probing and irritation, including *lal chitra* and the stick and leaves of a *lanka* (hot chili) plant. He explicitly draws on one case described by Norman Chevers, in which a Muslim woman in Bengal inserted a 4.5-inch branch of *lal chitra* fully into the uterus. Participating in the same logic of the case study and generalizable phenomena, he constructs a sociological explanation of abortion through physical evidence, like Webb, Chevers, and the contemporaneous textbooks of Lyon and others. In his description of the tools used to commit criminal abortion, Bandyopadhyay creates comprehensive taxonomies, including polygamous Muslim women and widows hoping to conceal their sexual indiscretions.[78] The sociological study of abortion concludes by detailing the wide array of local plants that were abortifacients, as if to guide the reader on how to commit the act itself. Indeed, Bandhyopadhyay describes how to mix herbs together into ingestible pastes that could induce abortion.

Bandhyopadhyay's study unites forensic analysis, a multilingual typology of sexually deviant women, and extensive knowledge of local poisons and plants used in abortions.[79] As his text produces a critique of women's unrestrained sexuality and the proclivity of women to commit abortion, it also provides detailed ways and tools that may be used to commit an abortion. Bandhyopadhyay, a social analyst who unites medical and sociological knowledge, openly acknowledges the importance of new forms of scientific knowledge in improving society. He asserts that forensic science was unique in its ability to illuminate the hidden acts and reveal those women who undermined the progress of Bengali society. Asserting the importance of medico-legal knowledge, *Gurbini Bandhab* offers one way in which the forensic scientific detection of abortion became essential to new social scientific studies of sexuality.

A Forensics of Deviant Female Sexuality

Let us turn back to the opening of this chapter, the autopsy of Kally Bewah's body. How do we understand the Jury of Inquest's insistence on condemning her body? Why did the jury assimilate a woman into the archives of criminal law by ruling that she and her sister be deemed criminal under the Indian Penal Code (sections 304 and 318)? Kally is ultimately a dead woman narrated as "rash and negligent" for committing a criminal abortion or miscarriage. After death, the body was not to be cremated on a funeral pyre but instead examined and adjudicated on the coroner's examination table.

The Indian woman enters the archive as a disembodied object, as a body, one that was to be opened, dissected, and brought to life through narratives of women's character and sexual typology. The woman is reduced to her body to be described, observed, memorized, and memorialized in text, to be replicated as a model to read the bodies of countless others. We receive fragmentary evidence of Kally's life distilled through the language of the coroner. This is the sole option through which we are to recover the social life of women. Yet to describe these archives as fragmentary would be to ignore a system of thought on the forensics of female sexuality that expanded and circulated widely, that institutionalized invasive practices of examination and evidence, and that soon permeated the social scientific study of Indian society. Case study after case study is filled with exhaustive descriptions that serve as an archive of social fact. We encounter a veritable cast of women who served as pedagogical tools in the detection of the crime of concealment: a Hindoo hag, a high-caste widow, a girl child, a Mussalmani widow, a prostitute.

In this chapter I have analyzed medico-legal narratives about Indian women's sexuality, the expansion of invasive forensic investigative techniques, and the role that forensics played in an expanding field of Bengali social scientific thought, a field explored in detail in the next chapter. Medico-legal knowledge was a site where scientific detail, legal authority, and sociological description converged to create new claims to scientific authority and legal objectivity. Legal medicine relied on a mode of circular thinking that united emerging fields of anatomical sciences, explanations of ancient Indian social custom, and new methods of sociological description. The widespread use of forensic medicine and examination by medical authorities as well as the police arm of the colonial state reveal the significance of the forensics of sexuality to new social scientific studies of everyday practices and intimate social relationships.

Colonial social analysts—military, medical, and legal authorities—described medical evidence of women's crimes as more useful and factual than the testimony of Indian women, as it revealed the real truth that hid behind the most secret crimes. Policemen, medical doctors, and colonial administrators sexualized the behavior of women, characterizing women who resided outside the domain of monogamous marriage as socially deviant, unchaste, and potentially criminal. In the next chapter I explore how the sexually deviant woman, criminalized and left open to public scrutiny by the colonial state, was cast by Bengali social scientists as outcast and of another time—out of sync, temporally, with the time of Indian social progress, much like Bandhyopadhyay in his assessment of the civilizational degradation of abortion.

Forensic medicine coalesced new modes to scientific authority, practices of governance, and social scientific description. Originating with these nineteenth-century practices and reports on forensic medicine, legal standards of medical evidence that unite corporeal observations and sexual typologies of women continue to be significant today in the prosecution of rape and infanticide cases. Forensic medical knowledge continues to travel from the particular physical features of the body to prejudices about women's chastity, past sexual history, and moral character.[80] Textbooks in contemporary South Asia often feature direct replications of these ideas, fashioned after authoritative colonial manuals and reports and only minimally revised, if at all. Despite calls to reform certain practices, namely assessments of the hymen and the "finger test" that unscientifically assesses the elasticity of the vagina, many authoritative textbooks reproduce nineteenth-century discussions of rape, virginity, abortion, and infanticide verbatim, especially in the assessment of the hymen as proof of sexual "habituation." This mode of circular reasoning—the travel between typologies of women's unchastity and sexual impropriety, physical evidence, and the fact of the event—has become commonsense in the collection of evidence, in the adjudication of legal cases, and in popular depictions of sexual violence.

4

Evolution

ETHNOLOGY AND THE PRIMITIVITY OF DEVIANT FEMALE SEXUALITY

THE IDEA OF sexual evolution permeated social scientific thought in colonial India. In 1911, a mandatory question appeared on the examination for all MA students in sociology at the University of Calcutta—the first advanced degree program in sociology in India.[1]

> "In no way is the moral progress of mankind more clearly shown than by the contrasting position of women among savages with their position among the most advanced of the civilized." Write an illustrative commentary on this dictum by describing the status of women amongst different peoples at different stages in the evolution of the race.[2]

For the first generation of students trained in sociology in India, the status of woman was the primary site of illustrative commentaries about the evolution of society. The unreferenced dictum in the exam question was the opening line in Herbert Spencer's chapter on the status of women in *The Principles of Sociology* (1874). Spencer's text was required reading for students across disciplines—history, philology, and sociology. In his theory of women's sexual subordination, Spencer provides his own illustrative commentaries on the "low status of women among the rudest people," comparing the promiscuity and social subordination of women among "savages" of the Americas, Central and South Asia, the Pacific Islands, Australia, and Africa.[3] By 1911, Spencer's comparative model of "primitive sex" could be invoked without citation: it was now axiomatic, a principle to be memorized, repeated, illustrated, and elucidated. The dictum was essential for social science in India, where woman's sexual evolution was the primary index of social and moral civilizational progress.

Indian social analysts did just that, creating a field of knowledge where they mapped Indian progress from savagery to civilization. The theory of evolution was an essential framework for evaluating Indian pasts and speculating about social futures. Critical for these models of Indian social evolution was the sexually deviant woman. She emerged as a key intermediary who challenged the temporal divide between modern man and primitive societies.[4] Medical doctors, professors, and jurists in Calcutta utilized the translation and transmutation of sexual ideas to create new theories of social progress that argued patriarchal monogamy was the culmination of civilizational development. In the introduction, we saw how novelist Saratchandra Chattapadhyay built a theory of female sexual deviance and social progress through the social scientific ideas of Spencer and others. For social analysts, the assessment of the progress of Indian society through female sexuality was crucial to understandings of who could participate in the modern world.[5]

Social analysts deployed evolutionary models from mid-nineteenth-century British and American ethnology (often termed "Victorian ethnology") to create new visions of the future for Indian society based in the idealization of monogamy.[6] The ethnological thought of Henry Maine, John McLennan, Johann Jakob Bachofen, and Lewis Henry Morgan (all contemporaries of Charles Darwin) fused comparative methods developed in philology with the natural sciences of the nineteenth century to argue for universalist models of linear progress for all human societies.[7] Ethnologists mapped custom and social organization onto a temporal scheme of human development, in which sexual practices defined civilizational stages along a universalist scheme of the stages of evolution.[8] This staging of custom in historical time, what Karuna Mantena has described as the "temporal horizon of the comparative method," prioritized social structures of marriage as the primary index of development.[9] European and American ethnologists claimed universalism in their nineteenth-century ethnological studies—studies that were, in actuality, based in empirical social scientific research conducted in colonial India.

Social scientific writing in India in the twentieth century was founded on this epistemic doubling: Bengali social analysts, deeply influenced by European ethnology, sought to map the place of India along universalist theories of evolution. Yet these universalist schemes were themselves created through the abstraction of early colonial studies of Indian "social custom"—the evidentiary basis for the theoretical comparativism of evolutionary thought. Alongside other so-called primitive societies, India functioned as a critical empirical referent for these universalist theories of comparative civilizations.[10] In the empirical data of primitive custom and marriage that constituted these linear, universalist theories of social evolution, social scientists in India recognized how Indian social practices functioned as exemplars of early social development. They then mapped Indian social practices in their own systematic philological and ethnological studies of Indian society. These men sought to account for colonial critiques of the "lag" of Indian social and political practices in accordance with these universalist schemes of social development.

Within models of social evolution in India, one concept stands out: the sexually deviant woman. In Bengali-language studies, she was variously named with the English term "prostitute" and a wide array of Bengali concepts, including *beshya* (a promiscuous woman), *ganika* (a woman had by many), *kulatadasi* (a woman fallen from the clan), *barangana* (a public woman), and *patita* (a fallen woman). Analysts deployed the concept of the prostitute to delineate diverse practices that were to be understood as sexually deviant and define progressive norms of gendered hierarchies of class, caste, race, community, and conjugal behavior. As these men produced novel models of social evolution through sexuality, they deployed this flexible, multilingual scheme, one that was to become a ubiquitous form of reasoning whereby all forms of female sexual desire and extramarital sexual behavior were correlated with the prostitute. These theories of evolution posited women's unrestrained sexual desire as dangerous to the possibility of linear social progress. Unrestrained female sexuality, named as the prostitute, was conceived of as *primitive*, both *lag* and *lack*: primitive, earliest in temporal development, understood to be a woman who acted solely through sexual instinct; lag, characterized as temporally out of sync with modern institutions and the attendant individual comportment; and lack, deficient of the very means of conscious restraint necessary for social and sexual development.[11]

The use of the concept of the prostitute as equivalent to different Bengali terms that describe sexually deviant women outside of the monogamous household was not incidental. I argue it was a systematic form of reasoning: a logic through which intellectuals sought to produce commensurability between universalist theories of social evolution and culturally specific social practices deemed to be backward. These social customs had become primary markers in colonial critiques of the *difference*, and failure, of Indian society.

Commensurability between universalist schemes and ideas of Indian social custom was achieved in large part through textual and epistemological parallels generated via the equation of Bengali and English categories of female sexuality. Through a logic that tied all forms of female sexual desire and public behavior to deviance, women's sexual desires and practices were homogenized, conflated, produced as equivalent in meaning, and deployed in new theories about Indian society. This process of conflation between English and Bengali terms was a primary feature of social scientific writing about the evolution of Indian society. The semiotics of female sexuality influenced a number of socio-scientific studies of Indian society in Bengali and English from the twentieth century. Theories that conceptualized female sexuality as a temporal question of civilization became foundational to the development of the social sciences in India. The concept of the prostitute served as a mediating idea that sutured sexual morality to science, and monogamy to an aspirational anti-colonial vision of modern society.[12]

Elite upper-caste Bengali men—medical doctors, dentists, university professors, and lawyers—authored books and journals on sexuality and social development. These writers included J. L. Chundra (active ca. 1911–1925), a professor at Calcutta Medical College and an editor of medical journals; Rafidin Ahmed (1890–1965), a dentist and activist who set up the first dental school in India; Gyanendrakumar Maitra (active ca. 1907–1935), a physician and author of numerous medical textbooks; Santosh Kumar Mukherji (active ca. 1922–1970), a doctor and prolific writer who won the Padma Shri Award for Medicine in 1962; and Radhakamal Mukerjee (1889–1968), the "father of Indian sociology" and author of dozens of books on economics, sociology, and philosophy. They created organizations for the improvement of Indian society, and held teaching and leadership positions in educational institutions, government, and nationalist political organizations. In their writings, evolutionary thought was brought together with an emerging *scientia sexualis* as well as comparative philology. These men used claims to a scientific, universalist evolution to promote new patriarchal structures based in hierarchies of gender, caste, and communal difference.[13]

This chapter accounts for the foundational place of deviant female sexuality in social evolutionary thought over the period between the 1860s and the 1950s. In the first part of the chapter, I analyze concepts of sexuality and patriarchal monogamy in European and American ethnology. I then explore the widespread impact of the field of ethnology on the ideas of a set of social analysts in eastern India who produced original theories of Indian social development in the first decades of the twentieth century. Their theories united the science of female sexuality with philology, biology, ethnology, psychology, and sociology to create original models for the evolution of Indian society. The unification of diverse sexual practices through classifications of deviant female sex constituted the social as a discrete domain of inquiry. These publications in critical social theory emerged in India at a moment when social scientific disciplines had not yet undergone disciplinary differentiation. A distinguishing feature of these publications was a claim to expertise about female sexuality through the blending of different fields of knowledge. In the last part of the chapter, I briefly touch on how these multidisciplinary understandings of primitivity and evolutionary development continue to shape social thought in postcolonial India.

Ethnological Thought and Indian Social Custom

Nineteenth-century ethnology served as a critical framework for defining Indian society as an object of modern social scientific study. A network of men invented foundational ideas that shaped social theory through the twentieth century—including the concepts of kinship, endogamy, exogamy, primitive promiscuity, and marriage and descent. These men, contemporaries of Charles Darwin (1809–1882), included Henry Maine (1822–1888), John Ferguson McLennan (1827–1881), Johann Jakob Bachofen (1815–1887), Herbert Spencer (1820–1903), and Lewis Henry Morgan (1818–1881). Their theories of social development used India as a comparative referent and empirical site.[14] Their ethnological theories widely influenced social scientific thought in India, including the earliest curricula in new academic departments that trained social scientists, doctors, and public intellectuals across India.[15]

In their theories of human evolution, ethnologists produced comprehensive, universalist schemes of human development in stages, from primitive society to modern society. Key to the staging of human evolution were the transitions between different stages of civilization, which were to be distinguished by the organization of a society and biological reproduction, from promiscuity to matrileany to polygamy to monogamy. Each developmental phase was demarcated by increasingly complex and institutionalized organization of sexual practices.

European and American ethnologists brought together different theories of biological and social evolution that had emerged in the natural sciences and philology. They fused these natural scientific and linguistic models to create new comprehensive comparative models of the origins and development of human societies from common characteristics of what they termed primitive societies. In their influential models of evolution, European ethnologists borrowed from ideas of monogenic linguistic and racial evolution from Indo-Aryan Indology popularized by Oxford Indologist Max Müller, a close associate of Henry Maine, as well as widely influential progressive models of positivist science from Auguste Comte, Jean-Baptiste Lamarck, and others who shaped the universalist theories of evolution in the first decades of the nineteenth century.[16]

William Jones and mid-eighteenth-century East India Company men produced extensive studies of Indian society that served as the empirical foundation for the nineteenth-century theories of social evolution of Maine, McLennan, Spencer, and others. These philologists and British ethnologists cited early colonial studies of "Indo-Aryan" society in ancient India as evidence of ancient social structures and languages in an earlier stage of civilization. By the 1850s and 1860s the field of ethnology was formalized as the science of social evolution, influenced by James Cowle Prichard's idea of ethnological evolution, the classification of peoples and races based in language classification.[17] This new field of integrative theories of primitive or traditional societies was based in a universalist, comparative scheme of social evolution. It became an influential field, essential to new comparative studies of law and racial development, as well as to the rapid expansion of taxonomy as the primary method for social scientific study.

Social evolution was a flexible concept. Writers utilized comparative models of human evolution to make a claim to scientific objectivity. Evolution was also critical to the assessment of societies along a unified linear model of progress, predicated on a common origin story of human society. Monogenism, the idea that man evolved from a singular origin, defined early twentieth-century ideas about Aryan origins that brought Indians racially in line with Europeans. Social analysts in India, responding to European models of civilization, proposed the modern reorganization of Indian society along a reified caste order centered on patriarchal monogamous marriage based in Aryan racial origins. Caste and racial hierarchies, structured through the patriarchal family, were foundational structures that defined Indian social evolution. The language of the singular origins of mankind mapped onto early colonial models of language families and philological stages of social evolution. Ethnology and Indology functioned in tandem in these new theories of social development: universalist models of ethnology were built on a foundational understanding of linguistic genealogy and the static nature of custom, where both language and social practice were used to describe the temporal statism of modern Indian society.[18]

In India, the term "ethnology" was also widely used by colonial administrators as well as intellectuals. In the introduction to his *Descriptive Ethnology of Bengal* (1872), Edward Tuite Dalton, colonial commissioner to Choto Nagpur and member of the Royal Asiatic Society of Bengal, proposed to hold an Ethnological Congress in Calcutta in 1866. This congress would have brought together "typical examples of the races of the Old World, to be made the subject of scientific study when so collected."[19] It never came to fruition. Dalton explains in his book that it was because of the possible political fallout that would result from the inevitable deaths of tribal peoples from around the world who would die on the dangerous journey to Calcutta. Despite the cancellation, in 1872 Dalton completed and published the report on ethnological races that had been commissioned in 1866.

One of the most important ethnological studies for Indian social thought was Sir Henry Maine's work of comparative jurisprudence. His ideas first appeared in *Ancient Law: Its Connection with the Early History of Society and Its Relation to Modern Ideas* (1861), which compared Hindu patriarchal law with ancient Roman law. He was influenced by the philologists of ancient India during his tenure as a member of the council general of the governor-general of India from 1862 to 1869. For Maine, patriarchy was key: it was not simply a natural instinct but an enduring transhistorical social form that exemplified an unchanging Hindu traditional society:[20]

> The Village Community of India is at once an organised patriarchal society and an assemblage of co-proprietors ... The Village Community is known to be of immense antiquity. In whatever direction research has been pushed into Indian history, general or local, it has always found the Community in existence at the farthest point of its progress. A great number of intelligent and observant writers, most of whom had no theory of any sort to support concerning its nature and origin, agree in considering it the least destructible institution of a society which never willingly surrenders any one of its usages to innovation. Conquests and revolutions seem to have swept over it without disturbing or displacing it, and the most beneficent systems of government in India have always been those which have recognised it as the basis of administration.[21]

Maine makes two connected arguments. First, he claims that patriarchy was the most enduring of all Indian social institutions, a social structure that harnessed women's sexuality through institutions of patriarchal marriage, descent, and inheritance. Second, he stressed the need not only for observational study, but a *theoretical* model that could trace the origins of this never-ending patriarchy in India. He expressed that the fact of an enduring Indian patriarchy was, in the present, only a passing observation for intelligent writers. Yet Maine argued that these observations did not account for why patriarchal society was a foundational social structure, an indestructible form that was the basis of social organization. Understanding patriarchy was critical to the administration of the rule of law.

Maine's stagist understanding of a timeless Indian patriarchy shaped culturalist policies that distinguished late British India from earlier legal reform projects of the East India Company. The patriarchal model was critical to Maine's theory that equated the social structures of ancient-village India with nineteenth-century Indian social custom—a model of the timelessness of Indian society that linked the study of ancient law to modern sociological studies. These ideas of social difference based in unchanging forms of culture justified what was to become a system of customary law, which institutionalized and entrenched a system of civil laws governing marriage, family, and property along lines of religious and communitarian difference.[22]

Maine's contemporaries disputed his understanding of the transhistorical patriarchal family of traditional society. They argued that the patriarchal family must instead be conceptualized as the culmination of the stages of social evolution. This understanding, of patriarchy as the *end* result of social evolution—indeed the most developed organizational form of civilized societies—was to become a central tenet in ethnological thought in the later 1860s, one that appears more broadly across social theory in early twentieth-century India.

Perhaps the strongest critique of the thesis came from John Ferguson McLennan, a Scottish jurist and ethnologist. His 1865 *Primitive Marriage* influenced understanding of social evolutionary thought and modern marriage in almost all studies in India from the late nineteenth century onward by arguing for matriarchy as the first form of social organization after primitivity. In *Primitive Marriage*, McLennan took as his subject the sexual practices of a primitive Indian society, which he compared to those of native peoples of the Americas and Pacific Islands.

McLennan's study influenced philological investigations of Sanskrit, as well as sociological studies of caste, race, and Aryanism.[23] McLennan's theory of marriage was built on the empirical study of Indian primitivity. He begins his study by arguing that marriage forms were to be used to stage human development and assimilate societies in a universal model of world progress:

> The chief sources of information regarding the early history of civil society are first, the study of races in their primitive condition; and, second, the study of the symbols employed by advanced nations in the constitution or exercise

of civil rights. From these studies pursued together, we obtain, to a large extent, the power of classifying social phenomena as more or less archaic, and thus of connecting and arranging in their order the stages of human advancement.[24]

In his comparative model of civilizations, McLennan argued that at the origin of human civilizations was an open system of sexual promiscuity, loosely organized through female polyamory and systems of bride capture. Emphasizing the importance of a polyandry—a women-centered model of biological descent—he described a female sexuality that was unrestrained compared to the "developed" sexual restraint of women in strict structures of patriarchal marriage and descent that characterized socially evolved societies. He cited the hill tribes of northeast India and the Nair of Kerala as exemplary of matrilineal forms of familial organization.[25]

These ideas of matriarchy at the earliest stages of civilization paralleled the arguments of Johann Jakob Bachofen, the Swiss philologist, ethnologist, and comparative jurist. In his influential work, Bachofen combined comparative studies of civilization with antiquarianism to form a comprehensive theory of the primitive promiscuity of unbound female sexuality. His *Das Mutterrecht* (Mother Right, 1861) argued that primitive man lived first in a state of promiscuity and sexual lawlessness, then transitioned to the stage of the "mother law," a model of early "gynecologic civilization" based in the social power of the mother and matrilineal forms of marriage and descent.[26] Like McLennan's model of bride capture and female-led polyamory, Bachofen's theory posited stages of sexual promiscuity and matriarchy as the predecessors of the most civilized form of marriage, patriarchal monogamy. He cited Roman law as well as a range of different early civilizations, including India, central Asian tribes, and indigenous peoples of America. He categorized the first stage of promiscuity as Hetaerism, a category named after the practices of the Hetaerae, the courtesans or concubines of ancient Greece. In Bachofen's stage of "Hetaerism," women were the common property of society, available to all men.[27] As we will see later in the chapter, social scientists would draw comparisons between Bachofen's Hetaerae courtesans of Greece and the Indian prostitute-courtesan nexus in new theories of Indian social development.

McLennan's posthumously published *Patriarchal Theory* (1885) continued his argument against the ancient origins of patriarchy. Maine's and McLennan's ideas were taken up and modified by many contemporaries. Most notably,

Edward Burnett Tylor drew on them in his *Primitive Culture* (1871). In this text, Tylor introduces the idea of civilizational "survivals" through a comparative analysis of primitive cultures, including Indian "tribes." Survivals were those processes, unchanging social customs, and enduring sexual practices of an earlier stage of civilization that appear in later stages of social development. The concept of survivals also came to widely influence social scientists who sought to account for civilizational lag in social custom through the idea of the prostitute as temporally out of sync.[28]

At the same time, jurist and social theorist Lewis Henry Morgan was conducting a countrywide ethnological survey of missionaries and administrators in America. He eventually collected hundreds of responses to his questionnaires with ethnological information about genealogical names and marriage structures among the native peoples of the Americas. He argued that the patriarchal family was the result of human development from what he termed "primitive promiscuity." The story of man, according to him, was one of gradually increasing restrictions upon the natural passions; man's evolution was a moral one, where each stage was an "unconscious reformatory movement" testifying to the "growth of the moral idea."[29] As Thomas Trautmann has demonstrated, Morgan's theory of primitive society was deeply influenced by philologist Max Müller. He hoped to prove through language and kin terms that native peoples of the Americas were Asiatic in origin. Like McLennan's, Morgan's theory placed the unrestrained sexuality of women at the first stage of development, what he termed "primitive promiscuity."[30]

For McLennan, Bachofen, and Morgan, the patriarchal monogamous family was the highest order of civilization. It was a fight to reach this stage, achieved through the constraint of primitive promiscuity in the evolved institution of monogamous marriage. These ethnological theories on the superiority of man and the control of female sexuality came to influence Charles Darwin in his evolutionary model of the subordination of women to men in *The Descent of Man, and Selection in Relation to Sex* (1871), where he applied his evolutionary ideas to human society.[31] Indeed, the ethnological model of evolution through patriarchal marriage came to dominate social-scientific arguments for monogamous heterosexuality across the modern world.[32]

Alongside the synthetic armchair ethnology, a fieldwork-based approach to colonial ethnographic studies emerged by the 1870s. These works included the widely influential studies of the tribes, castes, and races of India by H. H. Risley, W. W. Hunter, and others. Indeed, in 1891 Risley critiqued the ethnological studies of Maine, Lubbock, and others for their distant theoretical studies, which left him calling for firsthand *ethnographic* description by colonial administrators.[33] Risley's own study based on "personal acquaintance" with "primitives" was to be found in his definitive text released the same year, *The Tribes and Castes of Bengal* (1891). *The Tribes and Castes of Bengal* was a field-defining study, a foundational account that shaped the social scientific study of Indian society through the twentieth century (the cover from the first edition appears in Figure 11). Taken together, these synthetic comparative ethnologies of human evolution and field-based surveys of the colonial world like Risley's were to become formalized in the overlapping disciplines of modern sociology and anthropology.

Integrative nineteenth-century ethnological models of comparative civilizations depended on the *control of female sexuality* through the modern institution of monogamous marriage and patriarchal descent. I propose that key to these theories is the idea of unrestrained female sexuality as temporally primitive. The question of the control of women's sexuality for social evolution, outlined in European and American ethnology, became foundational for Indian social analysts in their own assessments of the progress of Indian civilization. Bengali social scientists found in ethnological theory a justification for increasingly strict forms of patriarchal marriage, for patriarchal strictures were the hallmark of Indian evolution. The sexual regulation of women and their reproductive capacity *by men* under increasingly developed patriarchal structures of marriage governed biological descent and ideas of property and inheritance. On the other hand, men's ability to restrain themselves from sexual instinct demonstrated their ability to make conscious decisions—essentially, to control their own nature, and thus nature itself.

The control of women's sexuality through patriarchy could be simultaneously the most traditional and the most modern social form. Patriarchal structures of marriage, descent, and inheritance institutionalized ancient law in customary legal codes that codified the textual origins of customary practices of distinct communities—most importantly, in claims to the customary origins of caste hierarchy. At the same time, an emerging group of social analysts in Bengal argued that patriarchal monogamy was the most modern, and developed, social institution. Here, then, was the simultaneous vacillation between—and the *merging* of—ancient patriarchal authority and the modernity of patriarchal monogamy marriage as the height of civilizational development. It was the temporal flexibility of monogamy, taken to be both ancient and developed, that made evolutionary social theories of patriarchy powerful for the institutional

FIGURE 11. Herbert H. Risley, *Tribes and Castes of Bengal* (1891), cover.

reorganization of Indian society along the lines of a "naturally" progressive patriarchal household.

Social Custom and the Rise of the Social Sciences

During the same period that universalist theories of social evolution were on the rise in Europe, social scientific inquiry intensified in colonial India. Perhaps no concept wielded more power in the rising social sciences than the idea of social custom. Women's subjugation could be named, predicted, and fixed as unchanging through this malleable concept that would come to dominate social research in the nineteenth century. Indeed European ethnology itself had roots in eighteenth-century universalist histories that posed the idea of timeless Indian social custom as pivotal to the fundamental divide between savagery and civilization.[34] Everything from James Mill's *The History of British India* (1817) to Georg Wilhelm Friedrich Hegel's *Lectures on the Philosophy of History* (delivered between 1822 and 1823) focused on the status of Indian women as the primary indicator of civilization versus degeneracy.[35] The status of woman was a key diagnostic of the stage of civilization: "The condition of the women is one of the most remarkable circumstances in the manners of nations," Mill writes in his *History*. "Among rude people, the women are generally degraded; among civilized people they are exalted."[36]

This understanding of woman as the index of civilizational status was not limited to colonial historians. From early in the nineteenth century, a growing number of English-educated elite in India actively contested colonial depictions of Indian unfitness for sovereignty and the backward nature of Indian social custom. Scientists, lawyers, teachers, and government officials reframed the place of custom to refute colonial critiques of Indian culture in their own theories of the reform and rejuvenation of society. Well-known social reformers, including Rammohan Roy and Ishwar Chandra Vidyasagar, wrote extensively on the status of women and the meaning of Hindu customs. They created elaborate theories in which custom was presented as the root of the unrestrained sexuality and a potential cause of prostitution for widows and Kulin polygamous wives.[37]

By the middle of the nineteenth century, Comtean positivism had become essential to social analysts in Bengal, influencing everyone from clergymen to lawyers to educators to natural scientists.[38] These men began to build institutions and networks that created an infrastructure in the colonial capital of Calcutta for academic inquiry in the sciences and social sciences. These organizations reflected a rich, conflicted intellectual culture that was emerging in Calcutta by the first decades of the nineteenth century. In 1825, the Society for Translating European Sciences was founded, which published a periodical on natural and biological sciences for an expanding readership.[39] First founded in 1835 with an English-medium curriculum, by 1851 the Calcutta Medical College had initiated Bengali-language courses in European medical sciences, where Allan Webb had put specimens on display just a few years before.

By the 1860s, scientific institutions spurred new organizations dedicated to the application of positivist scientific methods to the study of society. In 1867, a group of British and Bengali intellectuals came together under the guidance of Reverend James Long to found the Bengal Social Science Association.[40] It was led by prominent members of the colonial government, including Norman Chevers, who we encountered as a founder of the field of forensic medicine for India, and Dr. A. J. Payne, who we learned earlier was critical to new legal taxonomies of women under the Contagious Diseases Acts. More generally, the association's Bengali members were major figures from the local intelligentsia—literati, lawyers, and educators. Some familiar names include reformer Keshab Chandra Sen; prominent medical doctors Mahendra Lal Sircar and Kanny Lall Dey; and writers such as Peary Chand Mitra and Kaliprasanna Singha, whose texts I briefly address in the following chapter. By the 1870s, scientific and social scientific texts were regularly being translated from English, French, and German to Bengali. Lectures on Comte appeared in Bengali in the 1870s, and a Positivist Society was founded in Calcutta in 1873.[41]

From these different organizations came publications on social health that utilized a transnational language of scientific rationalism to critique and contest notions of Indian savagery and asserted Indian social autonomy through monogamous marriage.[42] Catering to an increasingly literate public, presses in North Calcutta produced these widely consumed chapbooks, manuals, almanacs, religious tracts, and pulp fiction.[43] The rapid rise of print publications aided the proliferation of many genres of writing in the Bengali language. By the second half of the nineteenth century publications on social life, health, the natural sciences, and medicine in Calcutta had dramatically expanded, including a diverse range of scientific texts that circulated across Europe, America, and India.[44]

This wide network of professionals promoted new norms of "appropriate" sexuality that would respond to the colonial critique of Indian civilization.[45] The unrestrained sexuality of women was tied to a wide range of social ills that required systematic inquiry, from the dangers of early menstruation and sexualization of girls to the excessive sexuality of women in and out of marriage.[46]

The female body became a critical site for the assessment of Indian society itself, as well as the primary mode through which social change could be wrought. Normative behavior was to be produced through a science of social and bodily discipline. Physical disease in women represented the degradation of social health, hindering the evolution of society.

By the first decades of the twentieth century, social analysis in India was deeply invested in evolutionary modes of thinking. Following the partition of Bengal in 1905, and the political and social organizing of the Swadeshi movement, social thought reached a new fervor. Brajendra Nath Seal (1864–1938), professor of philosophy at the University of Calcutta and widely respected member of the Brahmo Samaj, a monotheistic Hindu reform movement, championed the analytical power of social evolution in his "Address to the Universal Races Congress," held in London in 1911.[47] Like contemporaries who fused philology with ideas of scientific positivism, Seal authored the widely cited *The Positive Sciences of the Ancient Hindus* (1915). He saw India as key in the comparative studies of civilizational development, because for Seal, India was the origin of all civilizations. In his address, Seal argued for the importance of civilizational evolution in the making of social knowledge. Social evolution was what he termed "Genetic Anthropology," an essential model for understanding "Nationalism, Imperialism, Federationalism," on the path to universal humanity.

> Modern Science, first directed to the conquest of Nature, must now be increasingly applied to the organization of Society. But in this process, Science is no longer in the purely physio-chemical, or even the merely biological plane, but is lifted to the sociological and historical platform. A scientific study of the constituent elements and the composition of races and peoples or their origin and development, and of the forces that govern these, will alone point the way to a settlement of inter-racial claims and conflicts on a sound progressive basis.[48]

In Seal's theory, the methods of the natural sciences were essential for the study of social life and the historical development of society. In this project, the question of evolutionary origins was critical: an origin that could be found through the study of philological and comparative racial development. Seal would go on to present a series of widely influential public lectures at the University of Calcutta in 1917. In the lectures Seal proposed a universal comparative evolutionary method that could be used to study social practices across civilizations.[49] Seal's lectures on the civilizations and the comparative method were to become the basis of sociological study in India as part of Radhakamal Mukerjee's teachings in the Lucknow School of Indian Sociology and the many students he trained in sociology as part of the Department of Philosophy at the University of Calcutta. As the so-called father of Indian sociology, Mukerjee emphasized Seal's overwhelming influence on him and many others, describing Seal as a "legend in intellectual Bengal" from where he learned the "comparative method in the study of civilization."⁵⁰

The Indian Rationalistic Society and Sexual Evolution

Social evolutionary thought was formalized in educational institutions across India, while also being promoted by public intellectuals who looked to models of evolution to generate political and social thought. Founded in 1919, the Indian Rationalistic Society exemplified this development. A society of learned men, the Rationalistic Society cut across professional classes, including barristers, medical doctors, dentists, and natural scientists. For Indian Rationalists, science and reason superseded any religious affiliation, and they claimed to have members from all religious communities in Calcutta.

Modeled on Rationalist societies that had emerged in Europe, including the Rationalist Association in Britain founded in 1885 by publisher Charles Watts, the Indian Rationalistic Society became a primary publication venue for ideas of social evolution. Its periodical, the *Bulletin of the Indian Rationalistic Society*, included detailed theories of evolutionary thought and early studies of genetics, as well as essays on eugenics. The society also officially commissioned full-length monographs on rationalism and Indian society. Members of the Indian Rationalistic Society promoted evolutionary thought for the explicit purpose of creating a usable social science. These men included S. Wajid Ali (1890–1951), a Muslim barrister in the Calcutta High Court and a prominent short-story writer who later became the third presidency magistrate of Calcutta; and Rafi-din Ahmed (1890–1965), an American-trained dentist, a leader among Bengali Muslims who founded the first dental school in India in 1920. Other contributors included Torick Ameer Ali, a lawyer, author of a Mughal history book, son of Syed Ameer Ali, and founding member of the All-India Muslim League; and Nolini Mohun Chaterjee (1865–?), a barrister of the Calcutta High Court and author of *Le Védisme et l'origine des Castes* (Vedism and the origins of castes, 1919) and *The World Civilisation of Today; or, The Far East and the New West* (1925).⁵¹

In the inaugural issue's 1919 foreword, S. Wajid Ali declared that society as a whole must "feel convinced that science supplies us with the most reliable knowledge attainable about nature, both in its organic and inorganic aspects." He argued for a model of sociological analysis based in organic and inorganic science. This new science of society was the "cardinal object" of the Rationalistic Society. He declared that the road of science was the only way forward in the evolution of Indian society, for India was "full of archaic institutions and beliefs which are not defensible from a rationalist point of view."[52] Rationalism was thus a "momentous enterprise" necessary for country and humanity, one that could be used to reclaim an idealized precolonial past: "to win back the glory that once was ours, when this old Aryavarta [land of Aryas] was the proud home of seekers after truth."[53]

In the inaugural address delivered at the first meeting of the Rationalistic Society, Nolini Chaterjee likewise proposed that evolution be the singular mandate of Indian rationalism.

> The great principle of evolution is firmly established. It has increased rationalism among men, and by its light, unerring light, we find that the development of an organism proceeds from its activities; passivity has no place in it. The upward development of mind depends upon activity and plasticity All the biological laws which the rationalists have discovered are consonant to the laws of nature which meet us at every step in our existence. We may have to encounter many difficulties and opposition in this almost changeless east.[54]

Chaterjee lamented the static nature of Indian custom; in particular, he targeted "changeless" religious practices that he proclaimed had held India back in its evolutionary development. Chaterjee argued for a model of reason and religious revision that could address social custom through scientific rationalism. The meeting of the Rationalistic Society also included a discussion of eugenics and its importance for Indian development, and an extended exegesis on ethnological theories of social development through sex by Rafidin Ahmed.

Avowed rationalist Rafidin Ahmed (pictured in Figure 12) also published an essay in the first issue of the *Bulletin*. In his essay, titled "The Evolution of Sex," Ahmed provides a detailed study of the development of Indian society that combines philological, ethnological, and biological science. He extends Chaterjee's inaugural call for a science of Indian society based in evolutionary theory by arguing that sex was critical to social evolution. Ahmed begins by asserting the necessity of the study of sex for the race, despite a "repugnance" toward the subject:

DR. R. AHMED.

Dr. Ahmed is well known among the Hindusthanee Students in this country for his unselfish work for the Hindusthan Association. He is serving the Association for the last two years. He was general secretary in 1914, and we are confident that none

could do better than he in discharging the duties properly. His career as Vice-President (1915), is still more appealing, when though hard pressed by his own work, he is devoting ample time to keep up the spirit of the Association.

Dr. Ahmed stands as a candidate for the Presidency for 1916.

FIGURE 12. Rafidin Ahmed, photograph, *The Hindusthanee Student*, November 1915 issue.

To many of us, even now, the study of sex is abhorrent. The repugnance expresses an organic lack of sympathy with the aim of science, for many estimable people have no use for scientific analysis . . . they refuse to be curious as to how sex arose in the early ages of organic evolution. Many of our so-called educated men have an intellectual repugnancy to talk about "sex." To them to bring the facts of sex into broad daylight, is obscenity; to disclose the organic springs of love is to degrade man to the brute level . . . To us, students of biology, science is for the control of life, as well as for its enlightenment and therefore we think that the study of sex is likely to do much towards healthy-mindedness, towards lessening morbid brooding, towards a wholesome view of everything connected with the continuance of the race.[55]

Ahmed believed that racial evolution required an "ethnological history of mankind," which accounted for the development of sex from mammals to humans. Ahmed turns to the evolution of sex from unicellular organisms to multicellular organisms, from the sponge to polyps to birds and mammals. In Ahmed's scheme, the sexual differentiation between the male and the female was essential to the evolution of all species: "As we get higher up in the scale, we find that those species get on best which exhibit two distinct constitutions or forms, that is the male and female."[56]

In other words, for Ahmed it was the development of sexual difference, and the constituent changes that emerged with creation of the sexes, that drove social evolution. On the one hand, men became increasingly intense, energetic, and politically active. By contrast, women grew increasingly subservient, passive, and conservative through social evolution. Ahmed interprets this difference between men and women as a profound development, a necessary asymmetry of sex that aided human evolution: "the male more strongly individualised, the female more humanized and consequently adapted to the expression of the ideals of racial and social evolution."[57]

In this scheme of asymmetrical development, Ahmed argues that the control of female sexuality was critical to human evolution and advancement. He makes the argument through the language of racial unity. Man of the "race" would advance to the fullest state of civilization only by restraining himself from unrestrained women who had not correctly taken on their appropriate passive role, particularly the prostitute. In his ability to control his impulse, man would move from a state of promiscuity to a higher ideal of consciousness: "He has sex-impulses, no doubt, which spring up with tremendous organic momentum. But he has to think racially, socially, in relation to himself, and another beside himself. He knows he can purchase sexual gratification, but because he is self-conscious, he thinks twice before he satisfies his sex-impulses."[58]

A similar conceptual framework appeared in the essays and books of other society members. In a series of essays published across two years in the journal, Dr. Subodh Kumar Basu, a prominent medical doctor, justified the institution of monogamous marriage through a comprehensive theory of Indian social evolution. In "Marriage and Our Existing System," Basu develops a complex scheme of the evolution of reproduction from animals to humans. Marriage "between male and a female is a hundred times more vital to society than the individual life of each."[59] Like Ahmed, Basu offered a grand theory of sexual evolution from promiscuity to marriage. He details this theory through a sociological scheme of those clans and tribes that he argues were the first rudimentary organizations of sexual life:

> So in our list first comes promiscuity, the lowest form of sexual association and there is none lower morally and intellectually than promiscuity. Promiscuity means that all the women of a group, a herd or a tribe belong without rule or distinction to all the men. "The Agathyrses" (Scythians), says Herodotus, "have their women in common in order that they may be all brothers" ... Our own Mahabharat says "Women were unconfined and roved about at their pleasure, independent. Though in their youthful innocence they went astray from their husbands they were guilty of no offence. Swetaketu, son of Rishi Uddalak could not bear this custom and established the rule, that thenceforward wives should remain faithful to their husbands" ... Some say that the Holy festival of our country is the gasping mark of promiscuity ... General promiscuity have been followed by Hetairism ... The bride or purchased woman should make an act of Hetairism or prostitution before belonging to one man only.[60]

Basu offers comparative examples of prostitution across Cyprus, Armenia, Cambodia, and ancient Greece. In his theory, Herodotus was considered the authority for the history of ancient Greece, while the *Mahabharata* was held up as a definitive account of ancient Indian social practice. Like philologists and other ethnologists, Basu cites Swetaketu's originary dictum against women's sexual promiscuity as the first evolutionary event that moved Indian civilization away from primitive promiscuity, followed by the comparative stage of Hetairism, which he equated with prostitution. For India, "we also find this in our countries in Devadasis, Guruprasadee of Baisnav sect is another example of Hetairism in religious garb."[61] The social custom of holy religious festivals that continued in India were remnants of primitive promiscuity, where the earlier stages of civilization reemerged again in present-day India.

Basu insists that the theory of primitive promiscuity and its evolution into prostitution was essential to the study of Indian society: "Bachofen, McLenan [*sic*], Morgan, Lubbock, Bastian, Lippert, Kohler, Post Wilkim and many other sociologists hold that man originally lived in a state of promiscuity."[62] Basu looks to ethnology to create a model for the regeneration of India based in the theories of McLennan, Maine, and many others.⁶³ He synthesized these ideas to develop an evolutionary dialectic. Monogamy was framed as the sole evolutionary force for positive change, while prostitution was a persistent negative threat that stilted development:

> Therefore, when in course of the progressive evolution of societies monogamy came to be considered moral and legal, men became careful and mitigated its rigour by having recourse to concubinage and prostitution ... In our present regime, the family, however defective it may be still constituting the safest, and almost the only shelter for the child, and we cannot think of destroying this shelter before we have constructed a larger and better one.⁶⁴

In short, Basu presents marriage as the primary driver of social evolution. He frames this model of evolution in profoundly utilitarian terms, as the most efficient mode of social organization: "The institution of marriage has had no other object, it has no other origin, than the regulation of sexual union." Patriarchal marriage was not the result of natural instinct but the labor of the conscious intellect of man. Man was meant to overcome the natural sexual urge: "Let our instinct wane and reason wax regarding this institution of marriage, on which depends the future health, wealth, and prosperity of our nation."⁶⁵

Humans in early civilizations did not abide by any moral standards but instead practiced an elastic morality that reflected their evolutionary potential. Humans had over time abandoned promiscuity to set up rudimentary structures of prostitution "from general promiscuity to hetairism, from hetairism to polygamy and polyandry," eventually culminating in monogamous marriage.⁶⁶ Basu's idea of evolution and moral superiority quickly facilitated a scientific justification for social discrimination. He cites how "Mohamedans" and "Christians" continued in polygamy and even incestuous relationships. Basu insists that these archaic institutions persisted because of the "elasticity of morality even in sects which are living side by side as neighbors for centuries."⁶⁷ These remnants of primitive social practices required reason, a rational assessment of the stage of social evolution for the "progress of our race."

For these rationalists, the story of man's sexual evolution to monogamy was not meant to be a concept limited to specialists; rather, it was to be shared with a broad readership to spur greater social development. With this in mind, in 1919, the Indian Rationalistic Society published two books on social evolution and sexual development in Indian society. These popular publications, Sameer Chandra Mookerjee's *The Decline and Fall of the Hindus* (1919) and

Dhanapatinath Das's *Hindu Samajer Bartamon Abastha* (The present condition of Hindu society, 1919), circulated widely among social scientists and public intellectuals of the time. The English-language *Decline and Fall* was reviewed widely and cited by many nationalists of the period.[68]

In *The Decline and Fall of the Hindus*, S. C. Mookerjee sought to unite philological interpretations of Indo-Aryan origins of Indian society with a universalist ethnological model of the stages of the development of man. For Mookerjee, India was the best example of the first stages of social evolution, the most sophisticated of all ancient civilizations. But it had failed in the years following Mughal rule to fulfill its destiny as a modern civilization because of a perversion of true Hinduism. And what was "true Hinduism"? A state of religious unity? For Mookerjee, it was even greater. Indeed, it was the history of man's triumph over his animal instinct: "No country can show a greater or more heroic record than India, for taking systematised steps for the uplift of the sordid, selfish, clayey, fleshly, and brutish spirit in man and so subdue, shape and polish the animal in him by the infusion of that real light of self-knowledge, self-culture, self-reliance and righteousness as to make him the very image of God."[69]

In Mookerjee's analysis, present-day Hindu society had been falsely represented as degenerate in a universal scheme of racial advancement. In the eyes of the world, the Hindu had now fallen to the lowest depths of racial degeneracy. He proclaimed that Hindus were not seen as equivalent to "the Negroes, the Cannibals and savages with a black mark on their racial character." The global verdict was that the Hindu was plagued with racial failure. But Mookerjee believed that instead, India could still reclaim the legacy of the Indo-Aryan lineage and claim direct lineage of Indians from the Greeks, Etruscans, and Romans.[70] Ethnological analysis was required for Hindus to understand their present-day decline, their potential for evolution, and the steps that were to be taken for complete social development in modern India: "Come with me for a short while then to the Trans-Indian Vedic-age and see if any poison can be found there."[71]

Mookerjee's Gibbonian account of India's "decline and fall" rested on a complex theory of Indo-Aryan descent. He begins with the argument that Indians were derived from the Arctic Aryan races. The Aryan primitive religions and social conditions emerged from the Arctic, where they engaged in lax social practices of sexual immorality and indulged in beef-eating and alcoholism. According to Mookerjee, there was "no marriage amongst them nor was any status assigned to women . . . It is believed that in the ancient Indo-Aryan polity there existed what is called the degraded system of nationalisation of women."[72] By "nationalisation," he meant a social order in which men had access to any and all women. This degraded system of female sexual promiscuity was the hallmark of a primitivity overcome by Hindus.

Mookerjee then goes on to elaborately describe the migration of Aryans to South Asia, their blending with Mongolian tribes, and the hunter and gatherer societies of the subcontinent, which began to striate into new hierarchies—the basis of modern caste groups. Those who performed ancient ceremonies became Brahmans, and from there, "different kinds of work and labour had to be assigned according to aptitude and merit to the most capable of performing the task."[73] In Mookerjee's scheme, no less than eight forms of marriage emerged in the evolution of Indian society.

Key to Mookerjee's model of descent and intermarriage was an ethnological understanding of the evolutionary necessity of caste. For him, casteism—that is, caste hierarchy based on the subordination of those designated lower-caste or outcaste—was not a form of socioeconomic oppression. Rather, in his view, it had biological—indeed, evolutionary—roots that made it a natural stage of human development. Put simply, occupational specialization tied to caste was the result of racial difference, primitive sexual mixing, and social "fitness": "The riff-raffs of the Aryan and Non-Aryan communities likewise intermixed and became the Sudras, with gradations between them according to the quality of the mixture and their fitness for work, thus solving the then labour problems of the country."[74]

Female sexuality was critical to this scheme, as promiscuity could be mapped along the caste pyramid. In this model, the lowest-caste women were *necessarily* sexually promiscuous as a result of their evolutionary status. Hindu epics were cited as proof of this differentiated caste-based difference of sexual promiscuity and restraint:

> Read between the lines of our epics, the Ramayan and Mohabharat and you will see how by means of promiscuity and polygamy through the eight forms of marriage the peoples multiplied under the Brahmanic sway, and how in the background of deeds and exploits heroic there is the Brahmanic superiority discernible, leading Kshatriya or the kingly power by the hand, as it were, in everything.[75]

For Mookerjee, sexual promiscuity allowed India to populate the subcontinent, and was therefore a necessary step in Aryan migration. Eventually, however, in his scheme, Brahmans became the primary driver of social evolution.

They led the lower masses toward social development through the enforcement of institutions like marriage.

Like many of his contemporaries, Mookerjee emphasizes that the period under Muslim rule led to the degradation of a pure and socially progressive Hinduism. He provides a long exegesis on Buddhism in early India and the eventual perversion of Hindu caste practices under Muslims in medieval India. Mookerjee's critique of Brahmanical practices focuses on later Brahman practitioners who allowed for polygamy, the joint family structure, and forms of mendicant Hinduism that promoted promiscuity and the perversion of Hindu ideals. For Mookerjee, here was the first instance of the decline of the Hindus. This critique of Brahmans in modern India was really a call to return to older, purer ways.

Mookerjee ends his ethno-historical scheme by describing in evocative detail a dream he had of India's future. In the dream Mother India herself appeared to him, telling him of the natural progress of his country, and its rightful return to the height of evolution. In his conclusion, Mookerjee takes on the voice of Mother India as she speaks to him:

> The matter that is troubling you is the root of all evil in India which you do not seem to have been able to solve ... Cleanse your land of iniquities of your own doing first. That task is laid on *you* ... Your manhood cannot be strengthened unless the Shakti comes from your womanhood, which can't be made strong unless its girlhood is strengthened. Girlhood is the most sacred flower of every Race, but with you girlhood is shocked, slaughtered and debased ... India is being remade in the crucible of nature to be the befitting vessel for All Humanity, not for the selfish ends of any particular Nation or Race ... Cleanse your own Homes by the light of the spirit of Humanity, by the light of that idea that ye are all Brothers in India, irrespective of Colour, Caste or Creed.[76]

The perversion of social custom had led to the decline of the Hindus, the measure of man, or rather, the *shakti*, the power of men, was to be found in the "sacred flower" of girlhood. It was on Mookerjee to join with his rationalist brothers across communities to tell the world of a new era of Indian progress based in the cleansing of the home.

While Mookerjee developed a theory of sexual evolution based in a broad, more flexible theory of Hindu decline, Dhanapatinath Das focused more squarely on the danger of the prostitute in Hindu society. In his *Hindu Samajer Bartamon Abastha*, Das argues against the ill effects of what he termed the *patita*, the fallen woman. Das equates this Bengali term with the concept of the prostitute through extensive descriptions of acts of prostitution. Like many contemporaries, Das emphasizes that the "shameful profession" required a descriptive taxonomy. His schema includes the children of fallen women, widows, women who married outside of caste, child brides, and women in poverty. "Today, everyone believes that the *patita* is the greatest problem of our society," he declares in his opening passage. "This fear is correct."[77]

According to Das, women were most often seduced into the profession by men because they were unable to restrain their sexual desire. This inability was not to be seen as a condemnable fault; rather, it was simply the direct and inevitable result of women's sexual instinct, which required male vigilance and surveillance. Conscious restraint of sexual instinct was, after all, what differentiated man from woman, and what allowed modern man to overcome earlier stages of civilizational development. Why were women unable to restrain themselves? According to Das, it was the result of natural evolution and sexual reproduction:

> The mane of the lion attracts the lioness, the tail of the peacock attracts the peahen, and the voice of a male cuckoo bird attracts the female cuckoo bird. The power of primitive men is what attracted primitive women to them. You will always find that it is the man who arouses the sexual desires of a woman. If a *patita* gets a man who can fulfill her needs, then she would not open her door for other clients.[78]

Women who found pleasure in sexual freedom—in the state of primitive promiscuity—were the most dangerous threat. Primitive promiscuity thus was the civilizational state that could explain the persistence of the clandestine prostitute in modern Indian society. Like Basu, Das uses the language of natural selection (the cuckoo bird) to develop his theory of female sexuality. Das describes how the deviant woman differed from the natural sexuality of women: "When we talk about these *patita*, we think only of a group of women who take this life willingly . . . I have nothing to say about such women, except I can say that we must keep the drain clean so that it will not spread disease."[79] Das concludes his study with a call for a comprehensive analysis of the present-day *patita*. Only social scientific study would save modern man from the animalistic behavior and sexual promiscuity of primitive man. The present condition of Hindu society was precarious; the investigation and salvation of the prostitute was an important way forward.

A Primitive Within? The *Ganika* and Social Evolution

We have encountered a network of educated elites in Calcutta who created multidisciplinary theories of sexual evolution based on the "primitive within," a theory of female sexuality that combined sociological perspectives on Indian social custom with history and ethnology.[80] Gyanendrakumar Maitra, a medical doctor and writer, reframed discussions of scientific ideas about sexual excess around ideas of medical science and bodily evolution in his medical textbook, *Rati Yantradira Pida* (Sexual and venereal evils, 1923). He set out a theory of the biological and historical roots of sexual evil, employing female sexual excess as a window to understand the possibilities and failures of social evolution. Maitra's narrative reflected the popularity of circulating ideas about the evolution of society as well as the growing field of disciplinary history writing in colonial Bengal. With the rise of Bengali-language histories came a new intellectual fervor for accounts of the past that created scientific histories through rationalist methods. Maitra's *Rati Yantradira Pida*, while a medical textbook, could also be placed alongside an emerging literature on histories of the Bengali people, including Durgachandra Sanyal's *Banglar Samajik Itihas* (A history of Bengali society, 1910). In his study, Sanyal includes a lengthy introduction in which he develops a historical theory of Bengali social order based in the evolution of prostitution. His history is a classic in emerging genres of scientific history writing in Bengali.[81] For writers like Maitra and Sanyal, the scientific history of sexual evolution could be used to challenge colonial allegations of unfitness and provide a new model for Indian social progress.

From 1907 until 1930, Maitra published several original Bengali-language scientific and medical textbooks as well as translations of English medical textbooks.[82] His 1923 *Rati Yantradira Pida* was framed as an indispensable homeopathic guide to the harms of illicit sexual behavior and also included suggested remedies for sexual diseases. In a section titled in English "Venereal Disease and Prostitution" and in Bengali as "Ratijo Pida o Ganikagomon," Maitra wove an extraordinary narrative about the evolutionary biological roots of the *ganika*—a Sanskrit-derived term for a woman who is said to have multiple sexual partners.

Maitra fused gynecological science with philology, history, sociology, and ethnology to create a universalist narrative of evolution and its impact on Indian civilization, above all stressing the scientific value of his pursuit. He produced a novel theory of Indian prostitution and its ill effects on society.[83] In an extensive exegesis of the development of society, Maitra theorized the divide between nature and culture that animated debates about the progress of modern society in India. For him, the *ganika* was crucial, as her persistent appearance in modern society signified the difference between the cultural restraint of certain men and the dangerous nature of man's enslavement to sexual instinct. Maitra builds a complex theory that charts the divide between the nature of man and his ability to attain consciousness, a boundary demarcated through the haunting presence of the *ganika*.

Maitra did not intend to woo only specialists. Despite his claims to multidisciplinary authority and medical expertise, he explicitly addresses a general audience. This was because he believed, urgently so, that his ideas had immediate and widespread relevance: they could help solve the problem of the lag of Indian social practices through a definitive science of social evolution. Maitra directed his commentary toward a broad readership of upwardly mobile upper-caste Hindu men, whom he feared were haunted by the possibility of sexual disease and social degeneration. Maitra's books were examples of the hybrid genre of *daktari* publication, a genre that fused concepts from English textbooks circulating in Calcutta with original ideas on homeopathic and local remedies for different diseases.[84]

Like some textbooks on medicine in Bengali from the period, the pages largely feature Bengali typescript, with occasional English words scattered in the text (an example page from Maitra with English and Bengali typescript appears in Figure 13). However, unlike most medical books, which use English in titles or in the naming and definitions of disease, this text features English terms throughout the prose in English typescript and specifically creates textual parallels to show the equivalence of sexual concepts between Bengali and English.[85] These words seem to anchor major themes of the essay: "prostitute," "prostitution," "evolution," "civilization," "modern," "degenerate." Further, within the text, many scientific terms, like "phylogenetic" or "Consanguine," are transliterated into Bengali script.

Maitra created a hybrid account in two ways: First, he claims to explain both prostitution and the current state of Indian society through sexual practices. Second, he approaches this task by merging ancient historical accounts of Indian society with a schematic of evolutionary development in animal and human societies. Maitra narrates the evolution of society as a series of social forms that are modifications of one another. Like nineteenth-century ethnology, these transformations happened as a result of the disciplining of sexual desire, which he correlated with historical developments in Indian sexuality. He pairs degeneration with the possibility of social evolution. Invoking

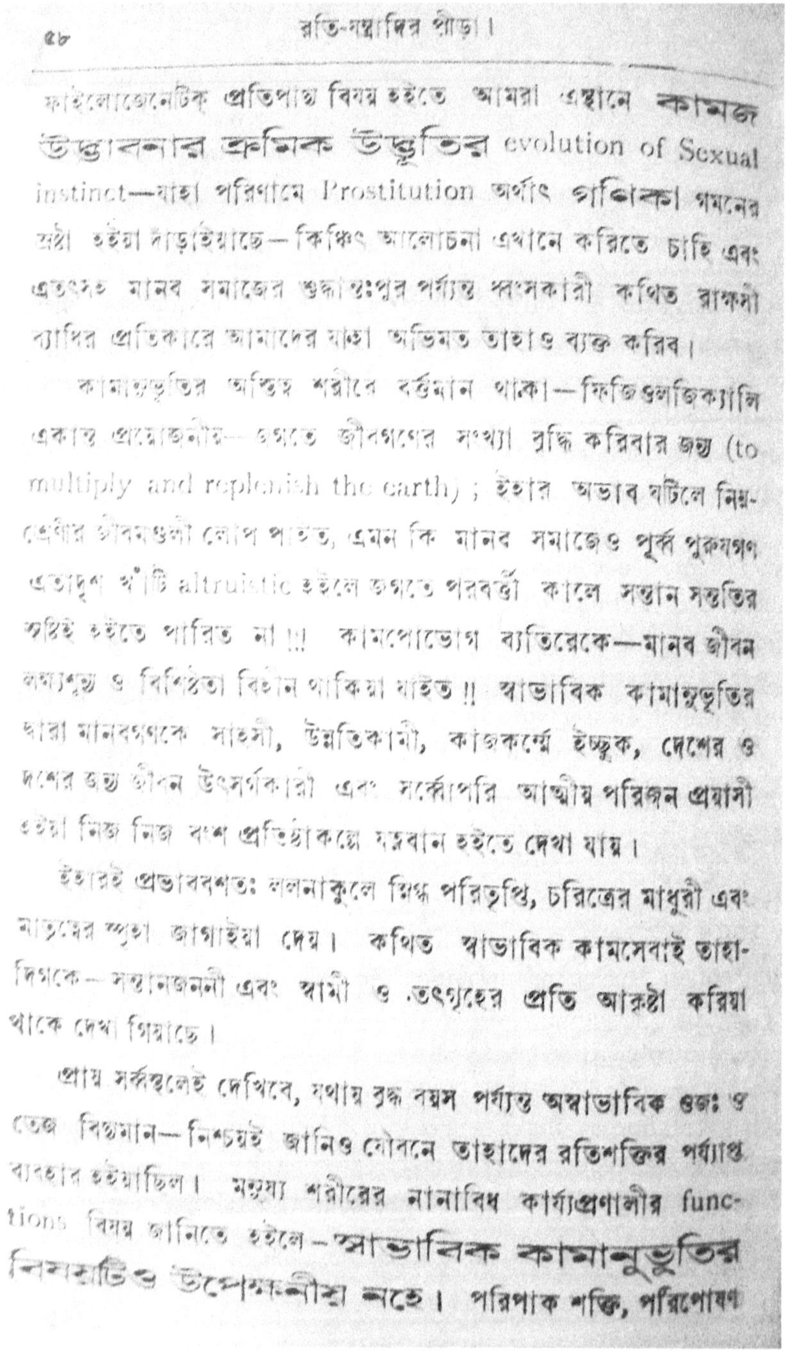

ফাইলোজেনেটিক প্রতিপাদ্য বিষয় হইতে আমরা এস্থানে কামজ উদ্ভাবনার ক্রমিক উদ্ভূতির evolution of Sexual instinct—যাহা পরিণামে Prostitution অর্থাৎ গণিকা গমনের সৃষ্টি হইয়া দাঁড়াইয়াছে—কিঞ্চিৎ আলোচনা এখানে করিতে চাহি এবং এতদ্দ্বারা মানব সমাজের শুদ্ধ অংশ পর্য্যন্ত ধ্বংসকারী কথিত রাক্ষসী ব্যাধির প্রতিকারে আমাদের যাহা অভিমত তাহাও ব্যক্ত করিব।

কামানুভূতির অস্তিত্ব শরীরে বর্ত্তমান থাকা—ফিজিওলজিক্যালি একান্ত প্রয়োজনীয়—জগতে জীবগণের সংখ্যা বৃদ্ধি করিবার জন্য (to multiply and replenish the earth); ইহার অভাব ঘটিলে নিম্নশ্রেণীর জীবমণ্ডলী লোপ পাইত, এমন কি মানব সমাজেও পূর্ব্ব পুরুষগণ এতাদৃশ খাঁটি altruistic হইলে জগতে পরবর্ত্তী কালে সন্তান সন্ততির সৃষ্টিই হইতে পারিত না !!! কামোপভোগ ব্যতিরেকে—মানব জীবন লাবণ্য ও বিশিষ্টতা বিহীন থাকিয়া যাইত !! স্বাভাবিক কামানুভূতির দ্বারা মানবগণকে সাহসী, উন্নতিকামী, কার্য্যকর্ম্মে ইচ্ছুক, দেশের ও দশের জন্য জীবন উৎসর্গকারী এবং সর্ব্বোপরি আত্মীয় পরিজন প্রয়াসী হইয়া নিজ নিজ বংশ প্রতিষ্ঠাকল্পে যত্নবান হইতে দেখা যায়।

ইহারই প্রভাববশতঃ ললনাকুলে বিশুদ্ধ পরিতৃপ্তি, চরিত্রের মাধুরী এবং মাতৃত্বের স্পৃহা জাগাইয়া দেয়। কথিত স্বাভাবিক কামসেবাই তাহাদিগকে—সন্তানজননী এবং স্বামী ও তৎগৃহের প্রতি আসক্তা করিয়া থাকে দেখা গিয়াছে।

প্রায় সর্ব্বত্রেই দেখিবে, যথায় বৃদ্ধ বয়স পর্য্যন্ত অস্বাভাবিক ওজঃ ও তেজ বিদ্যমান—নিশ্চয়ই জানিও যৌবনে তাহাদের রতিশক্তির পর্য্যাপ্ত ব্যবহার হইয়াছিল। মনুষ্য শরীরের নানাবিধ কার্য্যপ্রণালীর functions বিষয় জানিতে হইলে—স্বাভাবিক কামানুভূতির নিম্নগতি ও উপেক্ষনীয়া নহে। পরিপাক শক্তি, পরিপোষণ

FIGURE 13. Gyanendrakumar Maitra, *Rati Yantradira Pida* (1923), excerpted page.

nineteenth-century models of natural perfectibility in his discussion of human sexuality, he shows how sex could evolve into its ideal form—monogamous conjugality. Maitra suggests that the transformation of human behavior into disciplined civility was threatened by the possibility of degeneration, epitomized in the enduring presence of the *ganika*. Maitra poses the *ganika* as the negation of social evolution. Her continued existence in modern India signaled sexual perversion and a return to earlier, more degenerate forms of sexual barbarity.

In his multidisciplinary theory, Maitra creates a framework that links human sexual behavior to evolution in the natural world, those "lower animals" whose development reflected the progress of the human. He borrows extensively from Morgan's *Systems of Consanguinity and Affinity* (1871) and *Ancient Society* (1877), particularly Morgan's understanding of primitive promiscuity and kinship. He further builds on Tylor's idea of survivals, assigning the *ganika* to a primitive past, a persistent presence that exists despite the evolution of Indian society toward monogamous marriage. Maitra models the moral evolution of humans on this scheme of animal development; his theoretical model begins with the most primal animal urge, moves on to the appearance of male polygamy, and eventually arrives at women's adherence to monogamy in human societies. Maitra suggests that females carry the burden of attracting men to sexual intercourse, and it was evolutionary science that could explain the continued existence of *ganikagomon* in advanced forms of civilization where intercourse was meant to be channeled for reproduction. "In terms of scientific research," visiting the *ganika* "has an easy biological and physiological truth," as "lower animals reveal the natural inclination of men to mate with many women."[86] Women seduced men, as "sexual attraction of males originates in females and males naturally mate with many females."[87] As he saw it, the danger of desire was primarily carried in the female body, and it was her presence, rather than male urges, that threatened the evolution of man.

Maitra asserts the necessity of rationalism to understand the physiology of sexual desire and deviance. He begins the essay with a bold assertion, accusing social reformers who "seek to prevent venereal diseases and prostitution" of not bringing "into consideration *biological facts*."[88] Instead of claims of social reform, Maitra argues, one must use a "phylogenetic approach" to produce reasoned understandings of the prostitute. In his view, social reform was unreasonable because it lacked *scientific* reasoning and *objective* biological reasons for sexual deviance. Maitra insists that social reform must be rooted in science, not the *shastras*. His target is an "irrational" religious doctrine: "We do not want to mention any rules and regulations from the Shastras. We will only describe the rule of copulation that has been introduced in this society according to evolution."[89]

Maitra claims that physiologically, sexual instinct existed solely for the purpose of reproduction. Yet sexual pleasure (in men) was not simply utilitarian. On the contrary, the healthy male body *required* sexual pleasure: "We see that through normal sexual desire man becomes courageous, progressive, willing to work and to dedicate his life to his country, and careful to set up his own family."[90] In the study of sex, physical and social health could be analyzed as one. It was sexual desires—specifically, *normal* sexual desires—that allowed man to fulfill his position as a productive member of society. He harnessed sexual urges to find the power to work, and it was through sexual desire that man was able to "dedicate his life to his country," thereby epitomizing the ideal citizen. In healthy sexual desire, man found his masculinity and courage. For Maitra, man's sexual desire, when reproductive, was the primary genesis of an evolving society. Maitra posited that sexual urge in man was fundamental to the health of his body: "Like the power of digestion, nutrition and elimination, procreation is also necessary for keeping in good health."[91]

Men by nature were polygamous, and it was the "release of the litany of physical urges" that drove them to engage in coitus with more than one woman.[92] The sexual instinct in women, on the other hand, was natural only in relation to biological reproduction. Maitra argues that "normal sexual desire" developed in women in the form of "mild satisfaction, sweetness of character and motherly desires."[93] Women had reproductive urges, docile (feminine) yearnings—a desire not for sex but for children. Maitra uses the term *abhilamba*, which translates as both normal and natural, a melding of the biological basis of motherly desire in women and socially normal sexual desire. Female sexual desire became perverted whenever it was in excess of reproduction and was normal and natural when it led directly to progeny.

Women were "naturally monogamous" creatures, like their counterparts in lower animals, with the one known exception of the cuckoo bird.[94] Like Dhanapatinath Das's analysis of the prostitute in Hindu society, we again see the language of sexual selection through the analogous cuckoo bird. The urge for monogamous procreation was central to Maitra's description of appropriate sexuality in women and his differentiation of female sexuality from male sexuality. In discussions of monogamy Maitra tied women's desire to a biological urge for reproduction, arguing that unlike the incessant sexual drive in males, women felt urges solely "during the time of ovulation."[95]

For Maitra, the pivotal difference between humans and other animals was consciousness and the control of sexual behavior. Certain peoples were more advanced and benefited from their sexual evolution: "engaging elements that would fulfill their necessities, happiness and comforts. But to do all these things they had to deviate from primitive people. The attendant changes in man's sexual pleasure and sex life were not trivial."[96] In Maitra's narration of human sexuality, this moment was a turning point; it was the first time man "made proper generations," indeed the very "starting point of civilization."[97] In fact, this moment is also a turning point in the text, as it signals a transition from extensive discussions of the *natural* evolution of society and genealogy of the family unit into commentary on the *social* difference of sexuality in modern man.

This was a theory of the restraint of male sexuality through the control of female sexuality. Monogamy appeared only after man's long transformation of sexual practices:

> From my discussion, it can be easily understood that monogamy is a very modern concept, that it is difficult to make man consistent with principles, and that there are reasons behind illicit sexual unions of men and women who have gone astray! But from these words, one should not think that we are demeaning the institution of monogamy. There is no doubt at all that this method is the best way to spread the light of civilization to this world.[98]

Maitra argues that since early civilization, man had satisfied sexual desire beyond the need for reproduction, a habit not unlike eating and sleeping. It was this drive—the difficult, aspirational desire for monogamy—that was to be held up as the motor for civilization.

But what was the history of the prostitute in India? Maitra felt that there were no "proper histories" that could speak to the status of prostitutes in ancient India. It is here that we see the combination of ethnology and comparative analyses of ancient societies. The essay extensively discusses ancient histories of prostitution in Greek and Roman times. The history of ancient Greek civilization substituted for a genealogy of ancient India: "Archaeologically, our Indian civilization is the oldest of all the civilizations in the world but as we have no records of history, we have to follow what others have. So we have to say that the model of Greek civilization is found here in India."[99]

Maitra follows his comparative genealogy of ancient Greek women, Hetaerae, with extensive sociological analysis of the marginalization of the *ganika*. Here he creates a comparative analytic to Bachofen's theory of Hetaerism, or Greek prostitution, as parallel to primitive promiscuity. For Maitra, prostitution in Greek times was "a good example of how high educational systems for women should and should not be in our society."[100] The genealogy of the European prostitute revealed that education had the ability to pervert the natural appeals of the normal woman. Maitra emphasized a parallel perversion through education: "Virtuous wives are moving away from their delicacy, charm, and beauty and made cold-hearted and sullen through education."[101] Maitra argued that in Indian society, women who worked or moved outside of the home would "forget the sacredness and reproductive purpose of love." Instead of pursuing normal, civilized, family-oriented forms of sexuality, "they engage in beastly sexual intercourse" and passed on their "secret mental pursuit" of sexual desire to their children. Maitra warned of the deleterious effects of the animalistic nature in women, where "sexual instinct arises *beastly* desire in women in weak moments and disgraceful matters these *patitas* [literally, fallen women] are exposed and after this they become known as *ganika*."[102] Even if prostitution was outlawed, "new women will fill up" the ranks of the prostitute, providing a continual source of temptation for men. This was the paradox of modern society, where the natural sweetness of woman was perverted through modern institutions like education.

Withholding sex—here, presented as the harnessing of sexual power—was not to be seen as a perversion of nature. Rather, Maitra argued, "one should not think it is impossible to transfer sexual desire, which is natural, into a higher sphere."[103] The sexual instinct was to be restrained through the "moral attributes of *normal* men and women," and it was the "duty of doctors to bring the truth to the minds of every one of these men and women." Against those doctors that did not promote a civilized sexuality, Maitra asserted the power of science to help men reach true consciousness: "Medically as a physician, morally as a Hindu, and compassionately as a fellow human being, we record a solemn protest against this false treatment of sex. It is better for youth to live a content life."[104]

Through the concept of the *ganika*, which he equated with the prostitute, Maitra demarcated the divide between nature and culture. More critically, the *ganika* in the present revealed the *passage* back and forth between the nature/culture frontier. The *ganika* appears as a paradoxical concept in the text. She was the remnant of barbarity, the result of the undisciplined sexuality of primitive instinct, and the product of modernity, a perversion of the normal woman through modern institutions, particularly Western education. She served as a pivotal intermediary between the advancement of man and the potential return to his former primitive self.

Maitra's narrative of biological and historical advancement does not end with the rise to modern civilization in India. Rather, for Maitra, social evolution was precarious at every stage, since the most evolved social practices were the ones that required the most sophisticated forms of man's consciousness. Every excess threatened to produce social aberration, failure, and absolute degeneration. In Maitra's narrative, *ganikagomon* required a scientific, reasoned narrative of the origin and evolution of sexual desire through a precarious state of sexual control called modern marriage. The ideal monogamy was not natural. Instead, monogamous conjugality was won through the conscious departure of man from the primitive, and the prostitute was simply a remainder of older social orders, signaling a temporal lag that remained present in modern Indian society. The existence of the *ganika* in the modern world signified a radical disruption to this tenuous institution.[105] In Maitra's scheme, the *ganika's* continued presence threatened to precipitate civilized man's descent into his primitive, instinctual self.

Ethnology, Sociology, and the Traffic in Deviant Female Sexuality

Maitra's contemporaries also sought to explain the seemingly paradoxical persistence of the prostitute in modern Indian society. Between the 1920s and the 1960s, Santosh Kumar Mukherji, a prominent medical doctor in Calcutta, wrote extensively on social issues and medical science. He published many studies, on subjects ranging from Hindu worship, the partition of Bengal, disease treatments, prescriptions, and birth control, as well as a translation and study of the *Kamasutra*.[106] In 1968, he delivered a series of public lectures on the relationship between *dharma* and science; these lectures were later published in a volume titled *Shrishti, bhagabana, o sadhana* (1969). He stressed the significance of Hinduism in most of his scientific textbooks and social tracts. His pro-Hindu, anti-Muslim sentiments were most clearly expressed in *Boundary Problem in Bengal* (1943), in which he suggested the partition was a travesty for Hindus in Bengal and the result of Muslim agitation and greed. A similar bias can also be found in his attempts to define a distinct language for the Hindus of Bengal in his textbook, *Hindur Bangla* (1938). To underscore his expertise, Mukherji reproduced his various titles and memberships in medical and scientific organizations in all of his publications on the title page of his books (see Figure 14).

INDIAN SEX LIFE
AND
PROSTITUTION

BY

Dr. Santosh Kumar Mukherji, M.B.

Editor, Indian Medical Record; Formerly Lecturer, Calcutta Medical School and Member of Council of Presidents, Association Internationale de la Presse Medicale, Rome; Honorary Member, Institut Litteraire et Artistique de France, Paris; and Author of Infantile Cirrhosis of the Liver, Incompatibility in Prescriptions, Elements of Endocrinology, Birth Control for the Millions, Prostitution in India, Kama-Sutra, Psychology of Love and Sex etc.

ANIL KUMAR DAS GUPTA
BURNPUR, BURDWAN

FIGURE 14. Santosh Kumar Mukherji, *Indian Sex Life and Prostitution* (1934), title page.

In 1934, Mukherji published a 517-page study, *Prostitution in India*, that sought to trace and analyze the history of Indian sexual practices using the insights of a medical doctor who had "personally examined prostitute patients." *Prostitution in India* expanded on his study *Indian Sex Life and Prostitution*.[107] Mukherji modeled his study of the Indian prostitute from ancient to modern society on ethnology, particularly John McLennan's *Primitive Marriage* and Edward Westermarck's *The History of Human Marriage* (1891), as well as the philological study of ancient Indian sex life, including works by J. J. Meyer, H. C. Chakladar, and William Jones's *Sakuntala* (1789).

The book provides extensive readings of Sanskrit texts as the empirical basis of sexual and marriage practices that could be mapped onto comparative, universalist schemes of the stages of human development. Mukherji analyzes Sanskrit texts for the origins of female sexuality and then turns development of the prostitute from ancient to modern India. He integrates philology of ancient texts with ethnological theories of primitive tribal societies and a comprehensive sociology of prostitution in 1930s Calcutta. For Mukherji, marriage was the "product of civilization," and women became prostitutes because they were enslaved by their "animal nature."[108] The prostitute in society was the result of "degeneracy or reversions to the primitive man."[109] Through social evolution, marriage became important to "discourage sexual promiscuity."[110] Ultimately, in his scheme of social evolution, chastity became the sole imperative of the modern Hindu woman.[111]

Prostitution was the "by-product of marriage," a remnant of man's primitive instinct: "In the animal world, the mammals do not generally remain faithful to a single mate. In the prehistoric age men and women cohabited in the manner of birds and animals. Sexual promiscuity prevailed within the limits of each tribal group."[112] Textual proof of the origins of primitive promiscuity in Indian society, Mukherji notes, could be found in chapter 122 of the *Mahabharata*. He translates the text: "In ancient time the women were naked. They could roam and enjoy themselves at their own sweet will. They had not to live under the yoke of men. Even if they became attached from one man to another, no sin touched them. At that time, it was religious custom."[113] Again, primitive promiscuity is linked to the timelessness of Indian social and religious custom.

From the origin story of primitive promiscuity, Mukherji turns to evolutionary thought to develop a synthetic theory of social evolution for modern India based on Edward Dalton's ethnology of primitive societies in Bengal. Mukherji observes that apes remain faithful to a single sexual partner, and that "the male protects his mate and their young ones." By correlating the sociality of primate life to primitive man, he builds a crude model of family life for human societies. Then Mukherji lays out the three factors that explained the social evolution of Indians from primitive man: the transition from "periodic to constant sexual impulse in man," the development of occupations and associated labor of agriculture, and the evolution of man into distinct lines of family lineage and descent.

Throughout, Mukherji extensively cites Dalton's 1872 *Descriptive Ethnology of Bengal* as an *empirical* source for the primitives of Bengal. According to Mukherji, in the "Ho population" of Bengal there are women who are "saucy" and "full of spirits"—an inclination toward sexual promiscuity that appeared subdued in most seasons. However, these women rapidly became rabid in their sexual desire, using "gross language" in the season of the Magh feast: "Men and women become like animals in the indulgence of their amorous propensities there seems to be no restraint to their indulgence, it cannot be expected that chastity is preserved when the shades of night fall on such a scene of licentiousness and debauchery."[114] The Ho represented the continued presence of primitive promiscuity in contemporary India. In this telling, the Ho were presented as outside the time of progressive civilization. Temporality was thus key to understanding Indian sexual deviance and prostitution, as the continued presence of the prostitute testified to the continued existence of primitivity in contemporary life in India: "Prostitution has therefore rightly been described as a dark shadow out of the past falling now upon family life."[115] The scientific study of a primitive past was critical to understanding the colonial present.

Mukherji links these extensive discussions of primitivity and the history of sexual promiscuity by arguing that this historical development created a diverse array of different types of prostitutes who emerged over hundreds of years. Evolutionary theory necessitated a taxonomical classificatory project of the modern forms of the prostitute.[116] Mukherji's taxonomy parallels earlier lists and hierarchies of the many types of women who were prostitutes found in the colonial sociological survey.

In a chapter titled "Types of Prostitutes," Mukherji produces an elaborate taxonomy of women who had the potential to become prostitutes. His descriptions were exhaustive, and they included essentially all women, married or unmarried, of all castes, from upper-caste widows to outcaste servants. For Mukherji, any display of women's will—including public performances of dancing and theater, and even the clandestine sexual desire of a lonely housewife—made a woman a prostitute. As he describes the sexual danger of practices both inside and outside the conjugal home, he intentionally labels diverse social practices with the category of the prostitute to make commensurate a theory of Indian society that could be mapped onto a universalist scheme of social evolution.

Mukherji's taxonomy of women who were to be understood as clandestine prostitutes betrays his equation of sexual promiscuity and prostitution with the social practices of non-Brahmans, especially low-caste and outcaste Hindu women and *all* Muslim women. His detailed description of the categories of women who were prostitutes encompassed streetwalkers, performers, maid-servants, female cooks, women laborers in the mills of Calcutta, nurses, the *panwalli* (girls selling betel leaf), married Muslim women, and shop and telephone girls. His taxonomy includes old social types like the widow produced through custom, and new types of women who held jobs created through the colonial economy, from the nurse to the telephone girl. He even includes women in Hindu love marriages who did not see marriage as a permanent institution, whom he equates with concubines.[117] Mukherji produces a detailed description of each type of woman he includes in his taxonomy of the modern prostitute. He emphasizes the necessity of sociological description to expose the secret nature of these women's hidden sexual proclivities. For example, under the category "Maid Servant," Mukherji explains that the maid was the most pervasive and clandestine type of prostitute in society: "In towns most of the maid servants are clandestine prostitutes. Many of them work in the day and go to their room at night where they live with their paramours or receive visitors."[118]

With this taxonomy, Mukherjee also includes extensive transliterations of the categories in Hindustani and Bengali that were to be equated with the prostitute:

Dancing Girls

The dancing girls are generally known as *"tawaif."* In Bengal they are called *Vaiji* or *Taifawalli*. These women are prostitutes, though some of the *vaijis* have their so-called husbands who live with them. This device helps them to prevent any attempt at declaration of their residence as brothels ... The name of *Kamini* (popularly known as *Kanch Kamini*) is known to many people for her charities ... In Mysore such women are called *Kalavati* (artistes); but most of them are engaged in prostitution.[119]

Mukherji's equation of different types of women as prostitutes creates a uniform geography of women's sexual deviance across North and South India: the dancing girl of North India, the *tawaif*, is the *baiji* of Bengal, who is equivalent to the *kalavati* of Mysore. In footnotes to his book, he does more etymological work, where he names the many different Bengali words in Bengali script that were to be equated with the prostitute: *kulatadasi* (literally a woman outside of the clan), *kulata* (a bad woman or a woman outside of a clan), *swarini* (a self-assertive woman), *nati* (a woman actor/woman performer), *rupajiba* (literally, a woman who lives on her beauty), *magi* (a promiscuous woman), *beshya* (a promiscuous woman, commonly translated as "prostitute"), and many more.[120]

In Mukherji's scheme, perhaps no historical form of sexual promiscuity persisted as tenaciously as those brought by Muslim conquest.[121] Here he betrays his biases: the wives of all Muslim marriages (that he characterizes as temporary) were prostitutes. In his view, any Muslim woman outside of permanent structures of monogamous marriage should be classified as prostitutes. He moves from discussions about debased Muslim landlords and the clandestine promiscuity of women under Muslim rule in India to the continued degradation of social evolution as a result of British colonialism. In Mukherji's analysis, British colonialism magnified the sexual promiscuity of women in India introduced first by Muslims. He explains that the dangers of this promiscuity persisted, as Europeans introduced syphilis in India and were more diseased than Indians.[122]

In his account, enduring Muslim social practices that persisted into the present were temporally out of sync with modern Indian society:

> In Bengal the Hindu society does not tolerate concubinage and no person would dare to keep a concubine in his own house. This form of illegitimate sexual union is more common in Muhammedan society. A Muhammedan may delight in not more than four wives and as many concubines as he likes or can afford to maintain ... Concubinage or companionate marriage, by whatever name it may be called, cannot be tolerated by society.[123]

Mukherji's tropes are striking: the Muslim man kept as many women as he could afford to maintain, unlike the Hindu, who tended toward monogamy. Under the category of "Temporary Wives," Mukherji suggests that it was not only that Muslim men kept concubines but that their marriages were in themselves perverse.

Indeed, for Mukherji, most if not all Muslim marriage practices were to be understood as equivalent to prostitution:

> A large number of Muhammedan prostitutes practise prostitution with men of their own religion. These women take advantage of the peculiar system

of temporary marriage prevalent among the Shia sect of Muhammedans. Licentious men contract temporary marriages in order to enjoy the company of a woman . . . So long as these women are in the keeping of a man they are not classed as prostitutes.[124]

Mukherji, in linking Muslim marriage practices with prostitution, reflects the logic of the taxonomies of the prostitute in the surveys of the colonial state over sixty years before. This understanding, of Muslim sexuality as *inevitably* dangerous and always the result of a developmental lag appears in Mukherji as a kind of commonsense. Indeed, Mukherji's study reflects the way that women's sexual deviance and enslavement become one of the most enduring anti-Muslim ideologies in twentieth-century Hindu social thought. Mukherji argues that his historico-sociological project of naming and translating the history of prostitutes in Bengal, in their character, terminology, and social evolution, is fundamentally an ethical project—an ethical future, Mukherji imagines, that was to be built through the sexual strictures of patriarchal Hindu institutions.

Mukherji's definitive *Prostitution in India* was widely cited, and its republication in 1986 brought the text to a new generation of readers. It is still considered an authoritative text on the history of Indian prostitution, and has been regularly cited in the sphere of public health in the last twenty years—despite its blatant biases against lower-caste and Muslim women, and its deeply patriarchal vision of normative female sexuality. Mukherji has even been cited in studies of sex work and HIV in India that have influenced policy makers in India.[125]

In both Maitra's essay and Mukherji's text, the status of female sexual deviance signified the difference between the past and the present. Unrestrained desire was the remnant of a primitive past; the control of sexual desire was thus key to Indian social development in the present. These social scientific studies produce clear theories of sexual difference: a man could fall prey to instinct but had the capacity for conscious self-restraint and enlightenment; in contrast, a woman was constituted simply as being incapable of sexual restraint, with no will except the sexual drive. While they reinforced the necessity of sexual difference, these social analysts also marked a temporal difference in the ability of man to restrain his sexuality. Primitivity in Indian society came to an end in the moment of man's conscious restraint of sexual desire. The primitive could not be externalized. Indeed, the primordial form of man, his very *origin*, was found in the continued presence of the prostitute. There was an ever-present anxiety that the woman, fallen out of society, would inevitably become the ultimate temptation to man's devolution. This was a call to patriarchy and the control of female sexuality for the sake of a progressive Indian society. The evolution of society was disturbed by the perilous specter of the prostitute, the primitive *ganika*, whose continued existence would lead to the complete demise of civilization.[126]

These ethnological theories of sexual development became foundational for different fields of Indian social science in postcolonial India. In a 1956 lecture to the Indian History Congress, "Traces of Promiscuity in Ancient Indian Society," Ram Sharan Sharma, eminent ancient and medieval historian (1919–2011), employed these methods of uniting philological interpretation of Sanskrit text with the ethnological assessment of female sexuality. Sharma was author of over one hundred history books on premodern India. In his lecture, he traced women's sexual promiscuity in primitive societies through a philological and historical interpretation of the *Mahabharata* and *The Laws of Manu*. He began his address by connecting a genealogy of ethnological thought to ancient promiscuity:

> The German scholar Bachofen, who produced his epoch-making work *Mutterrecht* in 1861, was the first to suggest that a state of promiscuity preceded the establishment of the institution of marriage. His conclusions were reinforced by the researches of McLennan, Morgan, Lubbock, Bastian, Spencer and others.[127]

Sharma cites Johann Jakob Meyer's study of ancient Indian sex life and conducts his own positivist philological analysis of Sanskrit text. In his argument about the textual evidence in the *Puranas* and *Mahabharata*, he insists that women of ancient India were "licentious and self-willed, and indulge in sexual intercourse in the open."[128] This sexual promiscuity only ended with what we now know to be a familiar story, the legend of Swetaketu and his first stricture against primitive promiscuity. Swetaketu appears in Sharma's study, like so many from decades before, as the textual event that marks the origin of the marriage concept, an innovation and step toward civilization. Sharma correlated the Swetaketu event with ethnological timelines of social development, insisting that the Sanskrit texts were "in keeping with numerous other traditions" of ethnology. This correlation between epics and ethnological theory made Sanskrit text a source of scientific facts: "In view of these, it would not be correct to dismiss the Svetaketu legend as a fiction."[129] Ethnology, as a theory of primitive promiscuity to civilizational development, corroborated the tale of Swetaketu and his dictate against the sexual promiscuity of women in the *Mahabharata* as absolute social and historical fact.

Perhaps nowhere were models of sexual development more pervasive than in the formalization of Indian academic sociology. In his vast corpus of work, Radhakamal Mukerjee (1889–1968), the so-called father of Indian sociology and author of dozens of books on economics, sociology, and metaphysics, featured extended discussions of women's sexuality as the primary marker of civilizational development. Mukerjee was a leading proponent of the formalized social sciences in India, a primary training ground for sociology students. Mukerjee was trained in Calcutta and the founder of the Lucknow School of Indian sociology. Mukerjee was also influenced by the Scottish scientist, sociologist, and urban planner Patrick Geddes (1854–1932), who was the founder of the Bombay School of Sociology and whose 1889 study, *The Evolution of Sex*, focused on sexuality as a marker of social evolution.[130] Mukerjee created a model of multidisciplinary practice of social science for modern Indian society built on ethnological evolution. In multiple studies in his vast corpus of writing, Mukerjee theorized Indian society from primitive promiscuity to marriage and idealized monogamous marriage as metaphysical transcendence.[131]

For example, in his book-length treatise *The Horizon of Marriage* (1957), Mukerjee produces a definitive study of the metaphysical and moral realization of civilization, what he termed a "sexual sociology." The field of sociology, in this scheme, was at its foundation *sexual* sociology. He devotes his study to a unified biological, psychoanalytical, philological, and ethnological model of sexual evolution, with chapters ranging from "The Natural History of Sexuality" to "Primitive Marriage" to monogamy as "The Destiny of Sex."[132] In his treatise, he understands monogamy as the antithesis of primitive urge; monogamy is the sign of a "mature mind": "It is monogamy of a lasting kind ... that throws open the highest opportunities of personality development of normal man and woman."[133] Mukerjee extensively cites from the *Kamasutra* as an account of evolution from animalistic sexual urges, from biting among primitives, to higher, more civilized orders of sexual practices in marriage like soft kisses.[134] From the *Kamasutra*, Mukerjee finds ethnological social development; from the *Mahabharata*, he finds an ideal model for the restraint of female sexuality: "Marriage according to the Mahabharata is made in heaven. 'Monogamy is the state decreed by the god for women.'"[135]

The Epistemic Doubling of Indian Sexuality

This chapter has demonstrated that ideas about social evolution permeated the expanding field of the social sciences in colonial India. Social analysts in Bengal transmutated sexual ideas to produce idealized visions of Indian society based in sexual evolution to monogamy. The multilingual classification of deviant female sexuality shaped knowledge about the place of Indian society in universalist schemes of social evolution. The influence of these ideas is evident in texts ranging from exalted historical accounts of ancient India to the systematic sociological study of modern Indian society. Diverse social analysts utilized taxonomies of female sexual deviance to make equivalent incommensurate social practices. These social practices and types were mapped onto universalist schemes of social evolution. This project of commensurability was achieved in part through the textual and sociological equation of the category of the prostitute with numerous social classifications for women.

Bengali social analysts produced a multidisciplinary hermeneutic for female sexuality. These writers saw the mutable concept of the prostitute as the very genesis of social evolution. Deviant female sexuality—differently named *beshya, patita, ganika*—encompassed everything from the outcast slave woman to the Muslim dancing girl to the unrestrained housewife. These studies of prostitution and social evolution are not merely expressions of moral anxiety. Rather, they reveal a widespread form of reasoning that posited the concept of the prostitute as essential to the project of social scientific study: she was critical to making Indian society commensurate with an idealized evolving civilization.

Female sexual deviance was key to these emerging forms of social thought; it provided a mutable site used in the assessment of society. The Spencerian dictum about the status of woman could be used diagnostically: "In no way" could the "moral progress" of the Indian man be shown "more clearly" than by "contrasting the position of women among savages with their position among the most advanced of the civilized."[136] Deviant female sexuality—characterized as savage and primitive—was to be controlled in increasingly sophisticated structures of patriarchal marriage.

These social analysts were invested in a project of commensurability where they could produce equivalence between Indian social practices and transnational ideas about primitivity and evolved marriage. They utilized a broadly applicable logic that made diverse forms of social behavior (caste stricture, religious difference, class, gendered behavior; one's manner, speech, family relations; law) equivalent to prostitution. In this reasoning, the comprehensive study of female sexual transgression would account for the temporal lag of Indian social custom. It was not only a diagnostic of a primitive past but the basis for a kind of futurology, social theories that anticipated the potential development of Indian society. As I show in the next chapter, different Bengali publications, including popular literature and memoirs, utilized this vacillating idea of the sexually deviant woman as the past and future.

Through exhaustive taxonomies and claims to objective science, male social analysts sought to fix the prostitute as a fixed, singular, and homogenous concept. The concept of the prostitute was to do all of the descriptive work necessary to explain Indian social lag; it encompassed every form of social practice and sexual act that was temporally behind a modern society dominated by patriarchy. The prostitute, as a concept, could be identified and named, made commensurate and used in comparison to sexual practices across different times and places, and trafficked as a concept in the service of claims to a science of modern Indian society.

5

Veracity

LIFE STORIES AND THE REVELATION OF SOCIAL LIFE

WHY DO WOMEN become prostitutes? This question shaped the popular imagination about social life in the colonial city of Calcutta. The question of why women "fall" was posed by authorities across different domains who claimed that the answer was critical to the reform of society: if only the journey of the woman's fall could be elucidated fully, if only the reasoning of why women became prostitutes could be known in complete detail, only then would it be possible to understand the true nature of contemporary society. The answer was to be revealed in eyewitness accounts of prostitutes and in the "true" testimonials of women themselves.

In 1929, Manoda Devi published a confessional account of an "educated prostitute" in Bengali as *Shikshita Patitar Atmacharit*; nearly simultaneously, it appeared in English as *Autobiography of an Educated Fallen Woman*. Her book opens with a definitive answer to why women become prostitutes. The purported author, Manoda Devi, reflected that women had failed to recognize the sexual dangers they face in society: "It is just because I knew not the face of Satan in the days when I was young and pure, I—and why thousands like me, today live the abominable life of a prostitute."[1] Devi offers readers what she claims was the most intimate, most truthful account of the whole of society, one that remained hidden from public view:

> The autobiography of an educated fallen woman—many may doubt the idea behind it. Lives of great men, great as they are, are never the complete picture of humanity. My life itself is far from being great or noble, on the contrary its antithesis. But the ideal that has prompted me to write this book is

great and noble. A sinner and infamous woman as I am, I have nothing more to gain from this world in the nature of human praise. So I could chronicle the inner records of my life with greater sincerety [sic]. Great men, as they are, they are forced to conceal much. If one is to protect oneself from vices, one should know of its nature.²

Rather than in the promises of an elite political leader or a description of the nobility of upper-caste society, the voice of social truth was to be found in the autobiographical confession of the outcaste woman. Unlike great men who concealed social realities in their quest for praise, she was uniquely poised to reveal the reality of society to protect its future.

As we have seen across fields of knowledge, the search for the voice of the prostitute was critical to the project of social knowledge from its inception. In 1868, the year the colonial Contagious Diseases Act was passed, the newspaper *Amrita Bazar Patrika* ran an account of a man who purportedly surveyed two hundred-plus women to learn firsthand why women turned to the life of the *beshya*. In short summaries of the lives of anonymous women, the author of the article argued that women became prostitutes as a result of a combination of destitution, social exclusion, and most importantly, the failure of women to restrain their sexual passions.³

In 1870, the first "autobiography" of a woman who became a prostitute because of her sexual desires was published under the name Nabinkali Debi as *Kamini Kalanka* (A woman's shame). In 1923, the Calcutta Suppression of Immoral Traffic Act was introduced. Concurrent to the act came the Curjel Report on the condition of women in factories in Calcutta, which focused on the question of why women laborers became temporary wives and prostitutes.⁴ By the 1930s another comprehensive survey was under way, this time a project of policing. As Indrani Chatterjee demonstrates, the life histories of fifty women were collected and edited in 1935 by the Police Commissioner in Calcutta from what he claimed were firsthand testimonials.⁵ There were many other such measures to survey, interview, and come to know the prostitute. The "real" voices, gained through supposed interviews or testimonies of individual women, not only provided an expert view of the degradation of women, but served as a window into the whole of society. The voices of women, named as prostitutes by those reporting on these women's lives, were to be sought and documented across fields of knowledge as a justification of state and social intervention.

As print culture expanded, the emerging sciences of society became part of a widely influential popular imagination. Chapbook stalls sprung up on the streets and footpaths of Calcutta. Writers publishing in the world of the popular press utilized ideas of deviant female sexuality to reveal the truth of society. Writers saw the prostitute as the primary mode through which to narrate the secrets of social life. In these texts, the concept of the prostitute was ubiquitous.[6] The popular presses in North Calcutta published new texts that featured dramatic depictions of deviant female sexuality—particularly narratives about the fall of women into prostitution. Sexually deviant women abound in the pages of these diverse publications; fallen women were a central feature in songbooks, plays, novels, and memoirs.

In this concluding chapter I turn my gaze to popular texts, focusing on a set of lay sociologies and "prostitute autobiographies" in the rapidly expanding world of print in the period from the 1870s until the 1940s. In previous chapters, we have witnessed the rise of different domains of knowledge that utilized ideas of deviant female sexuality to comprehend the progress of Indian society. A broad, far-reaching epistemological project has come into view, where the mutable idea of the prostitute shaped practices of description in the legal survey, the pathological museum display, the scientific treatise, and the sociological taxonomy.

In this archive of popular texts, we see that ideas of deviant female sexuality exceeded the closed worlds of formal philology, the government-mandated survey, the pathological diagnosis of forensic science, and the theoretical models of ethnology. In exposés and autobiographies, writers claimed that the prostitute was essential for comprehending the dangers of society. In the analysis that follows, I show how the idea of the sexually deviant woman appeared as the secret of social life in scenes of impurity and pollution. These lay sociologies and life stories demonstrate the pervasive presence of a social imaginary that utilized the concept of the prostitute to create a regime of empirical truth.

These lay sociologies and "autobiographies" are a small but representative sample of numerous publications on the restraint and excesses of women's sexuality that appeared in popular print in the late nineteenth and early twentieth centuries. In these salacious texts the real authors are hard to name, as they often used a pseudonym or claimed a woman's voice. My interpretation stands in contrast to the historiographical urge to recuperate resistance and the agency of marginalized peoples from such texts—a project that reads archives at face value and finds voices through a search-and-rescue model of interpretation. These voices were collected, published, and repackaged in the social scientific enterprise in the service of state policy as well as a conservative social agenda of Hindu upper-caste elites.

I ask: What was achieved in the claim to the first-person witness of the prostitute or the voice of the prostitute herself? What claims to expertise and specialized knowledge are being made in these accounts? I analyze the critical place of the witness and expert in the popularization of the new sexual sciences of society. In the first part of the chapter I analyze men's accounts of female sexual deviance in the critique of timeless "social customs," focusing on debates about Hindu Brahman polygamy that intensified in the middle of the nineteenth century. These discourses about Hindu polygamy reemerged in the first decades of the twentieth century as primary objects of social science. Female sexual deviance was a potent critique of the continued existence of social customs, deployed by upwardly mobile elites in claims to authority and progress. In the second part of the chapter, I critically read texts that privilege the male eyewitness who writes the sexually deviant woman as the sociology of the city. In these accounts from the early decades of the twentieth century, the prostitute exposed the dangers of urban life hidden from view. In the final section, I explore the life stories of the fallen woman published between the 1920s and the 1940s. These autobiographies—purported to be in the women's own words—reflect a deep conservatism that defined female sexuality's role in this social scientific imaginary. Written in the first-person voice, these accounts privilege the position of the so-called prostitute in perceiving and critiquing social life. Even as they claimed to reveal the hypocrisy of society, these "autobiographies" made natural the terms of women's sexual exclusion and reasserted the primacy of patriarchal monogamy.

The Prostitute and the Revelation of Social Custom

Social scientific texts linked the pollution of women to the possible contamination of all of society. Social pollution was a potent accusation, a powerful form of stigmatization linked directly to caste discrimination used to control low-caste and outcaste bodies and peoples. The potential for social stigma followed women across their lifetimes—in social markers, their comportment, menstruation cycles, childbirth and childrearing, the sex of their children, widowhood, and even in death. But it was in death, in the proximity to the dead body, that the high-caste Hindu encountered the strongest form of impurity and the possibility of pollution. Death pervades the sexual sociologies of the previous chapters, from detailed descriptions of the act of infanticide to the forensic doctor's assessment of suspect women's bodies.

The privileged site of Hindu death scenes, the funeral pyre, was a powerful imaginary in sociological depictions of colonial Indian society. The pyre was a space of contrast, between the highest form of ritual practice conducted by the Brahman Hindu priest performing last rites and the enforced exclusion and subjugation of those people whose enforced labor was to clean, manage, and dispose of the bodies of the deceased. The pyre, while a place of mourning, was also a potential site of social impurity and condemnation. In popular descriptions of the sexually deviant woman, social degradation was staged in the scene of the cremation grounds. The woman at the funeral pyre—sometimes alive, sometimes dead, and sometimes soon to be dead through the act of *sati*— appeared in the earliest accounts of the colonial encounter in the paintings, photographs, and literature of European travelers.[7] The idea of the woman at the pyre was critical for Indian religious authorities and within the domain of popular Indian-language publications. The whole truth of society could be found at the volatile space of the cremation ground.

With the coming of new technologies of photography to India, numerous photographs and postcards of Hindu funeral pyres circulated around the world. These images trained a public across metropole and colony in new practices of viewing and social classification.[8] Take the example of an 1870s photograph of a funeral scene that appears on a postcard. It was likely taken by Samuel Bourne, a prolific British photographer who photographed peoples and places of the subcontinent and set up one of the earliest photography studios in colonial India. On the postcard, we confront an image of a woman staring directly into the gaze of the camera. Her stare seems mournful, even resentful—suspicious of the camera. The photograph captures the woman as she sits near the body of a widowed woman who is on top of a funeral pyre. The body of the widow appears small. It is folded, laid on top of a carefully assembled structure of wood logs. Her head is shaved and her body nude except for a small cloth around her hips. Several people surround the pyre, crouching as the priest performs funeral rites. The site of Nimtala, the famous site of funeral ghats in Calcutta, is recognizable by the large columns next to the Hooghly River. The caption of the photograph is simply "Burning Ghat, Calcutta."[9]

The pyre, a symbol of Hindu ritual practice and death, was an infinitely malleable site for the production of knowledge about Indian society. In a book produced around the same time as this photograph of Nimtala, we hear of another scene of a funeral at the ghat. In the 1873 *Kulakalima* (Black mark on the family), Yadavchandra Lahiri, a lawyer, describes the "true scenes" of everyday social life among polygamous Hindu Kulin Brahmans.[10]

In several scenes that describe the city and countryside, he explains how sexual deviance among polygamous Hindus was common among his contemporaries. In a scene set in a village, a prominent Kulin Brahman family mourned the death of their widowed daughter. Lahiri narrates how everyone had gathered near her funeral pyre to witness her cremation:

> Readers! Listen to what has happened at the Mukherjee house in the village next to yours. Everyone can hear the cries of the mother and the lamentation of the father as the whole community trembles with sadness. The widow girl of the Mukherjee family has died of tuberculosis. The news has spread all around. The entire village gathers to mourn her loss at her funeral pyre. Suddenly, a group of men in uniform arrive. They are unkind and in a great hurry, their eyes filled with a knowing dread. They run to the burning pyre and steal the dead body of the woman off of the burning funeral pyre.
>
> The men whisk the body away to the police station where a government doctor calmly performs a detailed post-mortem examination. The doctor cuts open the abdomen of the dead woman. Poison oozes from the body and a fully-formed fetus falls from her womb.[11]

Lahiri declared that the violence of the abortion resulted from greedy people who gave women too much freedom under the pretense of high-caste marriage. The details of the scene exposed the social conspiracy of Kulin Brahmans who hid their sexual indiscretions with elaborate explanations. The family hid the abortion from view and spread rumors about the daughter's illness with public performances of grief. Like the expert coroner who explained Kally's death, the doctor here exposes that the widow died from an alleged abortion. In Lahiri again the body testified to the Kulin widow's life and death, evidence of an unspoken social conspiracy to hide her sexual indiscretion and the subsequent loss of family caste status. Lahiri depicts the doctor as calm—an omniscient expert endowed with the ability to diagnose not only the truth of the widow's life and death but the secret ills of society. Lahiri's account demonstrates the reach of colonial forensic medicine into the popular imagination, a science that could expose the reality of the dangers of Hindu polygamy. It is classified as "sociology" alongside other texts on women, social ills, and customary marriage in Blumhardt's catalogue of Bengali books (see Figure 15).

In the nineteenth century, polygamy was a primary object of social critique and reform efforts. In India, polygamy is most often attributed to Muslim marriage practices; however, many different forms of Hindu polygamy were also practiced.[12] As Malavika Karlekar has demonstrated, Hindu Kulin polygamy

SOCIOLOGY.

Kalir nava ranga.. Nine Social Evils of the present Age. By Kālidāsa Mukhopādhyāya. pp. 22. 12mo. *Calcutta*, 1876.

Kanyāpaṇa-vināśikā. The Evils of Hindu Marriage Customs. By Kāśīnātha Dāsa Gupta. pp. 2, 55. 12mo. *Calcutta*, 1859.

Kaulīnya-saṃśodhinī. A Tract on the Evils of Kulinism. By Rāsavihārī Mukhopādhyāya. 2nd edition. pp. 13. 12mo. *Dacca*, 1871.

Kayek-khāni patra. Letters to a Wife on the Social, Domestic, and Intellectual Advancement of Women. pp. 49, 3. 12mo. *Calcutta*, 1882.

Ki holo. Strictures on existing Social Evils in Bengali Life. By Chandraśekhara Sena. pp. 18, 133. 12mo. *Calcutta*, 1875.

Kulakālimā. The Evils of the Marriage Customs of Kulin Brahmans. pp. 2, 105. 12mo. *Calcutta*, 1873.

Mādaka sevaner avaidhatā. A Tract against the Use of Intoxicating Drugs. By Gopālachandra Vandyopādhyāya. pp. 48. 12mo. *Calcutta*, 1865.

Marriage of Hindu. Widows. By Īśvarachandra Vidyāsāgara. *See* Vidhavāvivāha.

Nārīdharma. The Duties of Women. pp. 2, 43. 12mo. *Calcutta*, 1877.

Nārījātivishayaka prastāva. A Discourse on Woman. By Kālīprasanna Ghosha. pp. 242. *Calcutta*, 1869.

Nava Bābuvilāsa. An Exposure of the Vices of Bengali Bābus. By Pramathanātha Śarmā. pp. 2, 51. *Calcutta*, 1853.

Neśānāśaku Sabhā. An Appeal to Natives to join a Society founded for the Repression of Drunkenness. By Thomas Evans and J. H. Rouse. pp. 4. 12mo. *Calcutta*, 1876.

Paśudiger prati dayākaraṇa. The Duty and Advantages of Kindness to Animals. A prize essay by "Aliquis." Translated into Bengali by Gopīkṛishṇa Mitra. pp. 26. *Calcutta*, 1868.

Pativratādharma. The Duties of Wives towards their Husbands, illustrated by Pauranic stories and maxims. By Dayāmayī Devī. pp. 8, 52. 12mo. *Calcutta*, 1869.

Pativratopadeśa. The Duties of Wives towards their Husbands, compiled from Sanskrit authorities. By Padmalochana Nyāyaratna. 2nd edition. pp. 19. *Bardwan*, 1861.

Pātivratyadharmaśikshā. The Duties of Wives towards their Husbands, written in the form of a dialogue. By Śivachandra Jānā. pp. 58. 12mo. *Calcutta*, 1870.

Pātrīparīkshā. Rules for the Selection of a Girl in Marriage, by a consideration of her physical, social, and other qualifications. With quotations from Sanskrit authorities. By Rādhikānātha Ṭhākura. pp. 2, 66, 2. *Murshidabad*, 1880.

Sabhyatār itihāsa. History of Civilisation. By Śrīkṛishṇa Dāsa. Pt. I. pp. 2, 95. *Calcutta*, 1876.

Samāja-kuchitra. The Evils of our Society. By a Midnight Traveller. pp. 68. *Calcutta*, 1868.

FIGURE 15. J. F. Blumhardt, books listed under "sociology" in *Catalogue of the Library of the India Office: Bengali, Oriya, and Assamese Books* (1905).

in Bengal was an important subject of extended debate by the colonial state and Hindu elites. In Bengal, a system of polygamy practiced by Kulin Hindu Brahmans, the highest subcaste group among Brahmans, was unique to the region. Kulin Brahman marriage practices were not dictated in ancient Hindu *shastras*; rather, it was introduced in the eleventh century and expanded under the reign of Ballal Sen. In this period the Kulin subcaste was distinguished as the highest among the Brahman caste, the highest subcaste of all castes, a status determined by patrilineal inheritance.[13] The practice was described by administrator and ethnographer H. H. Risley as "hypergamous"; that is, it was maintained only through one's hereditary family and marriage into another Kulin line.[14]

Because they carried caste, Kulin men could marry any Brahman woman. In addition, they were able to engage in polygamous marriages because the caste was endogamous, and women were restricted only to intracaste marriage to a Kulin man. Marrying outside of the Kulin subcaste group, including to a non-Kulin Brahman man, would cause the woman and family to lose their status as Kulins. The marriage of a daughter into a good Kulin family was critical to the status and reputation of the family. The husband was not required to maintain his wives in his own home, nor was he required to cohabitate with any of his wives in their natal homes. Instead, Kulin women continued to reside with their own parents, uncles, or brothers.[15] Colonial officials, Bengali men, and some literate women debated the moral status of these practices of Hindu polygamy, resulting in extended discussions of the practice in legislative proceedings, social reform publications, and memoirs.[16]

According to popular accounts, Kulin marriage practices had become distorted with the coming of colonialism, leading to a perversion of Kulin polygamy.[17] As in colonial legal surveys and forensic medical textbooks, social analysts and reformers consistently linked polygamous marriages of Kulin Brahmans to problems of child marriage, early widowhood, and female sexual deviance. The most important rhetorical claim made by opponents of Kulin Brahmanism was to condemn it for causing high-caste Hindu women to become prostitutes. In this argument, the Kulin wife was particularly dangerous; this is because she held the distinction of being the highest of high-caste wives, yet she resided outside of the conjugal home and outside the protection of a husband.

The *sati* debates of the 1830s and the legislation that legalized widow remarriage in 1856 shaped debates about Kulin polygamy. Numerous petitions for a legal ban on Kulin polygamy led to an enquiry in 1866 that produced the "Report of the Committee Appointed in 1866 to Report on the Necessity of

Legislating on the Subject of Polygamy among the Hindus."[18] Yet it failed to produce a law; after the uprising of 1857, the colonial state was increasingly reluctant with possible state interventions into Indian social custom. Nevertheless, it spurred a sociological interest in Kulin polygamy.

Colonial officials and Hindu elites emphasized that Kulin wives practiced clandestine prostitution and hid their sexual deviance through abortion and infanticide to maintain their caste status. The prominent reformer Ishwar Chandra Vidyasagar, himself from a Kulin family, led the effort to pass a law permitting widow remarriage. He wrote an extended exegesis on the problem of Kulin Brahman polygamy, *Bahubibaha Rahit Haoya Uchit Kina Etadvisayak Bichar* (A proposal on the abolition of polygamy, 1871).[19] Like his exegesis on widow remarriage, Vidyasagar combines analysis of the present state of social practices with a philological approach, using textual interpretations from the *shastras* and *The Laws of Manu* to demonstrate the necessity of a colonial law against polygamy. His assertions of Sanskrit textual authority are reinforced with extensive sociological descriptions of contemporary Bengali society. He links polygamy to the widespread prevalence of adultery, sexual deviance, prostitution, and infanticide.

So why did Kulin wives become prostitutes? According to Vidyasagar, they were vulnerable to their own desires. The Kulin system was a failure because it did not safely transfer women from the protection of her father to the protection of her husband. This incomplete "traffic in women"—from father to spouse—endowed too much freedom on women who had the social legitimacy of marriage without any of the conjugal restraints or norms of respectability and status.[20] Critics of Hindu polygamy pushed for the legal enshrinement of monogamous marriage where the patriarch cohabitated with his wife and had the authority to surveil her movement at all points. Hindu social reformers also looked to change the terrain of social life through a broader project of sociological critique of polygamy.

This critique of Hindu polygamy is exemplified in Lahiri's depiction of the reality of Kulin polygamy in his book *Kulakalima*, which appeared in the aftermath of the failed legislative efforts. Lahiri proclaims the need for reason and truth in the face of social secrecy, asking his readers to "objectively view a society on the wheel of progress."[21] His sketches of social life claims to depict the real society that emerged from typical Kulin Brahman families. He links his text to social scientific organizations of the period, including the Bangiyo Navya Sampradaya (Society of Modern Bengalis on Tradition), a group that sought to revise social traditions for a modernizing society.[22] Lahiri asserts that the customs of Indian society were to be treated as objects of analysis to create a comprehensive view of social progress as a tree of civilization, where the "fruits, roots, and leaves of every tree" were to be examined to determine the origins of degeneration in contemporary society.[23] Rather than allowing society to develop naturally, Lahiri declares the necessity of arranging social life in a linear fashion, which he asserts was the only objective way to understand a social problem. Hindu society could be split into two parts: respectable people, and those depraved people who hid under the guise of respectability. As Lahiri argues, using ethnological ideas of marriage as the marker of evolution, "the civility of a society is decided according to its marital system."[24] Marriage reflected the fundamental "condition of its women, its culture of knowledge, and its mental and physical strength and moral courage."[25]

Lahiri thus positions himself not only as a social authority but as an expert witness. He describes a scene where a Kulin husband went to call upon his soon-to-be wife on his wedding day. Seeing her, he realized the woman's lap was "swollen"—she was pregnant even before the consummation of their marriage. Lahiri highlights the strange nature of the groom's response to his bride: "Instead of condemning her, the Kulin bridegroom chants rhymes and proclaims his divine power to impregnate his wife prior to the wedding night!"[26] For Lahiri, under the guise of the most respectable union, the Kulin Brahman would willingly commit himself to even the most disreputable marriages for the purpose of money. Lahiri describes how Kulin families killed fetuses endlessly to maintain the guise of respectability. Killing the fetus (*bhrunahatya*), rather than being a sign of sin, was what made them "*Kulinshashanka*" (the moon among the Kulins).[27]

In Lahiri's account, when the Kulin wife became pregnant illicitly because of her own "sexual weakness," she had "no choice but to take up prostitution." Yet the "glory of the Kulin family is not dimmed by hundreds of sinful acts."[28] It is a conspiracy of silence. Respectability intact, families continued to force their daughters into the customs of Hindu polygamy, knowing its often deadly outcomes. For Lahiri, this was the gravest mistake of a progressive society, for it withered away at the beauty of the woman and left her diseased. The "waves of youthfulness and the storm of lust" delivered even the most chaste of Kulin wives to deviance, producing a "shadow" over her face.

This associative form of reasoning, one that originated in legal and forensic investigations explored in the chapters "Repetition" and "Circularity," would be repeated across fields of knowledge. Early marriage based in caste strictures led to widowhood; widowhood exposed women to their own unfulfilled desires;

women's desire led to sexual transgression; sexual transgression led to prostitution; prostitution and sexual deviance led to pregnancy; pregnancy created a fear of expulsion from caste and society, and ultimately led to abortion and infanticide. The sign of the prostitute encompassed all associated forms of deviance: social, sexual, criminal.

By the first decades of the twentieth century, public discourse in Bengal about sexual deviance had largely shifted away from critiques of polygamy to focus instead on urbanization and its effects on economic change and family structure. Calls for the colonial state to legislate against Kulin polygamy had been common fifty years before. By the first decades of the twentieth century, while it was no longer subject to judicial reform, Kulin polygamy became an object of inquiry firmly within the domain of the formalized social sciences, particularly in the scientific study of caste. H. H. Risley's 1908 all-encompassing social scientific treatise *The People of India* features extensive discussions of Kulin polygamy. Risley was by this time the director of ethnography for India, an *officier d'académie* in France, and a member of anthropological societies from Rome to Berlin to London. According to Risley, based on his knowledge as the head of the census of India, Kulin polygamy had statistically declined significantly over the course of the nineteenth century due to a range of social and economic factors. Yet it had not been fully eliminated, a fact that Risley correlates with ethnological theories that posited monogamy as the most modern stage of civilization.

For Risley, the sociological study of caste could explain the persistence of polygamous marriage among the highest subcaste of Brahmans, a stage temporally behind modern stages of civilization in India. Risley argued that the persistence of social custom as a result of caste was the only way to explain the survival of polygamy—even among those men who called themselves modern. While men no longer toured the marriage market to "sell" their caste status in marriage, Kulin polygamy continued:

> The system, I am informed, has even now not wholly died out, but it prevails on a less outrageous scale; a connubial touring season is not so much in evidence; and educated opinion condemns it forcibly. According to a recent writer, however, "it is still in full force in East Bengal, where such an abominable practice of having many wives still exists." And an actual case was mentioned to me recently of a Kulin Brahman living in the neighbourhood of Calcutta who has more than fifty wives, duly entered in a register.[29]

Risley builds his understanding of Kulin Brahmanism on the work of the Hindu social analyst Babu Girindranath Dutt's study, *The Brahmans and Kayasthas of Bengal* (1906). Correlating with these local sociologies, Risley constitutes an original theory of hypergamy, or exaggerated endogamy, building on the idea of endogamy created by the ethnologist John F. McLennan. Caste hypergamy led to the perversion of the true values of marriage in Kulins, resulting in the commodification of marriage ("duly entered in a register" of wives) and female sexual deviance.

In his appendix to the voluminous *People of India,* Risley includes an extended overview of a 1907 controversy where intellectuals in Britain commented on the moral advances of colonialism against polygamy. Notably, the 1907 exchange on the persistence of Kulin polygamy includes a letter by Irish writer George Bernard Shaw (1856–1950), who reframes the problem not as one of morality but rather of excessive reproduction: "The population question is pressing hard on us."[30] It was now possible to reframe the negative effects of social custom as an urgent problem for the emerging demographic sciences of the colonies.

The sexually deviant woman, constrained by ritual and caste stricture, was, in the words of Risley's epigraph for *People of India*, "a little window that looketh upon a great world."[31] In texts that exposed the concealment of Kulin acts of adultery, prostitution, and abortion, women's sexual transgression was essential to view the reality of society. Lahiri created an elaborate argument for upwardly mobile high-castes who practiced monogamy in his critique of the highest subcaste of the Brahmans. Social critics like Lahiri and the petitioners against Kulin polygamy asserted authority by casting the Kulin woman as unbridled and the Kulin man as greedy, trafficking in fake marriages for money.

Critics of Hindu social customs asserted that women became prostitutes because of the failure of the anachronistic structures of polygamous marriage to restrain modern women. This claim to monogamy as a masculine protectionism pivoted on the restraint of women's sexuality through companionate marriage. Thus, they advocated for strictures against Hindu widow remarriage and Kulin Brahman polygamy. In their view, Kulin marriage reflects a social landscape of wives and widows who are always already prostitutes. The ubiquity of the prostitute was proof of a broken social system based in timeless social customs.

In critiques of Kulin marriage as the cause of female sexual deviance, social analysts achieved three major goals. First, through the cause of the prostitute, upwardly mobile castes demonstrated that they, unlike the rigid upper-caste Brahmans, were most capable of restraining the sexuality of the unbridled woman in monogamy. Second, we find a parallel critique of Kulin men's sexual norms that extended beyond the condemnation of women. The perversion of the colonial present manifested in the Kulin man who prostituted himself in the marriage market—who made a literal ledger of his clients. These men perverted the sanctity of marriage as they sought payment for marriage while their women were free to transgress sexual norms. Third, critics of Kulin polygamy established that the liberation of women from Kulinism would allow them to enter a form of monogamous marriage that provided protection of their chastity by their husbands. The high-caste woman was to be freed from social traditions that led to the perversion of culture and the failure of social development. However, she was not free to express or exhibit free will or desire in any way. Men were the sole agents of women's freedom; they liberated them from the harms of custom while restraining their lives and bodies through strictures of monogamy. The language of pity, intertwined with the authority of social scientific revelation, endowed upwardly mobile men like Lahiri with the power to assert patriarchal authority for the protection of women from their own sexuality.

The Prostitute and the Revelation of the City

We turn to another scene in an exposé of the prostitute, also set at a Hindu funeral pyre in the bustling city of Calcutta. The scene takes place in *Rater Kolkata* (Calcutta at night, 1923), by one Meghnad Gupta. The book offers different sketches of urban life. Published under the pseudonym "Meghnad Gupta," the book depicts a man walking across the landscape of the city of Calcutta and narrating the scenes that he observes in the city landscape.[32]

Rater Kolkata sketches different scenes of the city, among which we encounter Nimtala cremation grounds, depicted as a site of social pollution and degradation. In *Rater Kolkata*, at the Nimtala ghats, all depravities of social life came into view: "I have come frequently to the cremation grounds at Nimtala at midnight. I cannot say how many times different types of strange scenarios appear before my eyes."[33] The scenarios that are then described by the onlooker reveal the perversions and dangers of female sexual desire. In the language of the narrator, only at night could one confront Calcutta's true nature, a place that in the day appeared as a site of ritual. In reality, Gupta reveals, Nimtala was filled with immorality and danger. At Nimtala, high-caste men were cremated, and that was the moment that wives became widows. Gupta explains that in every scene of a funeral pyre of a high-caste Hindu husband, one could foresee the illicit pregnancy of his widow as a result of her sexual deviance. Gupta appears here as the omniscient viewer, one who can perceive a woman who becomes a prostitute at the moment of her transformation at her husband's funeral.

Gupta outlines his intentions to provide an objective account of the city at the outset of his study:

> Rater Kolkata is written only for adults. The picture of the past of Kolkata is available in Hutom. This book is also a *naksha* and the picture of the present in Kolkata is portrayed with honesty. This *naksha* will help cure the cataracts that have distorted people's eyes. Rater Kolkata will make everything clear to people. Perhaps the moralists will not be able to tolerate what I have depicted here, but I have no other option. This type of picture cannot be drawn elegantly or decently. To present the local ambience, I had to use crude language and uncover the picture of hell and sometimes I could not avoid erotic language. My only consolation is that Rater Kolkata is sacred like a Bible when it is compared to modern plays at the theater. If the reader looks carefully, he will see that I have named evil as evil . . .
>
> In this book there is no attempt to excite the reader unlawfully by using obscene language. I have seen the scenes in this book with my own eyes. Maybe, if I had depended on hearsay, I could have written more, but instead I have collected this information by wandering the streets and investigating the city like a detective. I have received the help of numerous first-class experts.[34]

Gupta's narrator is like a detective who investigates the truth of the crime. According to the author, he is compelled by the circumstance to narrate titillating details of city life to reveal the hidden truth of society. Gupta places his study in a distinct genre that emerged in the early nineteenth century in Bengal, the *naksha*, descriptive sketches of everyday life. The word derives from the Persian *naqshah*, meaning a map, drawing, sketch, or model, a new genre of prose writing on the city.[35] Yet Gupta's sketches were distinct from the *naksha* and social writings that preceded Rater Kolkata. Unlike the satirical sketches of the nineteenth century meant to provoke amusement in the reader, his work was presented as a true and serious snapshot of society, a work of eyewitness and comprehensive social analysis.

Gupta positioned himself both as an expert and moral authority who uncovered the true degradation of women, a man who had the moral right and objective mind to describe the reality of degraded womanhood. Rater Kolkata maps the sexual geography of different parts of Calcutta. Organized in nine scenes, the exposé moves from the street to Chinatown, from the brick houses of public women to the grounds of crematorium, and from Hindu festival processions to the stages of the theater district. Gupta offers readers an alternative map or palimpsest of the city, which they more likely thought of as a center of commerce or place of religious sites. He sets out to expose the injustice, cruelty, and perversion that he argues is hidden behind the façade of brick buildings, palaces, and Hindu temples and cremation grounds. Dispelling the misconception of Calcutta as the birthplace of civilization and heart of Empire, he proclaims:

> Kolkata! The Second City of the British, the capital city of India, Paris of the East, the meeting place of communities, a treasure for which the Bengalis feel pride, the birthplace of modern civilization, full of palaces! . . . But here, life and death live together like flower and thorn on the same branch.[36]

Like other social analysts, Gupta was contemptuous of all women outside of marriage, and felt that it was the ubiquity of the sexually deviant woman that required investigation and elucidation: "an abundance of women who are disguised as respectable, courageous and strong like the tiger," he writes.[37] However, these creatures were like tigers not because of their courage "but in violence and brutality."[38] These dangerous women would hide among people day and night, "like an unseen plague ready to ambush, in search of another victim."[39] The story of Calcutta at night, then, would reveal the moral or public health risk of female sexual deviance.[40]

After he dramatically depicts the city woman as wild animal, Gupta sketches the depravity of the Nimtala cremation grounds at night. Gupta narrates the scenes of desecration and pollution brought by the women who came to Nimtala. Gupta names these sexually deviant women as the *barbonita*—public women:

> The *barbonita* also come here frequently at night. Only they know why they come here. Do these women, worshippers of the body, like to see the terrible end of the body? How strange it is that this lifestyle committed to the body, this work of *barbonita*, is a specialty possible among Hindus of India. The women enter the cremation grounds intoxicated, staggering and drunk, and with them come notorious lascivious men. Even as they enter the cremation area, they do not stop hateful and obscene utterances about their lust. Swaying to and fro, they watch the dead bodies with no feeling, full of sinful

desire, chatting in lively voices. Their lustful noises fill the air in this place of mourning.

Sometimes, the *barbonita* also bring a dead body of a woman. The body comes, half naked, wearing only one cloth around the hips. The women remain drunk, drinking continuously. They shout the name Krishna in their shrill voices, breaking the silence of the night. The houses that surround the cremation area at Nimtala hear the shouting, and the people are filled with a strange unease. They know that the soul of the unfortunate woman who has died has been freed from the body, the body of an emaciated being, burdened with torture, pain, insults, and horrible diseases. There is no sign of lust left in this cold dead body of the *barbonita*. But her companions think nothing of it. They are not uneasy even when they see the cremation ground and the dead bodies of human beings. They poke fun at their dead companion in obscene language. They joke and make obscene gestures. This is the perverse scene of the cremation grounds.[41]

Gupta's account of Nimtala reveals not only the events at the cremation grounds; more significantly, it expresses his profound disdain for public women and their incivility. He is appalled by the willingness of women to see dead bodies and their indifference to the sanctity of ritual space. The dead body of a *barbonita* brought to the grounds by other women is simply discarded.

Gupta's account is populated with details of neighborhoods—what he calls common scenes in areas of the city, the pulse of dancing people in cars and alleys, and the mood of the landscape. He describes how the songs of women filled the streets of the city. Like folk song collections published at the turn of the twentieth century under the name *Beshya Sangeet, Baiji Sangeet* (Songs of the beshya, songs of the baiji), he claimed to capture the true voices of women through their songs.[42] The public woman was not solely the character of a salacious tale, but the domain of the lay sociologist, detective, criminologist, and the ethnomusicologist.

For Gupta, the world of public women was the refuge of men who fell prey to the indulgences of the city, away from the mundane world of demanding wives and tedious work. Gupta contrasted the nightlife of public women to the wives of the petty clerical workers. Only after these men indulged in bodily pleasures, eating rich mutton and fried food, drinking liquor, and sleeping with women would they stagger home to their wives.[43] No one believed that these were the same men who walked to the offices with heads hanging down in the morning, worn down by the gloomy toil of daily life. Nightlife thus stood in stark contrast to the grind of the new economy in rapidly urbanizing Calcutta, the dark drudgery that defined modern life in the colonial capital.

As Gupta tells the reader, in Calcutta at night, sexually deviant women lined the streets, animating the by-lanes and landmarks of the city. Famous and well-respected men of all religions came seeking their company, the very same men who gave speeches about social purity and morality by daylight. The women sung lewd songs and moved their bodies provocatively without shame or care. He describes the bodies and faces of these women. At this late hour, nobody could guess whether the face of the woman on the street was beautiful or ugly. They wore dramatic makeup and adorned their bodies with large, sparkling jewelry that lay heavy around their necks and provocatively hung on their breasts. Yet their beauty was a façade, for in the light of day, man could only see "the grotesque ugliness" concealed by "the woman adorned."[44] Underneath the artificial jewelry and makeup was nothing but a "decrepit woman, sagging, wrinkled, dying from disease."[45]

Even for those seemingly respectable men who stayed away from the dark alleyways of Calcutta at night, the sexually deviant woman was a constant presence in their lives. Gupta warned that all respectable families lived under the shadow of female sexual deviance, for they dangerously seduced men without appearing as prostitutes:

> In Calcutta, there is no person who does not go to a *barbonita*. The numbers of *barbonita* are unimaginable—even their numbers cannot be guessed seeing the census because there are innumerable *barbonita* who hide themselves behind different professions, so their names are not listed in the census report. For example, we can talk about the maidservants of a middle-class man's house. Many moralists do not go to the theater pretending that our theater halls are disgraced by the touch of women on the stage. But what is the identity of the maidservant in whose touch they spend their days and nights? Most of them are *barbonita*! Many men have sex with maidservants in their own houses. They exist in every locality in Kolkata . . . Indeed, we can say that every neighborhood of this city is pervaded by *barbonita*.[46]

Again we see that working-class women's sexuality was indeterminate, omnipresent, and dangerous, a threat to everyday life. Sexually deviant women in the city were insidious, "unimaginably vast in number." Their danger lay precisely in the concealment of their true identity as *barbonita*. Women entered the domestic space as maidservants, increasingly seen as a necessity for everyday middle-class life. Gupta proclaims that even when elite men declared to abide by higher moral values than the lower classes of men who visited street women, it was a lie. His description of the sexual indiscretions of these respectable men betrays the precarity of women laboring in domestic spaces. But he rhetorically blames women again and again for social degradation. It was the very presence of laboring women in the home, the maidservants, who were in actuality acting as prostitutes, that led inevitably to sexual deviance by men. There was no possibility in his scheme for sexual coercion or sexual violence against women.[47]

In a chapter on the types of *ganika*—the public or promiscuous woman—the reader encounters the now familiar pursuit of taxonomical classification of the many people who were prostitutes. In Gupta's lay sociology, all unmarried women, domestic laborers, widows, singers, dancers, and theater actors were prostitutes who served very different clientele. Meghnad Gupta, like his contemporary Santosh Kumar Mukherji's sociology of the many women who were prostitutes, argued that the type of prostitute could be distinguished by their locale and the style of their dwellings:

> There are classifications among *barbonita* in Calcutta. Those who stand on the road or by the lane are the prostitutes of the lowest class. They usually live in dirty one-story huts in darkness. The servants, the coolies, and lower-class poor people are worshippers of their beauty. The next class of *barbonita* live in two-story *mathkota* (mud-built) houses . . . Usually the mercantile clerical workers, shopkeepers, and lower ranking employees of the powerful go there in search of pleasure. Then there are women who live in one-story brick built houses . . . Their business of selling beauty is usually run with the help of clerks. The class above these *barbonita* is the highest class. There are two groups in this class—those who are fixed (*bandha*) and those who are free (*chuto*) . . . The women of this class are experts in singing and dancing.[48]

The Calcutta of Gupta's *Rater Kolkata* was a terrain made up of women who lived and died in a world fueled by sex, lies, and deceit. Moreover, these public women were susceptible to violent crimes because they used sex to earn an independent income.

Lay sociologies like *Rater Kolkata* claimed to document the reality of society, populated with men who bore witness to urban social life: the doctor, the legal authority, the expert witness of the city, the detective, and the police officer. Gupta's account was only one of numerous sociological studies on social purity written by British missionaries and Bengali social analysts between the

1870s and the 1930s. These studies traveled under the name *The Social Evil in Calcutta*, and became a veritable genre of their own, where the study of the prostitute was the necessary first step in any sociology of the city.[49] These studies include Robert Kerr's *The Social Evil in Calcutta* (1871), the anonymously authored *Social Evil in Calcutta* (1895), and J. N. Ghosh's *The Social Evil in Calcutta and Methods of Treatment* (1923). They feature the familiar taxonomies of the many women who were to be understood as prostitutes, the descriptions of neighborhoods, the accounts of dress and manner and song.

The sensational life and death of women also appears in the account of police officer Satyendranath Mukherjee in his *Murder of Prostitutes for Gain* (1930). In this exposé, Mukherjee explores the criminal underbelly of Calcutta with detailed descriptions of the murders and robberies of public women. His book features some of the first popularly published photographs of bodies as evidence, with photos from murder scenes of women he captions as prostitutes. The images include a nude photograph of a woman's body, offered as evidence of the prevalence of murder in Calcutta. Mukherjee asserts his authority as a detective and criminologist who has authoritatively studied a pervasive informal economy fueled by deception and violence.[50]

The Prostitute Autobiography

As the social analyst observed the reality of the social world through the concept of the prostitute in the exposé, the first-person testimonial of the Indian prostitute also drew circulating sociological ideas of female sexuality. By the 1930s these stories were familiar to a broad audience through popular texts that narrated the social danger of female sexual deviance, sexuality as a social disease, and the science of idealized heterosexual reproduction and domesticity. Among the pulp publications easily found in the footpath bookstalls were popular chapbooks that dramatized the scandal of romantic affairs and illicit life stories of women's fall into prostitution. In one such book we come upon another funeral pyre, another woman's body, and another set of suspicious circumstances in the anonymously authored *She Wasn't Ashamed: Autobiography of an Indian Prostitute* (1941). Throughout the narrative of *She Wasn't Ashamed*, the contemporary reader recognizes the archetypes of the many women who became prostitutes and the predictable narrative of a woman's fall from respectable society. Over the course of the "autobiography," the widow-turned-prostitute becomes the origin for all forms of social danger—from disease to the failure of heterosexual marriage and reproduction.

The book is structured as a three-way conversation between Leela, an Indian prostitute; Mrs. Turner, a British woman with obstetric knowledge; and Dr. Tej Bhan, an Indian doctor. In one tale narrated about the fall of women, Dr. Bhan describes how he rushed to the funeral pyre of a young widowed woman he knew, Sheela, her body ready for cremation. Against all odds, as the doctor evaluated the body, Sheela began to show signs of life.

> O Doctor! Can you come at once? Our girl who died this morning has been dragged down from the funeral pyre, for she betrays signs of returning consciousness. Our girl was the virgin widow of Seth Chuni Lal . . . I never knew she was ill, and I was their family doctor. But she was a widow and an ailing widow even in a wealthy family does not sometimes receive the attention she deserves. To work her late husband's salvation, and expiate her sins of omission and commission, what better fate than that of an early death! To this end they used to burn them at the funeral pyre with their husbands. But this was when the orthodox people had their way. Now it was different.
>
> I hastened to the cremation grounds . . . I pronounced that life was not extinct, and that she might survive.[51]

The doctor saves the young widow, still alive, from burning to death on the pyre. However, as Bhan ruefully notes, once she had been saved, she eventually runs away to become a prostitute, a young woman unable to restrain her sexual desires. *Sati* appears in the doctor's account as a timeless customary practice of social control that led to early death. But, according to Bhan, in modernizing India of the 1940s, widows were able to be saved: "Now it was different." With the end of *sati* in a now reformed society, contemporary society had a problem in the unrestrained sexuality of young widows.

The story of the prostitute's fall and eventual salvation through asceticism was not only recognizable but a subject of fascination as well as a cautionary tale for eager readers. Five editions of *She Wasn't Ashamed* were published in less than four years. Throughout the narrative of this sensational account, women are described in a highly sexualized manner. With a clear intent to titillate the reader, the account describes women as beautiful, with details about their initial innocence, sensual and attractive qualities, and sexual liaisons with men and women. The "autobiography" describes an elaborate world of prostitutes-turned-ascetics who live together after leaving the life of prostitution. The text sets forth an agenda for the recuperation and rescue of girls and women under the auspices of what appears to be the invented organization that publishes the account, the Women's Social Reform League. The "autobiography" produces a familiar logic that linked life stories of prostitutes with a number of social dangers, from widowhood to prostitution, failed pregnancies and abortions, and venereal disease. *She Wasn't Ashamed* also links the life of the prostitute to female homosexual desire. Dr. Bhan again attempts to save the misdirected prostitute from the dangers of that path of life: "Homosexuality . . . is a malady. Natural love is Nature's way to propagate the race, without which this creation of God would cease to exist."[52]

In this section, I analyze the proliferation of a genre of life writings (autobiography and memoir) by so-called prostitutes that emerged at the turn of the twentieth century. I do not treat these texts as narratives of the true interior selves of women; rather, I am interested in the way the autobiography, *atmacharit* (life tale), or *atmakatha* (life story) evolved into a popular form for the study and assessment of social life.[53] The genre of the first-person autobiography emerged as a tool for social analysis, a privileged perspective for revelation and critiques about society. These life testimonials function as a lay sexual sociology, where the woman supposedly speaks of her sexual pursuits and assesses society's hypocrisy through a true account of how she became a prostitute.

By the time *She Wasn't Ashamed* was published in 1941, the life story of the respectable woman turned-prostitute was a popular genre across colonial India.[54] According to these popular accounts, vulnerable young women, in their transition to womanhood, succumbed to their sexual desires. In Bengal these texts were published as early as 1870, in *Kamini Kalanka* (A woman's shame) by Nabinkali Debi.[55] *Kamini Kalanka* is a first-person confessional that describes the life of an upper-caste woman who has a love affair and eventually takes up the life of the prostitute. The text purports to be a memoir-novel. It begins with a declaration of the need for sympathy for fallen women. It traces the rise and fall of Binodini, who turns to the life of the prostitute after following her passions and eloping with a man who later leaves her. Binodini is only able to escape the life of the prostitute once she takes up an ascetic, spiritual life of deprivation and transcendence. *Kamini Kalanka* was critiqued in the press for producing a salacious tale of sexual deviance while claiming to be a true account of a woman's pitiable fall and redemption.

The call for pity for women again frames the story of the fallen woman in *Swarnabai* (1888). Swarnabai falls into prostitution because of her inability to control her sexual desires. She eventually finds salvation with the help of a British missionary woman in the lifestyle of a chaste, ascetic widow deprived of earthly pleasures.[56] The protagonist of Damodara Mukhopadhyay's *Nabina* (New woman, 1910) is a young widow residing in a village outside of Calcutta.

She cannot restrain her sexual desires and ends up in the city as a low-class prostitute. The text offers a direct critique of discourses of the "new woman": women given too much freedom and education were prone to sexual transgression. Nabina, now a low-class prostitute in the city, is finally rescued by a social reformer—the same man to whom she lost her chastity. He teaches her how to find fulfillment in a life of ascetic chastity and deprivation. The reading public had a formulaic answer for why a woman became a prostitute: women, left to their own devices, would fail to restrain their sexual desire. They were to be redeemed only in a lifestyle of absolute deprivation.[57]

Perhaps the most popular "autobiography" to be published in the period was *Shikshita Patitar Atmacharit* (1929). This life story of an educated "fallen woman" lays out a conservative defense of girl-child marriage and vehemently critiques the corruption of educated girls. Published under the pseudonym Manoda Devi, it tells the story of how an educated high-caste woman falls into the life of the prostitute. The *Atmacharit* was tremendously popular upon its publication, with four editions published within five months.[58] There were public debates about its authenticity at the time, with a legal case opened by the public prosecutor, who claimed it was a false autobiography of a fallen woman's life written by a man.[59]

Published at the height of renewed debates about the age of consent for girls, the narrative details the fall of Manoda Devi into the life of a *patita*, fallen woman. The story is as follows: Manoda, who is not married at the time of puberty, leaves the security of the *andarmahal* (inner quarters for women) for school, and succumbs to her "bodily passions."[60] The *Atmacharit* reinforced conservative ideas about the necessity for child marriage to prevent women's sexual promiscuity. She describes her sexual awakening during her independent tutorials with men succinctly: "I grew convinced, if there is desire, chance never lacks."[61] She describes how even the expertise of the doctor was no match for her desire: "With a coquettish smile I said, 'What a doctor!' But you should know that there are diseases which even your stethoscope cannot discover!"[62] Eventually, the "coquettish" Manoda succumbs to her desires, eloping with her married tutor.

A woman emboldened by her freedom from domesticity, Manoda travels across India with her lover. But this does not awaken her to the pleasures of freedom; rather, it shows Manoda the violence of Indian society: "Those who only roam in the realm of vision can acquire little knowledge about the hard realities of life. The world that I have seen so long in the pages of novels and the books I had read, melted away before me as soon as I came in direct touch with it."⁶³ She travels to Delhi, Bombay, and Srinagar but continues to feel uneasy. It is only when she sees the "place of the Puranas" that she finds the meaning of true womanhood in the *sati* who sacrifices herself on the funeral pyre:

> I know that if India had not the ideal of a Sati like Padmini, then humanity would have lost one of its guiding stars. In our Purans, we have heard of a Sati entering the fire in the Yagna of Daksha, here we see a Sati entering the fire with all the halo of sacrifice round her divine frame. The flickering flames did not touch the body of Padmini, it only turned to ashes the heads of the unholy.⁶⁴

The woman who throws herself into the burning pyre performs the most ideal deed of a woman. On the other hand, the liberated woman was only sinful at her death, burned to ashes. Within months of their marriage, Manoda's lover abandons her. Pregnant, she finds refuge back in Calcutta and suffers a stillbirth. As in popular accounts of abortion and infanticide among sexually deviant women, Manoda fails to produce healthy offspring. She loses social status and becomes a prostitute. While this happens, she offers extensive commentary and analysis of the failure of women's emancipation. According to Manoda, women's education and liberation were failed social projects; they proved that Indian society did not protect women in the safe transfer of their sexuality in sanctimonious marriage. Eventually, she ends up in an ashram for women ascetics but continues to harbor unrestrained sexual desires: "The seed of passion germinated within me."⁶⁵ Her account of her sexuality, the reason woman becomes the prostitute, reveals the dangers of society itself: "Whatever is hidden and forbidden, whatever is dark and polluted drag humanity into thousand maladventures."⁶⁶

Indeed, the "autobiography" takes on explicitly political themes and offers the allegedly true view from an insider perspective—the Child Marriage Restraint Act of 1929 and the participation of fallen women in anti-colonial politics.⁶⁷ In her narrative Manoda explicitly condemns the Sarda Act—which raised the age of marriage for girls to fourteen years of age—and expresses her outrage as social reformers claimed to protect women yet left young girls outside of marriage at the height of puberty.⁶⁸ Ultimately, Manoda offers the names of multiple "hypocritical" men, and her confessional reads more like a critique of the male leaders of contemporary political movements in Bengal in the 1920s. The supposed autobiographical perspective of the fallen woman exposed the hypocrisy of respectable men: they condemned the immorality of women yet frequently visited them; moreover, they failed to safeguard the sexuality of women by neglecting their wives and daughters.

In 1932, three years after Devi's controversial account was published, another first-person testimonial of a woman's sexual transgressions and social exclusion appeared in Calcutta under the title *Nurseyr Atmakatha* (Life story of a nurse). This account of a nurse builds a sustained critique of women leaving domestic space and entering the professional workforce. Narrated by the pseudonymous Parimalbala Dasi, it tells the story of a woman at the turn of the twentieth century who loses her chastity in her village. She then becomes a nurse in Calcutta and uses the title of nurse as a cover for her real work as a prostitute. The text describes the "destiny" of Parimalbala's life and her seemingly inevitable fall into disrepute. Under the claim of writing a narrative about a nurse, the memoir describes the life of Parimalbala, who suffers from the cruelty of social exclusion. The paradox, according to her, was that her sexual desires prevented her from achieving an ascetic's lifestyle.

Like Manoda Devi, the narrator experiences changes in her body and acutely senses her sexual desires in her adolescence. Despite these bodily changes, Parimalbala explains that her mind was still like a child's and that she was unable to comprehend the way men would respond to her physical development. A man, Haran, who worked in the house would linger after completing his tasks. She describes the depth of her fear late in the evening one day when she was washing utensils in the pond. Suddenly a group of men including Haran approached her from behind, covered her mouth, and muffled her screams. The story implies she was carried off, raped by multiple men for six days, and left at her father's house afterward. The text describes the event in indirect language: "They destroyed my virginity. Wherever my destiny was taking me, I was forced to go, helpless."[69]

After her abduction and rape, Parimalbala flees to her maternal uncle's home in Calcutta, where she is not welcomed. Alone, she decides to take up the profession of a nurse. Though the story from here on is ostensibly about her job, we are told little detail about her nurse training or her experiences as an independent wage earner. Instead, the reader encounters continuous descriptions of the sexual interactions Parimalbala has with men, including doctors and patients.

Parimalbala goes on to describe how eventually a man proposes marriage to her, but soon the marriage falls apart when she realizes she is in a polygamous marriage and is nothing but a maid. Following her abusive marriage, she becomes a high-class mistress, moving into a house of mistresses who live under the guise of reputable professions. Men visit these houses without fear of rumor. Following the convention of the "autobiography" of the fallen woman, she exclaims that the men who visited prostitutes lived under a mask of respectability:

> Men who came to us say that they hate to go to houses of prostitutes (*khankirbari*). But they come to us for their bodily satisfaction. They exist only in the darkness and commit all kinds of sin. But they are afraid of infamy. They are masked hypocrites. Underneath the veneer of respectability, they think only of us. These men purport to be conservative, to "protect society," yet they are the primary destroyers of society.[70]

Like Manoda's account, the confessional of the prostitute exposes the hypocrisy of men in society. According to Parimalbala, the woman left with nothing is like a *sati* immolated in the fire. In death, she only has the evil of sexual deviance: "She also jumps into the blazing fire just like an insect, but when she comes out of the fire, she is not ash but becomes something evil."[71] Again, like Manoda's account, *sati* appears in Parimalbala's account as the ideal action of a pure woman. On the other hand, the burning of the prostitute on the funeral pyre is the moment of transformation into social evil.

In a brief coda seven years later, we meet Parimalbala as an older woman who is attempting to take up the life of an ascetic. She was not to be redeemed, for she had "become so greedy" for sexual satisfaction and money. She ends her narrative with the tragedy that defined her life. "Today I cannot say to my son, 'all that you have heard is wrong, a lie. Your mother is pure and sacred.'"[72]

The prostitute "autobiography" thus functioned to prescribe the most conservative visions of society. It defined the prostitute as a perpetual threat to all womanhood and demonstrated how the empirical project of elucidating her fall was foundational to the study of society. The imagery of the woman burned on the funeral pyre reinforced the purity of the chaste wife, in contrast to the evil of the fallen woman. The prostitute's first-person account could be used to condemn everything from women's education, freedom from marriage, political leaders and social movements, to new circulating notions of sexual perversion—including homosexuality. She was the premier subject of social critique, critical to any project that revealed the reality of social life.

From the inception of the sciences of society in the nineteenth century, we have learned how she, the woman named prostitute, was to be endlessly studied, described, and classified. What was to be done when a woman had become a prostitute? By the first decades of the twentieth century she was the project of a new wave of social critique, recuperated by both elite men and women: the prostitute was to be exposed, rescued, and saved from the fallen lifestyle—with or without her consent. The life story of the fallen woman would always end in the same way: the woman could only be redeemed as an ascetic, stripped of desire or free will, for she existed in the service of an imagined future, one where she was entirely disappeared from view.

The Omnipresence of the Prostitute

In these popular texts, social analysts asked: Why exactly do women become prostitutes? As we have seen, this was a question posed across many fields of knowledge, with seemingly endless answers. Attempts to answer it even spurred new genres of articulation, but it never quite received a sufficient answer. Across lay sociologies and popular life stories, we encounter study after study that accounts for why women became prostitutes. Many reasons are given: because of deprivation, high-caste widowhood and other perversions of social custom, the immorality of the city at night, unmonitored puberty, the dangers of women's liberation, girls' education, the movement of women into the public sphere for employment and politics. These reasons could be linked to the most dangerous factor of all: the innate, and seemingly inevitable, failure of women to restrain their sexual desire when they encountered the "face of Satan."[73] The question led to prescriptive visions for healthy social futures. In the language of the "autobiography" of Manoda Devi, the revelation of the prostitute was the only way "to protect oneself from vices."[74] If the problem of prostitution was caused by the transgressive potential of female sexual desire itself, what could or should be done to solve it? What was the future for a society if the unmonitored woman no longer remained atop the funeral pyre, set ablaze in a test of her chastity?

One is left with countless dead women who appear again and again in the pages of texts across these fields of knowledge. As we have seen in the autobiographies, the potent image of *sati* as female chastity and sacrifice was indispensable over a century after the 1829 law against it was passed by the colonial state. *Sati* was the original site of the colonial imagination of Indian social life, and continued to be a contentious idea through the twentieth century. But in the new sciences of society the sexually deviant woman stood in contrast to the chaste *sati*, never immolated in a rite of chastity and sanctity. Her remains are instead desacralized through the lens of modern social science. They appear again and again in the colonial survey, the forensic textbook, and the popular chapbook sold on the footpath. We bear witness to the body of the Kulin widow swiftly taken away from the funeral pyre to be autopsied, the woman's body left without care by other women at the Nimtala cremation grounds, and the young woman who comes alive, denied the righteous cremation of the true virgin widow. In the scene of her death, the woman could be fixed in place as an exemplary object, disassembled and museumized, offered as scientific proof, written into view, and held up as scientific evidence of the dangers of woman's sexual deviance.

This chapter has explored the domain of popular texts, for it is in the expanding world of pulp publication that we see the widespread influence of this episteme that utilized deviant female sexuality to comprehend modern society. She was essential to defining the social as a bounded object of study—not only for doctors, social scientists, or colonial administrators but also for popular writers who claimed the position of the social analyst and created authoritative visions of the social future. Indeed, the specter of deviant female sexuality was everywhere, a potential danger, but also a sensational delight for a reading public. These texts sought to account for how women became prostitutes. The answer, for the lay social analysts, was that every woman had the potential to become sexually deviant, and it was perpetual surveillance in the institution of heterosexual monogamous marriage that would save women from their otherwise inevitable fall.

Afterword

THIS BOOK has tracked the extraordinary reach of an episteme that placed female sexual deviance, often named as the prostitute, at the heart of the modern sciences of society in India. A wide range of authorities argued that deviant womanhood was a problem that could not be easily solved. Rather, it was to be empirically studied, elucidated, described ad infinitum, scientifically consecrated, legally encoded, and constrained—all for the future of Indian society. In the process, women were described, put on trial, scrutinized in public view, forcibly indentured, imprisoned, examined against their will, and disassembled—on the autopsy table, in parts in the pathological specimen jar, and through photographs and accounts of the burning funeral pyre and postcards of the dancing girl.

This was a system of modern social thought premised on the absolute exhaustive study of the subject of deviant female sexuality, across genres, archives, and forms of authority. This project desperately and obsessively sought to detail and equate all forms of female sexual deviance to produce the prostitute as social *fact*. Over the course of this book, I have brought diverse archives together through a unified analytical framework. European, American, and Bengali social analysts searched ancient and medieval texts for sexual strictures for womanhood, constituting new models for a modern, progressive society based in premodern text. They created all-encompassing accounts of human history that made the sexually deviant woman the primary object of comparison in the evolutionary study of civilizations. Social scientific experts imagined, categorized, mapped, translated, reiterated, equated, diagrammed, charted, and condemned women to the status of prostitute. Popular writers claimed to tell all the secrets of society through the deviant woman, while the confessional "autobiographical" accounts of the prostitute claimed to tell the inner life of the fallen woman.

These archives are a testament to the profound empiricist desire that drove this epistemological project. Book after book comprehensively detailed female sexual deviance over thousands of pages of descriptions, taxonomies, graphs, charts, and diagrams. As an experience of archival encounter, this exhaustive knowledge economy is itself exhausting. One feels depleted from page after page of violent renderings of women as abject, stigmatized, primitive, and dangerously untethered, outside the time of modern society. As I have confronted these archives, I have deployed a critical hermeneutic to bring together seemingly disparate descriptive taxonomies and civilizational theories of primitive female sexuality across archives and bear witness to the heavily circulated images of bodies objectified in case studies and by the camera. These sciences of society were not solely projects of the colonial state but a key resource for theorizing by colonized men—men who asserted a claim to progressive politics by perpetuating the idea that Indian society was only to be liberated through the control and erasure of women's sexuality.

If this book is an account of the contempt for the transgressive woman that defined the modern sciences of Indian society, I want to end by engaging a very different project that sought to make women public, one that might be initially seen as a liberatory or utopic vision. I began this book with two paradigmatic imaginations of female sexual deviance in colonial India: Rudyard Kipling's 1888 short story about the exemplary timelessness of womanhood in what he described as the most ancient profession, and Saratchandra Chattapadhyay's use of pity in the consolidation of men's power in his hybrid essay on a woman's worth. I started with these two prominent men because these claims of omniscience—in the enduring idea of the prostitute as a self-evident member of the world's oldest profession and the paradigmatic object of social study—exemplified a project of social scientific discovery pursued by British colonial and Indian men.

To end, I turn to a work by a now well-known woman writer from Calcutta, Begum Rokeya Sakhawat Hossain, an early feminist thinker in India. Her short story "Sultana's Dream" was published in 1905, in the same historical moment as the emergence of these new fields of modern social thought. Today "Sultana's Dream" is celebrated for its radical world-making of a society where women rule the outside world and seclude men in the home.[1] Scholars have proclaimed Hossain's short story to be the first instance of feminist science fiction and a utopian vision of one of the first Muslim feminists. I am interested in Hossain's account not for its novelty as an early example of feminist science fiction or as a work written by a Muslim woman writer, but for the form of the story. Hossain's dream is a speculative project that imagines a radically different ideal future for Indian society.

Hossain's short story is narrated by a woman, Sultana, who, while thinking about the "condition of Indian womanhood," lapses into a dream-like state and emerges with a clear vision of a "distinctly" alternative world she calls "Ladyland."[2] Ladyland is a place where women reign supreme in public, innovating technologies and fostering peaceful statecraft, while men are socially secluded in the home. The women of Ladyland are never in excess because men—the sole source of their vulnerability and social failure—have been sequestered inside the domestic sphere. Women in Hossain's story are reasoned, rational, and moral. The story ends when Sultana suddenly wakes up from the dream, back inside the home.

So why end this book, a project about sexuality in the formalization of the sciences of society, with a curious fictional story about a dreamland ruled by women? What, if anything, do dreams have to do with modern social scientific study? Perhaps surprisingly, "Sultana's Dream" is not the first dreamscape concerned with the condition of Indian womanhood in this book. The reader may recall the work of S. C. Mookerjee of the Indian Rationalistic Society in his book *The Decline and Fall of the Hindus* (1919), his study on the evolution of modern Indian society based in the ideals of Aryan society. At the end of his evolutionary study, Mookerjee falls asleep. He narrates that Mother India comes to him in a dream.[3] He has a vision that the most idealized mother of the Indian nation commands him to restore Hindu society to its former glory—as a society that permanently eliminates the primitive, outcast sexually deviant woman through a new brotherhood of Indian men. A literal dream provides a vision and mandate for Mookerjee's speculative theory about a modern Indian society premised on patriarchal monogamy.

These two dreams, Hossain's and Mookerjee's, are contrasting visions of an idealized Indian society. In Hossain, what is striking is the clear absence of any discussion of women's sexuality, except obliquely. In Mookerjee, there is an insistence on the dangerous evolutionary excesses of women's sexuality to be disappeared in new social strictures. In Hossain, it is male exclusion from the public sphere which serves to protect the women from such "wild animals in the marketplace," while women are presented as naturally chaste without sexual desire.[4] In Mookerjee, the project of men's social surveillance of women in the public sphere is necessary in order for Hindu society to evolve. Hossain's Ladyland reverses the structure of Mookerjee's social seclusion of women and male political power to create a public where women's minds flourish and grow.

Yet here the two dreams coincide, for both Hossain and Mookerjee share the logic that women, *good* women, had no ability to control the conditions of their own sexuality, except in a homosocial world. The ideal societies of Mookerjee and Hossain, while starkly different from one another, had no place for public expressions of women's sexuality. What unites these two visions of society is that they are both speculative projects of social engineering based in hierarchies of naturalized sexual difference. What distinguishes them is that the whimsical story of Hossain is relegated to the status of fantasy and science fiction, while projects like Mookerjee's evolutionary theory would go on to shape the study of modern Indian society.

What happens to projects like Mookerjee's rationalist evolutionary theory of society when we take speculation to be the primary lens through which to understand these systems of social scientific thought? Would we have granted the status of objectivity and truth to these fields of knowledge? We have assumed the authority of these forms of knowledge because they claim to capture the whole of reality. We have endowed the forensic case study, the survey, and the sociological taxonomy with power because of the male author's assertion of his degrees, memberships, and affiliations and the way in which the page is organized—the *form* of the text—with its detailed narratives, extensive footnotes, citations, headings and subheadings, and the systematic visual illustrations of data in charts and graphs.

What if the thousands of pages of social scientific description we have encountered in this book could not claim the mantle of objectivity from their form alone? When placed alongside the brief story of "Sultana's Dream," the social world objectified by the diverse social analysts in this book reveals itself to be another type of speculative fiction, of men dreaming about the future of society. Their claims to scientific truth and their proclamations of a totalizing system of knowledge read more like a distorted social imaginary than a social science.[5] These men and their speculative sciences of society stand in stark contrast to Hossain's speculation of a peaceful public womanhood in her Ladyland. That is because, unlike Hossain, these men had the authority to initiate and institutionalize their vision, and soon thrived upon these processes of women's social exclusion, disembodiment, and erasure. Juxtaposed with Hossain's vision, the pernicious nature and the masquerade, the absurd performance of these sciences of society are fully revealed.

The documents of these men, their dreams, and their empirical accounts of the past and visions for ideal society are a project of futurity. The veneer of fact and authority hides disjointed conjectures and biased suppositions. Their claims to scientific objectivity hide speculation as the force that sustains this knowledge economy. Speculation governs the circular forms of reasoning where social analysts always turn to deviant female sexuality as explanation, construct the copious footnotes that fill more pages than the prose of the study itself, elaborate on the questionnaires that summarize Indian society through a transferable ideology of women's sexual deviance, and defer to ancient texts as indisputable doctrine about the past and present of Indian society. These textual practices, citational behaviors, and social prescriptions appear to be not unlike a system of rites with its own totems and taboos, a kind of worship at the altar of scientific objectivity. The civilizational logic that animates these archives, often treated as the remnant of a distant and more racially biased colonial past, appears instead as the quiet foundations of the theories that still hold sway in present-day studies of society. The pervasive influence of the form of reasoning that uses womanhood to map the failures of modern society appears everywhere.

And ultimately, no longer enchanted with the future promised to us by the sciences of society, we realize that the *fact* of deviant female sexuality is a grievous mistake.

ACKNOWLEDGMENTS

MY MOTHER, Dr. Rupa Chattopadhyay Mitra, is a stunning example of womanhood. She completed her PhD in statistics while raising my brother and me as a single mother and working full-time. She moved with children from Calcutta, India, to Shreveport, Louisiana, and then Fargo, North Dakota. In Fargo, she was the most committed professor in a special program dedicated to fostering first-generation, working-class, and older-than-average college students. Eventually she taught a five-five course load at a community college in Baltimore, Maryland. She consistently faced financial constraints, and often worked to the point of complete exhaustion while somehow always providing us with comfort and love. Like so many immigrants, she often held more than one job to support us and her family at home. She is the most dedicated teacher and scholar I know, as well as an accomplished artist, practicing the neglected arts of crochet and fine embroidery. She built a life against all odds in the face of social exclusion and judgment. That I now work on the intellectual history of women's social transgression is no accident. It will require many more books to document the incredible example of my mother and the power of womanhood that her life reveals. This book is a first step in bearing witness to how women's social exclusion has shaped how we understand and envision the present and future progress of our societies. It is a necessary first step in writing the accounts of people like my mother, who imagined differently, who persevered through intensely difficult circumstances because she desired a different life for herself and her children. I thank her for guiding me throughout my life.

Archivists and librarians have made this work possible in every way. My thanks most especially to Bidisha Chakraborty in the West Bengal State Archives, Bhawani Dutta Lane; Abhijit Bhattacharya at the Center for Studies in Social Sciences in Kolkata; the librarians at National Library, Kolkata; and numerous others who helped me survey and acquire materials at libraries, including Uttarpara Jaikrishna Library, Chaitanya Library, Bangiya Sahitya Parishad, Jadavpur University, the Asiatic Society, the British Library, the New York

Public Libraries, Widener Library at Harvard University, University of Pennsylvania Library, and Columbia University Libraries.

I had the privilege of learning from scholars committed to feminist scholarship in my advisors and mentors. I thank my PhD advisors, Gyanendra Pandey and Ruby Lal. They have taught me about the challenge and value of history writing. I deeply admire their commitment to rigorous scholarship and I am forever thankful to them for their guidance and incisive feedback. Clifton Crais and Pamela Scully have been thoughtful interlocutors and dedicated mentors. Lynne Huffer is a model scholar and wonderful mentor and teacher. I loved and respected the late Ivan Karp and continue to feel the privilege of friendship and intellectual engagement from the amazing Cory Kratz. During my PhD research, I had the opportunity to learn from the exceptional historian Samita Sen, my advisor during the Fulbright-Nehru fellowship, whose groundbreaking historical work on women workers has greatly influenced this project.

At Harvard University, I thank my colleagues who have created a warm and inviting space for intellectual engagement. Thank you to wonderful colleagues in Studies of Women, Gender, and Sexuality, including Robin Bernstein, Sarah Richardson, Robert Reid-Pharr, Françoise Lionnet, Afsaneh Najmabadi, Alice Jardine, Linda Schlossberg, Caroline Light, Michael Bronski, Mark Jordan, Amy Parker, Christianna Morgan, Ana Inoa, and members of the WGS Standing Committee. Thank you to Parimal Patil, Ahmed Ragab, and Afsaneh Najmabadi for exceptionally useful feedback on my manuscript. Ahmed Ragab has been endlessly generous to me as a mentor, collaborator, and colleague. Thank you to Parimal Patil for his dedicated mentorship and careful feedback on the manuscript. I have always aspired to reflect the masterful historiographic interventions of Afsaneh Najmabadi from afar, and have the benefit now to learn from her as my colleague. Thank you to Jane Kamensky for her intellectual generosity. Thank you also to Sunil Amrith, Jacqueline Bhabha, Karen Thornber, Ajantha Subramanian, and Vince Brown. Thank you to Dean Claudine Gay, Dean Lawrence Bobo, and Chris Kruegler for support for a manuscript workshop and for the production of the book. My sincere thanks to the Radcliffe Institute, especially Dean Lizabeth Cohen, Dean Tomiko Brown-Nagin, and the wonderful people at Radcliffe, including Meredith Quinn, for their support of me and this project.

Thank you to the community of friendship that surrounds me in Cambridge, including Genevieve Clutario, Lorgia García Peña, Medhin Paolos, Ju Yon Kim, and Lauren Kaminsky. Special thanks to Annabel Kim and Hannah Frydman, who have provided friendship, tea, and wonderful feedback on parts of the book. Thanks to wonderful friends in Katrina Forrester, Brandon Terry, George Paul

Meiu, Todne Thomas, Sai Balakrishnan, and Kirsten Weld. Thank you to friends and colleagues in the area, including Banu Subramaniam, Dwai Banerjee, Kareem Khubchandani, Sarah Pinto, Jyoti Puri, Carla Freeman, and Vivek Bald. I love the energy and commitment of scholars in the Black, Brown, and Queer reading group. My deepest thanks for the feedback and intellectual energy of friends and comrades in this community, including Eli Nelson, Gili Vidan, Shireen Hamza, Juanis Berrera, and so many others.

My deep gratitude and thanks to many mentors. Heather Love is an extraordinary mentor, a brilliant scholar, and a model of ethical scholarship. She has supported me every single step of this process, including providing me with invaluable and sensitive feedback that has transformed this manuscript. Thank you to Anjali Arondekar, who is the most fierce, intelligent, and laughter-filled critic there is. Her feedback to the manuscript has been essential for the revision of this book, and I am grateful for her commitment to fostering an unavowedly feminist sexuality studies for South Asia. My deep gratitude to Douglas E. Haynes for his amazing support throughout my time as a junior faculty member and for his detailed feedback on the manuscript. Thanks to Banu Subramaniam for fostering beautiful writing and giving me useful feedback on several chapters. My gratitude to Omnia El Shakry for her amazing intellectual guidance. Indrani Chatterjee has mentored me from my first visit to the British Library as a PhD student until today. I aspire to her archival rigor, kindness, and commitment to difficult historical questions. I am deeply grateful to Anupama Rao for her unwavering support of me and insightful feedback as I revised this project. Ashwini Tambe is amazing mentor, scholar, and editor, and I am lucky to have benefited from her mentorship and editorial guidance. Thanks to Sharon Marcus, a wonderful and incisive thinker who read the full manuscript and gave masterful comments. Ishita Pande has provided thoughtful feedback to my work in progress for several years and I look forward to thinking with her in the future. K. Sivaramakrishnan has always been generous with me with his time and ideas, and I thank him for giving me access and support as a PhD student and for his support every step beyond. Thank you to Asif Siddiqi, who has been a strong supporter of my work and a kind and thoughtful friend.

Thanks to many people who took time to think with me about this project at different stages, including Gayle Rubin, Mitra Sharafi, Ajay Skaria, Rachel Sturman, Projit Mukharji, Geraldine Forbes, Mytheli Sreenivas, Ramnarayan Rawat, Premesh Lalu, Gautam Bhadra, Sudipta Kaviraj, Ania Loomba, Suvir Kaul, Stefan Helmreich, Katherine Turk, Rochona Majumdar, Anand Yang, Geeta Patel, and Rachel Berger. Inderpal Grewal has generously mentored me at many steps in my career. Charu Gupta's intellectual curiosity and generosity are infectious, and I thank Charu for her critical engagement and generous warmth in Delhi. Thanks to Joan Wallach Scott, who generously met and spoke with me at length after years of fangirling her from afar. Thank you to professor Andrea Friedman, and to my teacher and mentor, the late Professor Leslie Brown. I have learned from the remarkable scholarship of many women, including Tanika Sarkar, Mrinalini Sinha, and Prathama Banerjee. Prathama Banerjee generously sent me incisive and thoughtful feedback on my work in progress. Her work asks critical questions that continue shape my research. In the first year of my PhD, Mrinalini Sinha sent me a handwritten note thanking me for a question that I had asked in a seminar. I thank her for her scholarship, and for giving me the courage to ask another question.

Thanks to institutions who funded and supported my research. Thank you to Harvard University Division of Social Science, the Radcliffe Institute, the Weatherhead Center for International Affairs, the Penn Humanities Forum (now Wolf Center for Humanities), the Consortium for Faculty Diversity Fellowship at Bowdoin College, the Fulbright-Nehru Fellowship to India, the American Institute of Indian Studies, and the Emory Laney Graduate School. Thank you to colleagues who have invited me for talks and provided extraordinary feedback on this project. Thanks to Sheila Jasanoff and the STS Circle at Harvard University; Ahmed Ragab, Eli Nelson, and the Science, Religion, and Culture Seminar at Harvard Divinity School; Homi Bhabha and the Mahindra Humanities Center; Todd Shepard and the Department of History at Johns Hopkins University; Premesh Lalu and the wonderful students and faculty at the University at the Western Cape; Karen Brown and Ajay Skaria at the University of Minnesota; Toronto Sexual Diversity Studies; Yale University; and the American Institute of Indian Studies Dissertation to Book workshop.

Many thanks to the wonderful people who sustained me in archives and in writing. Thanks to Navyug Gill, Ajitkumar Chittambalam, Sunandan KN, Debjani Bhattacharyya, Rohit De, Rohan Deb Roy, Erica Wald, Misha Chowdhury, Tarfia Faizullah, Margaret Boyle, Eric Beverley, Wanda Rivera-Rivera, Diala Shamas, Poulomi Saha, Tariq Omar Ali, Aniruddha Bose, Erica Wald, Krupa Shandilya, Uditi Sen, Onni Gust, Bindu Menon, Shinjini Das, Samaa Abdurraqib, Letitia Campbell, Zeb Tortirici, Anooradha Siddiqi, Angela Willey, Sandipto Dasgupta, Yuko Miki, Anand Venkatkrishnan, Dennis Yi Tenen, Manan Ahmed, Abeer Hoque, Mrinal Satish, Aparna Chandra, Ndidiamaka Oteh, Mana Kia, Andrew Liu, Robert Corber, Mara Mills, Madhavi Menon, Juned Shaikh, Amy Bhatt, Shailaja Paik, Asiya Alam, Krupa Shandilya, Greta

LaFleur, Daisy Rockwell, Anubhuti Maurya, Sarover Zaidi, Bodhisattva Kar, Hasan Siddiqui, Glenn Lopez, Satyaprasad Chattopadhyay, and Basundhara Chattopadhyay. I mourn the loss of my friend Quratulain Ali Khan, who shared a commitment to documenting women and the complexity of their lives. Thank you to the most amazing teacher, David Volk. My love to my extended family, Tamika Samuel and Jessica Schmidt. Kadji Amin is the best interlocutor and most wonderful friend. Thanks to my dear friend Nishaant Choksi, who read many parts of this project and gave me invaluable feedback. Thanks to Jeremy Kaplan-Lyman for his unending support of this project.

Thank you to generous editors at Princeton University Press, including Eric Crahan, Thalia Leaf, as well as the production editorial work of Sara Lerner. Thanks to Al Bertrand. They have helped me refine the ideas in this book and have seamlessly ushered the book through the publication process. Thanks to Ratik Asokan and Jessica Taylor for their editorial feedback, Moumita Som for her help during research trips with me to libraries across Bengal, and Sarah C. Smith and Judy Loeven for proofreading. Parts of chapters 4 and 5 have appeared in an earlier form in *Locating the Medical in South Asia* (Oxford University Press, 2018) and the journal *History and Technology*. I thank the editors and anonymous readers, especially Asif Siddiqi, Martin Collins, Guy Attewell, and Rohan Deb Roy.

My deepest thanks to Partha Chatterjee, whose scholarship has been transformative for my own. I thank Partha-da also for his generous friendship full of evergreen hits. Manan Ahmed is the most ethical and brilliant scholar I know. He has, as promised, read every single line of this book, often three or four times, with a vision and clarity of thought that has transformed my understanding of intellectual work. Thanks to the best cowriting group in the world, and my colleagues in XPmethod, Dennis Yi Tenen and Manan Ahmed. This book completes the first-book trilogy of our group.

My deepest love and thanks to my family, including the late Gopa Ray, who was the most effervescent woman, and my late grandmother, Manimala Chatterjee, who passed down her love of stories to me. Thanks to my uncle Avijit Chattopadhyay, who loves reading more than anyone I know. Thanks to my brother Rajarshi and my sister-in-law Tara, my uncle Biswajit Ray, Bipasha and Ron, Sourja and Trupti, Sanchari, and everyone in my family, especially my beautiful nieces and nephews. Jessica Schmidt is my best friend, sister, mentor, and Fargo soulmate. She is all things anyone would ever want in another human.

And again, thanks to my mother, Rupa Chattopadhyay Mitra. There are not enough words to say how much I love and thank her. I am happy and relieved that she will hold this book in her hands.

NOTES

Introduction: Excess, a History

1. See for example, A Member of the Royal Asiatic Society, *Sex Life in India* (1909); Mukherji, *Indian Sex Life and Prostitution* (1934); Meyer, *Sexual Life in Ancient India* (1929); Chakladar, *Social Life in Ancient India* (1929); Chakraberty, *Sex Life in Ancient India* (1963); Banerji, *Crime and Sex in Ancient India* (1980).

2. Building on Michel Foucault, in what he describes as a "grid of intelligibility of the social order," in his *The History of Sexuality*, vol. 1, 93.

3. "On the City Wall" in Kipling, *In Black and White*, 121–60.

4. On the fixity and lack of agency of India in the colonial imagination, see Inden, *Imagining India*, 1–6.

5. Kipling, "On the City Wall," 121.

6. Ibid., 127. Emphasis in original.

7. Ibid., 141.

8. I use the phrase "derivative discourse" from the title and introduction of Partha Chatterjee's foundational work on Indian nationalism, *Nationalist Thought and the Colonial World*, 1–36.

9. This project pursues a systematic evaluation of these terms and the widespread reasoning that allows for the ubiquity of the prostitute across modern social thought. For a critical evaluation of colonial legal practices of taxonomical naming, see Levine, "Orientalist Sociology and the Creation of Colonial Sexualities," 5–21; Wald, "From Begums and Bibis to Abandoned Females and Idle Women," 5–25. For a reading that refutes a self-evident equation of the term *devadasi* with prostitute in the context of overlapping British and Portuguese India, see Arondekar, "In the Absence of Reliable Ghosts," 100. Lucinda Ramberg reframes *devadasi* reforms in Karnataka through Mary John and Janaki Nair's term "sexual economies" to encompass caste stricture, sexual practice, and *devadasi* social relationships. See Ramberg, *Given to the Goddess*, 18–28.

10. The "woman for hire" appears throughout Corbin, *Women for Hire*; Walkowitz, *Prostitution in Victorian Society*, 2. Prostitution for historian Keely Stauter-Halsted is agentive, an "economic 'weapon of the weak.'" See Stauter-Halsted, *The Devil's Chain*, 5.

11. There are a wide range of studies on the prostitute as "sex worker" and a rich historiography on the legal regulation of commercial sex in the modern world. Studies on prostitution situated in Bengal include Indrani Chatterjee's foundational study, "Refracted Reality," 28–31; Ratnabali Chatterjee's important work on prostitution, "Prostitution in Nineteenth Century Bengal," 159–72, and "The Queens' Daughters"; Banerjee, *Under the Raj*; Chakraborty, *Sarkari Nothite*

Unish Shatoke Banglar Nari. On the regulation of prostitution in other parts of India, see Ballhatchet, *Race, Sex, and Class under the Raj*; Oldenburg, "Lifestyle as Resistance," 259–87; Philippa Levine's wide-reaching comparative colonial study across the British Empire, *Prostitution, Race, and Politics*; Ashwini Tambe's careful study of the productive nature of law in *Codes of Misconduct*; Legg, *Prostitution and the Ends of Empire*. In the comparative historiography of prostitution across the modern world, I am influenced by Luise White's attention to multilingual terminology and the many forms of domestic and affective labor related to sex work in her magisterial *Comforts of Home*. Foundational studies that locate the prostitute as sex worker and in the domain of the regulation of commercial sex in other comparative contexts include Stansell, *City of Women*; Guy, *Sex and Danger in Buenos Aires*; Gilfoyle, *City of Eros*; Bernstein, *Sonia's Daughters*; Hershatter, *Dangerous Pleasures*. Saheed Aderinto demonstrates how the regulation of prostitution was part of a larger domain of sexual politics in Nigeria in *When Sex Threatened the State*; on overlaps between the colonial regulation of prostitution and the emerging discourse of trafficking in the interwar Middle East, see Kozma, *Global Women, Colonial Ports*.

12. I am deeply influenced by Hortense Spillers and her thinking in a comparative context about the historical social marking that distinguishes Black womanhood, who opens her foundational essay with "Let's face it. I am a marked woman." See Spillers, "Mama's Baby, Papa's Maybe," 65–81.

13. I am thinking with David Halperin's formulation about homosexuality's "definitional incoherence" in response to Eve Kosofsky Sedgwick's critique of historical narratives of the "invention" of the homosexual in *Epistemology of the Closet*. This is what Halperin describes as the "unprecedented combination of . . . previously uncorrelated conceptual entities" in *How to Do the History of Homosexuality*, 12, 42.

14. On genealogy as a method, see Foucault, "Nietzsche, Genealogy, History," in *Language, Counter-Memory, Practice*, 139–64.

15. I build on the critical proposition of an anti-foundational genealogy of concepts in Foucault's essay "Nietzsche, Genealogy, History" and his study of the rise of the human sciences of philology, economics, and the biological sciences in *The Order of Things*. In my use of concept history, I build on Reinhart Koselleck's exegesis on the relationship of *Begriffsgeschichte* with the sociohistorical life of concepts. Concept history is first and foremost a methodological approach to source criticism. As Koselleck describes, "A concept must remain ambiguous in order to be a concept. The concept is connected to a word, but is at the same time more than a word: a word becomes a concept only when the entirety of meaning and experience within a sociopolitical context within which and for which a word is used can be condensed into one word." See *Begriffsgeschichte* and social history in Koselleck, *Futures Past*, 81, 85. The concept, as in Koselleck, "unites within itself a plenitude of meanings," encompassing different experiences and significations. The prostitute emerges as a concept that parallels that of "criminal tribes." The colonial state creates a concept, uses description of these peoples to represent the traits of the concept, then creates a state-led discourse of the domestication and liberation of those people who come to populate the concept. On criminal tribes, see Yang, "Dangerous Castes and Tribes," 108–27. My thanks to Ronald Inden for his many insights about the comparison between these concept histories. Thank you to Manan Ahmed for this line of inquiry.

16. Cohn, *Colonialism and Its Forms of Knowledge*, 44; cited in Guha, "Introduction" in Cohn, *Colonialism and Its Forms of Knowledge*, xxiii.

17. Guha, "Introduction," in Cohn, *Colonialism and Its Forms of Knowledge*, xxiii.

18. For archives where prostitute and prostitution also designate the regulation of male homosexuality, see Ross, "Sex in the Archives: Homosexuality, Prostitution, and the Archives de la Préfecture de Police de Paris," 267–90. Sexual difference is critical to these histories of sexual classification in colonial India. The prostitute was most often gendered as "woman" in these archives of modern social thought, for which I use the term "female" as an adjectival form. Other criminal laws facilitated the creation of other gender categories. Jessica Hinchy traces how the colonial classification of transgendered peoples under the category of "hijra" occurred through the Criminal Tribes Act of 1871, a history found in the B files of regional colonial archives. See Hinchy, "The Eunuch Archive," 127–46.

19. On Durkheim's understanding of the natural occurrence of social deviation in modern societies, see Durkheim, *The Rules of Sociological Method*; see also Durkheim on the necessity of ethnological evolution for a sociology of social limits in his "Debate on the Relationship between Ethnology and Sociology" (1907), in Durkheim, *Rules of Sociological Method*, 209–10. On Durkheim and the regulation of heterosexual conjugality and masculinity in modern France, see Surkis, *Sexing the Citizen*, 125–83. Here I am thinking with Foucault's study of normal and abnormal through moral interdictions around modern sexuality in *Abnormal*, built on the foundational history of science by Georges Canguilhem on the normal and the pathological in the biological sciences, *The Normal and Pathological*. I use the term "deviant" to encompass the history of the social scientific study of the interdiction against the anomaly, abherrant, abnormal, and pathological, consolidated into the study of the sociological category of "deviance" in the twentieth century. In using this term, I am influenced by Cathy Cohen's turn to deviance as a productive site of engagement at the intersection of feminist thought, queer theory, and Black studies. See Cohen, "Deviance as Resistance," 27–45. From Durkheim's foundational sociological studies of deviance emerged the study of stigma in the formalized discipline of sociology, most famously in American sociology by Erving Goffman in his *Stigma*. My own use of "stigma" as an analytic framework is influenced by this line of inquiry, of the social marking and shaming that leads to social exclusion of the spoiled identity that is socially condemned. On the formalized field of postwar deviance studies in the United States, including Goffman's conceptual innovation in the study of stigma as a critical reassessment of positivist approaches to the necessity deviance in sociology, see Love, "Doing Being Deviant," 74–95.

20. On the powerful reorganization of Bengali nationalist ideology around idealized upper-caste Hindu domesticity, see Sarkar, *Hindu Wife, Hindu Nation*. On the critical place of upper-caste conjugal domesticity in postcolonial India, see for example Basu and Ramberg (eds.), *Conjugality and Beyond*.

21. For a list of Bengali terms that the author suggests are equivalent and interchangeable with "prostitute," see Bandapadhyay, *Beshya Sangeet, Baiji Sangeet*, 44–45.

22. See Alexandre Parent-Duchâtelet in his field-defining *De la prostitution dans la ville de Paris, considérée sous le rapport de l'hygiène publique, de la morale et de l'administration: Ouvrage appuyé de documens statistiques puisés dans les archives de la Préfecture de police*, who historian Alain Corbin describes as "a veritable Linneaus of prostitution." According to Corbin, in a rather unfortunate depiction of the project of social science that he treats as a self-evident assessment of the true nature of "fallen women," Parent-Duchâtelet's study was "repeated so often in the literature on prostitution and inspired so many novelists," that according to Corbin, it likely

"determined to some extent the behavior of prostitutes itself." On the Linnean sensibility of Parent-Duchâtelet, see Corbin, *Women for Hire*, 6–7. Parent-Duchâtelet, followed by Baudelaire in *Fleurs du mal*, together produce a systematic understanding of the prostitute as a primary object of sociological and realist literary analysis in the urban landscape of Paris. Other social scientific studies of the prostitute proliferated across the modern world, including William Acton's key study in association with the English Contagious Diseases Acts in his 1857 *Prostitution Considered in Its Moral, Social, and Sanitary Aspects, in London and Other Large Cities and Garrison Towns*; William Sanger in New York City in his *History of Prostitution*; to Cesare Lombroso in Italy in his study, a founding text of the field of criminology, *A Donna Delinquente*. See also Merrick, *Work among the Fallen as Seen in the Prison Cells*; Ellis, *Studies in the Psychology of Sex*; in early Chicago sociology in the first decades of the twentieth century, situational sociology, or the definition of a social situation, is first articulated in William I. Thomas's study of the "unadjusted girl" in the racialized landscape of early twentieth-century Chicago, described in the foreword and in the study as "young prostitutes." See Thomas, *The Unadjusted Girl*, 16.

23. The turn of the nineteenth and twentieth centuries saw the rise of sexual sciences across the globe. However, to name the many texts that address ideas of sexuality only as "sexology" would be to reduce the transdisciplinary reach of these ideas and the primary role of social scientific study of sex and sexuality across disciplines. On sexual sciences, see Fuechtner, Haynes, and Jones, *A Global History of Sexual Science, 1880–1960*; Bauer, *Sexology and Translation*; Frühstück, *Colonizing Sex*; Bland and Doan, *Sexology in Culture*.

24. Weston, *Long Slow Burn*, 3.

25. Ibid., 4, 20.

26. Rubin, "The Traffic in Women," 157–210, and her reflection on this essay in her "The Problem with Trafficking" in her *Deviations*, 66–86. Ramberg troubles the stability and fictional performance of the kinship chart by returning to Rubin; see part III of Ramberg, "Trouble," in *Given to the Goddess*, 181–222.

27. Eve Kosofsky Sedgwick provocatively proposes that the hetero/homo divide was the central premise of Western thought. As Sedgwick begins her *Epistemology of the Closet*, "many of the major nodes of thought and knowledge in twentieth-century Western culture as a whole are structured—indeed, fractured—by a chronic, now endemic crisis of homo/heterosexual definition, indicatively male, dating from the end of the nineteenth century." See Sedgwick, *Epistemology of the Closet*, 1. The scholarship that follows Sedgwick's intervention about Western thought, however, takes the homo/hetero divide as a *universal* framework as the singular organizing mechanism for modern sexualities around the world. My thanks to Lynne Huffer for her insights on the foundational place of this definitional binary, and Afsaneh Najmabadi for her feedback on Sedgwick's project and the subsequent assumption in scholarship on the universality of this divide for global contexts. The prostitute is the critical site in the articulation of deviance and the normalization of heterosexual monogamy in colonial South Asia, complicating the homo/hetero divide as the primary structure for the making of social and sexual norms in colonial South Asia.

28. On India as episteme rather than exemplar, see Arondekar and Patel, "Area Impossible," 151–71.

29. In my thinking about deviant female sexuality as a central epistemic form, I build on scholarship on the history of women's sexuality and the history of women's classification as social

and sexual deviants, including comparative scholarship at the intersection of feminist and queer studies and Black feminist epistemologies. See the groundbreaking work of Vance, *Pleasure and Danger*, 1–28. In relation to racial difference and sexuality, I am influenced by Sarah Haley's innovative study of black women's deviance, which demonstrates that the concept of queer in the United States emerges *through* the violent racialized history of black women's categorization as deviants, as unruly bodies that defied sexual norms and transgressed social boundaries. See Haley, *No Mercy Here*, 1–16, 40. See also Marisa Fuentes's study on British colonial archives of women, sexuality, and slavery in colonial Barbados. Fuentes suggests that the archive of slavery "defies coherence," and, building on Michel-Rolph Trouillot and Black feminist historiography, proposes methods that trouble the self-evident "political project of agency" in *Dispossessed Lives*, 1, 3. Thanks to Robert Reid-Pharr for his feedback about comparative questions in archives of Black sexuality. At the intersection of comparative feminist and queer studies, I build on the work of Sharon Marcus, who questions habits of reading that recuperate hidden histories of "lesbian" pasts to instead argue for a practice of interpretation that accounts for the many forms of female desire that coexisted with Victorian heterosexual conjugality in *Between Women*, 1–22; see also Laura Doan's engagement with the unknowability of the past in archives of women's sexuality in *Disturbing Practices*, 1–26.

30. Anti-foundational methods have been essential in feminist history and histories of sexuality, as well as anti-foundational historiographic traditions from South Asia and the colonial world. I am especially influenced by the rich feminist historiography on colonial India, which I address later on in the introduction. In relation to critical feminist approaches to colonial forms of knowledge, see the groundbreaking essay by Lata Mani, "Contentious Traditions," 119–56. Perhaps the most sustained articulation of the historical contradictions in this project of recuperation can be found in Gayatri Chakravorty Spivak's essential critique of historical recuperation and the historical investigations of the Subaltern Studies collective that followed. See Spivak, "Can the Subaltern Speak?," 271–313. Critical feminist historians Joan Wallach Scott and Denise Riley produced field-changing foundational critiques of the unmediated recuperation of historical subjects, arguing that feminist history, at its inception, required methodology that troubled the very categories of woman and self-evident ideas of subaltern experience. See Riley, *"Am I That Name?"* and Scott, "The Evidence of Experience," 773–97.

31. As Arondekar provocatively asks: "What would it mean to let go of our attachments to loss, to unmoor ourselves, as it were, from the stakes of reliable ghosts?" See Arondekar, "In the Absence of Reliable Ghosts," 99; and her extended critique of recovery as the primary orientation of histories of sexuality in *For the Record*.

32. Afsaneh Najmabadi describes a parallel process in the "heteronormalization of eros and sex" as the singular model for modernity in modern Iran. See Najmabadi, *Women without Moustaches and Men without Beards*, 3.

33. See for example Puri, *Woman, Body, Desire in Post-Colonial India*; Sunder Rajan, *The Scandal of the State*; Menon, *Recovering Subversion*; Rege's essential study, *Writing Caste Writing Gender*; Chakravarti, *Gendering Caste*; on debates about sex work as labor in contemporary India, see Kotiswaran, *Dangerous Sex, Invisible Labor*; on sex work as part of a larger informal labor economy, see Shah, *Street Corner Secrets*.

34. Mani, "Contentious Traditions," 119–56; Yang, "Whose Sati?," 8–33.

35. Pioneering studies by Bernard S. Cohn, Ronald Inden, Gyanendra Pandey, Nicholas Dirks, Gyan Prakash, and others on the colonial recasting of concepts through scientific and social

scientific practices, notably in innovations in the study of populations around the world brought through the colonial census in India. These concepts, like kingship, communalism, and caste, demonstrate the sociological power of the colonial state—from its early Orientalist projects to its systematic surveys. The state characterized people as populations, assimilated them as sociological objects, and selectively narrated the essence of Indian peoples as without history, understood as naturally defined communities. See Cohn, *An Anthropologist among Historians and Other Essays*; Inden, *Imagining India*; Pandey, *The Construction of Communalism in Colonial North India*; Breckenridge and van der Veer, *Orientalism and the Postcolonial Predicament*; Chatterjee, *Texts of Power*; Cohn, *Colonialism and Its Forms of Knowledge*; Trautmann, *Aryans and British India*; Prakash, *Another Reason*; Chakrabarty, *Provincializing Europe*; Dirks, *Castes of Mind*. As Anjan Ghosh describes, the development of social scientific practices were "harnessed to this structure of governance," in his article "The Public Culture of Sociology in Calcutta" in *Doing Sociology in India*, 28.

36. William Jones, founder of the Asiatic Society and also a judge for the East India Company, translated *The Laws of Manu* and utilized his philological studies in his decisions in early colonial courts. Perhaps the most circulated text that depicted a romanticized (and erotic) vision of Indian womanhood in early projects of Indology was another translation of William Jones in his edition of Kalidasa's *Sakuntala*, which became an object of fascination for writers across Europe. See Thapar, *Sakuntala*.

37. On the rise of these organizations and disciplines in the world of nineteenth-century Bengal, see Chatterjee, "The Disciplines in Colonial Bengal," 9–29, in Partha Chatterjee (ed.), *Texts of Power*.

38. On the roots of a public sociology prior to the establishment of sociological disciplines in Calcutta, from the early rationalism of Anglo-Indian Henry Derozio and his Derozian followers to the connections between Tattwabodhini Sabha and the monotheistic Hindu reform movement, the Brahmo Samaj, see Ghosh, "The Public Culture of Sociology in Calcutta," 30–36. The Bengal Social Science Association was founded by Reverend James Long, and came to include major colonial officials and Indian intellectuals, including many who appear in this book, from Norman Chevers and Arthur J. Payne to Brahmo Keshab Chandra Sen to Bankim Chandra Chatterjee to Kaliprasanna Singha.

39. A distilled version of Comtean positivism had extraordinary reach in nineteenth-century Bengal, and positivist methods came to pervade much social and scientific study. Comte was first and most famously translated and interpreted for an English-speaking audience by John Stuart Mill, two years prior to the establishment of the Bengal Social Science Association. See his *Auguste Comte and Positivism, reprinted from the Westminster Review*. On the wide reach of positivist ideas and methods in Bengal, see Gupta, *Sociology in India*; and Forbes, *Positivism in Bengal*. My thanks to Omnia El Shakry for her feedback on the pervasive presence of Comtean positivism across the colonial world.

40. Over half of these educational institutions were built without state support. See Chatterjee, "The Disciplines in Colonial Bengal," in Chatterjee, *Texts of Power*.

41. Chatterjee, "Disciplines," 10, in Partha Chatterjee, *Texts of Power*; citing Basu, *The Growth of Education and Political Development in India, 1898–1920*, 107.

42. Patricia Uberoi, Nandini Sundar, and Satish Deshpande describe the colonial epistemic structures that organize the distinction between sociology proper and social anthropology, where sociology as a discipline claimed the study of modern industrial societies, while anthropology,

with its roots in colonialism, claimed the domain of the tribals, primitives, and premoderns. The context of colonial India posed a fundamental paradox, where colonial ethnographies of India formed the basis of modern knowledge in the emerging disciplines of both anthropology and sociology in the metropole and its colonies. They ask: Can we distinguish between these disciplines in the site of India that was simultaneously cast as an object of sociological study and as anthropological other? See their "Introduction: The Professionalisation of Indian Anthropology and Sociology: Peoples, Places, and Institutions," in *Anthropology in the East*, 6–7. On the many important foundational figures particularly for Calcutta, Pune, Bombay, and Lucknow, see also the essays and overview of the field in the introduction of Patel, *Doing Sociology in India*, xi–xxxviii; see also for Bombay, Juned Shaikh's innovative reading of photography as social science in "Imagining Caste," 491–514; on Aligarh Muslim University, see Lelyveld, *Aligarh's First Generation*; on Osmania University, see Datla, *The Language of Secular Islam*; on emerging disciplines in Tamil and Telugu, see, for example, Mantena, *The Origins of Modern Historiography in India*.

43. See, for example, Patrick Geddes, who founded the Bombay School of Sociology. Geddes, a Scottish biologist, sociologist, and foundational thinker for urban planning, published his coauthored ethnological treatise on sexuality with J. Arthur Thomson, *The Evolution of Sex*. Geddes was a proponent of close observation and ethnological evolutionism, what he described as a kind of sociological scientific method. Geddes became a significant influence for Bengali intellectual Radhakamal Mukerjee, cofounder of the Lucknow School of Sociology, who was deeply invested in sexual evolution.

44. See other uses of this phrase in the study of the colonial world. Partha Chatterjee uses the phrase the "Great Science of Society" to speak of Bankim Chattopadhyay's use of Comtean positivism and Spencerian evolutionary thought to create essentialist theories of Indian cultural difference. See Chatterjee, *Empire and Nation*, 44. Omnia El Shakry uses the phrase "science of society" to describe Egyptian intellectuals and their projects of social science as social engineering. See El Shakry, *The Great Social Laboratory*, 4.

45. J. F. Blumhardt, who compiled the essential catalog for the India office, featured the category of sociology in his 1905 catalog for Bengali books. Sociology featured texts on the status of women, in particular, on the control of women's sexuality. Themes included social evils, the fall of Hindu widows, Kulin Hindu polygamy, women's education, the use of the *Mahabharata* in modern domestic life, and the duties of the housewife. See Blumhardt, *Catalogue of the Library of the India Office*, 23–31.

46. The genre of "social reform" encompasses a wide array of texts, methods, and social and political concerns.

47. On the proliferative imagination of social reform, see Sarkar and Sarkar, *Women and Social Reform*, 1–12.

48. See the review titled "Pandita Ramabai Sarasvati" in Celarent, *Varieties of Social Imagination*, 104.

49. See his use of the term "social analyst" in Celarent, *Varieties of Social Imagination*, 98. Abbott (as Barbara Celarent) produced pseudonymous reviews of foundational books in sociology in *The American Journal of Sociology* between 2009 and 2015. They provide "a broad introduction to social thinking," and are based in authors "from the past and the other," with "30 of the 36 reviews" on the work of "authors outside of Europe and North America" who were most often not professional academics. See Celarent, *Varieties of Social Imagination*, ix–x.

50. I build on critical thinking about the status of description in the social sciences and practices of reading in humanistic inquiry. See Best, Love, and Marcus, "Building a Better Description," 1–21.

51. See Celarent on the marginalized peoples who made modern social thought, *Varieties of Social Imagination*, 138. Sudipta Kaviraj argues for the necessity to see political and social thought outside of traditional formalized academic disciplines in the context of censorship and control in colonial India, particularly in rich vernacular literary traditions of Bengal. See Kaviraj, *The Invention of Private Life*.

52. Many pioneering upper-caste women advocating for women's rights adhered to this view that the prostitute was the degradation of society. In perspectives that reflected the idealization of upper-caste womanhood, these ideologies of good womanhood as chaste womanhood reflect the reach of this epistemological project that saw the control of female sexuality as critical to the science of society. See, for example, Meera Kosambi's evaluation of the potential and possible limitations of Pandita Ramabai's vision of good womanhood, in Kosambi, *Pandita Ramabai*, 1–6. An exception to this adherence to sexual strictures as social good from Bengal can be seen in the example of Binodini Dasi, an acclaimed theater actor and performer who was herself considered "from the prostitute ranks." Binodini produces a nuanced critique of the indeterminacy of the concept of the fallen woman in her memoir. She refuses the easy equation of her life as a famed theater actor and the prostitute, yet also names herself through her position as a socially outcast woman. See Bhattacharya, *Binodini Dasi*. While there is a general adherence to the social condemnation of the prostitute, there are striking critiques of patriarchal neglect of women, including at the hands of other women in Bengali society. Such a critique can be found in the writing of Sarat Kumari Chaudhurani (1861–1920) in her "Adorer Na Anador" ("Beloved, or Unloved?," 1891). See Tharu and Lalita, *Women Writing in India*, 262–74.

53. This project enters the scholarship on nationalism in South Asian historiography through the provocation of Partha Chatterjee on the novel claims of Indian nationalists in the deployment of nationalism. As he asks in his paradigm-shifting *The Nation and Its Fragments*, who imagined the sovereign nation in colonial India? He suggests that, rather than solely being derivative of European nationalisms, Indian nationalist thought posed a radical difference from the "modular" forms of national society produced in the modern west. Political thought, as I argue for social thought here, rather than being solely derivative of a script already written in the West, must be seen as the novel deployment and reconfiguration of a set of social and political theories that circulated across the modern world. See his *The Nation and Its Fragments*, 3–13; for key ideas on idealized womanhood, gendered power, and Indian nationalism, see, for example, Sarkar, *Hindu Wife, Hindu Nation*; Sinha, *Colonial Masculinity* and her *Specters of Mother India*.

54. Models for multilingual intellectual histories of hybrid genres of social and political theory in Bengal include Banerjee, *Politics of Time*, and her current work on the political in Bengal in "Between the Political and the Non-Political," 323–39; Projit Mukharji demonstrates the significance of hybrid scientific/social scientific texts in the intellectual and social histories of Bengal in his book *Nationalizing the Body* and his ongoing project on race science. See Mukharji, "Profiling the Profiloscope," 376–96, and "The Bengali Pharaoh," 446–76.

55. Celarent, *Varieties of Social Imagination*, 197.

56. I build on Omnia El Shakry's study of the rise of human sciences in colonial Egypt among Egyptian intellectuals, see El Shakry, *The Great Social Laboratory*, 1–22.

57. See Tanika Sarkar and her radical reconfiguration of the history of anti-colonial nationalism, where "Hindu conjugality" sat "at the very heart of militant nationalism in Bengal." Sarkar, *Hindu Wife, Hindu Nation*; see also Chatterjee, *The Nation and Its Fragments*.

58. On Indian nationalism, see Chatterjee, *The Nation and Its Fragments*. In particular, see "The Nation and Its Women" on the "women's question."

59. This agenda was first set forth in the groundbreaking 1989 volume *Recasting Women*, which carefully revealed how "collusions" of British colonial and Indian nationalist patriarchies were integral to British colonial domination as well as a deeply exclusionary anti-colonial Indian nationalism. Ashwini Tambe skillfully maps the multiple sites of these "colluding patriarchies" between the colonial state and Indian elites through Indian feminist historiography, especially in scholarship on legal debates about marriage in her "Colluding Patriarchies," 587–600. See Sangari and Vaid, *Recasting Women*. All of the essays in the volume explore these collusions, from Lata Mani to Uma Chakravarti to Partha Chatterjee.

60. On women, gendered power, and structures of law, see Nair, *Women and Law in Colonial India*; Sturman, *The Government of Social Life in Colonial India*; on the critical place of gendered power in recasting the terms of modern Indian history, from domesticity to slavery, there is a rich field of scholarship. On changing ideas of idealized domesticity in Bengal, see Borthwick, *The Changing Role of Women in Bengal, 1849–1905*; Walsh, *Domesticity in Colonial India*; Majumdar, *Marriage and Modernity*; on the recasting of patriarchal power through debates about gender and women's subordination, see Sangari and Vaid, *Recasting Women*; Sinha, *Colonial Masculinity*; Forbes, *Women in Modern India*; Mani, *Contentious Traditions*; Sarkar, *Hindu Wife, Hindu Nation*; Sinha, *Specters of Mother India*; Ghosh, *Sex and the Family in Colonial India*; Sarkar, *Visible Histories, Disappearing Women*; Sreenivas, *Wives, Widows, and Concubines*; Sarkar, *Rebels, Wives, Saints*; Lal, *Coming of Age in Nineteenth-Century India*; critical histories of slavery, labor, and law include groundbreaking studies like Chatterjee, *Gender, Slavery, and Law in Colonial India*; and Sen, *Women and Labour in Late Colonial India*; on gendered power, sexuality, and the politics of difference, see Uberoi, *Social Reform, Sexuality, and the State*; Gupta, *Sexuality, Obscenity, Community*; John and Nair, *A Question of Silence?* On the critical place of caste discrimination and difference in the making of gendered power historically, see, for example, Rao, *The Caste Question*; Paik, *Dalit Women's Education in Modern India*; Gupta, *The Gender of Caste*.

61. I build on the study of gendered power, while emphasizing the question of sexuality to consider the foundational place of normative ideas of sexual difference, sexual desire, and sexual behavior and reproduction in the making of modern social thought. On gender as a "useful" historical category of analysis, see Joan Wallach Scott's essential "Gender," 1053–75. On the reductive use of gender as a historical category of analysis in the decades that followed Scott's essay, see Butler and Weed, *The Question of Gender*.

62. On the construction of communal difference as natural and timeless, see Pandey, *The Construction of Communalism in Colonial North India*; Gupta, *Sexuality, Obscenity, Community*. I thank Shrikant Botre and Ishita Pande for important insights about the question of caste in the sexual sciences of Maharashtra and North India at the Asian Studies Association conference, March 2017. See also Chandra's analysis of English education as the naturalization of caste dominance and sexual difference in *The Sexual Life of English*. On caste in Bengal, see Bandyopadhyay, *Caste, Protest, and Identity in Colonial Bengal*, and his *Caste, Culture, and Hegemony*; on the critical place of gender in the making of caste difference, see Rao, *The Caste Question*; *Gender and Caste*;

and "Caste, Colonialism, and the Reform of Gender," 239–64; Paik's important study on education and social mobility for women, *Dalit Women's Education in Modern India*; Gupta, *The Gender of Caste*. My thinking on the links between caste, gender, and the distinctions of theory and empiricism in disciplinary social science has also been influenced by the work of Sharmila Rege, especially her "Institutional Alliances between Sociology and Gender Studies," 2023–27, her *Writing Caste Writing Gender*, and her excellent editorial and commentary on B. R. Ambedkar's work in her *Against the Madness of Manu*; on the history of caste, bonded labor, and the collusion of upper-caste Indians and the state to uphold caste and bonded labor strictures, see Prakash, *Bonded Histories*; Rawat, *Reconsidering Untouchability*; Viswanath, *The Pariah Problem*.

63. Chatterjee, "Five Hundred Years of Fear and Love," 1333.

64. Here scientific knowledge is akin to Brahmanical knowledge in its exclusionary claims, building on Sunandan K. N., who argues that Brahmanical knowledge is recast as scientific expertise in the modern making of caste in Kerala. See Sunandan K. N., "From Acharam to Knowledge," 174–92.

65. Chandramukhi becomes the first in a long line of "fallen" women outside of marriage, labeled as the courtesan-prostitute, critical to the Indian cinematic imaginary. With *Devdas* came a preoccupation with the character of the courtesan-prostitute in Indian cinema. *Devdas* is the most remade film in Indian cinema history, produced in at least seven Indian languages in at least ten versions over the course of the twentieth century, with the latest made in 2018. *Devdas* was made as a film starting with the 1928 silent film. The cinematic version was made famous by the 1935 and 1955 films. *Devdas* was made first into a silent film, then simultaneously in Hindi, Bengali, and Assamese in 1935–1937 with songs and dialogue. It was made in Telugu and Tamil by 1953. The 1955 Hindi version, directed by Bimal Roy, brought *Devdas* to a broad audience. The movie was remade in 2002 with world famous actor Shah Rukh Khan as Devdas and Madhuri Dixit as Chandramukhi. It was again modernized in the popular Hindi retelling *Dev D* (2009), directed by Anurag Kashyap. The most recent version, *Das Dev*, was released in 2018.

66. Legend has it that Chattapadhyay collected hundreds of firsthand testimonials of "prostitutes" for a major treatise that were all allegedly lost in a fire in Burma. See Bandyopadhyay, "Chronicles of Love, Betrayal, and Prostitution in Late Colonial Bengal," 725.

67. Chattapadhyay, "Narir Mulya," 947–78. The language of monetary value with regard to womanhood is pervasive in these texts. See Geeta Patel and her exploration of the ubiquitous appearance of the language of value and worth as "techno-intimacy" across multiple genres in *Risky Bodies and Techno-Intimacy*.

68. The connection between this idea of the oldest profession (à la Kipling) and prostitution as primitive sexuality is made throughout social scientific studies from Bengal in the twentieth century. See, for example, Banerji, *Castaway of Indian Society*, 1.

69. For a comparative discussion of intellectual networks and cohering concepts, see Herling, *The German Gita*, 31.

70. For example, the indeterminacy of the concept of *vesya* or "prostitute" was critical to how Gandhi reframes the idea of *swaraj* in his *Hind Swaraj* (1908). Gandhi's use of *vesya* reflects a reasoning used by many of his contemporaries where the concept of prostitute is a key analogy for theories of the political capability of Indian society. See Ajay Skaria's reading of *swaraj* in "Only One Word, Properly Altered," 219–37.

71. For a comparative analysis in Britain, see Poovey, *Making a Social Body*, 91–97.

72. Durkheim, *The Rules of Sociological Method*, 7, 20. Or, reimagined more powerfully by Aimé Césaire: "My turn to state the equation: colonization = 'thingification.'" Césaire, *Discourse on Colonialism*, 42. Thanks to Omnia El Shakry for her insightful feedback to explore what methods are employed in this episteme.

73. Studies of colonial sexuality focus primarily on colonial control of sexuality and the colonial incitement to knowledge about sexuality and racial difference. Important studies of colonial sexuality include Stoler, *Race and the Education of Desire* and her *Carnal Knowledge and Imperial Power*; McClintock, *Imperial Leather*; on investigating sexuality across geographies and languages, see Babayan and Najmabadi, *Islamicate Sexualities* and the provocation from Inderpal Grewal and Caren Kaplan on writing sexuality in other parts of the world outside the binarism of modern and traditional in Grewal and Kaplan, "Global Identities," 663–79.

Chapter 1. Origins: Philology and the Study of Indian Sex Life

1. Ghose, *Rati-Sastram*, 21.
2. Ibid., 3.
3. Ibid., 5–6.
4. *Rati-Sastram* was enormously popular. Its first edition by S. C. Seal in Calcutta was rapidly republished in 1894, with a third imprint in 1904, a sixth edition by 1921. The book was republished by Nag Publishers in 1971 with at least two subsequent editions. Other versions were also published such as the *Rati-Sastram or, The Greatest Work on Hindu System of Sexual Science* (Calcutta: Sircar, 1908); *Science of Life, or Hindu System of Sexual Secrets: Parts I & II: Translated into English with Original Sanskrit Text* (Calcutta: Ganguly, 1909). The *Ratirahasya* is perhaps the most widely translated and circulated text after Burton's *The Kama Sutra*, and continues to be in print today. For publication details of six editions of Ghose between 1894 and 1977, see Zysk, *Conjugal Love in India*, 36–37.

5. A select, interpretive Hindu sexual sciences of the *Ratirahasya* appeared in Japanese in 1926. It also appeared in many Indian languages, differently titled as *Rati-Sastram, Ratirahasya*, and the *Koka-sastras*. Other editions include, in Hindi, Kokkoka and Kavi, *Kokasāra*; *The Rati Sastra Ratnavali*; Kokkoka, *Ratirahasya*; Nagarjuna and Deyer, *Rati Sastra*; printed in English in India, Upadhyaya and Raghavan, *Rati Rahasya of Pandit Kokkoka*; Jaya and Schmidt, *Kokkokam and Ratihasyam*; in Marathi in Jaisavala, *Marathi bhashenta Koka sastra*; in Oriya in Dasa, *Sacitri o brhat Koka-sastra ba Rati bijnana*; in Gujarati in Kokkoka and Nainasukha, *Vaidyamanotsava*.

6. Comfort, *The Koka Shashtra, Being the Ratirahasya of Kokkoka, and Other Medieval Indian Writings on Love*. This study became the basis of Comfort's *The Joy of Sex*. See Doniger and Kakar, *Kamasutra*, ii, note 61.

7. On the Hindu sexual sciences in modern India, see, for example, Fuechtner, Haynes, and Jones, *A Global History of Sexual Science, 1880–1960*; Botre and Haynes, "Sexual Knowledge, Sexual Anxieties," 991–1034; Pande, "Loving Like a Man," 675–92; Savary, "Vernacular Eugenics?," 381–97.

8. Turner, *Philology*, ix. Here, I am deeply influenced by Michel Foucault in his critical essay, "Nietzsche, Genealogy, History," where he argues: "History also teaches how to laugh at the solemnities of the origin. The origin makes possible a field of knowledge whose function is to recover it, but always in a false recognition due to the excesses of its own speech." See Foucault,

"Nietzsche, Genealogy, History," 143. I outline a field of knowledge whose function is to recover the origins of social life through philological inquiry into sexual difference and sexuality. See also Michel Foucault's extended engagement with philology as a foundational field (one of the three faces of knowledge alongside economics and biology) that claimed the status of science in the modern human sciences. See Foucault, *The Order of Things*, xvi–xxvi.

9. Turner, *Philology*, ix.

10. On the relationship of language families, ethnology, and race theory, see Trautmann's study *Aryans and British India*.

11. I build on scholarship that has demonstrated how the vast project of eighteenth-century and nineteenth-century Indology created essentialist understandings of the roots of Indian culture and society. Placing Indology at the very heart of the modern humanistic inquiry, Ronald Inden set forth an agenda for a sociology of knowledge that treats Indology as foundational for the modern human sciences. See Inden, *Imagining India*, 1. Inden describes how Indology embraced foundational "intellectual practices of the core social sciences" from history, anthropology, and "area studies," to psychology, economics, and sociology (3–4). Inden argues that through Indology, Hindu texts became the primary locus of a powerful essentialism that defined the colonial episteme, creating a select set of ancient Hindu texts that were canonized and held as exemplary of "the mind of India." See Inden, *Imagining India*, 4. Inden demonstrates how, within this dominant form of reasoning, ancient Hindu texts were the only evidence required to comprehend all parts of historical and contemporary Indian social life. In her influential essay "Whatever Happened to the Vedic Dasi?," Uma Chakravarti demonstrates how dominant anachronistic categories from Indology shaped gendered norms of womanhood in colonial India, most powerfully in the idea of the Aryan woman. The concept of Aryan womanhood was essential to the legal and social institutionalization of sexual difference and gendered power in colonial India. This selective philological understanding of an ancient past recuperated "lost" origins for the Indian woman as wife and mother, while foreclosing other forms of womanhood in India's precolonial past. See Chakravarti, "Whatever Happened to the Vedic Dasi?," 27–87.

12. Inden, *Imagining India*, 12–14. For Inden, the Indological study of Hinduism set forth a "epistemological procedure" where the ancient Hindu past, represented through exemplary, canonized text, became essential to any study of India, past or present. See Prakash, "Review of *Imagining India* by Ronald Inden," 602. On German Indology, see Pollock, "Deep Orientalism?," 76–133; see also Murti, *India*; Herling, *The German Gita*. Thank you to Manan Ahmed for this line of inquiry and thinking with me about the philological study of sex as foundational to modern social study. On the critical place of origins in the making of exclusionary visions of South Asia, see Ahmed, *A Book of Conquest*, 1–22.

13. An officer of the East India Company, Burton lived in Sindh, Gujarat, and Shimla. He famously traveled to Mecca where he disguised himself as a so-called native man, chronicled in his three-volume *Personal Narrative of a Pilgrimage to El-Medinah and Meccah (1855–1856)*. On Burton, see Lovell, *A Rage to Live*; Kennedy, *The Highly Civilized Man*.

14. Burton, *The Book of the Thousand Nights and a Night*. On the translations of this Arabic text, see Irwin, *The Arabian Nights*, 9–41.

15. See Daud Ali's introductory essay in his edited issue on *kamashastra* texts in the *Journal of Indian Philosophy*. Also see Doniger, *Redeeming the Kama Sutra*. Burton and Arbuthnot published texts as part of a fake literary society, "The Kama Shastra Society," to avoid censorship

and exempt the text from obscenity laws. On the reception of this text in England, see Grant, "Translating/'The' *Kama Sutra*," 509–16.

16. As Anjali Arondekar argues, scholars have at points reproduced this compulsive desire for the lost archives of Burton. She demonstrates how the rumor of Burton's report on same-sex practices shaped a desire for evidence of the perverse sexuality of the colonies, a longing that is reflected in practices of archival recuperation among scholars in the postcolonial world. See Arondekar, *For the Record*, 27–66.

17. See Ali, "Introduction," 2. See also Gautam, "The Courtesan and the Birth of Ars Erotica in the Kamasutra," 1–20.

18. My thanks to Anjali Arondekar for her formulation of a "phantasmatic empiricism" to explain these claims to textual authority.

19. On the limitations of Burton's translation and his Orientalist choices, including the widespread inclusion of the terms "yoni" and "lingam" despite not being features of the original Sanskrit, see Doniger in *Redeeming the Kama Sutra*, 156–57. See also Kumkum Roy's reading of the Sanskrit text in "Unravelling the Kamasutra," in *A Question of Silence?*, 52–76.

20. See, for example, Anne Hardgrove's reading of Indian translations of the *Kama Sutra* as a site for a conservative nationalist imaginary in "Nationalist Interpretations of the Kama Sutra," 97–106.

21. Ben Grant, "Translating/'The' *Kama Sutra*," 509–16.

22. Burton, *The Kama Sutra*, xv.

23. Ibid., xvii.

24. Ibid., vxiii. On the Scottish physician John Roberton (1776–1840), née Thomas Bell, see McGrath, *Seeing Her Sex*, 40–54.

25. Burton, *The Kama Sutra*, vxiii.

26. Arbuthnot and Burton, *Ananga-Ranga*, xii.

27. Ibid., viii.

28. Ibid., xii.

29. Burton, *The Kama Sutra*, 19.

30. Ibid.

31. Ibid.

32. Thapar, *Sakuntala*, 197–262. See also Figueira, *Translating the Orient*.

33. Franklin, *Sir William Jones*, 80–97.

34. Burton, *The Kama Sutra*, 131. See also Kumkum Roy's discussion of part of this excerpt and Burton's unusual representation of women in "Unravelling the Kamasutra," 68.

35. Arbuthnot and Burton, *Ananga-Ranga*, xi.

36. Ibid.

37. Schmidt was trained at Halle by the Indologists Karl Friedrich Geldner (1852–1929) and Richard Pischel (1849–1908). Geldner worked extensively on the *Rg Veda*, while Pischel wrote on Kalidasa's *Sakuntala*. Pischel influenced major writers, including Thomas Mann and Hermann Hesse. From his dissertation onward, Richard Schmidt focused his study primarily on erotic Sanskrit literature and became the Professor of Indian Studies at the University of Münster in 1910. For the history of Schmidt as part of a long tradition of Indologists at Halle University in Germany, see http://www.indologie.uni-halle.de/institutsgeschichte/.

38. Schmidt, *Beiträge zur indischen Erotik*, iv.

39. See Mani, "Contentious Traditions," 119–56; Banerjee, "Chanakya/Kautilya," 24–51.

40. With his longtime collaborator J. Jolly, Schmidt sought to improve upon the first translations done by Rudrapatna Shamasastry. Jolly and Schmidt, *Arthasastra of Kautilya*.

41. Schmidt, *Beiträge zur indischen Erotik*, iv.

42. Turner, *Philology*, 236–53.

43. Richard Schmidt, first preface to *Beiträge zur indischen Erotik* from June 1901, in *Beiträge zur indischen Erotik*, iv.

44. Schmidt, *Beiträge zur indischen Erotik*, iii.

45. On Weber's interpretation of the unchanging nature of the Hindu religion as essential to his theory of social change in the modern West, see Thapar, "Durkheim and Weber on Theories of Society and Race Relations Relating to Precolonial India," in *Cultural Pasts*, 21–51.

46. Schmidt, *Beiträge zur indischen Erotik*, 1–2. See also Iwan Bloch's reproduction of this passage in Bloch, *Anthropological Studies in the Strange Sexual Practises of All Races in All Ages: Ancient and Modern, Oriental and Occidental, Primitive and Civilized*, 34.

47. The study of ancient Indian sex defined modern sexological understandings of *ars erotica* that was to stand in contrast to *scientia sexualis*, famously described by Michel Foucault. See Foucault, *The History of Sexuality*, v. 1, 51–75. Schmidt's text was translated widely, including for an American audience in 1932 in Windsor's *The Hindu Art of Love*, and later an adapted edition, *Cultural and Anthropological Studies in the Hindu Art of Love*, which translated Schmidt's study and created a synthetic cultural and anthropological study of Hindu erotics.

48. Ellis, *Studies in the Psychology of Sex*, vol. 6, 129.

49. Bloch, *Anthropological Studies in the Strange Sexual Practises of All Races in All Ages*, 33–36; see also Iwan Bloch, *Indische Medizin* (Berlin: n.p, 1902).

50. Hirschfeld, *Weltreise eines Sexualforschers*, 238–40, quoted in translation in Windsor, *Cultural and Anthropological Studies in the Hindu Art of Love*, viii. On Hirschfeld's travels in India, see Fuechtner, "Indians, Jews, and Sex," 111–30.

51. W. D. Whitney came from a lineage of famous European Indologists. He trained under Edward Salisbury, who studied under Franz Bopp at the University of Berlin. C. D. Buck studied in Germany at Leipzig, and when appointed to the University of Chicago in 1892, became head of the Department of Indo-European Comparative Philology, where he taught classes in Sanskrit, as well as Latin, Greek, Avestan, Old Persian, Lithuanian, and Old Bulgarian. See Davis, *South Asia at Chicago*, 2–3.

52. Johann Jakob Meyer was born on April 25, 1870, to German immigrants in Michigan. In 1891 he graduated from Concordia College in Fort Wayne, Indiana, and then attended Concordia Theological Seminary in St. Louis, Missouri. From 1894 to 1900 Meyer studied at the University of Chicago. At Chicago, he focused on comparative linguistics and German literature and taught himself Sanskrit. He then became Professor of Sanskrit and Indo-European languages. After traveling to Europe, he translated his extended study of women and ancient sex life, which one German scholar credited as the greatest study in the nature of the Indian woman, wife, mother, or prostitute. See George, "Johann Jakob Meyer," 224–33.

53. Meyer's bibliography of translations and critical editions includes Kcemendra's *Samayamatrika* [Das Zauberbuch der Hetären or The spellbook of courtesans] and *Kavyasamgraha* [Erotic and esoteric songs]. Other texts include studies of ancient Hindu law, the *Puranas*, and histories of Indian political theories. See George, "Johann Jakob Meyer," 224–33.

54. Meyer, *Das Weib im altindischen Epos*, dedication page.

55. Meyer, *Sexual Life in Ancient India*, xi, 264–75.

56. Other work on the status of women in ancient societies includes the French woman scholar, Clarisse Bader, who may have been one of the only women scholars writing on ancient gender and sexuality at the time. See her *Femme dans l'Inde antique*, translated as *Women in Ancient India*.

57. Meyer, *Sexual Life in Ancient India*, 1.

58. Ibid., 2.

59. Ibid., 3.

60. Ibid., 4.

61. Ibid., 5.

62. Ibid., 5n1.

63. See Meyer's notes on the question of prostitution, *Sex Life in Ancient India*, 6, 271–73, and 476–78.

64. For a text that utilizes the philological study of sex as social critique of contemporary Indian social practices in the time of the publication of Katherine Mayo's *Mother India*, see Werner, *Indisches Liebesleben*. On the impact of Mayo's critique across the world, see Sinha's *Specters of Mother India*.

65. Indological inquiry intersected with the supposedly traditional practices of religious recitation of Sanskrit to create complex literate publics for reading erotics.

66. Banerjee, "Time and Knowledge," 30.

67. Ibid., 30. See also Chakrabarty, *Provincializing Europe*, 3–23, and an early articulation of this argument in Hobsbawm and Ranger, *The Invention of Tradition*, 1–14.

68. Ghose, *Rati-Sastram*, 61.

69. Ibid.

70. Ibid.

71. Chakladar, *The Aryan Occupation of Eastern India*, preface to the 2nd edition.

72. Chakladar's conception of the roots of Vedic Aryanism in Bengal influenced many writers, including Ray in his *Bangalir Itihas* and prominent Bengali anthropologist Nirmal Kumar Bose. See Hood, *Niharranjan Ray*, 21–24.

73. Chakladar, *Social Life in Ancient India*, 1.

74. Ibid., 26.

75. To date the text earlier than the fourth century C.E., Chakladar uses debates in the *Journal of the Department of Letters* of the University of Calcutta and works by A. Banerji-Sastri, J. Jolly and Richard Schmidt, Haraprasad Sastri and Batuknath Bhattacharya. Chakladar, *Social Life in Ancient India*, 50–51.

76. Chakladar, *Social Life in Ancient India*, 141.

77. See Ali's overview of books on the *Kamasutra* in his "Introduction," 1–13.

78. Mukherjee, *The Positive Background of Hindu Sociology*, 205. On the *Arthashastra*'s reemergence as a political text in Bengal, see Banerjee, "Chanakya/Kautilya," 24–51. As the *Arthashastra* functioned as a productive site for political self-imagining, Chakladar posits the *Kamasutra* as the unique source for the roots of a Hindu sociology in his *Social Life in Ancient India*.

79. Member of the Royal Asiatic Society, *Sex Life in India*.

80. See chapter 4, "Evolution." Books published by the Medical Book Company include Basu's rapidly republished *Kama-Sutra of Vatsyayana*, which had at least fourteen editions by 1958; Basu, *The Art of Love in the Orient*; Ray, *Ananga Ranga*; Mukherji, *Birth Control for the Millions*; Pandian, *Kokkokam*; Jaya and Schmidt, *Kokkokam and Ratihasyam*; Ray, *Kokkokam & Rati Rahasyam*; and a reproduction of the Arbuthnot and Burton book as Kalyanamalla, *Ananga Ranga*.

81. Basu published on sexual practices in English and Bengali. See Basu, *Bahumukhi mana, baharupi prema*; Basu, *Nara-narira younabodha*; Basu, *Youbanera yadupuri*; Basu, *The Art of Love in the Orient*. Thanks to Dr. Sharmadip Basu for these biographical and bibliographical references.

82. See chapter 2, "Repetition," for an extended discussion of colonial laws and prostitution and the rich historiography on the subject.

83. Basu and Sinha, *The History of Marriage and Prostitution*, vii.

84. Ibid., vii–viii.

85. Ibid., 108, 118.

86. Ibid., 1.

87. Ibid., 74–79.

88. Ibid., 29.

89. Ibid., 195.

90. Ibid., 23.

91. Ibid., 24.

92. Ibid., 25.

93. Ibid., 262.

94. Ibid., xxiii. See also the most recent edition of the book published in 2003 as *History of Prostitution in Ancient India*.

95. Mukherji's books include *Infantile Cirrhosis of the Liver*; *Elements of Endocrinology*; *Psychology of Image Worship of the Hindus*; *Boundary Problem in New Bengal*; *Srshti, Bhagabana, o Sadhana*; and *Modern Treatment*.

96. Mukherji, *Prostitution in India*, iii. This book serves as a self-evident source of facts for many studies that follow, including Biswanath Joardar's sociological studies, *Prostitution in Historical and Modern Perspectives* and *Prostitution in Nineteenth and Early Twentieth-Century Calcutta*.

97. Mukherji, *Prostitution in India*, vii.

98. Ibid., 6.

99. Ibid., 31.

100. Ibid., 70.

101. Ibid., 85–88.

102. Ibid., 219.

103. Mukherji's communal language appears explicitly in his *Boundary Problem of New Bengal*.

104. Mukherji, *The Kama Sutra of Vatsayana*, 17.

105. My thanks to Afsaneh Najmabadi for this insight into the productive epistemologies of taxonomies.

106. Mukherji, *The Kama Sutra of Vatsayana*, 216–17. See also the parallel taxonomy with more detail in Mukherji, *Prostitution in India*, 33.

107. Mukherji, *The Kama Sutra of Vatsayana*, 21. Mukherji's *The Kama Sutra* circulated widely with at least two editions published within four years.

108. See Hodges, *Contraception, Colonialism and Commerce*; Ahluwalia, *Reproductive Restraints*.

109. Mukherji, *Birth Control for the Millions*, 19.

110. Ibid., 20.

111. *San Francisco Chronicle*, December 11, 1917.

112. See Roy, *M. N. Roy Memoirs*, 186. Thanks to Projit Mukharji for this reference.

113. Chakraberty's works include *Principles of Education*; *Food and Health*; *Sexology of the Hindus*; *Endocrine Glands*; *National Problems*; *An Interpretation of Ancient Hindu Medicine*; *The Outline of Rationalism*; *The Racial History of India*, reprinted as *Racial Basis of Indian Culture*; and *Sex Life in Ancient India*.

114. See Sarton, "Review of *A Study in Hindu Social Polity*," 268. See also appendices in Chakraberty, *The Outline of Rationalism*, 1–33. He was reviewed in the Calcutta periodical *Amrita Bazar Patrika*, *Calcutta Medical Journal*, and *Modern Review*, as well as reviews in *The Madras Medical Journal* and *The Indian Medical Journal*, *Journal of the American Oriental Society*, and *Journal of the Royal Asiatic Society of Great Britain and Ireland*.

115. Chakraberty, *Sexology of the Hindus*, preface.

116. Ibid., 42.

117. Ibid., 49.

118. Ibid., 51–53.

119. Chakraberty cites the "iconoclast Mahmud of Ghazni," who at the destruction of the temple of Somanath, found 3,000 temple girls, who were then enslaved. See Chakraberty, *Sexology of the Hindus*, 116–17. Elsewhere, Chakraberty includes detailed commentary on the sexual tendencies of Muslims in India. In his *Cultural History of Hindus*, he describes how the "Moslems who idealize sexuality as an expression of their virility, a kind of prayer to their creator by displaying his creative energy, indulge in sexual excesses through their polygamous practice and mentality are degenerating." See Chakraberty, *Cultural History of Hindus*, 306. On the figure of Mahmud of Ghazni as the paradigmatic symbol of "Muslim despotism" and its effects on female sexuality in the colonial episteme, see Asif, *The Loss of Hindustan*.

120. See also his racial theory in Chakraberty, *Cultural History of Hindus*, 287–90. He emphasizes comparative racial differences in physiology between different racial types, from Mongols, Negroes, to Aryans, and Austro-Asiatics. From racial types, he moves to the *Puranas* and the *Mahabharata*, and finally, provides an extended analysis of *Kamasutra*. Ethnology became race science, which became comparative philology. Chakraberty, *Cultural History of Hindus*, 307. See also racial types and ancient texts in Chakraberty, *An Ethnic Interpretation of Pauranika Personages*, 61.

121. An notable example of the reach of this episteme can be found in the work of P. Thomas, a scholar based in Bombay, including *Women and Marriage in India*, a book reissued as recently as 2000 in India, and *Kama Kalpa; or, The Hindu Ritual of Love*.

122. Banerji, *The Castaway of Indian Society*; Banerji, *Crime and Sex in Ancient India*; chapter IV, on pornography, addresses "work dealing with or referring to prostitutes—*Kamasutra* on prostitution—*Kuttanimata*—*Desopadesa*—*Kalav*—Harlot's character and the evils of enjoying her," in Banerji, *Aspects of Ancient Indian Life*.

123. Ghose, *Rati-Sastram*, 21.

Chapter 2. Repetition: Law and the Sociology of Deviant Female Sexuality

1. Section 372, "Selling a minor for purposes of prostitution, etc." and Section 373, "Buying minor for purposes of prostitution, etc." from Chapter XVI: Of Offences Affecting the Human Body, Indian Penal Code of 1860, Indian Law Commission and Macaulay, *The Indian Penal Code, as Originally Framed in 1837*, 51–63.

2. A. H. Giles, Deputy Commissioner of Police in Calcutta to Secretary to Govt. of Bengal, in collected memoranda by officers consulted on the subject of forbidding the possession of girls under ten years of age by prostitutes, Judicial Branch, Judicial Department, October 1872, B. No. 252–335, West Bengal State Archives (hereafter WBSA).

3. Memoranda, October 1872, B. No. 252–335, WBSA.

4. A. Mackenzie, Officiating Secretary to the Government of Bengal, Judicial Department to H. L. Dampier, Officiating Secretary to the Govt. of India, October 17, 1872, Home Dept. Proceedings, July 1873, no. 156, National Archives of India (hereafter NAI).

5. As Bernard Cohn demonstrates, these practices of inquiry reflect the diverse "investigative modalities" of the colonial state—of observation, inquisition, enumeration, surveillance—that made India a critical site for the development of state technologies of knowledge. Cohn, *Colonialism and Its Forms of Knowledge*, 5–15.

6. Cohn, "The Census and Objectification in South Asia," *The Bernard Cohn Omnibus*, 230.

7. Lata Mani, in her essential 1989 article "Contentious Traditions," proposes that writing the history of law requires critically engaging the role of the question and answer in the constitution of "official knowledge." Mani, "Contentious Traditions," 121–22.

8. A. Mackenzie, Officiating Secretary to the Government of Bengal, Judicial Department, to H. L. Dampier, Officiating Secretary to the Govt. of India, October 17, 1872, Home Dept. Proceedings, July 1873, no.156, NAI.

9. On the constitution of the fact as a discrete unit of knowledge in the context of early modern Britain, see Poovey, *A History of the Modern Fact*.

10. On the penal code, see Chan, Wright, and Yeo, *Codification, Macaulay and the Indian Penal Code*, 34–38.

11. Stokes, *The English Utilitarians and India*; Stuy, "Macaulay and the Indian Penal Code of 1862," 513–57; Singha, *A Despotism of Law*; Yang, *Crime and Criminality in British India*. On the Police Act of 1861, see Gupta, *The Police in British India, 1861–1947*; Arnold, *Police Power and Colonial Rule*.

12. The uniform code built on Company laws from the early nineteenth century that saw prostitution as behavior in need of regulation. See Wald, "From Begums and Bibis to Abandoned Females and Idle Women," 5–25.

13. Indian Law Commission and Thomas Macaulay, *The Indian Penal Code, as Originally Framed in 1837*, 272.

14. On Contagious Diseases Acts and the resultant hospitals and jails, see Levine, *Prostitution, Race, and Politics*; on jails, see Arnold, "The Colonial Prison," 148–87.

15. Section 377 was rarely prosecuted in colonial India but was often used as a mode of intimidation. See Bhaskaran, "The Politics of Penetration," 15–29; Arondekar, "Time's Corpus,"

143–56; On the regulation of sexual difference through the scientific investigation of the gender non-normative body, see Arondekar, *For the Record*, 67–96.

16. Early sexual relationships, especially those between British men and Indian women, were regulated both through criminal law and especially through civil laws that sought to regulate marriage and the inheritance of property. Durba Ghosh's analysis of class difference in inheritance and fears of miscegenation in early colonial Bengal demonstrates the significance of interracial sexual relationships between British men and Indian women and the hierarchies that resulted. These racial intimacies shaped the development of the legal apparatus of civil law, from marriage to inheritance, in the early nineteenth century. See Ghosh, *Sex and the Family in Colonial India*, 1–34.

17. *Census of Bengal, 1881*, 15. See also Appadurai, "Number in the Colonial Imagination," in *Modernity at Large*, 314–39.

18. C. Bernard, Secretary to the Government of Bengal, Judicial Department, to All Divisional Commissioners and to the Commander of Police, Calcutta, April 19, 1872. Proposed measures for checking the practice of bringing up very young girls to the profession of prostitution, Judicial, Home Department, July 1873, NAI. Indrani Chatterjee powerfully demonstrates the link between the "buying and selling of girls" to the language of kinship and domesticity in gendered state discourses about slavery in the nineteenth century. See Chatterjee, *Gender, Slavery, and Law*, 221–22.

19. "Reply to an Enquiry by the Magistrate of Balasore as to whether he is empowered, with a view to their rescue, to enquire into cases of girls brought up for prostitution," Education Proceedings 57–61, October 1862, 25–27, WBSA.

20. W. C. Lacey, District Superintendent of Police, Cuttack forwarded to the Secretary to the Government of Bengal, July 26, 1867, Possession of Minor Girls, Judicial, WBSA.

21. C. S. Park, Magistrate of Tipperah to the Commissioner of Chittagong, June 5, 1872, Memoranda, October 1872, B. No. 252–335, WBSA.

22. Baboo Kasi Kenkur Sen, Magistrate of Rajshahye, to the Magistrate of Rajshahye, May 24, 1872, Memoranda, October 1872, B. No. 252–335, WBSA. See also letter from Police Commissioner of Calcutta to Secretary to the Government of Bengal, May 8, 1872, Memoranda, October 1872, B. No. 252–335, WBSA.

23. Baboo Kasi Kenkur Sen, to the Magistrate of Rajshahye, May 24, 1872, Memoranda, October 1872, B. No. 252–335, WBSA.

24. Magistrate of Dinajpore to Commissioner of Circuit Berhampore, May 15, 1872, Memoranda, October 1872, B. No. 252–335, WBSA.

25. Beverley, *Report of the Census of Bengal 1872*, 189.

26. Ibid., 188.

27. Ibid., 189.

28. Report on the Census of the Town and Suburbs of Calcutta, 1881, 139. See also Samita Sen's discussion of Vaishnavs among the laboring classes of women in Calcutta. Sen, *Women and Labour in Late Colonial India*, 201–4.

29. Bankim Chandra Chatterjee to the Magistrate of Moorshedabad, April 19, 1872, Memoranda, October 1872, B. No. 252–335, WBSA.

30. Ibid.

31. W. Wavell, Magistrate of Moorshedabad, to the Commissioner of Rajshaye, May 31, 1872, Memoranda, October 1872, B. No. 252–335, WBSA.

32. Ibid.

33. Ibid.

34. Mani, "Contentious Traditions," 119–56.

35. A. Abercrombie, Commissioner of Dacca to the Secretary to the Government of Bengal, Judicial Department, June 18, 1872, Memoranda, October 1872, B. No. 252–335, WBSA.

36. Ibid.

37. Ibid.

38. Babu Taraknath Mullick, Deputy Magistrate of Madaripur to the Magistrate of Backergunge, May 24, 1872; H. C. Sutherland to the Commissioner of Circuit, Dacca Division, May 31, 1872, Memoranda, October 1872, B. No. 252–335, WBSA.

39. D. R. Lyall, Magistrate of Dacca to the Commissioner of Dacca, May 15, 1872, Memoranda, Judicial Branch, Judicial Department, October 1872, B. No. 252–335, WBSA.

40. Ibid.

41. Magistrate of Dinajpore to Commissioner of Circuit Berhampore, May 15, 1872, Memoranda, October 1872, B. No. 252–335, WBSA.

42. Babu Taraknath Mullick, Deputy Magistrate of Madaripur to the Magistrate of Backergunge, May 24, 1872, Memoranda, October 1872, B. No. 252–335, WBSA.

43. Ibid.

44. As reported by Sutherland, *The Weekly Reporter, Appellate High Court,* vol. 12, 57.

45. Ibid., 55.

46. There is a robust historiography on the importance of the Contagious Diseases Act for regulating sexual commerce and defining new forms of colonial governance premised on racial difference, gender, and sexuality. See Ballhatchet, *Race, Sex, and Class under the Raj*; Philippa Levine has produced key research on the workings of the Contagious Diseases Acts in India and across the British Empire. In doing so, she establishes that racial hierarchies were produced through the law, from interracial relationships between British men and Indian women to the arrival of European women to the colonies. See Levine, *Prostitution, Race, and Politics*. Ashwini Tambe carefully traces how the Contagious Diseases Acts created prostitution as a site of social and legal production and a key site of legal imagination in *Codes of Misconduct*. Erica Wald suggests that the East India Company regulated prostitution in similar ways to the Contagious Diseases Acts long before the 1860s. See "From Begums and Bibis," 5–25. See also Legg, *Prostitution and the Ends of Empire*, 1–94. On prostitutes as a threat to the military and the security of colonial rule, see Levine, *Prostitution, Race, and Politics*, 44–45.

47. Philippa Levine describes the women who came under the Contagious Diseases Acts as sex workers and part of the sex trade in her comprehensive study of the working of the Contagious Diseases Acts across the empire. See Levine, "Orientalist Sociology," 11, and *Prostitution, Race, and Politics*, 133, 325. Ashwini Tambe describes the historical subjects in her book engaged in sex work and sex trade, but powerfully notes the problems with "presentist interpretation" for ancient and medieval practices of "non-marital sexual interaction," described as "'prostitution,' 'harlotry,' and 'courtesanship' by latter-day historians." See Tambe, *Codes of Misconduct*, xxii. In her article "From Begums and Bibis," Erica Wald importantly differentiates the types included in the early East India Company's use of the category. She reveals an early

sociology that sought to characterize women as prostitutes, including *begums* (women in relationships with British men), *nautch* girls, and *devadasi* women. Stephen Legg cautions against the use of "sex worker" for the historical term "prostitute." However, he describes his primary sources as an archive of sexual commerce. See Legg, *Prostitution and the Ends of Empire*, 9.

48. Proceedings of Department of Agriculture, Revenue and Commerce, August 12, 1871, Working of Contagious Diseases Act, 165, NAI. On petitions against classification, see Stuart Hogg, Commissioner of Police, Calcutta to the Secretary to the Government of Bengal, Judicial Department, 2nd December 1869, 5–6, WBSA.

49. *Census of Calcutta and Its Suburbs* (Calcutta: Bengal Secretariat Press, 1871), 8.

50. *Census of Calcutta and Its Suburbs* (Calcutta: Bengal Secretariat Press, 1891), 31.

51. Dr. Payne, Superintendent of Lock Hospitals, Calcutta, to Stuart Hogg, Commissioner of Police, dated March 29, 1870, 8, WBSA.

52. Dr. Payne, Superintendent of Lock Hospitals, Calcutta, to Stuart Hogg, Commissioner of Police, Judicial Department, dated March 29, 1870, WBSA.

53. Working of Lock Hospitals, Medical Branch, File no. 68, August, 20–22, 1879; Legality of Arrests By Police Under CD Acts, Medical Branch, File 68, November 4, 1879, WBSA.

54. Dr. Payne, Superintendent of Lock Hospitals, Calcutta, to Stuart Hogg, Commissioner of Police, dated March 29, 1870, WBSA.

55. Banerjee, *Dangerous Outcast*, 153.

56. Stuart Hogg, Commissioner of Police, Calcutta, to the Secretary to the Government of Bengal, Judicial Department, 2 December 1869, 2, WBSA.

57. Dr. Payne, Superintendent of Lock Hospitals, Calcutta, to Stuart Hogg, Commissioner of Police, dated March 29, 1870, 18, WBSA.

58. Ibid., 15.

59. Ibid., 2.

60. Ibid.

61. Surgeon Major Payne, Superintendent of Lock Hospitals to Stuart Hogg, Commissioner of the Police, February 1, 1871, p. 674, Oriental and India Office Collections (hereafter OIOC).

62. Ibid.

63. Stuart Hogg, Commissioner of Police, Calcutta, to the Secretary to the Government of Bengal, Judicial Department, 2 December 1869, 3, WBSA.

64. Stuart Hogg, Commissioner of Police, Calcutta, to the Secretary to the Government of Bengal, Judicial Department, 2 December 1869, 7, WBSA.

65. Lock Hospitals, Dum Dum and Barrackpore, General Department, 1878, 7, WBSA.

66. Horace Cockerell, Secretary to the Government of Bengal, Judicial, Political and Appointments Department to Secretary, Government of Bengal, Home Department, 11 July 1878, 1338, OIOC.

67. Proceedings of Department of Agriculture, Revenue and Commerce, August 12, 1871, Lock Hospitals in the Bengal Presidency, Index no. 10, pros. No. 16, Working of Contagious Diseases Act, 161–62, NAI.

68. Proposal for the amendment, Medical branch, File no. 8, number 17–19, July 1879, NAI.

69. S. C. Bayley, Officiating Secretary to the Government of Bengal, Judicial Dept., to the Secretary, to the Government of India, 19 June 1871, 73, NAI.

70. Stuart Hogg, Commissioner of Police for the Town and Suburbs of Calcutta, to the Secretary to the Government of Bengal, Calcutta, March 8, 1871, WBSA.

71. Stuart Hogg, Commissioner of Police, Calcutta, to the Secretary to the Government of Bengal, Judicial Department, 2 December 1869, 5, WBSA.

72. Ibid.

73. Levine comments on the indexes that point to the previous existence of petitions in a range of archives. See Levine, *Prostitution, Race, and Politics*, 222.

74. Surgeon Major A. Payne to Commissioner of Police, Calcutta, February 1, 1871, 674, OIOC.

75. Accusation brought against the police by certain prostitutes of Calcutta. Observations of the Govt. of India, Home Dept., on the subject of prostitution. San. Proceedings 1–3, August 1869, 1, WBSA.

76. Accusation brought against the police by certain prostitutes of Calcutta, 1–3, WBSA (emphasis added).

77. Accusation brought against the police by certain prostitutes of Calcutta, 5, WBSA.

78. On the movement against the Contagious Diseases Acts among British feminists, see Burton, *Burdens of History*, 127–70. On details of the repeal of the official Contagious Diseases Acts across the empire, see Levine, *Prostitution, Race, and Empire*, 91–145.

79. On the British feminist movement to repeal the Contagious Diseases Act in India, see Burton, *Burdens of History*; Andrew and Bushnell, *The Queen's Daughters in India*.

80. H. H. Risley reproduces every ethnographic question, including exemplary kinship diagram structures in *The Tribes and Castes of Bengal: Ethnographic Glossary*, vol. 2, 148–73.

81. On children, see Hunter, *A Statistical Account of Bengal*, vol. 10, 346; each of Hunter's studies followed the same structure, from "Topography and General Aspects of the District," to "The People," which gave the statistical enumeration of the peoples of the district, classified based on marriage, caste groups, religion, etc. See Hunter, *A Statistical Account of Bengal*, vols. 1–20.

82. On female infanticide in colonial India, see Vishwanath, "Female Infanticide," 2313–18; Bhatnagar, Dube, and Dube, *Female Infanticide in India*.

83. For a useful discussion of a comparative colonial history of infanticide, see Scully, "Narratives of Infanticide in the Aftermath of Slave Emancipation in the Nineteenth-Century Cape Colony, South Africa," 88–105.

84. See for example W. Macpherson, Officiating Judge, to the Secretary to the Government of Bengal, Legislative Department, April 6, 1877, Application of section 302 of IPC, Proceedings 10–39, August 1877, WBSA.

85. On Rao's indictment of the colonial state, see Ganachari, "Infanticide in Colonial Western India," 902–6.

86. Padma Anagol uses the phrase "infanticidal woman." See Anagol, "The Emergence of the Female Criminal in India," 73–93.

87. W. Macpherson, Officiating Judge, to the Secretary to the Government of Bengal, Legislative Department, April 7, 1877, Application of section 302 of IPC, Proceedings 10–39, August 1877, 123–24, WBSA.

88. J. M. Lewis, Sessions Judge of Bhagulpore to Secretary to the Govt. of Bengal, Judicial Department, Questions regarding the application of section 302 of IPC in case of a woman killing her illegitimate child directly after birth, Judicial File 58, Proceedings 10–39, August 1877,

101, WBSA. On investigations that linked women's sexual deviance to abortion, see chapter 3, "Circularity."

89. S. C. Bayley, application of section 302 of IPC, Proceedings 10–39, August 1877, 127, WBSA.

90. "Measures for putting a stop to the practice of police officers making enquiries into the pregnancy of widows," Judicial Proceedings of the Government of Bengal, Proceeding 76, Feb. 1861, WBSA.

91. W. Macpherson, Officiating Judge, to the Secretary to the Government of Bengal, Legislative Department, April 6, 1877, Questions regarding the application of section 302 of IPC, Proceedings 10–39, August 1877, 124, WBSA.

92. C. B. Garrett, Sessions Judge of Dacca to the Secretary to the Government of Bengal, Judicial Department, application of section 302 of IPC, Proceedings 10–39, August 1877, 119, WBSA.

93. L. R. Tottenham, Sessions Judge of Midnapore, to the Secretary to the Government of Bengal, Judicial Department, November 27, 1876, Questions regarding the application of section 302 of IPC, Proceedings 10–39, August 1877, 112, WBSA.

94. R. F. Rampini, to the Secretary to the Government of Bengal, Judicial Department, November 27, 1876, Questions regarding the application of section 302 of IPC, Proceedings 10–39, August 1877, 113, WBSA.

95. Baboo Juggadanund Mookerjee, Junior Government Pleader, High Court, to the Superintendent and Remembrancer of Legal Affairs, February 21, 1877, Questions regarding the application of section 302 of IPC, Proceedings 10–39, August 1877, 121, WBSA.

96. Questions regarding the application of section 302 of IPC, Proceedings 10–39, August 1877, WBSA. On the rationale of punishment and the irrationality of crime see Stuy, "Macaulay and the Indian Penal Code of 1862," 546; and Wiener, *Reconstructing the Criminal*, 48–49.

97. Indian Law Commission and Macaulay, *The Indian Penal Code, as Originally Framed in 1837*, 272. See also Sarkar's discussion of the law commission and infanticide in *Rebels, Wives, Saints*, 128–29.

98. See extensive exchanges on punishment in Questions regarding the application of section 302, WBSA.

99. On gendered systems of British imperial indenture and precarious conditions of indentured women's lives, see Bahadur, *Coolie Woman*.

100. S. C. Bayley, Secretary to the Government of Bengal, Judicial Department, to the Secretary to the Government of India, Legislative Department, Questions regarding the application of section 302 of IPC, Proceedings 10–39, August 1877, WBSA.

101. Letter from S. C. Bayley, Secretary to the Government of Bengal, Judicial Department, to the Secretary to the Government of India, Legislative Department, application of section 302 of IPC, Proceedings 10–39, August 1877, 128, WBSA.

102. Special account of cases of infanticide to be given in future Police reports of Calcutta and Bengal, Judicial File 211, Proceedings 15–16, Nov. 1882, WBSA.

103. Cases in which women are guilty of infanticide, Judicial File 237, Proceedings 57–58, Feb 1880, WBSA.

104. District and Sessions Judge Chittagong to the Secretary to the Government of Bengal, November 24, 1881, Statistics of Infanticide in India, File 211, Proceedings B 398–432,

February 1882. Instructions regarding the embodiment in provincial Police Reports, or in the resolution recorded by Local Governments thereon, of cases of women convicted of infanticide, Police, File P-3R-35 (1–4), Proceedings 28–32, October 1900, WBSA.

105. On late nineteenth-century debates about the welfare of women and critiques of the colonial state by Bengali men, see Sinha, *Colonial Masculinity*.

106. *Amrita Bazar Patrika*, May 30, 1889, 6.

107. Ibid.

108. The Government of Bengal received a petition on April 7, 1887, from inhabitants of Calcutta for the restriction of social vice in Calcutta, Index, WBSA.

109. A. H. Giles, Collected memoranda on the subject of forbidding the possession of girls, WBSA; Calcutta Vigilance Association, *The Calcutta Suppression of Immoral Traffic Bill 1923*.

110. Samita Sen has described colonial depictions of the dangerous woman factory worker, including as a prostitute. See her *Women and Labour in Colonial India*. See also Sarkar, *Bengal 1928–1934*, 62; Banerjee, *Men, Women, and Domestics*.

111. Curjel, "Women's Medical Service in India," File No. 2-R20/1923, April 1923, Commerce Branch, WBSA.

112. Thompson, *Census of India, 1921*, vol. 5, 897.

113. Indrani Chatterjee innovatively rereads a 1935 report by the commissioner of police in Calcutta submitted to the League of Nations, which sought to systematically detail the "life histories of fifty prostitutes." "Refracted Reality," 28–31.

Chapter 3. Circularity: Forensics, Abortion, and the Evidence of Deviant Female Sexuality

1. "Letter from the Coroner of Calcutta to the Secretary to the Government of Bengal, Judicial Department, dated 14th December 1885," Judicial Department, Judicial Branch, F.N. 343, No. B 334 & 335, January 1886, WBSA. This coroner's report from 1885 appears in an inquiry by the Jury of Inquest into the creation of an asylum for widows, a request swiftly dismissed by the Government of Bengal.

2. Letter from the Coroner of Calcutta to the Secretary to the Government of Bengal, December 1885.

3. Ibid.

4. In 1871, the Coroner's Act established the official position of coroner and endowed the coroner with the right to inquire and judge the circumstances of death, whether accidental or intentional. The act created the Inquest as an official judicial proceeding with the right to view the body by the coroner and jury in attendance and the right to call witnesses. The coroner acted as a judge of the cause of death in criminal proceedings. Coroner's Act, Act 4 of 1871, 27 January 1871.

5. "Letter from the Coroner," WBSA.

6. The coroner's report of Kally's death appears in the B files of the Judicial Branch of the Government of Bengal because of a query into the possibility of making an asylum for widows, which is summarily dismissed as not the concern of the colonial government. Ranajit Guha explores the question of who lays claim to the archive of a fragmented testimony in his "Chandra's Death," 135–65.

7. On legal medicine in India in relation to rape adjudication, see Kolsky's dissertation "'The Body Evidencing the Crime,'" 278–347; and her article "'The Body Evidencing the Crime,'" 109–30. In Europe, see Crawford, "Legalizing Medicine"; on forensics in the colonies, see Jentzen, "Death and Empire"; Fahmy, "The Anatomy of Justice," 224–71; for an excellent comprehensive study of legal medicine in twentieth-century China, see Asen, *Death in Beijing*.

8. The question of colonial difference has long shaped the historiography on South Asia. Most notably, it was argued by Partha Chatterjee, captured in his phrase the "rule of colonial difference" in his *The Nation and Its Fragments*, 19. For further discussion of textbooks of medical jurisprudence and Chatterjee's rule of colonial difference in the context of colonial rape evidence and adjudication, see Elizabeth Kolsky's dissertation, "'The Body Evidencing the Crime,'" 278–347 and her article, "'The Body Evidencing the Crime,'" 109–30. See also Arondekar, *For the Record*, 67–96, as well as Ishita Pande's critical engagement with textbooks of medical jurisprudence in India, rape, and gendered notions of age in *Medicine, Race, and Liberalism in British Bengal*, 156–57.

9. I am highlighting an epistemological shift where authorities produced a claim to objectivity in their descriptions through detailed narratives of anatomy and social behavior. Michel Foucault traces this epistemological shift from evocative modes of description to that of expert description: "From what moment, from what semantic or syntactical change, can one recognize that language has turned into rational discourse? . . . A rather more meticulous gaze, a more measured verbal tread with a more secure footing upon things, a more delicate, though sometimes rather confused choice of adjective—are these not merely the proliferation, in medical language, of a style which, since the days of galenic medicine, has extended whole regions of description around the greyness of things and their shapes?" See Foucault, *The Birth of the Clinic*, xi.

10. Reagan, *When Abortion Was a Crime*, 1–18. I also build on the research of Supriya Guha's study of unwanted pregnancies in colonial and popular understandings of reproduction in colonial Bengal. See Guha, "The Unwanted Pregnancy in Colonial Bengal," 403–35.

11. See Katharine Park's key study of women, dissection, and the privileged status of the womb for the secrets of women, *Secrets of Women*, 26.

12. The naming of those women in forensic medical reports includes Chandra, Phulmoni, Shama, and many others. In his moving 1987 essay "Chandra's Death," Ranajit Guha produces a sketch of a community found in a testimony from nineteenth-century Bengal. The testimony Guha refers to concerns an "untamed fragment" on the death of a woman, Chandra, who dies from an abortion. In constructing a caste history and a kinship chart for the Bagdi caste in nineteenth-century Bengal, Guha relies on sociological descriptions from colonial ethnographer H. H. Risley's *The Tribes and Castes of Bengal* (1891) to correlate the information of the testimony. Guha's recuperation of the social world of the Bagdi caste depends on a critical colonial episteme of sociological fact mandated by the colonial testimony. This colonial episteme was also deployed in Risley's 1891 comprehensive sociological project produced at the same historical moment. Guha's reading of the social landscape is based in the mode and categories of description contained in the testimony itself, which resulted from a colonial legal regime and its mandates for detailed descriptions of the social reasons for abortion. See Guha, "Chandra's Death," 139. Perhaps the most cited example of medical writing on the female body in the colonial period is the medico-legal report concerning the child Phulmoni in debates over Age of Consent legislation in the late nineteenth century. Tanika Sarkar reads the in-depth medical description of

Phulmoni's body as representative of the horror of sexual violence and the complicity of the colonial state in child rape. Ishita Pande provides an innovative reading of the medico-legal assessment of Phulmoni in the making of Age of Consent Debates. She critically considers the centrality of the body in the making of claims to humanitarianism by the state and anti-colonial elites. See Pande, "Phulmoni's Body," 9–30.

13. For important inquiries into gender and science in India, see Guha, "The Nature of Woman," 23–38. Also see Guha, "A Science of Woman"; and Pande, *Medicine, Race and Liberalism in British Bengal*. Key studies where medico-legal description shapes debates include Sinha, *Colonial Masculinity*; Nair, *Women and Law in Colonial India*; and Sarkar, *Hindu Wife, Hindu Nation*. On the comparative development of gynecology in Britain and the United States, see Jordanova, *Sexual Visions*; Russett, *Sexual Science*; Moscucci, *The Science of Woman*; Bashford, *Purity and Pollution*.

14. The first textbook on legal medicine for India was Baynes, *Hints on Medical Jurisprudence, Adapted and Intended for the Use of Those Engaged in Judicial and Magisterial Duties in British India*, followed by Chevers, *A Manual on Medical Jurisprudence for Bengal and the Northwestern Provinces*. On other investigative forensic technologies developed in India, see Chandak Sengoopta's study of fingerprinting, *Imprint of the Raj*.

15. On the Evidence Act in relation to the IPC, see Chan, Wright, and Yeo, *Codification, Macaulay and the Indian Penal Code*, 34–38. On the medico-legal expert, see Kolsky, "The Body Evidencing the Crime," 16. On the codification of the criminal code, see Kolsky, "Codification and the Rule of Colonial Difference," 631–83.

16. Officials made claims to medico-legal evidence, in particular in cases of foeticide (sections 315 and 316), infanticide (section 315) and in its sentencing under the act of murder (section 302), and rape (section 376).

17. On anatomy in the making of racial difference, see Harrison, "Racial Pathologies," 187.

18. Webb, *Pathologica Indica; or, The Anatomy of Indian Diseases, Medical and Surgical*, 329–31 (typeface in original source).

19. Webb, *Pathologica Indica*, 333.

20. Ibid., ii–iv.

21. Ibid., 255–58.

22. Ibid., 57.

23. Ibid., viii. Emphasis in original.

24. Ibid., 256.

25. Ibid., 259–60.

26. Ibid.

27. Baynes, *Hints on Medical Jurisprudence*, 121.

28. On the development of nineteenth-century textbooks and the role of these textbooks in rape adjudication, see Kolsky, "The Body Evidencing the Crime," 278–347. These manuals were followed with publications by colonial administrators I. B. Lyon and J.D.B. Gribble. Gribble's *Outlines of Medical Jurisprudence for Indian Courts* appeared in 1885; three years later, Lyon published his *Medical Jurisprudence for India with Illustrative Cases*. Lyon's book continues to be published today, with at least eleven editions, most recently published in 2012. Eventually, the publication of a widely influential textbook by the Indian doctor and professor of medical jurisprudence in Agra, Jaising P. Modi, in 1920, came to define the field of forensic medicine.

NOTES TO CHAPTER 3

29. Since its publication, J. P. Modi's manual, which reproduced many of Chevers's ideas about of crimes of "Chastity," "Infanticide," and "Foeticide," has been crucial to the jurisprudence of rape, abortion (until its legalization), and infanticide. See Mitra and Satish, "Testing Chastity, Evidencing Rape," 51–58.

30. Chevers, *A Manual of Medical Jurisprudence for Bengal and the Northwest Provinces*, 460–532. For postcolonial textbooks, see Agnes, "To Whom Do Experts Testify?," 1859–66.

31. Chevers, *A Manual of Medical Jurisprudence for India*, 746.

32. Ibid., 712. On the colonial marginalization of Indian midwifery and the professionalization of obstetrics under the supervision of medical doctors, see Forbes, "Managing Midwifery in India," 152–72.

33. Harvey, *Report on the Medico-legal Returns Received from the Civil Surgeons in the Bengal Presidency during the Years of 1870, 1871, and 1872*, 295 (emphasis added).

34. Ibid., 305 (emphasis added).

35. Harvey, "Report on Medico-Legal Returns," *Indian Medical Gazette*, 309–10 (emphasis added).

36. Guha, "Chandra's Death," 135–40.

37. The authoritative claim for the case in the modern world, as Lauren Berlant describes, emerges in the abstraction of particularity into exemplarity. Berlant, "On the Case," 664.

38. Harvey, "Report on Medico-Legal Returns," 309.

39. "Review of Robert Harvey's Reports," *The Lancet*, July 8, 1876, 63.

40. Lyon, *Medical Jurisprudence for India, with Illustrative Cases* (1888), 376–77.

41. Lyon, *Medical Jurisprudence for India, with Illustrative Cases* (1921), 139 (emphasis added).

42. Chevers, *Manual of Medical Jurisprudence for India*, 725.

43. Baynes, *Hints on Medical Jurisprudence*, 128.

44. Chevers, *Manual of Medical Jurisprudence for India*, 251.

45. Chevers uses abortion to describe the different botanical agents available to use as abortifacients. In his text he describes these agents in detail, including: "(1) Arsenic. (2) Amalgum of Tin, Sulphate of Soda, Silicate of Potash (in one packet). (3) Sulphate of Copper. (4) Wood Charcoal. (5) Capsicum Seeds. (6) Upang, or 'Achyranthes Aspera.' (7) Chitta, 'Plumbago Zeylanica?' (8) Lall Chitra, 'Plumbago Rosea.' (9) Root of 'Nerium Oleander,' 6 inches long, tipped with Assafoetida. (10) Opium. (11) A powder containing Black Pepper, burnt Sulphate of Copper and Cantharides. (12) Assafoetida." Chevers, *Manual of Medical Jurisprudence for India*, 714.

46. See Arnold, *Toxic Histories*, 33–34. I have also learned about poisons and abortion in personal correspondence with Mitra Sharafi on the basis of her research, "Abortion and Medical Experts in the British Indian Courtroom," presented at the 16th Berkshire Conference of Women Historians, 2014, in her ongoing research on the history of medical jurisprudence in India.

47. Lyon, *Medical Jurisprudence for India* (1921), 275–76.

48. Jordanova, *Sexual Visions*, 51–52. On the procedure for the genital exam, see Gribble, *Outlines of Medical Jurisprudence for Indian Courts*, 239–43. The doctor was to examine the external genital organs, which displayed evidence of sexual deviance and potential involvement in prostitution if there were "syphilitic sores" (243), and detail whether the hymen was ruptured, any evidence of penetration, and the length of the vagina.

49. Chevers, *Manual on Medical Jurisprudence for India*, 712.

50. Chevers, *Manual on Medical Jurisprudence for Bengal*, 491.

51. Chevers, *Manual on Medical Jurisprudence for India*, 712.

52. Chevers, *Manual on Medical Jurisprudence for Bengal*, 705.

53. Lyon, *Medical Jurisprudence for India* (1921), 317.

54. Ibid., 33.

55. Lyon, *Medical Jurisprudence for India* (1888), 324.

56. In 1920, an Indian doctor and professor of medical jurisprudence, Jaising P. Modi, published *A Textbook of Medical Jurisprudence and Toxicology*, which heavily relied on the textbooks by Lyon and Chevers as guides. Modi's textbook is the authoritative reference book on medical jurisprudence in India, Pakistan, and Bangladesh today. These textbooks, based on Chevers's and Lyon's original manuals, insisted that women bring false claims of rape and required that the medical doctor or examiner determine the women's sexual character in their assessment of physical evidence in cases of rape. Elsewhere, Mrinal Satish and I have argued that these manuals use a parallel form of reasoning where women's sexual character is judged through prejudicial interpretations of evidence of genitalia, particularly the state of the hymen and the widespread use of the finger test. We closely analyzed textbook chapters on virginity and rape to demonstrate how textbooks treat the medical assessment of virginity as closely connected to determination of rape, as both chapters assess the state of the genitalia and prescribe the use of tests to determine the past sexual history of a woman. See the discussion of false charges, the assessment of the hymen, and the importance of injuries in forensic medical textbooks in Mitra and Satish, "Testing Chastity, Evidencing Rape," 51–55.

57. Chande, *The Police in India*, 72–88.

58. "Measures for putting a stop to the practice of Police Officers making enquiries into the pregnancy of widows," Judicial Proceedings of the Government of Bengal, Proceedings 76–78, Feb. 1861, and 326, April 1861, WBSA; "Interference of police with cases of illegitimate pregnancy with a view to prevent miscarriage," Judicial File 232, Proceedings 87–89. March 1881, WBSA; "Examination of women in criminal cases," Judicial File 830. Proceedings 19–25, December 1888, WBSA.

59. On the use of sexuality as blackmail in England and America, see McLaren, *Sexual Blackmail*. My thanks to Sharon Marcus for this reference and key connection between different kinds of blackmail.

60. "Measures for putting a stop," April 1861, WBSA.

61. Ibid.

62. "Interference of police with cases of illegitimate pregnancy with a view to prevent miscarriage," Judicial File 232, Proceedings 87–89. March 1881, WBSA.

63. "Measures for putting a stop," April 1861, WBSA.

64. Gribble and Heher, *Outlines of Medical Jurisprudence for India*, 267.

65. Gribble and Heher, *Outlines of Medical Jurisprudence*, 268.

66. Chew, "The Case of the 'Unchaste' Widow," 33–43.

67. "Examination of women in criminal cases," Judicial File 830. proceedings 19–25, December 1888, WBSA.

68. "Examination of women in criminal cases," December 1888, WBSA.

69. Quotation from the section on "Criminal Abortion" in Chevers, *Manual of Medical Jurisprudence for Bengal*, 489.

70. "Examination of women in criminal cases," December 1888, WBSA.

71. Chevers, *Manual of Medical Jurisprudence for Bengal*, 489 (emphasis added).

72. Bandhyopadhyay, *Gurbini Bandhab*.

73. See also Bandhyopadhyay's *Balchikitsa*, vol. 1, *The Diseases of Infancy and Childhood*.

74. Bandhyopadhyay, *Gurbini Bandhab*, 71.

75. Ibid., 72.

76. Ibid., 73.

77. Ibid.

78. Ibid., 74.

79. Ibid., 73.

80. See Baxi, *Public Secrets of Law*; Satish, *Discretion, Discrimination and the Rule of Law*.

Chapter 4. Evolution: Ethnology and the Primitivity of Deviant Female Sexuality

1. The degree was given starting in 1909 as part of the Department of Political Economy and Political Philosophy. Sociology then became part of the curriculum of the ancient department, owing to the discipline's roots in philological studies of India, and eventually became an independent department in 1921. The University of Bombay began the first Sociology Department in India in 1919.

2. "M.A. Examination 1911, Political Economy and Political Philosophy (B), Sociology Paper I," included in Appendix VIII of Primary Sources in Gupta, *Sociology in India*, 296.

3. Spencer begins his first preface to the book *The Principles of Sociology* by declaring on page v: "For the Science of Society, the word 'Sociology' was introduced by M. Comte." He then describes numerous savage tribes in his comparison of the low status of women, citing Winwood Reade on Africans in his *Savage Africa* (1862) and numerous other colonial ethnographies of Australia, Sumatra, Madagascar, and Brazil, and the Chippewa, Andamans, and Bushmen of South Africa. He describes the Bhils, Gonds, and Hill tribes of South Asia as examples of slight "modifications" on the complete savagery of women in the "rudest" tribes. Spencer was a loyal follower of Comtean Positivism and John Stuart Mill. Spencer's work had wide appeal to a growing intelligentsia who utilized his positivist model of social evolution to launch a critique of the racialized diagnosis of Indian civilization. References to his work appeared on all sociology syllabi by the first decades of the twentieth century. Spencer, *Principles of Sociology*, vol. 1, preface, 713–44. My thanks to Douglas E. Haynes for his suggestion about the conceptual link of subjected womanhood between Mill and Spencer.

4. By "man" here, I denote the archetypal subject of sociological, political, scientific, and philosophical thought deployed in evolutionary texts like Darwin's *The Descent of Man, and Selection in Relation to Sex*. On the critical place of the idea of primitive society in modern anthropology, see Kruper, *The Invention of Primitive Society*.

5. Social evolutionary thought also appears in debates about birth control and population. See Hodges, *Contraception, Colonialism and Commerce*; Ahluwalia, *Reproductive Restraints*; Sreenivas, "Birth Control in the Shadow of Empire," 509–37.

6. I build on Thomas Trautmann's study on Aryan descent and the connections between British ethnology and philology. See his *Lewis Henry Morgan and the Invention of Kinship* and *Aryans and British India*.

7. These ethnologists were contemporaries of Charles Darwin, whose influential *On the Origin of Species* was published in 1859, just after the transition to direct rule in India. The complexity of these ideas of evolution and their persistence through much social thought in the twentieth century is lost when simply referring to evolutionary thought as "Social Darwinism." See George Stocking's comprehensive study of ethnological thought, *Victorian Anthropology*. For a deeper engagement with global Darwin, see Elshakry, *Reading Darwin in Arabic, 1860–1950*.

8. These ethnological theories were related to the broader race sciences of the late nineteenth and early twentieth centuries. On the vernacular history of race science in India, in particular in relation to the prehistory of genetics, see Mukharji, including his "From Serosocial to Sanguinary Identities," 143–76; "Profiling the Profiloscope," 376–96; and "The Bengali Pharaoh," 446–76.

9. Mantena, *Alibis of Empire*, 82.

10. Found in the work of Henry Maine. See Mantena, *Alibis of Empire*, 1–20.

11. On the concept of the "primitive" Santal in Bengali thought, see Banerjee, *Politics of Time*, 1–39.

12. Thanks to Anjali Arondekar for this formulation of the "suturing" power of sexual ideas in a private communication.

13. We would benefit from historical studies that consider the role of colonialism in global ethnology, specifically in relation to comparative racial schemes of the Atlantic world. On African American contestations of American ethnology and polygeny, see Rusert, *Fugitive Science*.

14. For a critical and comprehensive overview discussion of these and other Victorian anthropologists, see Stocking, *Victorian Anthropology*. On Victorian anthropology and gender, see Fee, "The Sexual Politics of Victorian Anthropology," 23–39.

15. The reading list for the the first MA exam in sociology in 1911 included Auguste Comte, E. B. Tylor, Herbert Spencer, Max Müller, Henry Maine, Herbert Risley, and more. In particular, Herbert Spencer (1820–1903), whose *First Principles* (1860–1862) and later *Principles of Sociology* (first serialized from 1872–1894) were widely cited as the references for an authoritative method for the study of society across the Indian social sciences. See 1911 syllabus in Appendix VIII in Gupta, *Sociology in India*, 298.

16. On Lewis Henry Morgan, see Trautmann, *Lewis Henry Morgan and the Invention of Kinship*. On Maine and ideologies of indirect rule, see Mantena, *Alibis of Empire*, 1–20. On ethnology and sexual politics, see the important research of Elizabeth Fee, "The Sexual Politics of Victorian Social Anthropology," in *Clio's Consciousness Raised*; on ethnological theory, female friendship, and ideas of companionate marriage in Victorian England, see Marcus, *Between Women*, 191–222. In particular, Marcus details the ethnological theory of a Victorian woman and theoretical models that shaped early feminism in England. She cites one of the only women writing ethnology in the period, Edith Simcox. Judith Surkis explores the influence of these ethnological ideas on Durkheim, the discipline of sociology, and masculinity in France; see Surkis, *Sexing the Citizen*, 169, 171. I thank Sharon Marcus for her insightful feedback and suggestions about nineteenth-century evolutionary thought and these key references.

17. Trautmann, *Aryans and British India*, 132–33.

18. Here, I build on Thomas Trautmann's formative argument on the importance of British ethnological classification to philology. See Trautmann, *Aryans and British India*, 131–89.

19. Dalton, *Descriptive Ethnology of Bengal*, i–ii. This Ethnological Congress was perhaps the first to be attempted, to be followed in the 1870s by popular human exhibitions across Europe and America, including Paris, London, and New York. The comparative civilizations exhibit was formalized in the World's Fairs, with some of the largest exhibits of peoples at the Paris World's Fairs of 1878 and 1889 and the 1904 Fair in St. Louis. See Blanchard, *Human Zoos*.

20. On the creation of the analytic concept of patriarchy beginning with Maine through twentieth-century Marxist traditions, see Coward, *Patriarchal Precedents*. Thank you to Anupama Rao for this reference.

21. Maine, *Ancient Law*, 260–61.

22. On the institutionalization of customary law, see Sturman, *The Government of Social Life in Colonial India*, 1–32. On the role of Maine in the construction of late colonial culturalist policies, see Mantena, *Alibis of Empire*, 1–20.

23. McLennan's *Primitive Marriage* built on key ideas of primitive matriarchy of his contemporary, Johann Jakob Bachofen, a Swiss jurist, ethnologist, and philologist. See Bachofen, *Das Mutterrecht*.

24. McLennan, *Primitive Marriage*, 5.

25. On the Nair caste and the colonial critique of matriliny, see Arunima, *There Comes Papa*.

26. Bachofen, *Das Mutterrecht*, v.

27. Ibid.; Bachofen, *Myth, Religion, and Mother Right*.

28. On survivals in Tylor, see Ratnapalan, "E. B. Tylor and the Problem of Primitive Culture," 131–42.

29. Morgan, *Systems of Consanguinity and Affinity of the Human Family*, 493.

30. Trautmann, *Lewis Henry Morgan and the Invention of Kinship*, 177–78. See also Moses, *The Promise of Progress*, 186–88. While both McLennan and Morgan saw patriarchy as a later stage of social evolution, they disagreed on many aspects of "primitive" social forms. For Morgan's critique of McLennan, especially his invented terms "endogamy" and "exogamy," see Lewis Henry Morgan's "Note" on McLennan in *Ancient Society*, 509–23.

31. On the historical context of *The Descent of Man*, see Richard, *Darwin and the Making of Sexual Selection*, xvii–xxxiii.

32. Ethnological ideas of Maine, Morgan, and others widely influenced nineteenth-century historical and developmentalist thinking; most famously, they shaped the ideas of Karl Marx and the thinking of Friedrich Engels in his 1882 book, translated in 1902 as *The Origin of the Family, Private Property and the State*. Unsurprisingly, we see the widespread influence of this evolutionary model of development in the economic thought of colonial and postcolonial India.

33. "It is difficult to get rid of the impression that the writers were a long way removed from the subjects they were dealing with." Risley, "The Study of Ethnology in India," 238, 235–63.

34. Kruper, *The Reinvention of Primitive Society*, 20–36.

35. See Mill, *The History of British India*, vol. 1.

36. Ibid., 309.

37. See Sarkar, "Vidyasagar and Brahmanical Society," 118–45.

38. Bela Dutta Gupta's study of early social science organizations demonstrates the influence of positivism in nineteenth-century Indian social thought, see Gupta, *Sociology in India*. See also Forbes, *Positivism in Bengal*.

39. Gupta, *Sociology in India*, xv.

40. Ibid., 129–72.

41. Ibid., xviii. In 1877, Rajendralal Mitra suggested a new scheme of translation that included new Bengali terms as well as transliterated English terms. Partha Chatterjee has suggested that the question of translation was a particularly vexing problem in Bengali scientific writing; see Chatterjee, *Texts of Power*, 17.

42. On periodicals, see Bose, *Health and Society in Bengal*. On themes of masturbation and child marriage in these manuals, see Pande, *Medicine, Race and Liberalism in British Bengal*, 151–76.

43. Ghosh, "An Uncertain 'Coming of the Book,'" 23–55.

44. Mukharji, *Nationalizing the Body*, 77–83, 91.

45. Elsewhere, I have explored how Bengali medical doctors translated transnational ideas of nymphomania, hysteria, and the dangers of excessive sexual desire to create normative ideas of monogamous conjugality. Mitra, "Translation as Techné," 350–75.

46. See also a discussion of women's sexual pleasure in Guha, "The Nature of Woman," 23–38.

47. Seal, "Address to the Universal Races Congress," in Gupta, *Sociology in India*, 213.

48. Ibid.

49. Jha, *Historical Sociology in India*, 50.

50. Quoted in Madan, *Sociological Traditions*, 121.

51. Chaterjee, *Le védisme et l'origine des castes*; Chaterjee, *The World Civilisation of To-day; or, The Far East and the New West*.

52. Ali, "Foreword," 2.

53. Ibid.

54. Chaterjee, "Inaugural Address," 5.

55. Ahmed, "The Evolution of Sex," 18–19 (emphasis in original).

56. Ibid., 20.

57. Ibid., 23.

58. Ibid., 24.

59. Basu, "Marriage and Our Existing System," *Bulletin* 1, 74.

60. Ibid., 78.

61. Ibid., 78.

62. Ibid., 79.

63. Ibid., 79.

64. Ibid., 84.

65. Basu, "Marriage and Our Existing System," *Bulletin* 2, 51.

66. Basu, "Marriage and Our Existing System," *Bulletin* 1, 78.

67. Basu, "Marriage and Our Existing System," *Bulletin* 2, 51–52.

68. See, for example, Sastri, *Hindu Culture, an Exposition and a Vindication*, xi–xv; Chandra, *True India*; Ellam, *Swaraj*.

69. Mookerjee, *The Decline and Fall of the Hindus*, 2.
70. Ibid., 9.
71. Ibid.
72. Ibid., 15.
73. Ibid.
74. Ibid., 17.
75. Ibid.
76. Ibid., 83.
77. Das, *Hindu Samajer Bartamon Abastha*, 1, translation mine.
78. Ibid., page unknown.
79. Ibid., 2.
80. The phrase of the "primitive within" is framed through the Santal in Prathama Banerjee's account. See Banerjee, *Politics of Time*, 40–81.
81. Mukhopadhyay, "Evolution of Historiography in Bengali (1800–1947)." Thanks to Projit Mukharji for this reference.
82. Perhaps most well known for his *Stri Chikitsa*, (Calcutta: n.p., 1907, 1925), Maitra specialized in diseases of the digestive tract and wrote and translated textbooks on diarrhea, dysentery, and cholera.
83. Wood, *Clinical Gynaecology*.
84. See Mukharji, *Nationalizing the Body*.
85. Lydia Liu argues that translation of knowledge cannot be regarded as simply a "purely linguistic or literary matter" outside the framework of power in relation to imperialism. Liu, *Tokens of Exchange*, 1–12. See also volume 23 of *Theory, Culture, and Society* from 2006. I thank Indrani Chatterjee for her feedback and references on translation.
86. Maitra, *Sachitra Rati Yantradira Pida*, 60.
87. Ibid.
88. Ibid., 57. "Biological facts" appears in the English text of the original.
89. Ibid., 63.
90. Ibid., 58.
91. Ibid., 58.
92. Ibid., 58–60.
93. Ibid., 58.
94. Ibid. Darwin had used the cuckoo bird in *Origin of Species* (1859) to demonstrate the modification of instinct based on natural selection.
95. Ibid., 65.
96. Ibid., 61.
97. Ibid.
98. Ibid., 63.
99. Ibid., 65.
100. Ibid.
101. Ibid.
102. Ibid., 66 (emphasis added).
103. Ibid., 63.

104. Ibid., 64.

105. In a comparative context, see Elizabeth Fee's discussion of Victorian notions of heterosexuality in "The Sexual Politics of Victorian Anthropology," 23–39.

106. In 1962, Mukherji was awarded the Padma Shri award for medicine, the fourth highest civilian honor given by the government of India. He published many books, including books on Hindu worship, the partition of Bengal, modern treatment for diseases, prescriptions, and later birth control. He delivered a series of public lectures on the relationship between *dharma* and science in 1968, and he published these lectures in a volume titled *Shrshti, Bhagabana, o Sadhana*.

107. Mukherji, *Prostitution in India*; Mukherji, *Indian Sex Life and Prostitution*.

108. Mukherji, *Prostitution in India*, 2–4.

109. Ibid., 5.

110. Ibid.

111. Ibid., 19.

112. Ibid., 5.

113. Ibid.

114. Ibid., 8.

115. Ibid., 26.

116. Ibid., 33–36, 107–30.

117. Ibid., 107–30.

118. Ibid., 25.

119. Ibid., 110–11.

120. Ibid., 155.

121. On gender and communalism, see Gupta, *Sexuality, Obscenity, Community*.

122. Mukherji, *Prostitution in India*, 103.

123. Ibid., 113.

124. Ibid., 121–22.

125. See, for example, Estebanez, Fitch, and Nájera, "HIV and Female Sex Workers," 397; Nepal, "AIDS Denial in Asia," 133–41.

126. What Fee terms in a comparative context the "Victorian melodrama." See her discussion of this patriarchal claim in "The Sexual Politics of Victorian Anthropology," 37–39.

127. Sharma, "Traces of Promiscuity in Ancient Indian Society," 153.

128. Ibid., 154.

129. Ibid., 155.

130. Geddes and Thomson, *The Evolution of Sex*.

131. Although remembered for his work in the field of sociology, Mukerjee's oeuvre reached across disciplinary forms, including economics, Sanskrit philology, art history, metaphysics and ethics, psychology, and sociology. In his study with Narendra Nath Sengupta, the head of the department of experimental psychology at Calcutta University, Mukerjee linked social psychology and sexual evolution. See Mukerjee and Sengupta, *Introduction to Social Psychology*. The theme of sexual evolution appears across his oeuvre, including in *The Dimensions of Human Evolution*; *The Sickness of Civilization*; and *The Destiny of Civilization*.

132. Mukerjee, *The Horizon of Marriage*, index.

133. Ibid., 12–13.

134. Ibid., 210.

135. Ibid., 188.
136. Spencer, *Principles of Sociology*, vol. 1, 713.

Chapter 5. Veracity: Life Stories and the Revelation of Social Life

1. Devi, *Autobiography of an Educated Fallen Woman*, 3. I have used excerpts from the first English edition for historically specific translations of the text.

2. Ibid., 3.

3. *Amrita Bazar Patrika*, February 20, 1868, also cited in part by Ray, "Contesting Respectability," 143. A year later, in 1869, another daily, *Ananda Bazar Patrika*, conducted an inquiry and reported that ninety-percent of anonymous women denoted as prostitutes resorted to prostitution because of widowhood. *Amrita Bazar Patrika*, March 1869, as cited in Chakraborty, *The Condition of Bengali Women in the Second half of the Nineteenth Century*, 32.

4. See Sen, *Women and Labour in Late Colonial India*, 199–203.

5. Chatterjee, "Refracted Reality," 28–31.

6. The notion of the popular is a site of much debate in South Asia, often deployed, critiqued, and debated through the binary of elite and popular culture and politics. These debates shaped articulations of the place of an autonomous "subaltern politics" and scholarship that followed. Partha Chatterjee's notion of the popular in the postcolonial world both adheres to and exceeds the formal spaces of institutions and government in his *The Politics of the Governed*, 3. In this chapter, the public of popular print encompasses both literate and semi-literate populations. It is difficult to trace a precise reception history of pulp publications. Scholars have demonstrated that South Asian print cultures expand far beyond literate classes through oral narratives and traditions. The most comprehensive account of the pulp literature from North Calcutta's Battala presses can be found in Gautam Bhadra's magisterial study, *Nyara Battalay Jay Kawbar?* On the rise of Bengali-language publication at the turn of the century, see also Ghosh, *Power in Print*; Gupta and Chakravorty, *Print Areas*; for an important discussion of popular culture in print, see Banerjee, *The Parlour and the Streets*; a critical comparative site of book publication history can be found in Orsini, *Print and Pleasure*; the idea of the popular is also critical in scholarship on cinema. See Rachel Dwyer on the courtesan in film in her *Filming the Gods*.

7. See, for example, the paintings of Baltazard Solvyns and the analysis in Hardgrave, "The Representation of Sati," 57–80.

8. Chaudhury, *Afterimage of Empire*; Pinney, *The Coming of Photography to India* and *Camera Indica*.

9. "Burning ghat, Calcutta," a photo by Bourne and Shepherd, ca. 1870s. Photograph as part of the archives of Frances W. Pritchett, who cites eBay as the source of the photograph. Pritchett's website features an important collection of sketches, paintings, and photographs of the ghat from the colonial period. See Pritchett's online *Resources on South Asia*.

10. Yadavchandra Lahiri was a legal pleader in east Bengal. Lahiri, *Kulakalima*, 1.

11. Lahiri, *Kulakalima*, 14–15.

12. In social scientific texts of colonial administrators, Kulin polygamy in Bengal was often contrasted to the social practices of the Nayar caste of Kerala. On colonialism and Nayar reform, see Arunima, *There Comes Papa*.

13. Karlekar, "Reflections on Kulin Polygamy," 136–55.

14. Risley, *The People of India*, 164.

15. Chakrabarty, *Condition of Women in the Second Half of the Nineteenth Century*, 8–9, 18; Karlekar, "Reflections on Kulin Polygamy," 136–55.

16. Karlekar, "Reflections on Kulin Polygamy," 136–55.

17. There are numerous tracts, plays, novels, and lay sociologies that detail the social "evils" of Kulin Brahman polygamy. The holdings of the India Office offer diverse genres of writing on Kulin polygamy, including Ramnarayan Tarkaratna, *Kulina Kulasarvasva* (Calcutta: n.p., 1854); Krishnakamini Das, *Chittavilasini* (Calcutta: n.p., 1857); Dinabandhu Mitra, *Lilavati Natak* (Calcutta: n.p., 1867); Rashbehari Mukhopadhyay, *Ballali-Sansodhini* (Dacca: n.p., 1868); Srimati Nitambini, *Anurha Yuvati Natak* (Dacca: n.p., 1872); Kshetranath Bandyopadhyay, *Dukhini Kulina Kamini* (Calcutta: n.p. 1872); Lakshminarayan Chakravarti, *Kulina Kanya* (Calcutta: n.p., 1874); Chandranath Sarkar, *Sukumari Natak* (Calcutta: n.p., 1877); Srinath Singha, *Kularahasya Kavya* (Murshidabad: n.p., 1877); Sasankabihari Guha, *Babar Cheler Ma* (Nannar: n.p., 1882); Prasannakumar Bhattacharya, *Kulina Viraha* (Dacca: n.p., 1882); Haridas Bandyopadhyay, *Kulinakahini* (Calcutta: n.p., 1885); Pyarishankar Gupta, *Kaulinyamahima* (Bogra: n.p., 1894).

18. General Department, May 1866, Proceedings 74, 46–47, WBSA. The Report of 1866 was produced by a commission convened after men sent numerous petitions against Kulin polygamy with thousands of signatures to the colonial government. The commission included men involved in polygamy debates, including Ishwar Chandra Surma (Vidyasagar), Ramanauth Tagore, Joykissen Mookerjee, and Degumber Mitter.

19. On Vidyasagar's campaign against Hindu Kulin polygamy, see Hatcher, *Vidyasagar*, 135–36; for Vidyasagar on widow remarriage, see Sarkar, "Vidyasagar and Brahmanical Society," 118–45.

20. Rubin, "The Traffic in Women," 157–210.

21. Lahiri, *Kulakalima*, 1.

22. Ibid., 3–4.

23. Ibid., 1–2.

24. Ibid., 3.

25. Ibid.

26. Ibid., 12.

27. Ibid.

28. Ibid., 18.

29. Risley, *The People of India*, 187.

30. Ibid., cxlvi.

31. Ibid., cover page.

32. Gupta, *Rater Kolkata*. In the republication of *Rater Kolkata* in 2015, the editor attributes authorship to Hemandra Kumar Roy. See the preface to Roy (Meghnad Gupta), *Rater Kolkata*. Hemandra Kumar Roy was the author of numerous children's books and detective novels. The authorship of *Rater Kolkata* remains disputed. In other studies, *Rater Kolkata* has been cited as a pure reflection of the realities of the world of prostitutes in the first decades of the twentieth century. See, for example, Joardar, *Prostitution in Nineteenth and Early Twentieth Century Calcutta*, 17; Banerjee, *Dangerous Outcast*, 109–10.

33. Gupta, *Rater Kolkata*, 44.

34. Ibid., 13–14.

35. Scholars have suggested that this prose literature is a unique form. As Hans Herder has described, the contents of the *naksha* are defined as prose that attempted to "mirror" the social world in glimpses of Calcutta's social life. See Herder, "The Modern Babu and the Metropolis," 358–401. This genre of sketches of the public woman as city had appeared for almost a century before *Rater Kolkata*. These texts included Bhabanicharan Bandyopadhyay's sketches of archetypes of the city in *Nababubilash* (The merriment of the babu); *Dutibilas* (The merriment of the procurer); and *Nababibibilas* (The merriment of the bibi). In Bandyopadhyay's texts, the *babu* was a drunken, weak man who consorted with prostitutes in the new colonial city of Calcutta; the *duti* was the woman procurer of innocent women, the woman temptress who lured innocent women into prostitution; and the *bibi* was the new public woman or "prostitute" who defined the terrain of the city. Scholars like Sumanta Banerjee interpret Bhabanicharan Bandyopadhyay's texts as "literary documentations" of the realities of the lives of prostitutes; that is, as a true documentation of city life. See Banerjee, *Dangerous Outcast*, 74–77. Unlike Banerjee, I argue against an uncritical interpretation that sees these texts as a pure reflection of "real" prostitutes. Another precedent was the popular social sketches of Peary Chand Mitra in his *Alaler gharer dulal* (The pampered son of an elite family), and Kaliprasanna Singha, *Hutom Pyancha Naksha* (*The Observant Owl*). In these social sketches, the prostitute features prominently as an urban institution. In *Hutom*, for example, Singha depicts the owl as third-person narrator who describes the city as fortified by social and sexual deviance. From the Hindu religious festival, to the streets of the red-light district, to the very buildings of the city, "public women" built and sustained Calcutta. Mitra and Singha were members of the Bengal Social Science Association.

36. Gupta, *Rater Kolkata*, 15.

37. Ibid., 16.

38. Ibid., 15.

39. Ibid., 16.

40. Ibid., 17.

41. Ibid., 46–47.

42. Scholars have addressed these accounts of songs as the true voices of women, despite the dubious circumstance of their collection and the unstated relationship of these songs to other folk song traditions like Vaishnav music. See, for example, Bandhyopadhyay, *Beshya Sangeet, Baiji Sangeet*; Chowdhury, "Position of Prostitutes in Bengali Culture as Gleaned from Popular Literature," 239–56.

43. On the mundane life of the worker in the colonial city and the "dark ages" brought by colonial modernity, see Sarkar, "Renaissance and Kaliyuga" and "'Kaliyuga,' 'Chakri' and 'Bhakti,'" in his *Writing Social History*.

44. Gupta, *Rater Kolkata*, 18.

45. Ibid., 18–19.

46. Ibid., 33.

47. The sexuality of maid-servants and female domestic workers is an important theme in much literature; they appear as a major feature of short stories and novels as the most present sexual threat to men. Swapna Banerjee demonstrates how the female domestic servant is critical to the constitution of the middle classes, in Banerjee, *Men, Women, and Domestics*.

48. Gupta, *Rater Kolkata*, 33–34.

49. See Kerr, *The Social Evil in Calcutta*; the anonymous account, Verax, *Social Evil in Calcutta*; Ghosh, *The Social Evil in Calcutta and Methods of Treatment*. Published in the same year as the new 1923 Bengal Suppression of Immoral Traffic Law, Ghosh's *Social Evil* links the need for a taxonomy of prostitutes to an emerging social issue—modern sex trafficking and the need to save girls who were in danger of becoming prostitutes.

50. In his preface, public prosecutor Rai Bahadur Taraknath explains that the police play the role of protectors in society, as truly the "'Ma Bap' (mother and father) of several unfortunate poor people." Mukherjee, *Murder of Prostitutes for Gain*, preface.

51. Anonymous, *She Wasn't Ashamed: Autobiography of an Indian Prostitute*, 173–75.

52. Ibid., 109–10.

53. Recent work on autobiography has explored the rise of the genre of autobiography and the constitution of modern subjectivity in South Asia. Udaya Kumar suggests that the autobiography is first and foremost a public event rather than the expression of an already-constituted interiority. See Kumar, *Writing the First Person*. On women's memoirs and autobiographical writing, see Sen, *The Memoirs of Dr. Haimabati Sen*; Papanek, "Afterword," 58–85; Karlekar, *Voices from Within*; Sarkar, *Words to Win*; Bhattacharya, *Binodini Dasi*; Chakravarti, *Rewriting History*; Burton, *Dwelling in the Archive*; Malhotra and Lambert-Hurley, *Speaking of the Self*.

54. See, for example, Gupta, *Sexuality, Obscenity, and Community*.

55. Debi, *Kamini Kalanka*.

56. On *Swarnabai*, see Chatterjee, "Swarnabai," 329–47.

57. At the turn of the century, literate, high-caste women also began to write and publish memoirs and autobiographies. In these accounts, we see the emergence of a critique of patriarchal strictures by women. In the autobiography of Binodini Dasi, a famous stage actor on the Calcutta stage and writer of memoirs and poetry, we learn of her social exclusion and grief as a result of the social condemnation of her as a woman fallen out of respectable society. See Rimli Bhattacharya's exceptional critical edition of Binodini's work, Binodini Dasi, *My Story and My Life as an Actress*. In the unpublished memoir of Dr. Haimabati Sen, widowed at the age of ten, we learn of her sexual precarity as a young widow and the profound social exclusion that she felt as a result of her widowhood and her own desire to pursue education. She describes the way she, as a widow, was perceived as sexually promiscuous and as prostitute. See Sen, *The Memoirs of Dr. Haimabati Sen*. I thank Geraldine Forbes for her insights about the role of transgressive sexuality in this memoir.

58. See Ratnabali Chatterjee's insightful introduction to the 2011 critical edition of Devi's text, Chatterjee, "Introduction," in *The Autobiography of an Educated Prostitute*, iii–xix. The book was translated and published in both English and Hindi within a year of its original publication, and continues to be republished in contemporary India, with the most recent reprint of the autobiography in English and Bengali in 2011.

59. See Public Prosecutor to the Legal Remembrance, December 11, 1929, File No. 666/1929, Govt. of Bengal, Home (Political), WBSA. Ratnabali Chatterjee situates the autobiography in the context of 1920s Bengal and the controversy that surrounded it. See Chatterjee, "Introduction," iii–xix; see also Bandyopadhyay, "The Fallen and Noncooperation," 18–21.

60. The autobiography translates the *andarmahal* as "harem" in the first English edition, linking the colonial imaginary of Muslim women's exploitation and the sexuality of Hindu women. Devi, *Autobiography of an Educated Fallen Woman*, 14.

61. Ibid., 35.
62. Ibid., 34.
63. Ibid., 40.
64. Ibid., 46.
65. Ibid., 72.
66. Ibid., 148.
67. For example, women who organized as part of the first Non-Cooperation Movement. See Bandyopadhyay, "The Fallen and Noncooperation," 18–21; Albinia, "Womanhood Laid Bare," 428–30.
68. As Mrinalini Sinha demonstrates, the damning exposé *Mother India* by American woman Katherine Mayo sought to undermine the moral claims of Indian nationalists. The Sarda Act was the final act in a series of agitations that had begun in 1860. See Sinha, *Specters of Mother India* and her important work on the earlier age of consent debates in *Colonial Masculinity*.
69. Dasi, *Nurseyr Atmakatha*, 10. My sincere thanks to Shrimoy Roy Chaudhury for this reference and for giving me access to this source.
70. Ibid., 92.
71. Ibid., 96.
72. Ibid., 111.
73. Devi, *Autobiography of an Educated Fallen Woman*, 3.
74. Ibid.

Afterword

1. This may well be because of the story's brevity and accessibility to an English-language audience. See Hasanat, "Sultana's Utopian Awakening," 114–25; Hasan, "Commemorating Rokeya Sakhawat Hossain and Contextualising Her Work in South Asian Muslim Feminism," 39–59; Ray, *Early Feminists of Colonial India*.
2. Hossain, *Sultana's Dream*.
3. Mookerjee, *Decline and Fall of the Hindus*, 83. My thanks to Manan Ahmed for his insights on the politics of speculation.
4. Hossain, *Sultana's Dream*, n.p.
5. World-making is not exhausted by these men, colonial and Indian social scientists, and their genres of truth. The falsity of this claim is apparent when we turn to the work of poets, artists, and intellectuals, women like poet and essayist Meena Alexander and visual artist Shahzia Sikander, who demonstrate that the claim of form as truth is tenuous at best, and that there are other forms in which truth about women can be expressed with complexity, ambiguity, and whimsy. Their artistic and scholarly works are a kind of world-making that stands in stark contrast to the colonial social scientific form.

BIBLIOGRAPHY

Archival Records, Government Documents, and
Collections of Legal Proceedings

Census of Bengal. Calcutta: Bengal Secretariat Press, 1881.
Census of Calcutta and Its Suburbs. Calcutta: Bengal Secretariat Press, 1871.
Census of Calcutta and Its Suburbs. Calcutta: Bengal Secretariat Press, 1891.
Census of India. Delhi: Census Commissioner's Office, 1921.
1860 Indian Penal Code (IPC)
West Bengal State Archives (WBSA), Kolkata

> Commerce Department Proceedings, Government of Bengal
> Education Department Proceedings, Government of Bengal
> General Department Proceedings, Government of Bengal
> Judicial Department Proceedings, Government of Bengal
> Sanitation Department Proceedings, Government of Bengal

National Archives of India (NAI), New Delhi

> Department of Agriculture, Revenue and Commerce, Government of India
> Home Department Proceedings, Government of India

Oriental and India Office Collections (OIOC), British Library, London

> Military Department Records, India Office
> Public and Judicial Department Records, India Office

Newspapers and Periodicals

Amrita Bazar Patrika
Ananda Bazar Patrika
The Ango Indian
Antahpur
Anubikshan
Baigyanik Dampatya Pranali
Bamabodhini Patrika
Bangabani
Bangamahila

Bangasamaj
The Bengalee
Calcutta Review
Chikitsa Sammilani
Dasi
Friend of India
Hindoo Patriot
The Indian Medical Gazette
Indian Mirror
The Indian Observer
The Lancet
Pravasi
San Francisco Chronicle
Somprakash
The Statesman
Swasthya
Tattvabodhini Patrika

Primary and Secondary Sources

Acton, William. *Prostitution Considered in Its Moral, Social, and Sanitary Aspects, in London and Other Large Cities and Garrison Towns.* London: John Churchill and Sons, 1857.

Aderinto, Saheed. *When Sex Threatened the State: Illicit Sexuality, Nationalism, and Politics in Colonial Nigeria, 1900–1958.* Urbana: University of Illinois Press, 2015.

Agnes, Flavia. "To Whom Do Experts Testify? Ideological Challenges of Feminist Jurisprudence." *Economic and Political Weekly* 40, no. 18 (April 30–May 6, 2005): 1859–1866.

Ahluwalia, Sanjam. *Reproductive Restraints: Birth Control in India, 1877–1947.* Urbana: University of Illinois Press, 2010.

Ahmed, Rafidin. "The Evolution of Sex." *Bulletin of the Indian Rationalistic Society* 1, nos. 1–7 (June–Dec. 1919): 18–25.

Albinia, Alice. "Womanhood Laid Bare: How Katherine Mayo and Manoda Devi Challenged Indian Public Morality." In *Sarai Reader* 5, edited by Monica Narula, Shuddhabrata Sengupta, Jeebesh Bagchi, Geert Lovink, and Lawrence Liang, 428–30. Delhi: Center for the Study of Developing Societies, 2005.

Ali, Daud. "Introduction." *Journal of Indian Philosophy* 39, no. 1 (February 2011): 1–13.

Ali, Wajid. "Foreword." *Bulletin of the Indian Rationalistic Society* 1, nos. 1–7 (June–Dec. 1919): 2.

Anagol, Padma. "The Emergence of the Female Criminal in India: Infanticide and Survival under the Raj." *History Workshop Journal* 53 (Spring 2002): 73–93.

Andrew, Elizabeth W., and Katharine C. Bushnell. *The Queen's Daughters in India.* London: Morgan and Scott, 1898.

Appadurai, Arjun. *Modernity at Large: Cultural Dimensions of Globalization.* Minneapolis: University of Minnesota Press, 1997.

Arbuthnot, F. F., and Richard F. Burton. *Ananga-Ranga (Stage of the Bodiless One); or, The Hindu Art of Love (Ars Amoris Indica).* London: Kama Shastra Society of London and Benares, 1885.

Arnold, David. "The Colonial Prison: Power, Knowledge and Penology in Nineteenth-Century India." In *Subaltern Studies VIII: Essays in Honour of Ranajit Guha*, edited by David Arnold and David Hardiman, 148–87. New Delhi: Oxford University Press India, 1994.

Arnold, David. *Police Power and Colonial Rule: Madras, 1859–1947*. New Delhi: Oxford University Press, 1986.

Arnold, David. *Toxic Histories: Poison and Pollution in Modern India*. Cambridge: Cambridge University Press, 2016.

Arondekar, Anjali. *For the Record: On Sexuality and the Colonial Archives*. Durham, NC: Duke University Press, 2009.

Arondekar, Anjali. "In the Absence of Reliable Ghosts: Sexuality, Historiography, South Asia." *differences* 25, no. 3 (December 2014): 98–122.

Arondekar, Anjali. "Time's Corpus: On Temporality, Sexuality and the Indian Penal Code." In *Comparatively Queer: Crossing Times, Crossing Cultures*, edited by Jarrod Hayes and William Spurlin, 143–56. New York: Palgrave, 2010.

Arondekar, Anjali, and Geeta Patel. "Area Impossible: Notes toward an Introduction." *GLQ: A Journal of Lesbian and Gay Studies* 22, no. 2 (2016): 151–71.

Arunima, G. *There Comes Papa: Colonialism and the Transformation of Matriliny in Kerala, Malabar, c. 1850–1940*. New Delhi: Orient Longman, 2003.

Asen, Daniel. *Death in Beijing: Murder and Forensic Science in Republican China*. Cambridge: Cambridge University Press, 2016.

Asif, Manan Ahmed. *A Book of Conquest: The Chachnama and Muslim Origins in South Asia*. Cambridge, MA: Harvard University Press, 2016.

Asif, Manan Ahmed. *The Loss of Hindustan: Tari'kh-i Firishta and the Work of History*. Forthcoming.

Babayan, Kathryn, and Afsaneh Najmabadi. *Islamicate Sexualities: Translations across Temporal Geographies of Desire*. Cambridge, MA: Harvard University Press, 2008.

Bachofen, Johann Jakob. *Das Mutterrecht*. Stuttgart: Verlag von Krais & Hoffman, 1861.

Bachofen, Johann Jakob. *Myth, Religion, and Mother Right; Selected Writings of J. J. Bachofen*. Translated by Ralph Manheim. Princeton, NJ: Princeton University Press, 1967.

Bader, Clarisse. *Femme dans l'Inde antique: Études, morales, et littéraries* (1867). Translated as *Women in Ancient India*. London: Kegan Paul, Trench, Trubner and Co., 1925.

Bahadur, Gaiutra. *Coolie Woman: The Odyssey of Indenture*. Chicago: University of Chicago Press, 2013.

Ballhatchet, Kenneth. *Race, Sex, and Class under the Raj: Imperial Attitudes and Policies and their Critics, 1793–1905*. London: Palgrave Macmillan, 1985.

Bandapadhyay, Devajit. *Beshya Sangeet, Baiji Sangeet*. Calcutta: Subarnarekha, 2001.

Bandhyopadhyay, Harinarayan. *Balchikitsa, The Diseases of Infancy and Childhood in Bengali*, vol. 1. Calcutta: G. P. Roy and Co. Press, 1873.

Bandhyopadhyay, Harinarayan. *Gurbini Bandhab*. Calcutta: G. P. Roy and Co. Press, 1875.

Bandyopadhyay, Aparna. "Chronicles of Love, Betrayal, and Prostitution in Late Colonial Bengal." *Proceedings of the Indian History Congress* 75 (2014): 723–28.

Bandyopadhyay, Bhabanicharan. *Dutibilas*. Calcutta: n.p., 1826.

Bandyopadhyay, Bhabanicharan. *Nabababubilash*. Calcutta: n.p., 1825.

Bandyopadhyay, Bhabanicharan. *Nababibibilas*. Calcutta: n.p., 1831.

Bandyopadhyay, Haridas. *Kulinakahini*. Calcutta: n.p., 1885.
Bandyopadhyay, Kshetranath. *Dukhini Kulina Kamini*. Calcutta: n.p., 1872.
Bandyopadhyay, Sandip. "The Fallen and Noncooperation." *Manushi* 53 (July–August 1989): 18–21.
Bandyopadhyay, Sekhar. *Caste, Culture, and Hegemony: Social Dominance in Colonial Bengal*. Delhi: Sage, 2004.
Bandyopadhyay, Sekhar. *Caste, Protest, and Identity in Colonial Bengal: The Namasudras of Bengal, 1872–1947*. Surrey: Curzon, 1997.
Banerjee, Prathama. "Between the Political and the Non-Political: The Vivekananda Moment and a Critique of the Social in Colonial Bengal." *Social History* 39, no. 3 (2014): 323–39.
Banerjee, Prathama. "Chanakya/Kautilya: History, Philosophy, Theater and the Twentieth-Century Political." *History of the Present* 2, no. 1 (Spring 2012): 24–51.
Banerjee, Prathama. *Politics of Time: "Primitives" and History-Writing in a Colonial Society*. Oxford: Oxford University Press, 2006.
Banerjee, Prathama. "Time and Knowledge." In *Political Science*. Vol. 3, *Indian Political Thought*, edited by Pradip Kumar Datta, Sanjay Palshikar, and Achin Vanaik, 28–62. Delhi: Oxford University Press India, 2013.
Banerjee, Sumanta. *Dangerous Outcast: The Prostitute in Nineteenth Century Bengal*. Calcutta: Seagull Books, 1998.
Banerjee, Sumanta. *The Parlour and the Streets: Elite and Popular Culture in Nineteenth Century Calcutta*. Calcutta: Seagull Books, 1989.
Banerjee, Sumanta. *Under the Raj: Prostitution in Colonial Bengal*. New York: Monthly Review Press, 1998.
Banerjee, Swapna. *Men, Women, and Domestics: Articulating Middle-Class Identity in Colonial Bengal*. Delhi: Oxford University Press, 2004.
Banerji, Sures Chandra. *Aspects of Ancient Indian Life: From Sanskrit Sources*. Calcutta: Punthi Pustak, 1972.
Banerji, Sures Chandra. *The Castaway of Indian Society: History of Prostitution in India since Vedic Times, based on Sanskrit, Pali, Prakrit, and Bengali Sources*. Calcutta: Punthi Pustak, 1989.
Banerji, Sures Chandra. *Crime and Sex in Ancient India*. Calcutta: Naya Prokash, 1980.
Bashford, Alison. *Purity and Pollution: Gender, Embodiment and Victorian Medicine*. New York: Palgrave Macmillan, 1998.
Basu, Aparna. *The Growth of Education and Political Development in India, 1898–1920*. Delhi: Oxford University Press, 1974.
Basu, B. N. *Kama-Sutra of Vatsyayana: The Hindu Art of Love*. Calcutta: Medical Book Company, 1926.
Basu, N. K. *The Art of Love in the Orient*. Calcutta: Medical Book Co., 1944.
Basu, N. K. *Bahumukhi mana, baharupi prema*. Calcutta: N. K. Basu, n.d.
Basu, N. K. *Nara-narira younabodha*. Calcutta: N. K. Basu, 1931.
Basu, N. K. *Youbanera yadupuri*. Calcutta: Girindrachandra Som, 1936.
Basu, N. K., and S. N. Sinha. *The History of Marriage and Prostitution*. Calcutta: The Bengal Social Hygiene Association, 1933.
Basu, N. K., and S. N. Sinha. *History of Prostitution in Ancient India: Up to the Third Century A.D.* Kolkata: Shree Balaram Prakasani, 2003.

Basu, Srimati, and Lucinda Ramberg, eds. *Conjugality and Beyond: Sexual Economy, State Regulation and the Marital Form in India*. Delhi: Women Unlimited, 2015.
Basu, Subodh Kumar. "Marriage and Our Existing System." *Bulletin of the Indian Rationalistic Society* 1, nos. 1–7 (June–Dec. 1919): 74–85.
Basu, Subodh Kumar. "Marriage and Our Existing System." *Bulletin of the Indian Rationalistic Society* 2 (July 1920): 50–58.
Baudelaire, Charles. *Fleurs du mal*. Paris: Poulet-Malassis et de Broise, 1857.
Bauer, Heike, ed. *Sexology and Translation*. Philadelphia: Temple University Press, 2015.
Baxi, Pratiksha. *Public Secrets of Law: Rape Trials in India*. Delhi: Oxford University Press, 2014.
Baynes, C. R. *Hints on Medical Jurisprudence, Adapted and Intended for the Use of Those Engaged in Judicial and Magisterial Duties in British India*. Madras: Messrs. Pharaoh and Co., 1854.
Berlant, Lauren. "On the Case." *Critical Inquiry* 33, no. 4 (Summer 2007): 664.
Bernstein, Laurie. *Sonia's Daughters: Prostitutes and Their Regulation in Imperial Russia*. Berkeley: University of California Press, 1995.
Best, Stephen, Heather Love, and Sharon Marcus. "Building a Better Description." *Representations* 135, no. 1 (2016): 1–21.
Beverley, H. *Report of the Census of Bengal 1872*. Calcutta: Secretariat Press, 1873.
Bhadra, Gautam. *Nyara Battalay Jay Kawbar?* Calcutta: Chhatim Books, 2011.
Bhaskaran, Suparna. "The Politics of Penetration: Section 377 of the Indian Penal Code." In *Queering India: Same-Sex Love and Eroticism in Indian Culture and Society*, edited by Ruth Vanita, 15–29. New York: Routledge, 2002.
Bhatnagar, Rashmi Dube, Renu Dube, and Reena Dube. *Female Infanticide in India: A Feminist Cultural History*. Albany: State University of New York Press, 2005.
Bhattacharya, Prasannakumar. *Kulina Viraha*. Dacca: n.p., 1882.
Bhattacharya, Rimli, ed. and trans. *Binodini Dasi: My Story and My Life as An Actress*. New Delhi: Kali for Women, 1998.
Blanchard, Pascal, ed. *Human Zoos: Science and Spectacle in the Age of Colonial Empires*. Liverpool: Liverpool University Press, 2008.
Bland, Lucy, and Laura Doan, eds. *Sexology in Culture: Labeling Bodies and Desires*. Chicago: University of Chicago Press, 1998.
Bloch, Iwan. *Anthropological Studies in the Strange Sexual Practises of All Races in All Ages: Ancient and Modern, Oriental and Occidental, Primitive and Civilized*. New York: Anthropological Press, 1933.
Bloch, Iwan. *Indische Medizin*. Berlin: n.p., 1902.
Blumhardt, J. F. *Catalogue of the Library of the India Office: Bengali, Oriya, and Assamese Books*. vol. 2, Part 4. London: Eyre and Spottiswoode, 1905.
Borthwick, Meredith. *The Changing Role of Women in Bengal, 1849–1905*. Princeton, NJ: Princeton University Press, 1984.
Bose, Pradip Kumar, ed. *Health and Society in Bengal: A Selection from Late Nineteenth Century Periodicals*. New Delhi: Sage Publications, 2006.
Botre, Shrikant, and Douglas E. Haynes. "Sexual Knowledge, Sexual Anxieties: Middle-Class Males in Western India and the Correspondence in Samaj Swasthya, 1927–53." *Modern Asian Studies* 51, no. 4 (2017): 991–1034.

Breckenridge, Carol A., and Peter van der Veer, *Orientalism and the Postcolonial Predicament: Perspectives on South Asia*. Philadelphia: University of Pennsylvania Press, 1993.
Burton, Antoinette. *Burdens of History: British Feminists, Indian Women, and Imperial Culture, 1865–1915*. Chapel Hill: University of North Carolina Press, 1994.
Burton, Antoinette. *Dwelling in the Archive*. New York: Oxford University Press, 2003.
Burton, Richard F. *The Book of the Thousand Nights and a Night*. Benares: Kamashastra Society, 1885.
Burton, Richard F. *The Kama Sutra of Vatsayana*. London: The Kama Shastra Society, 1883.
Burton, Richard F. *Personal Narrative of a Pilgrimage to El-Medinah and Meccah (1855–1856)*. London: Longman, Brown, Green, Longmans, and Roberts, 1857.
Butler, Judith, and Elizabeth Weed, eds. *The Question of Gender: Joan W. Scott's Critical Feminism*. Bloomington: Indiana University Press, 2011.
Calcutta Vigilance Association. *The Calcutta Suppression of Immoral Traffic Bill 1923: An Explanation and Some Objections Advanced*. Calcutta: O.P. Works, 1923.
Canguilhem, Georges. *The Normal and Pathological*. Translated by Carolyn R. Fawcett and Robert S. Cohen. New York: Zone Books, 1991.
Celarent, Barbara. *Varieties of Social Imagination*. Chicago: University of Chicago Press, 2017.
Césaire, Aimé. *Discourse on Colonialism*. Translated by Joan Pinkham. New York: Monthly Review Press, 1972.
Chakladar, Haran Chandra. *The Aryan Occupation of Eastern India*. Calcutta: Indo-Aryan Publications, 1962 [1925].
Chakladar, Haran Chandra. *Social Life in Ancient India: Study in Vatsyayana's Kamasutra*. Calcutta: Brhattara Bharata Pariṣad, 1929.
Chakrabarty, Dipesh. *Provincializing Europe: Postcolonial and Historical Difference*. Princeton, NJ: Princeton University Press, 2000.
Chakrabarty, Usha. *Condition of Women in the Second Half of the Nineteenth Century*. Calcutta: Usha Chakrabarty, 1963.
Chakraberty, Chandra. *The Cultural History of Hindus*. Calcutta: Vijaya Krishna Brothers, 1946.
Chakraberty, Chandra. *Endocrine Glands*. New York: Omin and Co., 1923.
Chakraberty, Chandra. *An Ethnic Interpretation of Pauranika Personages*. Calcutta: Firma K. L. Mukhopadhyay, 1971.
Chakraberty, Chandra. *Food and Health*. Calcutta: R. Chakraberty, 1922.
Chakraberty, Chandra. *An Interpretation of Ancient Hindu Medicine*. Calcutta: R. Chakraberty, 1923.
Chakraberty, Chandra. *National Problems*. Calcutta: R. Chakraberty, 1923.
Chakraberty, Chandra. *The Outline of Rationalism*. Calcutta: Vijaya Krishna Bros, 1938.
Chakraberty, Chandra. *Principles of Education*. Calcutta: Ramchandra Chakraberty, 1922.
Chakraberty, Chandra. *Racial Basis of Indian Culture*. New Delhi: Aryan Books International, 1997.
Chakraberty, Chandra. *The Racial History of India*. Calcutta: Vijaya Krishna Bros., 1944.
Chakraberty, Chandra. *Sex Life in Ancient India: An Explanatory and Comparative Study*. Calcutta: Mukhopadhyay Publishers, 1963.
Chakraberty, Chandra. *Sexology of the Hindus: A Study in the Hindu Psychology of Sex with Modern Interpretations*. 3rd edition. Calcutta: Vijaya Krishna Publishers, 1938[?].
Chakraborty, Bidisha. *Sarkari Nothite Unish Shatoke Banglar Nari*. Calcutta: Prova Prakashani, 2002.
Chakraborty, Usha. *The Condition of Bengali Women in the Second Half of the Nineteenth Century*. Calcutta: Published by Usha Chakraborty, 1963.

Chakravarti, Lakshminarayan. *Kulina Kanya*. Calcutta: n.p., 1874.
Chakravarti, Uma. *Gendering Caste: Through a Feminist Lens*. Delhi: Sage, 2018.
Chakravarti, Uma. *Rewriting History: The Life and Times of Pandita Ramabai*. Delhi: Kali for Women, 1998.
Chakravarti, Uma. "Whatever Happened to the Vedic Dasi? Orientalism, Nationalism and a Script for the Past." In *Recasting Women: Essays in Colonial History*, edited by Kumkum Sangari and Sudesh Vaid, 27–87. Delhi: Kali for Women, 1989.
Chan, Wing-Cheong, Barry Wright, and Stanley Yeo. *Codification, Macaulay and the Indian Penal Code: The Legacies and Modern Challenges of Criminal Law Reform*. London: Ashgate, 2013.
Chande, M. B. *The Police in India*. New Delhi: Atlantic Publishers and Distributors, 1997.
Chandra, Harish. *True India*. Calcutta: Equitable Literature Home, 1931.
Chandra, Shefali. *The Sexual Life of English*. Durham, NC: Duke University Press, 2009.
Chaterjee, Nolini. "Inaugural Address." *Bulletin of the Indian Rationalistic Society* 1, nos. 1–7 (June–Dec. 1919): 5.
Chaterjee, Nolini. *Le védisme et l'origine des castes*. Calcutta: S. C. Chowdhury, 1919.
Chaterjee, Nolini. *The World Civilisation of To-day; or, The Far East and the New West*. Calcutta: Calcutta Book Co., 1925.
Chattapadhyay, Saratchandra. *Devdas*. Calcutta: Deja, 1995 [1917].
Chattapadhyay, Saratchandra. "Narir Mulya." In *Sarat Rachanabali* 3, 947–78. Calcutta: Deja Publishers, 2004.
Chatterjee, Indrani. *Gender, Slavery, and Law in Colonial India*. Oxford: Oxford University Press, 1999.
Chatterjee, Indrani. "Refracted Reality: The 1935 Calcutta Police Survey of Prostitutes." *Manushi* 57 (March–April 1990): 28–31.
Chatterjee, Partha. *Empire and Nation: Selected Essays*. New York: Columbia University Press, 2010.
Chatterjee, Partha. "Five Hundred Years of Fear and Love." *Economic and Political Weekly* (May 30, 1998): 1330–36.
Chatterjee, Partha. *The Nation and Its Fragments*. Princeton, NJ: Princeton University Press, 1993.
Chatterjee, Partha. *Nationalist Thought and the Colonial World: A Derivative Discourse*. London: Zed Books, 1986.
Chatterjee, Partha. *The Politics of the Governed: Reflections on Popular Politics in Most of the World*. New York: Columbia University Press, 2004.
Chatterjee, Partha. *Texts of Power: Emerging Disciplines in Colonial Bengal*. Minneapolis: University of Minnesota Press, 1995.
Chatterjee, Ratnabali. "Introduction." In *The Autobiography of an Educated Prostitute*, by Manoda Devi, iii–xi. Calcutta: Aruna Prakashan, 2011.
Chatterjee, Ratnabali. "Prostitution in Nineteenth Century Bengal: Construction of Class and Gender." *Social Scientist* 21, nos. 9/11 (1993): 159–72.
Chatterjee, Ratnabali. "The Queens' Daughters: Prostitutes as an Outcast Group in Colonial India." *CMI Report*. Bergen: Chr. Michelsen Institute, 1992.
Chatterjee, Ratnabali. "Swarnabai: Nitikatha naa Pornography." In *Bangalir Battala*, edited by Adrish Biswas and Anil Acharya, 329–47. Calcutta: Anushtup, 2013.
Chaudhury, Zahid. *Afterimage of Empire: Photography in Nineteenth-Century India*. Minneapolis: University of Minnesota Press, 2012.

Chevers, Norman. *A Manual on Medical Jurisprudence for Bengal and the Northwestern Provinces.* London: Carbery, 1856.

Chevers, Norman. *A Manual of Medical Jurisprudence for India: Including the Outline of a History of Crime against the Person in India.* Medical Heritage Library. London: Calcutta, 1870.

Chew, Dolores. "The Case of the 'Unchaste' Widow: Constructing Gender in 19th-Century Bengal." *Colonialism, Imperialism, and Gender* 22, nos. 3 and 4 (Fall/Winter 1993): 33–43.

Chowdhury, Anindita Roy. "Position of Prostitutes in Bengali Culture as Gleaned from Popular Literature." In *Popular Literature and Pre-modern Societies in South Asia*, edited by Surinder Singh and Ishwar Dayal Gaur, 239–56. Delhi: Dorling Kindersley, 2008.

Cohen, Cathy. "Deviance as Resistance: A New Research Agenda for the Study of Black Politics." *Du Bois Review: Social Science Research on Race* 1, no. 1 (2004): 27–45.

Cohn, Bernard S. *An Anthropologist among Historians and Other Essays.* New York: Oxford University Press, 1987.

Cohn, Bernard S. "The Census and Objectification in South Asia." *The Bernard Cohn Omnibus.* New Delhi: Oxford University Press, 2004.

Cohn, Bernard S. *Colonialism and Its Forms of Knowledge: The British in India.* Princeton, NJ: Princeton University Press, 1996.

Comfort, Alex. *The Joy of Sex.* New York: Crown Publishing Group, 1972.

Comfort, Alex. *The Koka Shashtra, Being the Ratirahasya of Kokkoka, and Other Medieval Indian Writings on Love.* London: George Allen and Unwin, 1964.

Corbin, Alain. *Women for Hire: Prostitution France.* Cambridge, MA: Harvard University Press, 1990.

Coward, Rosalind. *Patriarchal Precedents: Sexuality and Social Relations.* London: Routledge, 1983.

Crawford, Catherine. "Legalizing Medicine: Early Modern Legal Systems and the Growth of Medico-legal Knowledge." In *Legal Medicine in History*, edited by Michael Clark and Catherine Crawford, 89–116. Cambridge: Cambridge University Press, 1994.

Dalton, Edward T. *Descriptive Ethnology of Bengal.* Calcutta: Office of the Superintendent Government Printing, 1872.

Darwin, Charles. *The Descent of Man, and Selection in Relation to Sex.* London: J. Murray, 1871.

Darwin, Charles. *On the Origin of Species by Means of Natural Selection.* London: J. Murray, 1859.

Das, Dhanapatinath. *Hindu Samajer Bartamon Abastha.* Calcutta: The Indian Rationalistic Society, 1919.

Das, Krishnakamini. *Chittavilasini.* Calcutta: n.p., 1857.

Dasa, Narayanacandra. *Sacitri o brhat Koka-sastra ba Rati bijnana.* Karnataka: Narayana Pustakalaya, 1939.

Dasi, Binodini. *My Story and My Life as an Actress.* Edited and translated by Rimli Bhattacharya. Delhi: Kali for Women, 1998.

Dasi, Parimalbala. *Nurseyr Atmakatha.* Calcutta: n.p., 1932.

Datla, Kavita. *The Language of Secular Islam: Urdu Nationalism and Colonial India.* Manoa: University of Hawaii Press, 2013.

Davis, Richard. *South Asia at Chicago: A History.* Chicago: Committee on Southern Asian Studies at the University of Chicago, 1985.

Debi, Nabinkali. *Kamini Kalanka.* 2nd edition. Calcutta: Adharchandra Sarkar, 1886.

Devi, Manoda. *Autobiography of an Educated Fallen Woman.* Calcutta: Sakha Press, 1930[?].

Dirks, Nicholas B. *Castes of Mind: Colonialism and the Making of Modern India.* Princeton, NJ: Princeton University Press, 2001.
Doan, Laura. *Disturbing Practices: History, Sexuality, and Women's Experience of Modern War.* Chicago: University of Chicago Press, 2013.
Doniger, Wendy. *Redeeming the Kama Sutra.* Oxford: Oxford University Press, 2016.
Doniger, Wendy, and Sudhir Kakar, eds. *Kamasutra.* Oxford: Oxford University Press, 2002.
Durkheim, Émile. "Debate on the Relationship between Ethnology and Sociology" (1907). In Émile Durkheim, *Rules of Sociological Method.* Edited by Steven Lukes and translated by W. D. Halls, 209–10. New York: Free Press, 1982.
Durkheim, Émile. *The Rules of Sociological Method: And Selected Texts on Sociology and Its Method.* New York: Simon and Schuster, 2014.
Dwyer, Rachel. *Filming the Gods: Religion and Indian Cinema.* London: Routledge, 2006.
Ellam, John E. *Swaraj: The Problem of India.* Delhi: Concept Publishing Company, 1930.
Ellis, Henry Havelock. *Studies in the Psychology of Sex.* Philadelphia: F. A. Davis Co., 1901.
Elshakry, Marwa. *Reading Darwin in Arabic, 1860–1950.* Chicago: University of Chicago Press, 2013.
El Shakry, Omnia S. *The Great Social Laboratory: Subjects of Knowledge in Colonial and Postcolonial Egypt.* Stanford, CA: Stanford University Press, 2007.
Engels, Friedrich. *The Origin of the Family, Private Property and the State.* Moscow: Foreign Languages Publishing House, 1891.
Estebanez, P., K. Fitch, and Rafael Nájera. "HIV and Female Sex Workers." *Bulletin of the World Health Organization* 71, no. 3–4 (1993): 397–412.
Fahmy, Khaled. "The Anatomy of Justice: Forensic Medicine and Criminal Law in Nineteenth-Century Egypt." *Islamic Law and Society* 6, no. 2 (1999): 224–71.
Fee, Elizabeth. "The Sexual Politics of Victorian Anthropology." *Feminist Studies* 1, no. 3/4 (Winter–Spring, 1973): 23–39.
Fee, Elizabeth. "The Sexual Politics of Victorian Social Anthropology." In *Clio's Consciousness Raised: New Perspectives on the History of Women,* edited by Mary S. Hartman and Lois Banner. New York: HarperCollins, 1974.
Figueira, Dorothy. *Translating the Orient: The Reception of Sakuntala in Nineteenth-Century Europe.* Albany: State University of New York Press, 1991.
Forbes, Geraldine. "Managing Midwifery in India." In *Contesting Colonial Hegemony: State and Society in Africa and India,* edited by Dagmar Engels and Shula Marks, 152–72. London: German Historical Institute, 1994.
Forbes, Geraldine. *Positivism in Bengal: A Case Study in the Transmission and Assimilation of an Ideology.* Calcutta: Minerva Associations, 1975.
Forbes, Geraldine. *Women in Modern India.* Cambridge: Cambridge University Press, 1996.
Foucault, Michel. *Abnormal: Lectures at the Collège de France, 1974–1975.* New York: Picador, 2004.
Foucault, Michel. *The Birth of the Clinic: An Archaeology of Medical Perception.* Translated by A. M. Sheridan. London: Routledge, 1973.
Foucault, Michel. *The History of Sexuality.* Vol. 1. Translated by Robert Hurley. New York: Vintage, 1990.
Foucault, Michel. "Nietzsche, Genealogy, History." In *Language, Counter-Memory, Practice: Selected Essays and Interviews,* edited by D. F. Bouchard, 139–64. Ithaca, NY: Cornell University Press, 1977.

Foucault, Michel. *The Order of Things*. New York: Routledge, 1989.

Franklin, Michael J., ed. *Sir William Jones: Selected Poetical and Prose Works*. Cardiff: University of Wales Press, 1995.

Frühstück, Sabine. *Colonizing Sex: Sexology and Social Control in Modern Japan*. Berkeley: University of California Press, 2003.

Fuechtner, Veronika. "Indians, Jews, and Sex: Magnus Hirschfeld and Indian Sexology." In *Imagining Germany, Imagining Asia: Essays in Asian-German Studies*, ed. Veronika Fuechtner and Mary Rhiel, 111–30. Rochester, NY: Camden House, 2013.

Fuechtner, Veronika, Douglas E. Haynes, and Ryan M. Jones, eds. *A Global History of Sexual Science, 1880–1960*. Berkeley: University of California Press, 2018.

Fuentes, Marisa. *Dispossessed Lives: Enslaved Women, Violence, and the Archive*. Philadelphia: University of Pennsylvania Press, 2016.

Ganachari, Aravind. "Infanticide in Colonial Western India: The Vijay Lakshmi Case." *Economic and Political Weekly* 38, no. 9 (Mar. 1–7, 2003): 902–6.

Gautam, Sanjay K. "The Courtesan and the Birth of Ars Erotica in the Kamasutra: A History of Erotics in the Wake of Foucault." *Journal of the History of Sexuality* 23, no. 1 (January 2014): 1–20.

Geddes, Patrick, and J. Arthur Thomson. *The Evolution of Sex*. New York: Humboldt Publishing, 1889.

George, Dieter. "Johann Jakob Meyer." *Zeitschrift der Deutschen Morgenländischen Gesellschaft* 118, no. 2 (1968): 224–33.

Ghose, Abinash Chandra. *Rati-Sastram; or, The Hindu System of Sexual Science*, 2nd edition. Delhi: Nag Publishers, 1971 [1894].

Ghosh, Anindita. *Power in Print: Popular Publishing and the Politics of Language and Culture in a Colonial Society*. Oxford: Oxford University Press, 2006.

Ghosh, Anindita. "An Uncertain 'Coming of the Book': Early Print Cultures in Colonial India." *Book History* 6 (2003): 23–55.

Ghosh, Anjan. "The Public Culture of Sociology in Calcutta." In *Doing Sociology In India: Genealogies, Locations, and Practices*, edited by Sujata Patel, 29–46. Delhi: Oxford University Press, 2011.

Ghosh, Durba. *Sex and the Family in Colonial India: The Making of Empire*. Cambridge: Cambridge University Press, 2006.

Ghosh, J. N. *The Social Evil in Calcutta and Methods of Treatment*. Calcutta: published by the author, 1923.

Gilfoyle, Timothy J. *City of Eros: New York City, Prostitution, and the Commercialization of Sex, 1790–1920*. New York: Norton, 1992.

Goffman, Erving. *Stigma: Notes on the Management of Spoiled Identity*. Englewood Cliffs, NJ: Prentice-Hall, 1963.

Grant, Ben. "Translating/'The' Kama Sutra." *Third World Quarterly* 26, no. 3 (2005): 509–16.

Grewal, Inderpal, and Caren Kaplan. "Global Identities: Theorizing Transnational Studies of Sexuality." *GLQ: A Journal of Lesbian and Gay Studies* 7, no. 4 (2001): 663–79.

Gribble, J.D.B. *Outlines of Medical Jurisprudence for Indian Courts*. Madras: Higginbotham, 1885.

Gribble, J.D.B., and Patrick Heher. *Outlines of Medical Jurisprudence for India*. Madras: Higginbotham, 1892.

Guha, Ranajit. "Chandra's Death." In *Subaltern Studies V*, edited by Ranajit Guha, 135–65. Delhi: Oxford University Press, 1985.
Guha, Ranajit. *Subaltern Studies V: Writings on South Asian History and Society*. Delhi: Oxford University Press, 1985.
Guha, Sasankabihari. *Babar Cheler Ma*. Nannar: n.p., 1882.
Guha, Supriya. "The Nature of Woman: Medical Ideas in Colonial Bengal." *Bulletin (Centre for Women's Development Studies)* 3, no. 1 (1996): 23–38.
Guha, Supriya. "A Science of Woman." PhD diss., University of Calcutta, 1996.
Guha, Supriya. "The Unwanted Pregnancy in Colonial Bengal." *The Indian Economic & Social History Review* 33, no. 4 (1996): 403–35.
Gupta, Abhijit, and Swapan Chakravorty, eds. *Print Areas: Book History in India*. Delhi: Permanent Black, 2004.
Gupta, Anandswarup. *The Police in British India, 1861–1947*. New Delhi: Concept, 1979.
Gupta, Bela Dutta. *Sociology in India: An Enquiry into Sociological Thinking and Empirical Social Research in the Nineteenth Century with Special Reference to Bengal*. Calcutta: Centre for Sociological Research, 1972.
Gupta, Charu. *The Gender of Caste*. Seattle: University of Washington Press, 2015.
Gupta, Charu. *Sexuality, Obscenity, Community: Women, Muslims, and the Hindu Public*. Delhi: Permanent Black, 2001.
Gupta, Meghnad. *Rater Kolkata*. Calcutta: Naba Bharat Machine (91/2 Mechua Bazar Street), 1923.
Gupta, Pyarishankar. *Kaulinyamahima*. Bogra: n.p., 1894.
Guy, Donna J. *Sex and Danger in Buenos Aires: Prostitution, Family, and Nation in Argentina*. Lincoln: University of Nebraska Press, 1991.
Haley, Sarah. *No Mercy Here: Gender, Punishment, and the Making of Jim Crow Modernity*. Chapel Hill: University of North Carolina Press, 2016.
Halperin, David. *How to Do the History of Homosexuality*. Chicago: University of Chicago Press, 2002.
Hardgrave, Robert L., Jr. "The Representation of Sati: Four Eighteenth Century Etchings by Baltazard Solvyns." *Bengal Past and Present* 117, nos. 1–2 (1998): 57–80.
Hardgrove, Anne. "Nationalist Interpretations of the Kama Sutra: K. Rangaswami Iyengar and the Respectability of Ancient Texts." *Translation Today* 6, nos. 1 & 2 (2009): 97–106.
Harrison, Mark. "Racial Pathologies: Morbid Anatomy in British India, 1770–1850." In *The Social History of Health and Medicine in Colonial India*, edited by Biswamoy Pati and Mark Harrison, 173–94. London: Routledge, 2009.
Harvey, Robert. "Report on Medico-Legal Returns." *Indian Medical Gazette*. December 1, 1875: 309–14.
Harvey, Robert. *Report on the Medico-legal Returns Received from the Civil Surgeons in the Bengal Presidency during the Years of 1870, 1871, and 1872*. Calcutta: Calcutta Central Press Co., 1876.
Hasan, Mohammed Mahmudul. "Commemorating Rokeya Sakhawat Hossain and Contextualising Her Work in South Asian Muslim Feminism." *Asiatic* 7, 2 (2013): 39–59.
Hasanat, Fayeza. "Sultana's Utopian Awakening: An Ecocritical Reading of Rokeya Sakhawat Hossain's 'Sultana's Dream.'" *Asiatic* 7, 2 (2013): 114–25.
Hatcher, Brian. *Vidyasagar: The Life and After-life of an Eminent Indian*. London: Routledge, 2014.

Herder, Hans. "The Modern Babu and the Metropolis." In *India's Literary History: Essays on the Nineteenth Century*, edited by Stuart Blackburn and Vasudha Dalmia, 358–401. Delhi: Permanent Black, 2004.

Herling, Bradley L. *The German Gita: Hermeneutics and Discipline in the German Reception of Indian Thought, 1778–1831*. New York: Routledge, 2006.

Hershatter, Gail. *Dangerous Pleasures: Prostitution and Modernity in Twentieth Century Shanghai*. Berkeley: University of California Press, 1997.

Hinchy, Jessica. "The Eunuch Archive: Colonial Records of Non-Normative Gender and Sexuality in India." *Culture, Theory, and Critique* 58, no. 2 (2017): 127–46.

Hirschfeld, Magnus. *Weltreise eines Sexualforschers im Jahre 1931/32*. Frankfurt am Main: Eichborn, 2006.

Hobsbawm, Eric, and Terence Ranger. *The Invention of Tradition*. Cambridge: Cambridge University Press, 1983.

Hodges, Sarah. *Contraception, Colonialism and Commerce: Birth Control in South India, 1920–1940*. London: Ashgate, 2008.

Hood, John W. *Niharranjan Ray*. Delhi: Sahitya Akedemi, 1997.

Hossain, Rokeya Sakhawat. *Sultana's Dream*. Chennai: Tara Books, 2015.

Hunter, W. W. *A Statistical Account of Bengal*. Vols. 1–20. Delhi: D. K. Publishing House, 1973.

Inden, Ronald. *Imagining India*. Oxford: Basil Blackwell, 1990.

Indian Law Commission and Thomas Macaulay. *The Indian Penal Code, as Originally Framed in 1837*. London: Higginbotham, 1888.

Irwin, Robert. *The Arabian Nights: A Companion*. London: Alan Lane, 1994.

Jaisavala, Bainarama. *Marathi bhashenta Koka sastra*. Aligaṛh: Bainirama enda san, 1938.

Jaya, Yato Dharma Tato and Richard Schmidt. *Kokkokam and Rati-Rahasyam: The Secret of Love*. Calcutta: Medical Book Company, 1949.

Jentzen, Jeffrey M. "Death and Empire: Legal Medicine in the Colonization of India and Africa." In *Medicine and Colonialism: Historical Perspectives in India and South Africa*, edited by Poonam Bala, 159–74. London: Pickering & Chatto, 2014.

Jha, Hetuka. *Historical Sociology in India*. New York: Routledge, 2016.

Joardar, Biswanath. *Prostitution in Historical and Modern Perspectives*. New Delhi: Inter-India Publications, 1983.

Joardar, Biswanath. *Prostitution in Nineteenth and Early Twentieth Century Calcutta*. New Delhi: Inter-India Publications, 1985.

John, Mary E., and Janaki Nair, eds. *A Question of Silence?: The Sexual Economics of Modern India*. London: Zed Books, 1998.

Jolly, J., and R. Schmidt. *Arthasastra of Kautilya*. Lahore: Punjab Sanskrit Book Depot, 1923.

Jordanova, Ludmilla. *Sexual Visions: Images of Gender in Science and Medicine between the Eighteenth and Twentieth Centuries*. New York: Harvester Wheatsheaf, 1989.

Kalyanamalla. *Ananga Ranga: Stage of the Bodiless One, the Hindu Art of Love*. Calcutta: Medical Book Company, 1961.

Karlekar, Malavika. "Reflections on Kulin Polygamy: Nistarini Debi's Sekeley Katha." *Contributions to Indian Sociology* 29, nos. 1–2 (1995): 136–55.

Karlekar, Malavika. *Voices from Within: Early Personal Narratives of Women*. Delhi: Oxford University Press, 1991.

Kaviraj, Sudipta. *The Invention of Private Life: Literature and Ideas*. New York: Columbia University Press, 2015.
Kennedy, Dane. *The Highly Civilized Man: Richard Burton and the Victorian World*. Cambridge, MA: Harvard University Press, 2009.
Kerr, Robert. *The Social Evil in Calcutta*. Calcutta: T. S. Smith, 1871.
Kipling, Rudyard. *In Black and White*. New York: The Lovell Company, 1899.
K. N., Sunandan. "From Acharam to Knowledge: Claims of Caste Dominance in Twentieth-Century Malabar." *History and Sociology of South Asia* 9, no. 2 (2015): 174–92.
Kokkoka. *Ratirahasya*. Kasi: Babu Thakur Das, 1909.
Kokkoka and Narayaṇacandra Dasa. *Sacitri o bṛhat Koka-ṣāstra ba Rati bijnana*. Kaṭaka: Narayana Pustakalaya, 1939.
Kokkoka, and Ananda Kavi. *Kokasāra*. Delhi: Brahma Press, 1873.
Kokkoka, and Ananda Kavi. *The Rati Sastra Ratnavali*. Madras: S. Mürthy & Co., 1905.
Kokkoka, and Sarabhai Manilal Nawab Naiṇasukha. *Vaidyamanotsava: Ane Kavi Ananda viracita Kokasara*. Ahmedabad: Sarabhai Manilal Nawab, 1946.
Kolsky, Elizabeth. "The Body Evidencing the Crime: Gender, Law and Medicine in Colonial India." PhD diss., Columbia University, 2005.
Kolsky, Elizabeth. "'The Body Evidencing the Crime': Rape on Trial in Colonial India, 1860–1947." *Gender & History* 22, no. 1 (2010): 109–30.
Kolsky, Elizabeth. "Codification and the Rule of Colonial Difference: Criminal Procedure in British India." *Law and History Review* 23, no. 3 (2005): 631–83.
Kosambi, Meera, ed. *Pandita Ramabai: Life and Landmark Writings*. London: Routledge, 2016.
Koselleck, Reinhart. *Futures Past: On the Semantics of Historical Time*. New York: Columbia University Press, 2004.
Kotiswaran, Prabha. *Dangerous Sex, Invisible Labor: Sex Work and the Law in India*. Princeton, NJ: Princeton University Press, 2011.
Kozma, Liat. *Global Women, Colonial Ports: Prostitution in the Interwar Middle East*. Albany: SUNY Press, 2017.
Kruper, Adam. *The Invention of Primitive Society*. London: Routledge, 1988.
Kruper, Adam. *The Reinvention of Primitive Society: Transformations of a Myth*. London: Routledge, 2005.
Kumar, Udaya. *Writing the First Person: Literature, History, and Autobiography in Modern Kerala*. Delhi: Permanent Black, 2016.
Lahiri, Yadavchandra. *Kulakalima*. Calcutta: Srinath De and Co., 1873.
Lal, Ruby. *Coming of Age in Nineteenth-Century India: The Girl-Child and the Art of Playfulness*. New York: Cambridge University Press, 2013.
Latour, Bruno. *Aramis or the Love of Technology*. Cambridge, MA: Harvard University Press, 1996.
Legg, Stephen. *Prostitution and the Ends of Empire: Scale, Governmentalities, and Interwar India*. Durham, NC: Duke University Press, 2014.
Lelyveld, David. *Aligarh's First Generation: Muslim Solidarity in British India*. Princeton, NJ: Princeton University Press, 1978.
Levine, Philippa. "Orientalist Sociology and the Creation of Colonial Sexualities." *Feminist Review* 65, no. 1 (2000): 5–21.

Levine, Philippa. *Prostitution, Race, and Politics: Policing Venereal Disease in the British Empire*. New York: Routledge, 2003.

Liu, Lydia. *Tokens of Exchange: The Problem of Translation in Global Circulations*. Durham, NC: Duke University Press.

Lombroso, Cesare. *A Donna Delinquente*. Translated as *The Criminal Woman, the Prostitute, and the Normal Woman* by Nicole Hahn Rafter and Mary Gibson. Durham, NC: Duke University Press, 2004 [1893].

Love, Heather. "Doing Being Deviant: Deviance Studies, Description, and the Queer Ordinary." *differences* 26, no. 1 (2015): 74–95.

Lovell, Mary S. *A Rage to Live: A Biography of Richard and Isabel Burton*. New York: Norton, 1988.

Lyon, Isidore B. *Medical Jurisprudence for India with Illustrative Cases*. Calcutta: Thacker, Spink, & Co., 1888.

Lyon, Isidore B. *Medical Jurisprudence for India with Illustrative Cases*. Calcutta: Thacker, Spink, & Co., 1921.

Madan, T. N. *Sociological Traditions: Methods and Perspectives in the Sociology of India*. New Delhi: Sage Publications, 2011.

Maine, Henry. *Ancient Law*. London: John Murray, 1861.

Maitra, Gyanendrakumar. *Sachitra Rati Yantradira Pida*. Calcutta: Maitra and Sons, 1923.

Maitra, Gyanendrakumar. *Stri Chikitsa. Diseases of Women and Their Homeopathic Treatment*. Calcutta: Maitra, 1907.

Majumdar, Rochona. *Marriage and Modernity: Family Values in Colonial Bengal*. Durham, NC: Duke University Press, 2009.

Malhotra, Anshu, and Siobhan Lambert-Hurley. *Speaking of the Self: Gender, Performance, and Autobiography in South Asia*. Durham, NC: Duke University Press, 2015.

Mani, Lata. "Contentious Traditions: The Debate on Sati in Colonial India." *Cultural Critique* 7 (Autumn 1987): 119–56.

Mani, Lata. *Contentious Traditions: The Debate on Sati in Colonial India*. Berkeley: University of California Press, 1998.

Mantena, Karuna. *Alibis of Empire: Henry Maine and the Ends of Liberal Imperialism*. Princeton, NJ: Princeton University Press, 2010.

Mantena, Rama. *The Origins of Modern Historiography in India: Antiquarianism and Philology, 1780–1880*. New York: Palgrave Macmillan, 2012.

Marcus, Sharon. *Between Women: Friendship, Desire, and Marriage in Victorian England*. Princeton, NJ: Princeton University Press, 2009.

Mayo, Katherine. *Mother India*. London: Cape, 1927.

McClintock, Anne. *Imperial Leather: Race, Gender, and Sexuality in the Colonial Contest*. London: Routledge, 1995.

McGrath, Roberta. *Seeing Her Sex: Medical Archives and the Female Body*. Manchester: Manchester University Press, 2002.

McLaren, Angus. *Sexual Blackmail: A Modern History*. Cambridge, MA: Harvard University Press, 2002.

McLennan, John Ferguson. *Primitive Marriage: An Inquiry into the Origin of the Form of Capture in Marriage Ceremonies*. Edinburgh: Adam and Charles Black, 1865.

Member of the Royal Asiatic Society. *Sex Life in India*. Calcutta: Medical Book Company, 1952 [1909].

Menon, Nivedita. *Recovering Subversion: Feminist Politics beyond the Law*. Delhi: Permanent Black, 2004.

Merrick, G. P. *Work among the Fallen as Seen in the Prison Cells*. London: Ward, Lock and Co., 1890.

Meyer, Johann Jakob. *Sexual Life in Ancient India: A Study in the Comparative History of Indian Culture*. New York: Barnes and Noble, 1953 [1929].

Meyer, Johann Jakob. *Das Weib im altindischen Epos*. Leipzig: Heims, 1915.

Mill, James. *The History of British India*. Vol. 1, 1st edition. London: Baldwin, Cradock and Joy, 1817.

Mill, John Stuart. *Auguste Comte and Positivism, reprinted from the Westminster Review*. London: N. Trubner and Co., 1865.

Mitra, Dinabandhu. *Lilavati Natak*. Calcutta: n.p., 1867.

Mitra, Durba. "Translation as Techné: Female Sexuality and the Science of Social Progress in Colonial India." *History and Technology* 31, no. 4 (2015): 350–75.

Mitra, Durba, and Mrinal Satish. "Testing Chastity, Evidencing Rape: Impact of Medical Jurisprudence on Rape Adjudication in India." *Economic & Political Weekly* 49, no. 41 (2014): 51–58.

Mitra, Peary Chand. *Alaler Gharer Dulal*. Calcutta: n.p., 1858.

Modi, Jaising P. *A Textbook of Medical Jurisprudence and Toxicology*. Calcutta: Butterworth & Co., 1920.

Mookerjee, Sambhu Chandra. *The Decline and Fall of the Hindus*. Calcutta: Indian Rationalistic Society, 1919.

Morgan, Lewis Henry. *Ancient Society; or, Researches in the Lines of Human Progress from Savagery through Barbarism to Civilization*. New York: Henry Holt and Co., 1877.

Morgan, Lewis Henry. *Systems of Consanguinity and Affinity of the Human Family*. Washington, DC: Smithsonian Institution, 1870.

Moscucci, Ornella. *The Science of Woman: Gynaecology and Gender in England, 1800–1929*. Cambridge: Cambridge University Press, 1990.

Moses, Daniel Noah. *The Promise of Progress: The Life and Work of Lewis Henry Morgan*. Columbia: University of Missouri Press, 2009.

Mukerjee, Radhakamal. *The Destiny of Civilization*. Bombay: Asia Publishing House, 1964.

Mukerjee, Radhakamal. *The Dimensions of Human Evolution*. London: Macmillan & Company Ltd., 1963.

Mukerjee, Radhakamal. *The Horizon of Marriage*. Calcutta: Asia Publishing House, 1957.

Mukerjee, Radhakamal. *The Sickness of Civilization*. Bombay: Allied Publishers, 1964.

Mukerjee, Radhakamal, and Narendra Nath Sengupta. *Introduction to Social Psychology: Mind in Society*. New York: D. C. Heath and Company, 1928.

Mukharji, Projit. "The Bengali Pharaoh: Upper-Caste Aryanism, Pan-Egyptianism, and the Contested History of Biometric Nationalism in Twentieth-Century Bengal." *Comparative Studies in Society and History* 59, no. 2 (2017): 446–76.

Mukharji, Projit. "From Serosocial to Sanguinary Identities: Caste, Transnational Race Science and the Shifting Metonymies of Blood Group B, India c. 1918–60." *Indian Economic and Social History Review* 51, no. 2 (2014): 143–76.

Mukharji, Projit. *Nationalizing the Body: The Medical Market, Print, and Daktari Medicine*. New York: Anthem Press, 2009.

Mukharji, Projit. "Profiling the Profiloscope: Facialization of Race Technologies and the Rise of Biometric Nationalism in Inter-war British India." *History and Technology* 31, no. 4 (2015): 376–96.

Mukherjee, Benoy Kumar. *The Positive Background of Hindu Sociology: Introduction to Hindu Positivism*. Delhi: Motilal Banarsidass, 1985 [1937].

Mukherjee, Satyendranath. *Murder of Prostitutes for Gain*. Calcutta: Jnan Printing Works, 1930.

Mukherji, Santosh Kumar. *Birth Control for the Millions*. Calcutta: Medical Book Company, 1945.

Mukherji, Santosh Kumar. *Boundary Problem in New Bengal*. Calcutta: Hindusthan Socialist Party, Badur Bagan Street, 1947[?].

Mukherji, Santosh Kumar. *Elements of Endocrinology*. Calcutta: Indian Medical Record Book Depot, 1924.

Mukherji, Santosh Kumar. *Indian Sex Life and Prostitution*. Burdwan: Anil Das Gupta, 1934.

Mukherji, Santosh Kumar. *Infantile Cirrhosis of the Liver*. Calcutta: Indian Medical Record Book Depot, 1922.

Mukherji, Santosh Kumar. *The Kama Sutra of Vatsayana*. Calcutta: Oriental Agency, 1945.

Mukherji, Santosh Kumar. *Modern Treatment*. Calcutta: Mukherjee, 1979.

Mukherji, Santosh Kumar. *Prostitution in India*. Delhi: Inter-India Publications, 1986 [1934].

Mukherji, Santosh Kumar. *Psychology of Image Worship of the Hindus*. Calcutta: Oriental Agency, 1947[?].

Mukherji, Santosh Kumar. *Srshti, Bhagabana, o Sadhana*. Calcutta: Institute of National Culture, 1969.

Mukhopadhyay, Rashbehari. *Ballali-Sansodhini*. Dacca: n.p., 1868.

Mukhopadhyay, Subodh Kumar. "Evolution of Historiography in Bengali (1800–1947)—A Study of the Pattern of Growth." In *Historiography in Modern Indian Languages, 1800–1947: Report of the National Seminar Held at Santiniketan, from 11th March to 13th March 1985*. Calcutta: Naya Prokash, 1987.

Murti, Kamakshi. *India: The Seductive and Seduced "Other" of German Orientalism*. London: Greenwood Press, 2001.

Nagarjuna, Siddha, and K. Deyer. *Rati Sastra*. 2nd edition. Amritsar: Steno House Agency, 1953 [1933].

Nair, Janaki. *Women and Law in Colonial India: A Social History*. Delhi: Kali for Women, 1996.

Najmabadi, Afsaneh. *Women without Moustaches and Men without Beards: Gender and Sexual Anxieties of Iranian Modernity*. Berkeley: University of California Press, 2005.

Nepal, Binod. "AIDS Denial in Asia: Dimensions and Roots." *Health Policy* 84, no. 2 (2007): 133–41.

Nitambini, Srimati. *Anurha Yuvati Natak*. Dacca: n.p., 1872.

Oldenburg, Veena Talwar. "Lifestyle as Resistance: The Case of Courtesans of Lucknow, India." *Feminist Studies* 16, no. 2 (Summer 1990): 259–87.

Orsini, Francesca. *Print and Pleasure*. New Delhi: Permanent Black, 2009.

Paik, Shailaja. *Dalit Women's Education in Modern India: Double Discrimination*. London: Routledge, 2014.

Pande, Ishita. "Loving Like a Man: The Colourful Prophet, Conjugal Masculinity and the Politics of Hindu Sexology in Late Colonial India." *Gender & History* 29, no. 3 (November 2017): 675–92.

Pande, Ishita. *Medicine, Race, and Liberalism in British Bengal*. New York: Routledge, 2010.

Pande, Ishita. "Phulmoni's Body: The Autopsy, the Inquest and the Humanitarian Narrative on Child Rape in India." *South Asian History and Culture* 4, no. 1 (Jan. 2013): 9–30.

Pandey, Gyanendra. *The Construction of Communalism in Colonial North India*. Oxford: Oxford University Press, 1990.

Pandian, Ativira Rama. *Kokkokam*. Calcutta: Medical Book Company, 1949.

Papanek, Hanna. "Afterword: Caging the Lion, a Fable for Our Time." In *Sultana's Dream*, edited by Rokeya Sakhawat Hossain, 58–85. New York: Feminist Press of the City University of New York, 1988.

Parent-Duchâtelet, Alexandre. *De la prostitution dans la ville de Paris, considérée sous le rapport de l'hygiène publique, de la morale et de l'administration: Ouvrage appuyé de documens statistiques puisés dans les archives de la Préfecture de police*. Paris: J. B. Baillière et fils, 1857 [1836].

Park, Katharine. *Secrets of Women: Gender, Generation, and the Origins of Human Dissection*. New York: Zone Books, 2006.

Patel, Geeta. *Risky Bodies and Techno-Intimacy: Reflections on Sexuality, Media, Science, Finance*. Seattle: University of Washington Press, 2017.

Patel, Sujata, ed. *Doing Sociology in India: Genealogies, Locations, and Practices*. Delhi: Oxford University Press, 2011.

Pinney, Christopher. *Camera Indica: The Social Life of Indian Photographs*. Chicago: University of Chicago Press, 1997.

Pinney, Christopher. *The Coming of Photography to India*. London: British Library, 2008.

Pollock, Sheldon. "Deep Orientalism? Notes on Sanskrit and Power Beyond the Raj." In *Orientalism and the Postcolonial Predicament: Perspectives on South Asia*, edited by Carol A. Breckenridge and Peter Van der Veer, 76–133. Philadelphia: University of Pennsylvania Press, 1993.

Poovey, Mary. *A History of the Modern Fact: Problems of Knowledge in the Sciences of Wealth and Society*. Chicago: University of Chicago Press, 1998.

Poovey, Mary. *Making a Social Body: British Cultural Formation, 1830–1864*. Chicago: University of Chicago Press, 1995.

Prakash, Gyan. *Another Reason: Science and the Imagination of Modern India*. Princeton, NJ: Princeton University Press, 1999.

Prakash, Gyan. *Bonded Histories: Genealogies of Labor Servitude in Colonial India*. Cambridge: Cambridge University Press, 2003.

Prakash, Gyan. "Review of *Imagining India* by Ronald Inden." *The American Historical Review* 97, no. 2 (April 1992): 601–2.

Pritchett, Frances W. *Resources on South Asia*. http://www.columbia.edu/itc/mealac/pritchett/00fwp/.

Puri, Jyoti. *Woman, Body, Desire in Post-Colonial India: Narratives of Gender and Sexuality*. London: Routledge, 1999.

Ramberg, Lucinda. *Given to the Goddess: South Indian Devadasis and the Sexuality of Religion*. Durham, NC: Duke University Press, 2014.

Rao, Anupama. "Caste, Colonialism, and the Reform of Gender: Perspectives from Western India." In *Gendering Colonial India: Reforms, Print, Caste, and Communalism*, edited by Charu Gupta, 239–64. Delhi: Orient Blackswan, 2012.

Rao, Anupama. *The Caste Question: Dalits and the Politics of Modern India*. Ranikhet: Permanent Black, 2009.

Rao, Anupama. *Gender and Caste*. Delhi: Kali for Women, 2003.

Rati-Sastram; or, The Greatest Work on Hindu System of Sexual Science. 2nd edition. Calcutta: Sircar, 1908.

Rati Sastra Ratnavali, An Excellent Treatise on Hindu Men and Women in Simple English Prose, Translated from Sanskrit Verses. Madras: S. Mürthy & Co., 1905.

Ratnapalan, Laavanyan. "E. B. Tylor and the Problem of Primitive Culture." *History and Anthropology* 19, no. 2 (2008): 131–42.

Rawat, Ramnarayan S. *Reconsidering Untouchability: Chamars and Dalit History in North India*. Ranikhet: Permanent Black, 2012.

Ray, Bharati. *Early Feminists of Colonial India: Sarala Devi Chaudurani and Rokeya Sakhawat Hossain*. New Delhi: Oxford University Press, 2002.

Ray, Bidisha. "Contesting Respectability: Sexuality, Corporeality and Non-'Bhadra' Cultures in Colonial Bengal." PhD diss., University of Manchester, 2008.

Ray, Niharranjan. *Bangalir Itihas: Adiparva*. Calcutta: n.p., 1949.

Ray, T. *Ananga Ranga*. Calcutta: Medical Book Company, 1944.

Ray, T. N. *Kokkokam & Rati Rahasyam*. 2nd edition. Calcutta: Medical Book Company, 1960.

Reagan, Leslie J. *When Abortion Was a Crime: Women, Medicine, and Law in the United States, 1867–1973*. Berkeley: University of California Press, 1997.

Rege, Sharmila. *Against the Madness of Manu: B.R. Ambedkar's Writings on Brahmanical Patriarchy*. Delhi: Navayana Publishers, 2013.

Rege, Sharmila. "Institutional Alliances between Sociology and Gender Studies: Story of the Crocodile and the Monkey." *Economic and Political Weekly* 32, no. 32 (1997): 2023–27.

Rege, Sharmila. *Writing Caste Writing Gender: Narrating Dalit Women's Testimonios*. Delhi: Zubaan, 2006.

"Review of Robert Harvey's Reports." *The Lancet*, July 8, 1876, 63.

Richard, Evelleen. *Darwin and the Making of Sexual Selection*. Chicago: University of Chicago, 2017.

Riley, Denise. *"Am I That Name?": Feminism and the Category of "Women."* London: Macmillan, 1988.

Risley, Herbert H. *The People of India*. Calcutta: Thacker, Spinck, and Co., 1908.

Risley, Herbert H. "The Study of Ethnology in India." *The Journal of the Anthropological Institute of Great Britain and Ireland* 20 (1891): 235–63.

Risley, Herbert H. *The Tribes and Castes of Bengal*. Calcutta: Bengal Secretariat Press, 1891.

Ross, Andrew Israel. "Sex in the Archives: Homosexuality, Prostitution, and the Archives de la Préfecture de Police de Paris." *French Historical Studies* 40, no. 2 (2017): 267–90.

Roy, Hemandra Kumar [Meghnad Gupta]. *Rater Kolkata*. Kolkata: Urbi Prakasana, 2015.

Roy, Kumkum. "Unravelling the Kamasutra." In *A Question of Silence? The Sexual Economics of Modern India*, edited by Mary E. John and Janaki Nair, 52–76. London: Zed Books, 1998.

Roy, M. N. *M.N. Roy Memoirs*. Bombay: Allied Publishers, 1964.

Rubin, Gayle. "The Problem with Trafficking: Afterthoughts on 'The Traffic in Women'." In *Deviations: A Gayle Rubin Reader*, 66–86. Durham, NC: Duke University Press, 2011.

Rubin, Gayle. "The Traffic in Women: Notes on the 'Political Economy' of Sex." In *Toward an Anthropology of Women*, edited by Rayna Reiter, 157–210. New York: Monthly Review Press, 1975.

Rusert, Britt. *Fugitive Science: Empiricism and Freedom in Early African American Culture*. New York: NYU Press, 2017.

Russett, Cynthia Eagle. *Sexual Science: The Victorian Construction of Womanhood*. Cambridge, MA: Harvard University Press, 1989.

Sangari, Kumkum, and Sudesh Vaid. *Recasting Women: Essays in Colonial History*. Delhi: Kali for Women, 1989.

Sanger, William. *History of Prostitution*. New York: Harper and Brothers, 1858.

Sarkar, Chandranath. *Sukumari Natak*. Calcutta: n.p., 1877.

Sarkar, Mahua. *Visible Histories, Disappearing Women: Producing Muslim Womanhood in Late Colonial Bengal*. Durham, NC: Duke University Press, 2008.

Sarkar, Sumit. "Vidyasagar and Brahmanical Society." In *Women and Social Reform in Modern India: A Reader*, edited by Tanika Sarkar and Sumit Sarkar, 118–45. Bloomington: Indiana University Press, 2008.

Sarkar, Sumit. *Writing Social History*. Delhi: Oxford University Press, 1997.

Sarkar, Tanika. *Bengal, 1928–1934*. New Delhi: Oxford University Press, 1988.

Sarkar, Tanika. *Hindu Wife, Hindu Nation: Community, Religion, and Cultural Nationalism*. Bloomington: University of Indiana Press, 2001.

Sarkar, Tanika. *Rebels, Wives, Saints: Designing Selves and Nations in Colonial Times*. Ranikhet: Permanent Black, 2009.

Sarkar, Tanika. *Words to Win: The Making of "Amar Jiban": A Modern Autobiography*. New Delhi: Kali for Women, 1999.

Sarkar, Tanika, and Sumit Sarkar, eds. *Women and Social Reform in Modern India: A Reader*. Bloomington: Indiana University Press, 2008.

Sarton, George. "Review of *A Study in Hindu Social Polity*." *Isis* 7, no. 2 (1925): 268.

Sastri, K.S. Ramaswami. *Hindu Culture, an Exposition and a Vindication*. Calcutta: S. Ganesan, 1922.

Satish, Mrinal. *Discretion, Discrimination and the Rule of Law: Reforming Rape Sentencing in India*. New York: Cambridge University Press, 2017.

Savary, Luzia. "Vernacular Eugenics? Santati-Śāstra in Popular Hindi Advisory Literature (1900–1940)." *South Asia: Journal of South Asian Studies* 37, no. 3 (2014): 381–97.

Schmidt, Richard. *Beiträge zur indischen Erotik*. 3rd edition. Berlin: Hermann Barsdorf Publishers, 1922.

Science of Life, or Hindu System of Sexual Secrets: Parts I & II: Translated into English with Original Sanskrit Text. Calcutta: Ganguly, 1909.

Scott, Joan Wallach. "The Evidence of Experience." *Critical Inquiry* 17, no. 4 (1991): 773–97.

Scott, Joan Wallach. "Gender: A Useful Category of Historical Analysis." *American Historical Review* 91, no. 5 (1986): 1053–75.

Scully, Pamela. "Narratives of Infanticide in the Aftermath of Slave Emancipation in the Nineteenth-Century Cape Colony, South Africa." *Canadian Journal of African Studies* 30, no. 1 (1996): 88–105.

Sedgwick, Eve Kosofsky. *Epistemology of the Closet*. Berkeley: University of California Press, 1990.
Sen, Haimabati. *The Memoirs of Dr. Haimabati Sen: From Child Widow to Lady Doctor*. Translated by Tapan Raychaudhuri and edited by Geraldine Hancock Forbes. New Delhi: Roli Books Ltd., 2000.
Sen, Samita. *Women and Labour in Late Colonial India: The Bengal Jute Industry*. Cambridge: Cambridge University Press, 1999.
Sengoopta, Chandak. *Imprint of the Raj: How Fingerprinting Was Born in Colonial India*. London: Macmillan, 2003.
Shah, Svati. *Street Corner Secrets: Sex, Work and Migration in the City of Mumbai*. Durham, NC: Duke University Press, 2014.
Shaikh, Juned. "Imagining Caste: Photography, the Housing Question, and the Making of Sociology in Colonial Bombay, 1900–1939." *South Asia: Journal of South Asian Studies* 37, no. 3 (2014): 491–514.
Sharafi, Mitra. "Abortion and Medical Experts in the British Indian Courtroom." Paper presented at the 16th Berkshire Conference of Women Historians, Toronto, 2014.
Sharma, Ram Sharan. "Traces of Promiscuity in Ancient Indian Society." *Proceedings of the Indian History Congress* 19 (1956): 153–57.
She Wasn't Ashamed: Autobiography of an Indian Prostitute. Lahore: All India Women's Social Reform League, 1941.
Singha, Kaliprasanna. *Hutom Pyancha Naksha*. Calcutta: n.p., 1862.
Singha, Radhika. *A Despotism of Law: Crime and Justice in Early Colonial India*. Oxford: Oxford University Press, 1998.
Singha, Srinath. *Kularahasya Kavya*. Murshidabad: n.p., 1877.
Sinha, Mrinalini. *Colonial Masculinity: The "Manly Englishman" and the "Effeminate Bengali" in the Late Nineteenth Century*. Manchester: Manchester University Press, 1995.
Sinha, Mrinalini. *Specters of Mother India: The Global Restructuring of an Empire*. Durham, NC: Duke University Press, 2006.
Skaria, Ajay. "Only One Word, Properly Altered: Gandhi and the Question of the Prostitute." *Postcolonial Studies* 10, no. 2 (2007): 219–37.
Spencer, Herbert. *First Principles*. London: G. Mainwaring, Williams & Norgate, 1860–62.
Spencer, Herbert. *Principles of Sociology*. Vol. 1. New York: D. Appleton and Company, 1893 [1875].
Spillers, Hortense J. "Mama's Baby, Papa's Maybe: An American Grammar Book." *Diacritics* 17, no. 2 (1987): 65–81.
Spivak, Gayatri Chakravorty. "Can the Subaltern Speak?" In *Marxism and the Interpretation of Culture*, edited by Cary Nelson and Lawrence Grossberg, 271–313. Urbana: University of Illinois Press, 1988.
Sreenivas, Mytheli. "Birth Control in the Shadow of Empire: The Trials of Annie Besant, 1877–1878." *Feminist Studies* 41, no. 3 (2015): 509–37.
Sreenivas, Mytheli. *Wives, Widows, and Concubines: The Conjugal Family Ideal in Colonial India*. Bloomington: Indiana University Press, 2008.
Stansell, Christine. *City of Women: Sex and Class in New York, 1789–1860*. Urbana: University of Illinois Press, 1987.
Stauter-Halsted, Keely. *The Devil's Chain: Prostitution and Social Control in Partitioned Poland*. Ithaca, NY: Cornell University Press, 2015.

Stocking, George. *Victorian Anthropology*. New York: The Free Press, 1987.
Stokes, Eric. *The English Utilitarians and India*. Oxford: Clarendon Press, 1959.
Stoler, Ann Laura. *Carnal Knowledge and Imperial Power: Race and the Intimate in Colonial Rule*. Berkeley: University of California Press, 2002.
Stoler, Ann Laura. *Race and the Education of Desire: Foucault's History of Sexuality and the Colonial Order of Things*. Durham, NC: Duke University Press, 1995.
Sturman, Rachel. *The Government of Social Life in Colonial India: Liberalism, Religious Law and Women's Rights*. Cambridge: Cambridge University Press, 2012.
Stuy, David. "Macaulay and the Indian Penal Code of 1862: The Myth of the Inherent Superiority and Modernity of the English Legal System Compared to India's Legal System in the Nineteenth Century." *Modern Asian Studies* 2, no. 3 (July 1998): 513–57.
Sunder Rajan, Rajeswari. *The Scandal of the State: Women, Law, and Citizenship in Postcolonial India*. Durham, NC: Duke University Press, 2003.
Surkis, Judith. *Sexing the Citizen: Morality and Masculinity in France, 1870–1920*. Ithaca, NY: Cornell University Press, 2006.
Sutherland, David. *The Weekly Reporter, Appellate High Court*. Vol. 12. Calcutta: Thacker, Spink, and Co., 1870.
Tambe, Ashwini. *Codes of Misconduct: The Regulation of Prostitution in Colonial Bombay*. Minneapolis: University of Minnesota Press, 2008.
Tambe, Ashwini. "Colluding Patriarchies: Sexual Reform in Colonial India." *Feminist Studies* 26, 3 (2000): 587–600.
Tarkaratna, Ramnarayan. *Kulina Kulasarvasva*. Calcutta: n.p., 1854.
Thapar, Romila. *Cultural Pasts: Essays in Early Indian History*. Oxford: Oxford University Press, 2000.
Thapar, Romila. *Sakuntala: Texts, Readings, Histories*. New Delhi: Kali for Women, 1999.
Tharu, Susie, and K. Lalita. *Women Writing in India: 600 BC to the Present*. Vol. 1. New York: The Feminist Press at CUNY, 1991.
Thomas, P. *Kama Kalpa, or, The Hindu Ritual of Love*. Bombay: D. B. Taraporevala Sons and Co., 1960.
Thomas, P. *Women and Marriage in India*. London: George Allen and Unwin, 1939.
Thomas, William I. *The Unadjusted Girl: With Cases and Standpoint for Behavior Analysis*. Boston: Little, Brown, and Co., 1923.
Thompson, W. H. *Census of India, 1921*. Vol. 5. Calcutta: Superintendent Government Printing, 1923.
Thomson, J. Arthur. *The Evolution of Sex*. New York: Humboldt Publishing, 1889.
Trautmann, Thomas. *Aryans and British India*. Berkeley: University of California Press, 1997.
Trautmann, Thomas. *Lewis Henry Morgan and the Invention of Kinship*. Berkeley: University of California Press, 1988.
Turner, James. *Philology: The Forgotten Origins of the Modern Humanities*. Princeton, NJ: Princeton University Press, 2014.
Uberoi, Patricia, ed. *Social Reform, Sexuality, and the State*. New Delhi: Sage Publications, 1996.
Uberoi, Patricia, Nandini Sundar, and Satish Deshpande, eds. *Anthropology in the East: Founders of Indian Sociology and Anthropology*. Calcutta: Seagull Books, 2007.
Upadhyaya, S. C., and V. Raghavan. *Rati Rahasya of Pandit Kokkoka: The Hindu Secrets of Love*. Bombay: Taraporevala, 1981 [1965].

Vance, Carole, ed. *Pleasure and Danger: Exploring Female Sexuality*. London: Routledge and Kegan Paul, 1984.

Verax. *Social Evil in Calcutta*. Calcutta: Calcutta Central Press Co., 1895.

Vishwanath, L. S. "Female Infanticide: The Colonial Experience." *Economic and Political Weekly* 39, no. 22 (2004): 2313–18.

Viswanath, Rupa. *The Pariah Problem: Caste, Religion, and the Social in Modern India*. New York: Columbia University Press, 2014.

Wadley, Susan S. "Women and the Hindu Tradition." *Signs: Journal of Women in Culture and Society* 3, no. 1 (1977): 113–25.

Wald, Erica. "From Begums and Bibis to Abandoned Females and Idle Women: Sexual Relationships, Venereal Disease and the Redefinition of Prostitution in Early Nineteenth-Century India." *Indian Economic and Social History Review* 46, no. 1 (2009): 5–25.

Walkowitz, Judith. *Prostitution in Victorian Society: Women, Class and the State*. Cambridge: Cambridge University Press, 1980.

Walsh, Judith. *Domesticity in Colonial India: What Women Learned When Men Gave Them Advice*. Lanham, MD: Rowman & Littlefield, 2004.

Webb, Allan. *Pathologica Indica; or, The Anatomy of Indian Diseases, Medical and Surgical: Based Upon Morbid Specimens from All Parts of India in the Museum of the Calcutta Medical College; Illustrated by Detailed Cases, with the Prescriptions and Treatment Employed, and Comments, Physiological, Practical and Historical*. Calcutta: W. H. Carey, 1848.

Werner, B. *Indisches Liebesleben*. Berlin: P. J. Oestergaard, 1928.

Weston, Kath. *Long Slow Burn: Sexuality and Social Science*. New York: Routledge, 1998.

White, Luise. *Comforts of Home: Prostitution in Colonial Nairobi*. Chicago: University of Chicago Press, 1990.

Wiener, Martin. *Reconstructing the Criminal: Culture, Law, and Policy in England, 1830–1914*. Cambridge: Cambridge University Press, 1990.

Windsor, Edward. *Cultural and Anthropological Studies in the Hindu Art of Love*. New York: Falstaff Press, 1937.

Windsor, Edward. *The Hindu Art of Love*. New York: Falstaff Press, 1932.

Wood, James C. *Clinical Gynaecology*. Philadelphia: Boericke & Tafel, 1897.

Yang, Anand A. *Crime and Criminality in British India*. Tucson: University of Arizona Press, 1986.

Yang, Anand A. "Dangerous Castes and Tribes: The Criminal Tribes Act and the Magahiya Doms of Northeast India." In *Crime and Criminality in British India*, 108–27. Tucson: University of Arizona Press, 1985.

Yang, Anand A. "Whose Sati? Widow Burning in Early 19th Century India." *Journal of Women's History* 1, no. 2 (1989): 8–33.

Zysk, Kenneth G. *Conjugal Love in India: Ratisastra and Ratiramana*. Leiden: Brill, 2002.

IMAGE CREDITS

1. Richard Schmidt, *Kamasutram: Die indische Ars Amatoria des Vatsyayana* (Berlin: Barsdorf, 1904), cover.
2. N. K. Basu and S. N. Sinha, *The History of Prostitution* (Calcutta: Calcutta Hygiene Association, 1929), 194.
3. Santosh Kumar Mukherji, *Indian Sex Life and Prostitution* (Calcutta: Anil Kumar Das Gupta, 1934), 88.
4. Chandra Chakraverty, Photograph with Ernst Sekunna, German Intelligence Officer, undated, George Grantham Bain Collection, Library of Congress.
5. Handwritten letter from Deputy Magistrate Bankim Chandra Chatterjee to Government of Bengal, "Collected Memoranda by Officers Consulted on the Subject of Forbidding the Possession of Girls under Ten Years of Age by Prostitutes," Judicial Branch, Judicial Department, October 1872, B. No. 252–335, West Bengal State Archives.
6. A. Mackenzie, Officiating Secretary to the Government of Bengal, Judicial Department to H. L. Dampier, Officiating Secretary to the Govt. of India, October 17, 1872, Home Dept. Proceedings, July 1873, no. 156, National Archives of India.
7. Chart of Infanticide Cases in Bengal, 1871–1875, Shahabad in A. V. Palmer letter dated November 17, 1876, in "Response to Questions regarding the application of section 302 of IPC in case of a woman killing her illegitimate child directly after birth," Judicial File 58, Proceedings 10–39, August 1877, West Bengal State Archives.
8. Allan Webb, *Pathologica Indica; or, the Anatomy of Indian Diseases, Medical and Surgical: Based upon Morbid Specimens from All Parts of India in the Museum of the Calcutta Medical College; Illustrated by Detailed Cases, with the Prescriptions and Treatment Employed, and Comments, Physiological, Practical and Historical* (Calcutta: W. H. Carey, 1848), title page.
9. Norman Chevers, *A Manual of Medical Jurisprudence for India* (Calcutta: Thacker, Spink & Co., 1870), title illustration page and title page.
10. I. B. Lyon, *Medical Jurisprudence for India, with Illustrative Cases* (Calcutta: Thacker, Spink, & Co., 1921), 582.
11. Herbert H. Risley, *The Tribes and Castes of Bengal: Ethnographic Glossary,* vol. 2 (Calcutta: Bengal Secretariat Press, 1891), cover.
12. Rafidin Ahmed, photograph, *The Hindusthanee Student* 2, no. 3 (November 1915): 19.

13. Gyanendrakumar Maitra, *Rati Yantradira Pida* (Calcutta: n.p., 1923), 58.
14. Santosh Kumar Mukherji, *Indian Sex Life and Prostitution* (Calcutta: Anil Kumar Das Gupta, 1934), title page.
15. J. F. Blumhardt, *Catalogue of the Library of the India Office: Bengali, Oriya, and Assamese Books*, vol. 2, Part 4 (London: Eyre and Spottiswoode, 1905), 29.

INDEX

Note: Page numbers in italic type indicate illustrations.

Abbott, Andrew, 12–13, 221n49, 222n51
Abercrombie, Alexander, 74
abortion: as act of concealment, 88–94, 103, 112, 122, 123–24, 185; alleged prevalence of, 68, 93–94, 109–10, 112, 115, 122–23, 129; case studies of, 113–21; caste linked to, 109–10; circular reasoning concerning, 101–2, 105–6, 114, 121, 124, 128, 131–32; deviant female sexuality linked to, 88–91, 103; difficulties in detecting, 88–91; forensic evidence of, 19, 99–132; institutionalization of forensics of, 124–31; among Kulin Brahmans, 109, 121, 181, 185; methods of, 115–21, 130, 241n45; prohibition of widow remarriage linked to, 109, 112, 115, 122–23; prostitution linked to, 122, 129; rape and, 122–24; scientific approach to, 115, 120; sociological types of women, 113–21; surveillance associated with, 90–91, 124–31; violence of, 90–91, 93, 103, 111, 113–21. *See also* infanticide
Acton, William, 7
Ahmed, Rafidin, 136, 148, 149–51, *150*
Alexander, Meena, 253n5
Ali, S. Wajid, 148–49
Ali, Syed Ameer, 148
Ali, Torick Ameer, 148
All-India Muslim League, 148
Amrita Bazar Patrika (newspaper), 96, 177

Ananga-Ranga, 29–30
Anangaranga, 25, 28, 29, 32, 34, 47, 59
Anarkhali, 54
Anthropos (journal), 38
antiquarian study. *See* philology
Arbuthnot, Forster Fitzgerald, 27, 226n15
Archer, W. G., 24
archives, 3–6, 14, 203, 204; colonial legal, 62, 63, 65, 67, 69, 78, 84, 85, 88, 98; forensic, 101, 103, 114, 131; methods to approach, 9, 20–22, 178, 207, 219n29, 219n31; philological, 39; of popular publications, 178, of prostitution, 217n18; sexuality and the, 219n29, 219n31
Arondekar, Anjali, 9, 28, 215n9, 218n28, 219n31, 227n16, 227n18, 233n15, 244n12
artha (wealth, property), 32, 36, 44–45
Arthashastra, 32, 34, 36, 44, 53
Aryans, 25–26, 43, 45, 48, 57, 60, 138. *See also* Indo-Aryans
asceticism, 195–201
Asiatic Society of Bengal, 10, 31
Augustine, Saint, 17
autobiographies: of high-caste women, 252n57; of "prostitutes," 20, 176–79, 194–201

Bachofen, Johann Jakob, 134, 137, 141, 142, 152, 163, 172
Bader, Clarisse, 229n56
Ballhatchet, Kenneth, 216n11, 234n46

279

Bandhyopadhyay, Harinarayan, *Gurbini Bandhab* (A guide to pregnancy), 128–31
Bandyopadhyay, Bhabanicharan: *Dutibilas* (The merriment of the procurer), 251n35; *Nababibibilas* (The merriment of the bibi), 251n35; *Nababubilas* (The merriment of the babu), 251n35
Banerjee, Prathama, 41, 222n54, 244n11, 247n80
Banerjee, Sumanta, 215n11, 249n6, 250n32, 251n35
Banerji, Sures Chandra, 61
Bangiyo Navya Sampradaya (Society of Modern Bengalis on Tradition), 184
barangana (public woman), 129, 135
barbonita (public woman), 190–93
Barua, B. M., 47
Basu, J. N., 47
Basu, Nripendra Kumar, 27, 47, 230n80, 230n81; *The History of Prostitution*, 47–52
Basu, Subodh Kumar, 151–53
Bayley, S. C., 84, 90, 95
Baynes, C. R., 110, 117
Bell, Thomas, *Kalogynomia: or the Laws of Female Beauty*, 29
Bengali social thought: and ancient sexuality, 26, 40–61, 152, 154–55, 163, 167, 172, 174; and forensics, 129, 130; importance of, 10–14; and philology, 26–27; prostitute concept in, 7; sexuality and social development in, 6, 134–36, 147, 148, 171, 174; social authority/control grounded in theories of, 14–16, 22, 27, 143, 203, 204, 206, 222n53. *See also* modern social thought
Bengal Social Hygiene Association, 47
Bengal Social Science Association, 11, 146, 220n38
beshya (promiscuous woman, prostitute), 49, 71, 135, 170, 177, 191. See also *vesya*
Beshyasangeet, Baijisangeet (Songs of the beshya, songs of the baiji), 191, 217n21, 251n42

Bewah, Kally, 99–101, 103, 106, 131, 181
Bhide, Shivaram Parashuram, 28
Black feminist thought, 216n12, 217n19; and history, 219n29
blackmail/extortion, 84–85, 90, 103, 125–26
Bloch, Iwan, 36, 48, 53, 228n46
Blumhardt, J. F., 181, 221n45; sociology books catalogued by, 182
body, forensics of abortion and, 99–101, 105–7, 110–21, 131–32
Bombay School of Sociology, 173, 221n43
Book of The Thousand Nights and a Night, 27, 29
Bopp, Franz, 228n51
Bose, S. C., *The Hindoos as They Are*, 39
Bourne, Samuel, 180
Brahmans: intellectuals, 14; caste hierarchy, 42, 71; widows, 67; 155–56, 180. *See also* Kulin polygamy
Brahmo Samaj, 147
Buck, Carl Darling, 36, 228n51
Buddhism, 156
Bulletin of the Indian Rationalistic Society (journal), 148–49
Burckhardt, Johann Ludwig, 110
Burton, Richard F., 26, 27–32, 34, 35; *Kama Sutra of Vatsayana*, 26, 27–32, 34, 35

Calcutta, 81–83, 145–46, 158, 176, 188–93
Calcutta High Court, 78, 127
Calcutta Medical College, 11, 104, 108, 146
Calcutta Suppression of Immoral Traffic Act (1923), 47, 97, 177
Calcutta University. *See* University of Calcutta
Cantonment Acts (1864), 69, 78
caste: abortion linked to, 109–10; "Chandals," 42, 71; female sexuality linked to, 14; menstruation and, 42–43; naturalization of, through social scientific theories, 15–16; polygamy linked to, 186–87; social evolution and, 138, 155; Vaishnav disregard for, 70–71, 73. *See also* Hindu upper castes; lower castes

INDEX 281

census of Bengal (1881), 69
census of India (1871), 80
census of India (1891), 80
census of India (1921), 97–98
Chakladar, H. C., 27, 43–45, 56, 167; *The Aryan Occupation of Eastern India*, 43; *Social Life in Ancient India*, 43–44, 48, 53
Chakraberty, Chandra, 27, 57–61, 58; *Ancient Indian Sex Life*, 57; *The Racial History of India*, 57; *Sexology of the Hindus*, 57, 59
Chakravarti, Uma, 26, 226n11
Chambers, E. W., 99–101
Chaterjee, Nolini Mohun, 148, 149
Chattapadhyay, Saratchandra, 16–18, 134, 204; *Devdas*, 16; "Narir Mulya" (The value of a woman), 17–18
Chatterjee, A., 47
Chatterjee, Bankim, 71–74; letter from, 64
Chatterjee, Indrani, 177, 215n11, 223n60, 233n18, 238n113
Chatterjee, Partha, 102, 213n8, 221n44, 222n53, 239n8, 246n1, 249n6
Chattopadhyay, Nisikantha, 38
Chevers, Norman, *A Manual of Medical Jurisprudence*, 10, 110–12, *111*, 115–17, 122, 123, 127, 130, 146, 242n56
child marriage, 197–98
Child Marriage Restraint Act (1929), 198
Chowdhury, K. C., 47
chowkidar (watchman), 90–91, 126
Chundra, J. L., 136
clandestine prostitutes, 50, 55, 63, 70–72, 78, 80–83, 93, 97, 157, 169, 184
Cockerell, Horace, 84
Cohen, Cathy, 217n19
Cohn, Bernard, 65, 219n35, 232n5
colonial difference, 102, 135, 239n8
colonial India. *See* India
colonial knowledge, 3, 9–11, 27; and ethnology, 137–45; feminist historical approaches to, 219n30; forensic, 101–3; as multidisciplinary 12–14; postcolonial and subaltern historical approaches to, 219n35
Comfort, Alex, 24

communalism. *See* Muslims: anti-Muslim sentiment
Comte, Auguste, 11, 138, 145, 146, 220n39
concept history, 2, 6, 8, 216n15. *See also* prostitute concept
concubinage, 54, 82, 153, 169, 170
Contagious Diseases Act (1868), 47, 68, 69, 78–86, 97, 98, 122, 146, 177, 234n46
Cantonment Acts (1864), 69, 86
contraception, 56
control of female sexuality: central to Indian social life, 2, 6, 8, 15, 22, 24, 42, 143, 221n45, 222n52; Contagious Diseases Act and, 78–86; criminal laws related to, 68–69; forensics and, 128; infanticide and abortion linked to, 91; *kama* texts written for, 31–32; monogamous marriage as means of, 187; necessity of, 56–57; patriarchal, 8, 9, 143, 188; philological bases of, 24–25, 31; social evolution and, 142–43, 151; widow remarriage as means of, 94
coroners, 238n4
courtesans, 4, 30, 31, 35, 45, 46, 51, 54, 55, 75, 86, 141, 234n47; in film, 224n65, 249n6
Cowell, Edward, 51
Criminal Procedure Code (1861), 104
cuckoo birds, 157, 162
Curjel, Dagmar, and Curjel Report, 97, 177
custom/tradition: associated with abortion and infanticide, 87–89, 91, 94, 102, 103, 108, 109, 111, 123, 128; colonial conceptions of, 9–10, 65, 145; critiques of, 179–88; ethnology and, 134, 137–45, 149, 158; female sexual deviance and, 19, 53, 74, 167; *kama* texts as means to understanding, 44; law linked to, 140; in lay sociologies, 179, 181, 184, 185; philology and, 25, 39; prostitution and, 18, 77; as racial difference, 102, 135; rationalism vs., 149, 152, 156; sciences of society and, 145–48; social evolutionary theory based on studies of, 134; universalist theories and, 145

daktari publication, 159
Dalton, Edward Tuite, 167; *Descriptive Ethnology of Bengal*, 10, 138–39, 168
dancing girls, 75, 169
Darwin, Charles, 134, 137; *The Descent of Man*, 142, *On the Origin of Species*, 244n7
Das, Dhanapatinath, *Hindu Samajer Bartamon Abastha* (The present condition of Hindu society), 154, 156–57
Dasi, Binodini, 222n52, 252n57
Dasi, Parimalbala (pseudonym), *Nurseyr Atmakatha* (Life story of a nurse), 199–200
Debi, Nabinkali, *Kamini Kalanka* (A woman's shame), 177, 196
degeneration, social, 128, 130, 154, 159, 161
Devdas (film), 16, 224n65
Devi, Manoda (pseudonym), *Shikshita Patitar Atmacharit* (Autobiography of an Educated Fallen Woman), 176, 197–99, 201
deviance, concept of, 6–7
deviant female sexuality: abortion linked to, 88–91, 103; autobiography and, 194, 195, 196, 198, 200; comparative approach to, 60; contemporary debates concerning, 9; definition of, 6, 217n19, 218n29; as fact, 203, 207; forensic evidence of, 19; fundamental nature of, 31; history of, 16–22; infanticide linked to, 87–96; Kulin polygamy as a cause of, 181–87; in lay sociologies, 189–94; meaning of, 6–7; in modern social thought, 1–2, 8, 9, 203; originary role of, 3; philology and, 19, 23–61; the prostitute as proxy for, 1, 6, 7; role of, in colonial/postcolonial knowledge of India, 6–9, 14–15, 22; social evolution and, 133–36; taxonomies of, 49, 50, 53, 55, 63, 65, 71–77, 82, 89, 98, 119, 130, 157, 168, 169, 171, 174, 193, 194, 204; and truth, 19–20. *See also* female sexuality; promiscuity: primitive; prostitute concept
Dey, Baboo Kanny Lall, 110, 146

dharma (law), 32, 36, 44–45
Dharmaśastra, 44
dhobi (washerman), 90, 125–27
Doan, Laura, 219n29
Dulong, M., 117
Durkheim, Emile, 6, 217n19
Dutt, Babu Girindranath, *The Brahmans and Kayasthas of Bengal*, 187
Dutt, R. C., *History of India*, 53

East Bengal and Assam Disorderly Houses Act (1907), 96
East India Company, 138, 140, 234n46, 234n47
education: growth of, in late nineteenth century, 11; women corrupted by, 164
Ellis, Havelock, 53; *Studies in the Psychology of Sex*, 36
Elphinstone, Mountstuart, 51
El Shakry, Omnia, 221n44
endogamy, 187
Engels, Friedrich, 8
ethnology: deviance and, 6; female sexuality as subject of, 8, 17; fieldwork-based approach to, 142–43; Indian social thought and, 48, 137–45; and social evolution, 6, 8, 38, 134; universalist models in, 15
Eulenburg, Albert, 36
evidence. *See* forensics
evolution/social evolution, 133–75; anti-Muslim bias, 16; caste and, 16, 138, 155; comparative approach to, 134–35, 138; control of female sexuality and, 142–43, 151; deviance and, 6, 7; deviant female sexuality and, 133–36; early decades of theories of, 244n7; *ganika* and, 158–65; and history of prostitution, 167–71; in Indian social thought, 147–48; institutionalization of, 148–57; marriage as index of, 134; monogamous marriage as culmination of, 151–53; patriarchy as culmination of, 140–42; rationalist accounts of, 148–57; sexuality and, 1–2, 11,

17–19, 38–39, 48, 134, 149–51, 163; stadial theories of, 137; universalist models of, 134–38, 174

extortion. *See* blackmail/extortion

Female Infanticide Act (1870), 87

female sexuality: caste linked to, 14; comparative approach to, 19, 39–40, 108–9; criminal laws related to, 68; duality characteristic of, 42; excessive/unrestrained, 6, 18, 21, 24, 31–32, 34, 42, 51, 53, 56–57, 60, 73, 76, 87, 91, 130, 135, 141–43, 145–46, 157, 162, 164, 171, 195, 197–98; exploitation of theories concerning, 15; homosexual, 196; Indological study of, 19, 25–40; law and, 19, 62–98; nationalism linked to, 14; objectification of, 65, 67; philology and, 23–25; popular readership on, 25; Sanskrit and, 23–25, 31, 41–46; scientific approach to, 29, 34–35, 41–42; timeless essence of, 41–42. *See also* deviant female sexuality; promiscuity: primitive; sexual difference

foeticide. *See* abortion

forensics, 19, 99–132; of abortion, 99–100, 104–21, 128–31; case studies in, 113–21; institutionalization of, 124–31; of rape, 123–24

Foucault, Michel, 215n2, 216n15, 225n8, 239n9

Fuentes, Marisa, 219n29

funeral pyres, 180–81, 188–91, 195

Galton, Francis, 6

gang rape, 55, 199

ganika (woman with many partners), 45, 46, 55, 135, 158–65

Garrett, C. B., 93

Geddes, Patrick, 173, 221n43

Geldner Karl Friedrich, 227n37

gender, 4, 6, 14, 61, 135, 136, 174, 226n11; in the making of caste, 223n62; history, 15, 223n60, 234n46; labor and, 9;

nonnormative, 69, 217n18; transgendered people, 217n18; violence, 9;

genital examinations, 78, 86, 111–12, 120, 124–28, 241n48, 242n56

geography, 44

Ghose, Abinash Chandra, *Rati-Sastram*, 23, 41–43, 225n4

Ghosh, J. N., *The Social Evil in Calcutta and Methods of Treatment*, 194

Ghosh, S., 47

Giles, A. H., 62–63, 97

Goethe, Johann W., 31

good womanhood, 48, 222n52

Great Unchastity Case (1873), 127

Greece, 30

Gribble, J.D.B., *Outlines of Medical Jurisprudence for India*, 126

Guha, Ranajit, 239n12

Gupta, Meghnad (pseudonym), *Rater Kolkata* (Calcutta at night), 188–93, 250n32

Haddon, Alfred C., 17

Haley, Sarah, 219n29

harems, 54, 76, 252n60

Hartland, Edwin Sidney, *Primitive Paternity*, 39, 48

Harvey, Robert, 112–16, 117, 122, 123

Hegel, Georg Wilhelm Friedrich, *Lectures on the Philosophy of History*, 145

Heher, Patrick, *Outlines of Medical Jurisprudence for India*, 126

Herder, Hans, 251n35

Herodotus, 152

Hetaerism, 30, 141, 152, 163–64

Hindoo Kama Shastra Society, 28, 226n15

Hindu College, 11

Hinduism: essentialist view of, 26, 139–40; theory of evolutionary development of, 154–56

Hindu upper castes: exploitation of social scientific theories by, 6, 13–16; marriage ideal of, 6, 7, 14, 15–16. *See also* Brahmans; Kulin polygamy

Hirschfeld, Magnus, 36, 40, 53; *Sexual-pathologie*, 48
historiography, 158; Black feminist, 219n29; colonial, 54; colonial difference in, 239n8; comparative feminist, 4, 219n13, 223n59; on Contagious Diseases Acts, 234n46, 234n47; nationalism, 222n53; postcolonial and subaltern, 219n35; of prostitution, 4, 215n11
Hogg, Stuart, 80–81, 83–84
homosexuality, 8, 196, 218n27
Hossain, Begum Rokeya Sakhawat, "Sultana's Dream," 204–6
Hunter, William Wilson, 86, 142; *A Statistical Account of Bengal*, 10
hymen, 114, 124, 132, 241n48, 242n56
hypergamy, 187

Inden, Ronald, 25, 226n11, 226n12
indenture, 87, 95, 96
India: duality characteristic of, 35, 38; essentialist view of, 226n11; role of the concepts of the prostitute and deviant female sexuality in, 2–9, 14–15; sexuality as key to nature of, 29–30, 32, 35, 39; timeless essence of, 2, 19, 26, 30, 35, 38, 39, 44
Indian Evidence Act (1872), 104
Indian Medical Record (journal), 52
Indian Penal Code (1860), 62, 68–70, 84, 87, 97, 98, 100, 104, 124, 131
Indian Police Act (1861), 124
Indian Rationalistic Society, 148–49, 153
Indo-Aryans, 137–38, 154. See also Aryans
Indology: in America, 36; and ancient texts, 10; and female sexuality, 19, 25–40; and Indian education, 11; modern social thought grounded in, 26, 226n11; and prostitute concept, 7; as science of society, 12; and sexuality, 36; significance of, in nineteenth century, 25–26; and study of *kama*, 28. See also philology
Indrajit, Bhagavanlal, 27
infanticide: as act of concealment, 88–94; alleged prevalence of, 68, 93–94, 122–23; in Bengal, 87–96; chart of cases of, 92; custom blamed for, 87–89, 91, 94; deviant sexuality blamed for, 89–90, 93; pity for women accused of, 88; punishment for, 90, 94–96; surveillance associated with, 90–91; surveys on, 87–89, 93. See also abortion
Institute of Sexual Science, 36

Joardar, Biswanath, 52
Jones, William, 10, 30–31, 138, 220n36; *Sakuntala*, 167
jute mill employees, 97

Kalidasa, 30
kama (desire/love/sex), 26, 27–32, 34, 36, 44–45
Kamasutra, 25, 27–29, 31, 32, 34, 41, 43–45, 47, 48, 51, 53, 55, 59, 173
Karlekar, Malavika, 181
Kautilya, 45
Kerr, Robert, *The Social Evil in Calcutta*, 194
Kipling, Rudyard, 204; "On the City Wall," 2–3
Kokasastra, 24, 25, 45
Kolsky, Elizabeth, 102, 239n8, 240n15, 240n28
Kosselleck, Reinhart, 216n15
Krafft-Ebing, Richard, *Psychopathia Sexualis*, 34
Kulin polygamy, 63, 75, 76, 109, 122, 145, 180–81, 183–88

lag, civilizational, 16, 135, 142, 156, 159, 172, 175
Lahiri, Yadavchandra, *Kulakalima* (Black mark on the family), 180–81, 184–85, 187
Lal Kunwar, 54
Lamarck, Jean-Baptiste, 138
The Lancet (journal), 115
law: ancient Hindu, as cause of prostitution, 76; custom linked to, 140; female sexuality and, 19, 62–98; regulation of prostitution, 47, 78–86, 96–97; on sexual and reproductive behavior, 68

Law Commission for India (1837), 68, 94
lay sociologies, 8, 13, 20, 178, 188–94, 196
Legg, Stephen, 216n11, 235n47
Legislative Council of Bengal, 47
Levine, Philippa, 216n11, 234n46, 234n47
Lizzat al-Nisa, 29
Lombroso, Cesare, 7
Long, James, 146
lower castes: prostitution linked to, 49; theories of the body concerning, 16
Lowis, J. M., 89
Lubbock, John, 17, 142, 152, 172
Lucknow School of Indian Sociology, 148, 173, 221n43
Lyall, D. R., 75
Lyon, Isidore B., *Medical Jurisprudence for India*, 115, *118*, 119–20, 122–24, 130, 240n28, 242n56

Mackenzie, A., 63, 65; summary of survey responses, *66*
Macpherson, W., 90
Mahabharata, 17, 25, 30, 31, 37–38, 44, 48, 51, 52, 53, 59, 152, 172, 173
maidservants, 97, 169, 192–93, 251n47
Maine, Henry, 8, 17, 134, 137, 138, 139–40, 141, 142, 153
Maitra, Gyanendrakumar, 136, 247n82; *Rati Yantradira Pida* (Sexual and venereal evils), 158–65, *160*
male sexuality, 48, 143, 161–62, 188. *See also* sexual difference
Manava-Dharmasastra (Laws of Manu), 31
Mani, Lata, 65, 219n30, 232n7
Mantena, Karuna, 134
Manu, and *Laws of Manu*, 32, 45, 74, 76, 172, 184
Manusmriti, 25, 48, 53
Marcus, Sharon, 219n29, 244n16
marriage: the control of female sexuality through, 8, 9, 11, 17, 37, 45, 48, 53, 54, 57; as index of social evolution, 134; McLennan's theory of, 140–41; prostitution compatible with, 74–76; role of, in colonial/postcolonial knowledge of India, 86; upper-caste Hindu, 6, 14. *See also* monogamous marriage; "nika" marriage; polygamy; widow remarriage
Maspero, Gaston, 17
matriarchy, 140–41
McGregor, James, 107
McLennan, John, 8, 17, 48, 134, 137, 138, 140–42, 152, 153, 172, 187; *Patriarchal Theory*, 141; *Primitive Marriage*, 39, 53, 140–41, 167
Medical Book Company, 46–47
medical jurisprudence. *See* forensics
menstruation, 41, 42, 108, 146, 179
Meyer, Johann Jakob, 26, 36–40, 48, 167, 172, 228n52; *Sexual Life in Ancient India*, 37, 53
Mill, James, *The History of British India*, 145
Mill, John Stuart, 17
Mitra, Peary Chand, 146; *Alaler gharer dulal* (The pampered son of an elite family), 251n35
Mitra, Rajendralal, 40
modern social thought: and ancient sexuality, 40–46; colonial vs. Indian uses of, 12; evolutionary theory's influence on, 147–48; institutions of, 10–11; *Kamasutra* as significant text for, 41–46; limited and distorted nature of, 20; objectifying nature of, 7–8, 20–21; overview of, 9–14; philology as basis of, 24, 26; role of the concepts of the prostitute and deviant female sexuality in, 1–9, 18–22, 203. *See also* Bengali social thought; sciences of society
Modi, Jaising P., *A Textbook of Medical Jurisprudence and Toxicology*, 242n56
Moll, Albert, 34
monogamous marriage: control of female sexuality through, 187; as culmination of social evolution, 151–53, 165, 173; natural to women, 162; as norm/ideal, 6, 7, 9, 14, 16, 17, 62, 128, 142, 161, 173; patriarchal structure of, 143; protective function of, 187–88; sex legitimized only within, 7, 37, 62, 69

monogenicism, 138
Mookerjee, Sameer Chandra, *The Decline and Fall of the Hindus*, 153–56, 205–6
Mookerjie, Baboo Juggadanund, 94
Morgan, Lewis Henry, 8, 134, 137, 142, 152, 172; *Ancient Society*, 161; *Systems of Consanguinity and Affinity*, 161
Mukerjee, Radhakamal, 136, 148, 173, 221n43, 248n131; *The Horizon of Marriage*, 173
Mukharji, Projit, 222n54, 244n8
Mukherjee, Satyendranath, *Murder of Prostitutes for Gain*, 194
Mukherjee, S. C., 97
Mukherji, Santosh Kumar, 27, 52–56, 136, 165–71, 193, 248n106; *Birth Control for the Millions*, 56; *Indian Sex Life and Prostitution*, 166; *Prostitution in India*, 52–55, 167–71; *Sex Life and Prostitution in India*, 52
Mukhopadyay, Damodara, *Nabina* (New woman), 196–97
Müller, Max, 25, 40, 51, 137, 142
Mullick, Babu Taraknath, 75–77
Mullick, Bulloram, *Home Life in Bengal*, 39
museum, pathological, 104–8
Muslims: anti-Muslim sentiment, 15, 16, 60, 123, 165, 170–71; and "nika" marriage, 74–76, 82; prostitution associated with, 54, 60, 71, 74–76, 170–71; sexual deviance imputed to, 5, 7, 14, 16; in social evolutionary theory, 156; theories of the body concerning, 16

Nagpur, Choto, 138
Najmabadi, Afsaneh, 219n32
naksha (everyday-life sketches), 189, 251n35
nationalism: Chakraberty and World War I, 57; female sexuality linked to, 14
new woman, 196–97
"nika" marriage, 74–76, 82
Nimtala, 180, 188–91

Orientalism, 27, 30

Panchasayaka, 59
Pande, Ishita, 240n12
Parent-Duchâtelet, Alexandre, 7, 217n22
patriarchy: ancient and modern aspects of, 143; in anti- and postcolonial movements, 22; central to Indian social life, 143; collusion of colonial and Indian, 223n59; control of female sexuality through, 8, 9, 143, 188; as culmination of social evolution, 140–43; Hindu, 54; as Indian social progress, 172, as timeless feature of Hindu society, 139–40
Payne, Arthur J., 110, 122, 129, 146
Payne, Robert, 80–84
philology: American Indo-European, 36; Chakraberty's use of, 58–61; essentialism linked to, 226n11; and female sexuality, 19, 23–61; and history of prostitution, 46–56; and Indian custom/tradition, 44; modern social thought based on, 24, 26; overview of, 25; on sexuality and reproduction, 108; significance of, in nineteenth century, 25, 36. *See also* Indology
Pischel, Richard, 227n37
police: complaints against, 78, 84–85; and the Contagious Disease Acts, 80–86; detection of abortion and infanticide, 90, 95, 181; exposé by, 194; genital exams conducted by, 124–26; powers of, 68, 128; surveillance conducted by, 124; taxonomy by the Commissioner of, 62–63; testimonials collected by, 177
polyandry, 141
polygamy: Bengali, 129; caste linked to, 186–87; critiques of, 181, 183–88; Muslim, 75–76; natural to men, 162; in social evolution, 153; women's objection to, 63. *See also* Kulin polygamy
popular culture, 249n6
population control, 56, 187
positivism, 19, 45, 145–46, 220n39, 221n44
Positivist Society, 146

Prichard, James Cowle, 138
primitive promiscuity. *See* promiscuity: primitive
promiscuity: caste linked to, 155; legendary end of, in India, 52–53; primitive, 17, 31, 38–39, 53, 133, 141–43, 152, 157, 161, 163, 167–68, 172
prostitute concept: children and, 70; comparative approach to, 49; comparative instances of, 7; diversity and scope of, 4–5, 49–50, 55–56, 62–63, 67, 69, 72–79, 86, 97, 135, 169; in feminist discourse, 4; history of, 2–9; in Indian film, 224n65; positivist analysis of, 19; as proxy for deviant female sexuality, 1, 5, 6; role of, in colonial/postcolonial knowledge of India, 2–9, 16–22, 67, 69, 77–79, 135–36, 174–75, 201–2, 216n15; sexual primitivity and, 17–18; as sex workers, 4–5; social issues seen through perspective of, 5, 8, 77–82, 98, 200. *See also* deviant female sexuality; prostitution
prostitution: abortion linked to, 122, 129; appeals from women accused of, 85–86; autobiographical accounts of, 20, 176–79, 194–201; caste linked to, 49; clandestine, 50, 55, 63, 70–72, 78, 80–83, 93, 97, 169, 184; comparative study of, 49, 152; compatible with marriage, 74–76; criminal laws on, 68; diversity and scope of, 193; explanations of, 176–77, 197, 201; Kulin polygamy linked to, 183–85; means of addressing, 77, 80; Mukherji's history of, 167–71; Muslims linked to, 54, 60, 71, 74–76, 170–71; origins of, 46–57; rape linked to, 123; regulation of, 47, 78–86, 96–97; in social evolutionary theory, 156–59; surveys on, 62–77; taxonomies of, 49–50, 53–56, 71–74, 77, 82, 157, 168–69, 193–94; Vaishnav Hinduism associated with, 70–71, 73. *See also* prostitute concept; trafficking, of women and children

Puranas, 48, 172
pyres. *See* funeral pyres

questionnaires. *See* surveys and questionnaires

race: Aryan theories of, 48; Chakraberty's theories of, 57, 59–60, 231n120; Indians distinguished by, 57, 60; sexuality linked to, 59–60; social evolution and, 138
racial difference, 4, 8, 16, 25, 27, 57–60, 102, 116, 119, 137, 138, 147, 151, 154, 155; and sexuality, 219n29
Ramabai, Pandita, 222n52; *The High Caste Hindu Woman*, 39
Ramakrishna, 38
Ramayana, 17, 25, 37–38, 44, 48, 51, 53
Rampini (judge), 93–94
Rao, T. Madhav, 88
rape, 122–24, 199. *See also* gang rape
Rationalist Association, 148
Rationalistic Society. *See* Indian Rationalistic Society
Ratirahasya (also known as *Koka Shastra*), 23–24, 47, 59, 225n4, 225n5
Raur, Sukhimonee, 78
Rege, Sharmila, 224n62
Reis and Rayyat (newspaper), 96
reproduction, as purpose of sex, 24, 76, 157, 161–62; birth control and, 55–56
Rg Veda, 43, 44, 48, 59
Riley, Denise, 219n30
Risley, Herbert Hope, 142–43, 183; *The People of India*, 186–87; *A Statistical Account of Bengal*, 86; *The Tribes and Castes of Bengal*, 11, 86, 143, 144, 239n12
Roy, Hemandra Kumar, 250n32
Roy, M. N., 57
Roy, Rammohan, 145
Royal Asiatic Society of Bengal, 139
Rubin, Gayle, 8, 218n26

Sakuntala (Indian tale), 30–31, 220n36
Salisbury, Edward, 228n51

Sanger, William, 7
Sanskrit: epics, 18; and ethnology, 140, 158, 167, 172; and female sexuality, 7, 23–61; and Hindu Kulin polygamy, 184; and history of prostitution, 46–56; sociological inquiry based in, 30; universal applicability of, 24–26, 29. *See also* Indology
Sanyal, Durgachandra, *Banglar Samajik Itihas* (A history of Bengali society), 158
Sarda Act, 198
Sarkar, Benoy Kumar, 45
Sarkar, Tanika, 14, 223n57, 239n12
Sarton, George, 57
sati (widow immolation), 10, 17, 26, 65, 77, 109, 180, 183, 195, 198, 200, 201
Satish, Mrinal, 241n29, 242n56
Schmidt, Richard, 26, 32, 34–41, 227n37; *Beiträge zur Indischen Erotik* (Contribution to the study of Indian erotics), 32, 34, 38; *Kama Sutram*, 32, 33, 41
Schmidt, Wilhelm, 38
sciences of society: casteism and communalism in, 15–16; and colonial expansion, 9–14; custom, 145–48; defined, 12, 221n44; female sexuality as object of, 29; *Kama Sutra* as example of, 28–29; and popular print, 177; rationalism and, 149; speculative nature of, 206–7. *See also* modern social thought
scientia sexualis, 136
scientism, 11–12
Scott, Joan Wallach, 219n30, 223n61
Seal, Brajendra Nath, 147–48
Sedgwick, Eve Kosofsky, 216n13, 218n27
Sekunna, Ernst, 58
Sen, Baboo Kasi Kenkur, 70–71
Sen, Ballal, 183
Sen, Haimabati, 252n57
Sen, Keshab Chandra, 146
Sex Life in India (anonymous), 46–47
sexology, 8, 36, 48
sexual difference, 36, 56, 72, 151, 171

sexuality: Bengali social analysts on, 40–46; comparative approach to, 32, 34; detailed accounts of, 35, 59; evolution and, 1–2, 11, 17, 19, 38–39, 134, 149–51, 163; hetero/homo division of, 8, 218n27; human nature revealed by study of, 29; in Indian society, 29–30, 32, 35, 39; interracial, 233n16; *Kama Sutra* and, 27–32; race linked to, 59–60; rationalist accounts of, 148–57; role of, in colonial/postcolonial knowledge of India, 60; scientific approach to, 34, 39–41, 58–61; sociological approach to, 57–61; timeless essence of, 35–36; universalist approach to, 29, 40. *See also* deviant female sexuality; female sexuality; male sexuality; promiscuity
Sharma, Ram Sharan, 172
Shastras, 76, 161–62, 183, 184
Shaw, George Bernard, 187
She Wasn't Ashamed (anonymous), 194–96
Sikander, Shahzia, 253n5
Sil, R. D., 51
Singha, Kaliprasanna, 146; *Hutom Pyancha Naksha* (The observant owl), 251n35
Sinha, S. N., 27; *The History of Prostitution*, 47–52
Sircar, Mahendra Lal, 146
social analysts: on ancient sexuality, 40–46; backgrounds/fields of, 13, 40, 56, 146; claims to expertise, 16; defined, 12–13; exploitation of social scientific theories by, 15–16, 22, 40–41; study of social evolution by, 134–35
social custom. *See* custom/tradition
Social Evil in Calcutta (anonymous), 194
social evolution. *See* evolution/social evolution
social pollution, 16, 23, 179
social reform, 4, 5, 12, 15, 39, 45, 47, 94, 161, 183, 184, 198
social science. *See* modern social thought; sciences of society

social thought. *See* modern social thought
Society for the Acquisition of General Knowledge, 11
Society for Translating European Sciences, 146
sociology: abortion case studies and, 113–21; deviant female sexuality as basis of, 9; as a discipline, 12, 221n45; Indian, 11, 173, 243n1; Indian society as object of, 12, 18, 26, 30; lay, 13, 20; positivist, 16, 17, 18, 20; in relation to anthropology, 220n42; Sanskrit texts as basis of, 30; sex as subject of, 57–61; sexual, 173
sodomy, 54, 69
Spencer, Herbert, 6, 17, 133–34, 137, 138, 172, 174, 243n3; *The Principles of Sociology*, 133
Spillers, Hortense, 216n12
stigma, 1, 6, 9, 22, 72, 124, 179
surveillance: abortion/infanticide as object of, 90–91, 124–31; citizen engagement in, 90–91, 125–27
surveys and questionnaires: on infanticide, 87–96; on prostitution, 62–77, 98
survivals, Tylor's concept of civilizational, 142, 161
Swadeshi movement, 11, 147
Swarnabai (anonymous), 196
Swetaketu, 52–53, 152, 172

Tagore, Rabindranath, 38
Tambe, Ashwini, 234n46, 234n47
Tattwabodhini Sabha (Truth-seekers Society), 11
temporary marriage/wives, 54, 75–76, 82, 170–71, 177
Thapar, Romila, 220n36, 228n45
Thoinot, Leon Henri, *Medicolegal Aspects of Moral Offenses*, 48
Tod, James, *Annals and Antiquities of Rajasthan*, 38
Tottenham (judge), 93
trafficking, of women and children, 17, 47, 62, 68–70, 96–97

Trafficking Prevention Acts (1920s–1930s), 96–97
Trautmann, Thomas, 142
truth: cremation ground as site of, 180; deviant female sexuality and, 19–20; distrust of Indian women, 93, 123–25, 127–28, 242n56; forensics as means of determining, 103, 123–25, 181, 242n56; prostitutes as source of, 177–78
Tylor, Edward Burnett, 161; *Primitive Culture*, 142

University of Calcutta, 11, 43, 45, 133, 147
University of Chicago, 36, 228n51, 228n52
upper castes. *See* Hindu upper castes

Vaishnav Hinduism, 70–71, 73
"Vande Mataram" (national song), 72
Vatsayana, *Kamasutra*, 28, 29, 32, 43, 48. See also *Kamasutra*
Vedas, 44
venereal disease, 82, 83, 86, 122, 158
Verner, W. H., 71
vesya (prostitutes/courtesans), 30, 49. See also *beshya*
Vidyasagar, Ishwar Chandra, 94, 145, 184
virginity, 124, 242n56

Wald, Erica, 234n46, 234n47
Walkowitz, Judith, 4
Ward, William, 110
Waring, E. J., *Pharmacopoeia for India*, 117
Watts, Charles, 148
Wavell, W., 74
Webb, Alan, *Pathologica Indica*, 10, 104–10, 105, 112, 115, 117, 130, 146
Weber, Max, 34
Westermarck, Edward, *The History of Human Marriage*, 167
Weston, Kath, 8
Weysse, A. W., *Medicolegal Aspects of Moral Offenses*, 48
Whitney, William Dwight, 25, 36, 51, 228n51

widow remarriage: abortion linked to prohibition of, 109, 112, 115, 122–23; legalization of, 94, 183; prohibition of, 45, 71; prostitution linked to prohibition of, 74, 76–77

widows: abortions by, 99–100, 107, 109, 112, 115, 122–23, 125; inheritance of, 127; regarded as prostitutes, 62–63, 74; surveillance of, 125–26. See also *sati*

Wilson, H. H., *Select Specimens of Theatre of the Hindoos*, 30

womanhood: Aryan, 26, 48, 226n11; Black, 216n12; degradation of, 17, 189; genital exam as a violation of, 85; Hindu, 37, 42; as historical method, 21, 219n29, 223n60, 223n61; monetary value of, 224n67; normative, 10, 14, 222n52; prostitution as threat to, 200; *sati* as ideal, 198; in "Sultana's Dream," 205–26; timelessness of Indian, 204; transition to, 196. *See also* deviant female sexuality; female sexuality

A NOTE ON THE TYPE

This book has been composed in Arno, an Old-style serif typeface in the classic Venetian tradition, designed by Robert Slimbach at Adobe.

GPSR Authorized Representative: Easy Access System Europe - Mustamäe tee
50, 10621 Tallinn, Estonia, gpsr.requests@easproject.com

www.ingramcontent.com/pod-product-compliance
Lightning Source LLC
Chambersburg PA
CBHW021653230426
43668CB00008B/608